WHY I BELEIVE

in

The Beauty & Truth of the Catholic Faith

John L. Fontana

Dedication

To my first Catholic teachers: My parents-Anthony and Evelyn Fontana

& to My Spiritual Director: My Godfather- Monsignor Charles Mallett

Contents

Introduction 1

Chapter One Spencer Adrain 8

Chapter Two Dead Man Walking 37

Chapter Three Siblings 51

Chapter Four THE BIBLE 63

Chapter Five Sola Scripture 80

Chapter Six Know Your Church 98

Chapter Seven Know Your Church Part 2 116

Chapter Eight Confession 141

Chapter Nine The Last Supper 159

Chapter Ten Eucharist 182

Chapter Eleven WOUNDS 215

Chapter Twelve Believe It or Not 226

Chapter Thirteen Believe it or Not-Part Deux 260

Chapter Fourteen Purgatory Is for Real 279

Chapter Fifteen Satan 299

Chapter Sixteen Hell 330

Chapter Seventeen Heaven 342

Chapter Eighteen Heaven on Earth 378

Chapter Nineteen Powerful Weapons 393

Chapter Twenty Conclusion 428

Footnotes 445

Introduction

As I sit down and introspect on those precious 65 years of my life, a lot comes to mind that leaves me pondering over many factual things. In today's world, where my faith and identity are sometimes challenged, I could have been born anywhere—into any culture, any race, to parents of varying means, in a country at peace or one ravaged by war, in a nation that cherishes religious freedom or one that persecutes faith. The possibilities are endless. As I navigated through the tumultuous water of life, I realized that my initials were not in my hand; the only thing that we can change about ourselves is after birth. Walking my readers through my childhood, I was born where I was meant to be, a white male, to Catholic parents in the small town of Abbeville, Louisiana. My childhood unfolded in a neighborhood called Mount Carmel Heights, just a short ten-minute walk from Mount Carmel Elementary and Vermilion Catholic High School. Every detail of my upbringing, from the streets I walked to the schools I attended, was part of God's plan for me, and with time this belief is only strengthening. And I know that I have been blessed with this unique journey, one that has shaped the person I am today. As I continue to reflect on my life, it is clear to me that so much of who I

am today has been shaped by forces beyond my control. The family I was born into, the time and place of my birth, my education, and the values instilled in me—these were all set in motion before I had any voice or control over them. And yet, as I stand here today, I know that these aspects of my life have not only defined me but also anchored me in a deeper understanding of faith and identity.

In this fast-paced era, where questions about identity are often framed by the lens of race, gender, and social class, we easily forget the deeper meaning of life, the core purpose of our existence. The unspoken feeling of almost every individual who has yet to explore the profound reality of life is that we all could have been born as anyone, anywhere, under vastly different circumstances. Well, I have come to terms with life's reality, and the earlier you accept the truth, the peaceful your life becomes. For me, I was blessed to be born into a community where tradition and faith were pillars of daily life. Had I been born somewhere else in the world, perhaps in a war-torn country, to different parents, or to a different culture, who knows how my experiences would have shaped my outlook on life? Yet, even in the face of such randomness, there was a purpose in my birth, in my upbringing. The circumstances of my life were not simply the result of chance; they were part of a divine plan. My parents, devout Catholics, made sure that I was not only raised with religious values but that a faith-filled community also surrounded me. My neighborhood, Mount Carmel Heights, was not just a physical location—it was a place steeped in the spirit of the Catholic Church, a place where everyone knew each other and looked out for one another. With over one hundred kids in the neighborhood, we had endless games of football, baseball, kick-the-can, firecracker fights, as well as just hanging out at each other's homes. The presence of Mount Carmel Elementary and Vermilion Catholic High School within walking distance meant that my education was rooted in Catholic principles, where faith was not separate from learning but intertwined with every lesson.

This upbringing, this foundation of faith and community, shaped my identity in profound ways. I was taught early on that my Catholic faith in God was the anchor of my life. I was also taught that my identity as a child of God transcended the circumstances of my birth—whether I was born in Louisiana or anywhere else, my worth was not tied to my race, class, or nationality. It was tied to my relationship with God and my willingness to live out His will in my life. This understanding has given me a deep sense of gratitude and humility, and it has also given me the strength to navigate a world that is increasingly divided by identity politics and shifting cultural norms.

As I look back on my journey, I also see how God's hand has guided me through the highs and lows of life. It was not always easy, and at times, I faced challenges that tested my faith and resolve. But I believe these trials, as difficult as they were, were not random. They were part of a divine design to refine my character, strengthen my faith, and remind me of the importance of perseverance. There were moments in my life when I questioned why things unfolded the way they did, and I couldn't stop my mind from thinking. Why was I born into a family that embraced faith so wholeheartedly, while others around me struggled to find meaning in their lives? Why was I spared from the suffering that many others experience, simply by virtue of where and when I was born? These questions have often led me to a deeper reflection on the nature of providence—that we are all part of a grand, mysterious plan that is not always easy to understand but is always for our ultimate good.

As the world changes and new ideologies emerge, it becomes increasingly important to hold firm to the values that have shaped us into who we are. In an age where many are questioning the role of religion in public life and where the lines between right and wrong seem to blur more each day, I find myself returning to the teachings of my faith. These teachings have always served as a compass, guiding me through the challenges and uncertainties of life. I often reflect on the lessons I learned at Mount Carmel Elementary and Vermilion Catholic High School. The nuns and priests who taught me

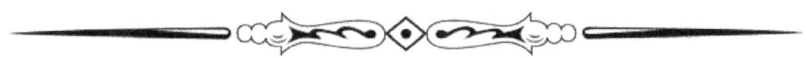

were not only educators—they were mentors who instilled in me the belief that faith is not merely an abstract concept, but a living, breathing force that must be expressed through actions. In a world that increasingly questions traditional beliefs, my faith has only grown stronger, for I have seen the strength it gives me in the face of adversity. It has taught me that, even in the most difficult circumstances, God's love is steadfast, and His plan for us is greater than anything we could ever imagine.

At the same time, I have realized that while my faith and identity may seem unshakable, they do not make me immune to the complexities of modern life. In fact, it is precisely because I have been grounded in these values that I feel a responsibility to stand firm in my beliefs, especially when they are challenged. Today's world is full of voices that seek to undermine or redefine the foundations of faith and family. Yet, I remain steadfast in my conviction that the truth of God's love and purpose for our lives remains unchanged, regardless of the trends and tides of culture. As I conclude this reflection on the past 65 years of my life, I am filled with a sense of gratitude for the path that God has led me down. I am aware that my life could have unfolded in countless ways, but I believe that I am exactly where I am meant to be. My faith, my family, and my community have shaped me into the person I am today, and I am committed to living out that identity with humility, purpose, and grace. In this changing world, I understand that there will always be voices challenging my faith, my identity, and my values. But I also know that I can face these challenges with confidence because my identity is not bound to the transient labels of the world but to the eternal truths of my faith. I could have been born anywhere, to anyone, under any circumstances—but God chose me to be born here, in this place, with this purpose. And for that, I am eternally grateful to have been raised in the Catholic Faith.

For millions of Catholics worldwide, their faith is not simply a set of beliefs; it is a way of life, a source of deep truth, beauty, and purpose. The Catholic Church, with its rich history and timeless

doctrines, is viewed as the true faith established by Jesus Christ, handed down through the apostles, and guided by the Holy Spirit. From the very beginning, Catholics have believed that their Church is the authentic expression of Christ's teachings—an unbroken continuation of His message through the ages. This conviction is rooted in several key aspects of the Catholic tradition: the authority of the Church, its sacred worship, the universality of its mission, and its call to holiness. Catholics are drawn to the Church's historical continuity, confident in the apostolic succession that traces its leadership directly back to Saint Peter, whom they believe was appointed by Jesus as the rock upon which His Church would be built. The Church's teachings, preserved in both Sacred Scripture and Sacred Tradition, form the foundation of their lives, offering wisdom and guidance that remains relevant through the ages. The beauty of Catholic worship, particularly the celebration of the Eucharist, is seen as a direct encounter with the living Christ, whose presence nourishes both body and soul.

Moreover, Catholics are united not just by shared beliefs but by a deep sense of community that transcends time and space. The Church's universality—the fact that it welcomes all people, regardless of nationality or background—reflects its belief that the gospel is meant for everyone. Catholics believe that the Church's doctrines, grounded in faith, hope, and charity, provide a pathway to eternal life with God. Through prayer, sacraments, and acts of service, they strive to live lives of holiness, guided by the truth of the gospel and the promise of salvation. In the Catholic faith, the union of sacred tradition, personal encounter with God, and the universal call to love and serve others shapes a profound, enduring devotion. For those who believe, it is this combination of historical integrity, spiritual richness, and transformative grace that makes Catholicism not just a religion but the true path to knowing Christ and fulfilling His mission on earth. In a world increasingly characterized by skepticism and relativism, the question of belief takes on profound significance.

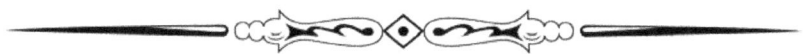

"Why I Believe" invites readers on a journey to explore the rich tapestry of Catholicism, illuminating the reasons behind its enduring appeal and transformative power. This book seeks to answer not just the questions of "what" we believe but why I believe those beliefs matter both personally and community. At its core, the Catholic faith is a profound narrative woven through centuries of tradition, theology, and human experience. It offers a comprehensive understanding of life's deepest questions: Who are we? What is our purpose? How do we find meaning in suffering and joy? This exploration reveals that belief is not merely an intellectual assent to doctrines but an invitation to engage with the divine mystery that permeates our existence. The beauty of the Catholic faith has inspired rituals, artistic paintings, music, books, and palaces of worship, highlighting how these expressions serve as conduits to the sacred. Each chapter offers insights into the theological principles that underpin Catholics beliefs, providing a framework for understanding the faith's relevance in today's world. Readers will encounter stories of saints, theologians, and ordinary believers whose lives exemplify the profound impact of faith on personal and societal levels.

"Why I Believe" is not just for devout Catholics or the curious inquirer, it is for anyone seeking a deeper understanding of spirituality and community in an often-fragmented society. By examining the interplay between faith, reason, and culture, this book aims to foster a dialogue that transcends denominational lines, inviting all to appreciate the universal truths that lie at the heart of the Catholic tradition. Through its exploration of the beauty and truth found within Catholicism, "Why I Believe" offers a compelling vision of hope, inviting all to rediscover the richness of beliefs and its capacity to transform hearts and minds. Walk with me as we examine some exciting beliefs of the Catholic faith as we explore the foundations of a faith that has shaped civilizations and continues to inspire over a billion Catholics around the globe.

SPENCER ADRAIN

Chapter One
Spencer Adrain

"I have a hard time believing some of the events that happened over 2000 years ago." Spencer continued, "Don't get me wrong—I believe in Jesus and what He did, but some parts of the story are difficult for me to grasp fully." He expressed his doubts and the journey that led him to be a firm believer. In the fall of 2022, while pursuing a master's degree in athletic training at LSU, I had the privilege of working with both the men's and women's swim teams. During this rotation, I got to meet with Spencer, a swimmer from California who quickly became popular for his infectious enthusiasm and uplifting energy, driving many crazy. While Spencer was expressing his doubts, it reminded me of my journey of faith - of the many questions I had struggled with when I was at LSU back in 1978 and even as an older man. "I understand," I replied, offering reassurance. "Faith, like any relationship, grows through questioning and searching. You're not alone in this." I smiled and continued, "There was a time when even the closest followers of Jesus – the Apostles - didn't fully understand everything about Him. But, as they

sought the truth, the Holy Spirit illuminated their hearts and minds. And He will do the same for you."

In that moment, as I spoke to Spencer about the importance of holding onto faith amidst doubt, I found myself reflecting on my journey. I thought about all the times I had questioned, struggled, and yet, with each passing year, the beauty and depth of the Catholic faith had become even more meaningful. It was this very journey—the ongoing search for truth in the face of uncertainty—that inspired me to write *Why I Believe: The Beauty & Truth of the Catholic Faith*. My story isn't one of absolute certainty but rather a narrative of wrestling with doubt, learning to trust, and embracing the mysteries that come with faith. Like Spencer, the Apostles, and countless others throughout history, we all face our moments of struggle. Yet, amid it all, the truth of Jesus Christ shines through. I reminded Spencer in that moment, "You don't need all the answers right now. Faith is a journey. Keep searching, keep asking, and the answers will come. The beauty of faith isn't in having everything figured out but in the willingness to move forward with an open heart." Let's take a step back in biblical history to understand the struggles faced by the early believers and the challenges they encountered as they navigated their own faith journeys.

For centuries, the Israelites awaited the arrival of the Messiah, as prophesied in their holy scriptures. Jesus, indeed, was the promised Savior, but His arrival was not as they had imagined. The Creator, God Himself, walked among them for salvation—but many failed to recognize Him. Was He too ordinary in appearance? The Scriptures tell us that He had "no form or majesty that we should look at Him, and no beauty that we should desire Him." His beginnings were humble—so much so that His parents, unable to afford the more expensive sacrificial lamb, offered two doves instead. His roots were unremarkable; He came from Nazareth, a small, despised town, so obscure that it was often seen as backward and insignificant. Even the Apostle Nathanael, when Philip spoke of Jesus, questioned, "Can anything good come out of Nazareth?" In His own hometown, He was

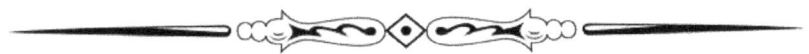

met with rejection, even to the point of them trying to throw Him off a cliff. But Jesus remained calm, moving through them without fear or hesitation. His mission was never about prestige or status. He didn't need wealth, age, race, or gender to build relationships with others. In fact, He often sought out those with tarnished reputations—the sinners, the outcasts. In an era when women were treated as property, Jesus defied cultural and societal norms. He asked a Samaritan woman for water, brought a widow's dead son back to life, welcomed the tearful repentance of a prostitute, and accepted costly perfume from a woman whose love for Him was boundless. He told the astonished scribes, "It is not the healthy who need a doctor, but the sick. I have not come to call the righteous, but sinners to repentance."

In a time of political and social turmoil, the Savior of the world shattered all expectations. The people were anticipating a powerful military leader to come and overthrow their oppressors, not a humble, unassuming figure like Jesus. Yet, it was only those with open hearts, minds, and eyes who indeed saw Him for who He was— the long-awaited Messiah. Despite their physical ailments and sinful natures, they pressed toward Him with desperation, crying out for healing—both for their bodies and souls. These were the ones who recognized that the Savior had come, not to lead a revolution of power but to offer His own life as the ultimate sacrifice, bringing salvation to all who believed in Him.

Yes, the people of Israel, longing for deliverance, were eagerly awaiting the arrival of the Messiah—the Savior promised in the Scriptures who would restore God's kingdom. They expected a king who would free them from Roman oppression and usher in a reign of peace and justice. When King Herod heard the news of the long-awaited Messiah's birth, he recognized the potential threat to his own rule. Herod summoned the chief priests and scribes to learn where Christ was to be born. Fearing the loss of his throne, he ordered the brutal massacre of all male infants under the age of two in Bethlehem and its surrounding areas. This heinous act tragically fulfilled the prophecy from Jeremiah: *"A voice was heard in Ramah, lamenting*

and sobbing bitterly, for Rachel is weeping for her children, and no one can console her."

In times of crisis and doubt, as we see in the lives of the people of Israel and even in the story of King Herod, faith can be tested, questioned, and, at times, rejected. This is the biggest trail for a believer. Our persistence in the face of adversity is what matters the most. Yet, through it all, the beauty and truth of God's plan remains unwavering. Even in our darkest moments, God's will continue to unfold, reminding us that no matter how much we struggle or falter, His promises will always triumph. This truth— that God's love and plan are constant, even when we can't see them—has been a guiding light throughout my own journey of faith. It is this steadfast beauty, this assurance that God's truth endures through all things, which deepens my belief in the Catholic faith and strengthens my trust in His unfailing love.

In *The Chosen*, Director Dallas Jenkins depicts the Apostles referring to John the Baptist as "Crazy John," a title that reflects his radical way of life. Living in the wilderness, surviving on honey and locusts, and wearing camel hair, John's unconventional lifestyle, combined with his fiery preaching of repentance and the coming Messiah, made him stand out. It's no surprise that some might have questioned his sanity. But the reality of John's mission was far deeper and more profound than any surface-level eccentricity. John, six months older than Jesus, was uniquely aware of the "Word" even when he was in his mother Elizabeth's womb. When Elizabeth, pregnant with John, encountered her cousin Mary, carrying the infant Jesus, John leapt for joy within her, filled with the Holy Spirit.

From the very beginning, John's life was destined for something extraordinary—to prepare the way for the Lord, as prophesied in the book of Isaiah. John's message was clear: "Repent, for the Kingdom of God is at hand." When he saw Jesus, he declared, *"Behold the Lamb of God, who takes away the sin of the world"(John1:29)* This was a powerful testimony from John that

Jesus was indeed the Messiah, the One for whom he had been preparing the way. John even testified, "I myself have seen and have testified that this is the Son of God." These words, "I have seen," are a profound declaration of faith that would resonate throughout the Gospels and become a cornerstone of my own belief in the truth of Christ's identity and mission. John's clarity of purpose was a question for many to wonder if he was the Christ, and some even asked him directly. In his humility and honesty, John answered, "I am not the Christ, but there is someone greater coming after me, someone so powerful that I am not worthy to untie the straps of His sandals. He will baptize you with the Holy Spirit." John knew his role was to point to Jesus, not to claim the glory for himself, and his unwavering testimony to the truth, even in the face of rising opposition, is a testament to his deep faith.

But John's journey also reveals the complexities of faith. Despite his bold proclamation of Jesus' identity, he faced profound challenges. He condemned the immortal actions of King Herod, which led to his imprisonment. While in prison, John's doubt began to surface. Perhaps, it was the physical suffering or the isolation of imprisonment, but in a moment of vulnerability, John sent his disciples to Jesus, asking, *"Are You the one who is to come, or should we expect someone else?"* (Matt11:3) It was a moment of deep human doubt, a reminder that even the greatest saints can struggle with uncertainty. Yet, despite his doubts, John's story is ultimately one of beauty and truth. His life and ministry show us the depths of God's love, the power of humility, and the beauty of truth, even when it is difficult to comprehend. John's unwavering testimony, even in the face of personal suffering, points us back to the truth of Christ, a truth that remains steadfast and unchanging, no matter the challenges we face.

Jesus 'response to John's disciples was both compassionate and powerful. He didn't rebuke John's doubt; instead, He pointed to His miracles as proof of His divine mission. *"Go back and tell John what you have seen and heard,"* Jesus said. *"The blind receive sight,*

the lame walk, those who have leprosy are cleansed, the deaf hear, the dead are raised, and the poor have the good news proclaimed to them."(Matth11:4-6) Jesus reminded John and all who would listen that His works revealed the beauty and power of God's plan unfolding in the world. Even though John's doubts were met with this assurance, his journey ultimately led to martyrdom. Yet, Jesus spoke of him with the highest reverence, saying, "*I tell you, among those born of women, there is no one greater than John.*" (Matt11:9)These words from Jesus speak highly of John's greatness, adding the profound humility and truth that marked his life. John's faith, even in the face of doubt, pointed directly to the truth of Jesus Christ.

John's story resonates deeply with my own faith experience. Like John, I faced moments of uncertainty and struggle, questioning God's plan for me or His presence. And as I interact with people, I have reached to a conclusion, that God test his dear believers with moment of despair to see whether they will be firm in their belief or be easily trapped with the challenges around. But, even in those moments of trials, the beauty and truth of my faith shine even brighter, revealing upon us the divine help of God. Faith is not a static state but a journey—one filled with questions, challenges, and moments of doubt. Yet, through it all, God's promises remain true. Just as Jesus reassured John's disciples, we, too, are reminded that God's work is evident in the world around us. Through His miracles, His Word, and the life of the Church, we encounter the truth of God's love and presence, even amid our own doubts. The Bible offers only a few brief glimpses into the childhood of Jesus: The Holy Family's flight to Egypt, their return to Nazareth, and the occasion when, at twelve years old, Jesus was found teaching in the Temple after being separated from His parents for three days. The scribes and rabbis who were astonished by the wisdom of this young boy may have been among those who later prosecuted Him as an adult. These fleeting moments raise more questions than answers, yet they quietly remind us that Jesus' early years were filled with mystery and purpose, even before His public ministry began.

We now turn to a pivotal moment in Jesus' adult life, one that marks the beginning of His mission: His return to Nazareth. The people in His hometown had heard the rumors—the extraordinary reports of His teachings and miracles spread throughout Galilee. The Jesus they had known as a child had become something of a legend. Curiosity filled the synagogue that day, with locals eager to see if the stories were true, if the boy they had watched grow up was the remarkable figure He had become. Some of the elders, His childhood friends, and the families that had known Him might have struggled to reconcile the humble carpenter's son they remembered with the man standing before them now. As was customary, Jesus was invited to read from the Scriptures. He stood and unrolled the scroll of the prophet Isaiah. What happened next was nothing short of revolutionary. Jesus read aloud: *"The Spirit of the Lord is upon me because He has anointed me to bring good news to the poor. He has sent me to proclaim release to the prisoners and recovery of sight to the blind, to let the oppressed go free, and to proclaim the year of the Lord's favor"* (Luke 4:18-19). This was a profound declaration, but it was the next words that truly shook the synagogue: *"Today, this Scripture has been fulfilled in your hearing" (Luke 4:21).*

In that moment, Jesus was not just quoting prophecy—He was declaring that He was the fulfillment of it. He was announcing that He, the one standing before them, was the long-awaited Messiah. The room buzzed with excitement, awe, and confusion. The local people who had watched Him grow up could hardly believe what they were hearing. How could this man, whom they had seen in His youth, now stand before them, claiming to be the fulfillment of God's promises?

The reaction of the elders in the synagogue that day was one of shock and outrage. The people who had known Jesus for years could not fathom that the child they had watched grow up in their small town was now declaring Himself the fulfillment of Scripture. To them, His words seemed nothing short of blasphemy. The tension quickly escalated into a furious mob, and they drove Jesus out of town, pushing Him to the edge of a cliff with the intent to throw Him

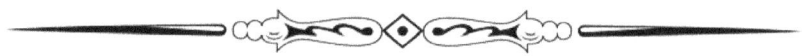

down. But, as the Gospel recounts, Jesus calmly walked through the crowd and went on His way. He was guided by the divine force and amid the uprising tension, he didn't lose his composure and remained firm. In this moment, Jesus spoke a poignant truth: "A prophet is not without honor except in his hometown, among his relatives, and in his own house." His own people, those who should have recognized Him, rejected Him, and He could perform only a few miracles, healing a few sick people, because of their lack of faith. This powerful scene highlights a sobering reality: even when miracles are performed right in front of us, belief is not always born from what we see. The people of Nazareth had witnessed Jesus' power, yet their hearts were closed, and they couldn't accept the truth.

At the height of His public ministry, Jesus drew crowds by the thousands and inspired many disciples. Yet, when it came to choosing His closest companions, He didn't choose scholars, priests, or political leaders. Instead, He called twelve ordinary men: fishermen like Peter, James, Andrew, and John; Matthew, a tax collector despised by his peers; Simon the Zealot, a political radical; and others like Thomas, Jude, Nathanael, Philip, Bartholomew, and James the Less. None of them came from the religious elite or held positions of influence. They were humble, uneducated, and struggling to make a living under a foreign occupation. Yet, despite their ordinariness, Jesus chose them to be His Apostles.

The word "apostle" comes from the Greek *apostolos*, meaning "one who is sent." In Aramaic, the term is *shaliah*, which referred to an official representative of the Sanhedrin, with the full authority to speak and act on behalf of the council. The apostles were entrusted with the same rule by Jesus—to speak on His behalf and to carry out His mission with the power He bestowed upon them. They were sent to proclaim the Kingdom of God, to heal the sick, and to cast out demons. What makes this even more remarkable is that they were ordinary, fallible men. They were not distinguished by any inherent greatness or position of power but by their willingness to serve and openness to God's call. When the Holy Spirit descended upon the

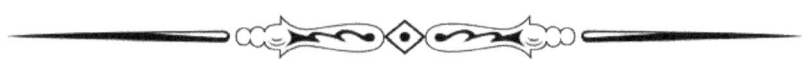

apostles at Pentecost, everything changed. What had begun with ordinary men became a movement that transformed the world. They were filled with divine revelations and spoke with a newfound authority. They preached with boldness, conviction, and power—ordinary men, empowered by the Holy Spirit, doing extraordinary things. Through them, the Church was born. Matthias, who replaced Judas, joined the eleven, and together, they laid the foundation for what would become the Catholic Church, a global community that now spans 1.3 billion people worldwide.

Everything changed at Pentecost. As recorded in Acts 2:1–4, the Holy Spirit descended upon them with power: *"When the day of Pentecost arrived, they were all together in one place. Suddenly, a sound like the blowing of a violent wind came from heaven and filled the whole house where they were sitting. They saw what seemed to be tongues of fire that separated and came to rest on each of them. All of them were filled with the Holy Spirit and began to speak in other tongues as the Spirit enabled them."* This moment marked the beginning of something extraordinary—a new era in Christian history- the Church. The Holy Spirit, descending upon the apostles, empowered them to preach boldly and to spread the message of Christ to the world. That very day, about three thousand people were baptized, and the inaugural of the Church took place. In Acts 2:42, we see the early Church as a community devoted to the apostles' teaching, to fellowship, to the breaking of bread, and prayer. These pillars became the foundation of Christian life and doctrine. Before the New Testament was entirely written, the apostles' teachings were the guiding authority on how to live as followers of Christ. What we now call the New Testament is, in essence, a Spirit-inspired record of the apostles' teachings. It's through these sacred texts, handed down through the ages, that we come to know the truth of Christ and His mission.

The Catholic faith is rooted in this rich history, where the Holy Spirit continues to guide and inspire the Church's teachings and practices. It is through this divine inspiration that we come to

understand the fullness of God's love and truth. And it is through the celebration of the Eucharist, the fellowship of believers, and the life of prayer, that we continue to experience the presence of the Holy Spirit in our lives. This is the beauty and truth of the Catholic faith—the same Holy Spirit who descended on the apostles at Pentecost continues to empower us today, filling us with the grace and wisdom to live out our faith in the world.

Growing up Catholic, I learned about the apostles as larger-than-life figures - saints with halos, unshakable in faith and radiant in holiness. I admired them deeply for their courage and for the sacrifices they made to build the church. I believed, and still believe, that their faithfulness earned them their heavenly reward. They were often depicted as saints—larger-than-life figures, heavenly beings with halos, representing the pinnacle of spirituality and holiness. I admired them for their unwavering dedication to establishing Jesus's Church and their willingness to endure suffering and even death for His glory. And, in my heart, I believed—and still do—that their faithfulness and sacrifice earned them their place in heaven. But as I grew older, I understood something even more beautiful and profound: the apostles didn't start as saints. They were ordinary men—fishermen, tax collectors, and zealots—just like the rest of us. They had their flaws, weaknesses, and doubts. They were not exempt from sin. In fact, Peter himself, the bold leader of the apostles, once said to Jesus, *"Depart from me, Lord, for I am a sinful man"* (Luke 5:8). This moment reveals something significant about the nature of the apostles' journey—they, too, struggled with their humanity. They were not perfect, but they were open to God's grace, which made all the difference. This realization is one of the reasons I believe in the beauty and truth of the Catholic faith.

The Church is built on the foundation of these flawed, imperfect men who were transformed by their encounter with Christ. Their imperfections didn't disqualify them from being chosen; instead, it was through their weaknesses that God's strength shone through. In their failures and their moments of doubt, God worked

miracles. They were not saints because of their greatness, but because they allowed God's grace to work through them. This is a powerful reminder, everyone. Like the apostles, we are all a work in progress. The Catholic faith teaches us that holiness is not about being perfect, but about being open to God's transformative love. It is through our willingness to be molded by God, despite our flaws, that we come to know His greatness and goodness. We are all called to sainthood, not because we are flawless, but because we allow God's grace to redeem and sanctify us. The apostles' journey from ordinary men to extraordinary witnesses of Christ is a testament to the power of grace, and it inspires me to continue growing in faith, knowing that God's love can transform even the most imperfect of us.

The journey of the apostles began with a simple act of faith. The first two apostles to demonstrate faith in Jesus were Andrew and John. As disciples of John the Baptist, they were present when John pointed to Jesus and declared, "Behold the Lamb of God," and immediately followed Jesus. Moved by what they saw in Him, they stayed with him that day. Andrew, filled with joy at having found the Messiah, quickly sought out his brother Simon, telling him, "We have found the Messiah," and brought him to Jesus. In this simple yet profound moment, their lives changed forever.

What strikes me about this is how Andrew and John's faith began not with grand miracles, but with a quiet invitation to follow— a call they responded to with trust and eagerness. They didn't need miracles to believe. They believed because they encountered Jesus and recognized something unique about Him, even before witnessing His works. Their faith was a choice, rooted in identifying who Jesus was. And it wasn't a faith without testing. As they journeyed with Jesus, their faith was stretched in many ways.

Over the next three years, the apostles accompanied Jesus and saw firsthand His miraculous works. They witnessed Jesus heal the sick, cast out demons, and perform acts that defied natural law, such as feeding thousands with only a few loaves of bread and fish,

calming storms with a single command, and walking on water. They saw Him raise the dead, bringing back to life the son of a widow in Nain, Jairus's daughter, and Lazarus, who had been dead for four days. These were astonishing acts of divine power, and yet, despite the overwhelming evidence of Jesus's authority, there were still moments of doubt and fear. There were times when the apostles' faith wavered, moments when they failed to fully grasp the depth of who Jesus was and his purpose in the world. But there was this one moment, one extraordinary experience, that set three of the apostles—Peter, James, and John—apart. Jesus took them up a high mountain, where they witnessed His Transfiguration. In that moment, Jesus was transformed before their eyes, His clothes changed into dazzling white, and He spoke with Moses and Elijah. Then, the voice of God came from the cloud, declaring, "This is my beloved Son. Listen to Him."

This was not just a miracle; it was a direct and personal revelation from God. The apostles saw Jesus as He truly is, and they heard God's command to listen to Him. This was an experience of divine confirmation, a moment of absolute clarity about the identity and mission of Jesus. For me, this story embodies the beauty and truth of the Catholic faith. The apostles were ordinary men, much like us, struggling with doubt and uncertainty, yet they were invited into an extraordinary relationship with God. They didn't believe because they had everything figured out or because they had seen every miracle, but because they were open to the truth revealed through Jesus, a truth that was confirmed in their hearts and minds. This is why I believe in the beauty and truth of the Catholic faith—the call to follow Jesus is not based on our own perfection or understanding, but on the trust that He is who He says He is. Jesus invites us to listen to Him, just as God the Father called the apostles to do.

The Transfiguration is a moment of divine revelation that reminds me of the power of God's voice and presence in our lives. It challenges me to listen, to trust, and to believe, even when I don't have all the answers. It reminds me that faith is not about having all

the proof or understanding of every mystery. It is about recognizing the truth of who Jesus is and responding to His call to follow Him with an open heart. This is the beauty of the Catholic faith—the way God reveals Himself to us, not just through grand miracles, but through the quiet moments of faith and trust, leading us closer to Him.

When I was in the Church of the Transfiguration in the Holy Land, I reflected on why Jesus chose only three of His apostles—Peter, James, and John—to witness the Transfiguration on the mountain, rather than taking all twelve. It's a question that invites deeper contemplation, highlights the personal and mysterious nature of Christ's call. I once came across an interpretation that offered a profound perspective on this choice. It is suggested that Jesus selected Peter because of his deep love for Him, James because he would be the first apostle to be martyred, and John because he was the one whom Jesus loved the most. Each apostle had a unique relationship with Christ, and in choosing them, Jesus revealed something special about their roles in His plan.

Peter, widely known for his passionate love and bold declarations of faith, was chosen because of his deep commitment to Jesus. Though flawed and prone to doubt, Peter had an unwavering love toward Christ. Jesus saw in Peter the potential to lead His Church after His departure, and this moment on the mountain was a glimpse of the glory and authority that would one day be entrusted to him. The Transfiguration was a moment of deep confirmation for Peter, a glimpse of Christ's divine nature that would strengthen him in his future mission, particularly when faced with persecution and his eventual martyrdom. James, who would later become the first of the apostles to die for his faith, was chosen because of the special role he was to play in the unfolding of God's plan. The glory revealed to him on the mountain foreshadowed the ultimate sacrifice he would make as the first martyr among the apostles.

His witness to the Transfiguration was a sign that he would be a steadfast witness to the truth of Christ, even in the face of death. His

faithfulness, even unto martyrdom, was part of the testimony that would build the foundation of the Church. And then there is John, who is often described as the apostle whom Jesus loved most. John, often called the beloved disciple, shared a unique intimacy with Jesus. He was the one who leaned on Jesus at the Last Supper and stood at the foot of the cross. For John, the Transfiguration wasn't just a display of divine power—it was a deeply personal invitation into the heart of God's love. His later writings echo that love, forming a theology of communion that continues to resonate within the Church.

In the face of witnessing numerous miracles—some accounts list anywhere from 36 to 40—it's striking how the apostles still struggled to grasp the full scope of Jesus's mission. The Gospel of John even alludes to the impossibility of fully documenting all that Jesus did, noting that "there are many other things that Jesus did; if every one of them were written down, I suppose that even the world itself could not contain the books that would be written" (John 21:25). The apostles were privileged to witness countless signs of God's power and grace. Yet, they often failed to comprehend the deeper truth of Jesus's purpose. They continued to expect a political Messiah who would overthrow the Roman oppressors and establish a Jewish kingdom, rather than understanding Jesus's mission of mercy, forgiveness, and salvation for all people.

Throughout the Gospels, we see Jesus firmly rebuking the apostles for their lack of faith. He calls them "O you of little faith" multiple times (Matthew 6:30, 8:26, 14:31, 16:8). In the Gospel of Mark, He rebukes them twice: first for their fear and lack of faith when He calms the storm (Mark 4:40), and later for their "hardness of heart" when they refuse to believe the testimony of those who saw Him resurrected (Mark 16:14). And then there's Philip's request during the Last Supper, "Show us the Father," to which Jesus responds, "Have I been with you all this time, Philip, and you still do not know me?" (John 14:9). Even after all they had seen, they still struggled to grasp the depth of who Jesus truly was. This consistent struggle of the apostles has always resonated with me. Their journey

reflects the reality of faith, it's not always easy, and it's often messy. The apostles, despite walking alongside Jesus and witnessing His miracles, were still human. They had doubts, fears, and misconceptions. They did not immediately understand the fullness of His mission, and they even failed in the most crucial moments. At the Last Supper, Peter boldly declared his loyalty, *"I will lay down my life for you"* (John 13:37), yet when Jesus was arrested, all of them fled in fear. They scattered, abandoning Him when He needed them most. It was only after the resurrection, when they encountered the risen Christ and received the Holy Spirit, that they were finally able to understand and proclaim the full message of Jesus's life, death, and resurrection.

This imperfection of the apostles never diminishes their faith—it amplifies it. Their failures, doubts, and misunderstandings make their eventual transformation and unwavering commitment to Christ even more beautiful and overpowering. It's a reminder that faith is a process. It's not about being perfect or having everything figured out. It's about being open to the truth, even when we don't fully understand it. Jesus met the apostles where they were, with all their flaws and limitations, and gradually revealed to them the fullness of His mission.

After Jesus's crucifixion and burial, the apostles found themselves in hiding, consumed by fear and grief. They had given up everything to follow Him—abandoning their families and livelihoods in the hope that He was the Messiah, the one who would bring salvation to Israel. But now, the man they believed to be their Savior had been brutally scourged, crucified, and buried in a tomb. Their dreams and hopes were shattered. The depth of their sorrow and confusion must have been overwhelming. They had watched Him die in the most humiliating way, and now they feared they would share the same fate. Then, on the morning after the Sabbath, everything changed.

Mary Magdalene and several other women went to the tomb to anoint Jesus's body. But they found the tomb empty. When a man—whom she mistook for the gardener—talked to her, she replied in sorrow, *"Sir, if you have carried Him away, tell me where you have put Him, and I will take Him away (John 20:11)."* It was only when Jesus spoke her name— "Mary"—in that moment, everything clicked. In an instant, her sorrow was replaced by joy, and she recognized Him, alive. Her encounter with the risen Lord transformed her despair into a triumphant proclamation: *"I have seen the Lord"* !(John 20:17) She ran to tell the apostles, eager to share the news. But when she burst into the upper room to announce the miracle, the apostles dismissed her words. They refused to believe her testimony, seeing it as nonsense. In the culture of the time, the testimony of women was not given the same weight as that of men. Yet, Mary's experience is a beautiful testament to the truth that the risen Jesus first revealed Himself to the humble and the marginalized, to the faithful women who had followed Him. Peter and John, despite their doubts, ran to the tomb to investigate. They found it empty, with the linen clothes lying undisturbed and the head cloth neatly rolled up. Even in the face of this evidence, the apostles struggled to understand. It wasn't until Jesus appeared to them later that their disbelief began to be overcome.

Another challenging moment came when Jesus appeared to the apostles in the absence of Thomas. Upon hearing that Jesus was alive, Thomas famously declared, *"Unless I see the mark of the nails in His hands and put my finger into the place where the nails were, and my hand into His side, I will not believe."(John 20: 25)* A week later, Jesus appeared again, with Thomas present, and invited him to touch His wounds. Overcome with awe and disbelief, Thomas fell to his knees and declared, *"My Lord and my God." Jesus responded, "You have believed because you have seen me. Blessed are those who have not seen and yet have believed."* (John20:28-29) Thomas, often called "Doubting Thomas," is sometimes criticized for his skepticism. But in truth, all the apostles struggled with doubt and fear. Peter, for instance, could be seen as a bigger doubter than Thomas. While

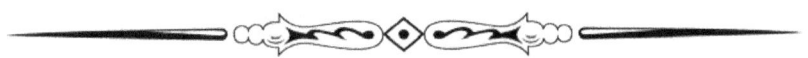

Thomas demanded physical proof of the resurrection, Peter had already denied Jesus three times in His darkest hour, even after walking with Him for years, witnessing His miracles, and hearing His teachings. Peter's denials were a powerful testament to the human fragility of faith. Yet, after the resurrection, Jesus allowed Peter to reaffirm his love three times, restoring him to his mission. Jesus didn't rebuke Peter for his failure; He restored him with love and grace, showing that even our deepest flaws do not disqualify us from His call.

This journey of doubt and restoration is something I can relate to deeply, which is why I believe so strongly in the beauty and truth of the Catholic faith. Like Thomas and Peter, I have had my own moments of doubt and struggle. There have been times when I, too, have questioned God's plan or been overwhelmed by the weight of the world. But what gives me hope is that, just as Jesus met the apostles where they were, He meets us where we are. He doesn't condemn us for our doubts but invites us into a deeper relationship with Him, a relationship founded not in perfect faith but on trust in His goodness and mercy. The story of the apostles' doubts and Jesus's patient, loving responses reveals the heart of the Catholic faith. It's not about always having unshakable certainty—it's about trusting in Jesus, even when we struggle to understand. The faith of the apostles was built on encounters with the risen Christ, and it was in those encounters that their faith was strengthened. Just as Thomas's encounter with the risen Jesus transformed his doubt into worship, so too can our struggles and doubts lead to deeper faith and greater intimacy with God. This is the beauty of the Catholic faith: it teaches us that faith is a journey, often marked by questions and challenges, but ultimately leading us into the arms of a merciful and loving Savior who calls us to believe—even when we cannot see.

Jesus's renaming of Simon to Peter, meaning "rock," is a powerful moment that speaks to the foundation of the Church. When Jesus said, *"On this rock, I will build my Church,"* He wasn't just calling Peter a name, He was assigning him a purpose—one that

would carry the weight of future generations. Peter's role was the rock on which the Church would be built; it was not merely a symbolic title, but a profound calling to lead, serve, and be a pillar of faith. Peter's faith in Jesus seemed strong, especially when he boldly declared at the Last Supper, "Even if everyone else falls away because of you, I will never fall away." His words were filled with confidence, even bravado. Yet, Jesus knew the depth of Peter's heart and warned him, *"Before the cock crows, you will deny me three times."* Despite his strong commitment and his witness to Jesus's miracles—the healing of his mother-in-law, his presence during the Transfiguration—Peter's faith was tested in the crucible of fear. When the moment came, Peter denied Jesus three times, just as Jesus had foretold.

This failure is one of the most humanizing aspects of Peter's story. His denial didn't mean he lacked faith, but rather that, under the intense pressure of the moment, he faltered. His actions reveal a profound truth about human nature: even those who love and follow Jesus deeply, have seen His miracles and heard His teachings, are not immune to fear, doubt, and failure. The apostles, like all of us, were deeply human. Jesus chose them, and yet, they were not perfect. They struggled, they stumbled, and they faced moments of profound weakness.

I observe the same pattern in my life, just like Peter, we all falter. But now my approach has changed; now I don't allow fear or doubt to take control of my thoughts. But the story of Peter reminds me of many beautiful lessons, when a Jesus's apostles can go astray, and feel weak in his faith then I'm an ordinary human being. And feeling weak in your faith is also a test from your lord. It reminds me that failure is not the end—it's an opportunity for renewal and restoration. God's grace is always greater than our mistakes, and His call to us is never rescinded because of our flaws. This is the beauty of the Catholic faith: it teaches us that, even in our brokenness, we are still chosen, still called, and still loved by God. We are not defined by our failures, but by the truth of His love and the purpose He gives us,

just as Peter was defined by the rock of his faith, despite his moments of doubt. While it took the Apostles a long time to grasp who Jesus was, others understood Jesus was the Savir right from the beginning. We shall look at a few of them.

Mary's acceptance of her role as the mother of God stands as one of the most powerful testimonies of faith in the catholic tradition. When the Angel Gabriel appeared to her – a young, unmarried girl and announced that she would bear the son of God, she didn't hesitate. Instead, she replied with grace and humility, embracing God's decision. Mary replied, *"I am the servant of the Lord. Let it be done to me according to your word." (Luke1:38)* Her yes to God was not just a momentary acceptance, but a complete surrender to God's will that reshaped the salvation history. This act of trust and obedience is not only beautiful but deeply inspiring. Mary's faith is a model for all of us, showing that when we accept God's call, no matter how daunting it may seem, we are participating in the unfolding of a greater divine plan. In a comparable way, the prophet Simeon, guided by the Holy Spirit, expressed his deep faith when he encountered the infant Jesus in the temple. Simeon had been promised that he would not die until he had seen the Messiah, and upon holding the baby Jesus, he praised God, saying, "Now, Lord, you may dismiss your servant in peace, for my eyes have seen your salvation." Simeon's words reflect a deep recognition that the long-awaited Savior had come. His faith, grounded in the promises of God, was fulfilled in that moment, and he saw the truth of God's plan unfold before his eyes. The elderly prophetess Anna also witnessed this fulfillment, speaking of the child to all who were waiting for the redemption of Jerusalem. Both Simeon and Anna are examples of how the Holy Spirit works in our lives, leading us to recognize the presence of God even in the most unexpected circumstances. Their faith was not based on signs and wonders, but on a deep trust in the promises of God.

The story of the woman who had been hemorrhaging for twelve years is a deeply moving example of the transformative power of faith. Physically suffering and socially outcast, knowing that her

condition would have rendered her ceremonially unclean in the eyes of society, isolating her from family and community. She will be isolated and blamed for a sin she never committed. She was, in many ways, an outcast; she had every reason to give up hope. Yet, she chose to believe, she was of the faith that simply touching the edge of Jesus's cloak could bring her healing. Her faith was so simple, yet profound—she didn't need a grand spectacle or public acknowledgment. Maybe she did not know that Jesus was truly the Messiah, but she just knew, in her heart, that Jesus had the power to heal her, and that was enough. When she touched His garment, Jesus noticed immediately. He said, *"Someone touched me; I felt power leave me."(Luke 8:46)* This is a beautiful reminder that, even in a crowd of people, God sees us individually, He sees our faith, our need, and He responds. The woman's act of faith, born out of desperation and hope, was enough to bring forth the healing she longed for. When Jesus tells her, *"Daughter, your faith has healed you," (Luke 8:48)* it's a reminder that faith, no matter how small or humble, is powerful. It's not the grandeur of the act, but the trust in God that opens the door to His mercy and grace.

In *The Chosen*, this scene is brought to life in the most powerful way. We see the woman's desperation, her struggle to make her way through the crowd, and her quiet determination to reach Jesus. The portrayal of her faith—raw and vulnerable yet full of hope—is moving and relatable. It reminds me that faith doesn't need to be loud or extraordinary; sometimes, it's the quiet, humble belief that God is watching and whatever I do be it good or bad will be written in my deed book. This belief leads us far more and makes us content believers. This beautiful story teaches us that God meets us where we are, in our struggles and our faith, however imperfect or small it may seem. Jesus doesn't need a grand display of faith—He responds to the sincere heart that reaches out to Him. And that, to me, is the most satisfying revelation of his powers and divine love toward mankind.

Another beautiful encounter occurs at the well, where Jesus speaks with a Samaritan woman. In a time of deep division and animosity between Jews and Samaritans, Jesus broke down barriers by speaking to this woman, someone society would have considered an outsider. Yet, Jesus revealed to her that He was the source of the "living water" that could quench her thirst forever. The woman, overwhelmed by this revelation, immediately became a witness to others, bringing them to Jesus. Many of them came to believe in Him, not just because of her testimony, but because they encountered Him for themselves. This scene demonstrates the transformative power of God's love, which knows no boundaries. It teaches me that no matter our background, mistakes, or past, God's grace is available to all who seek Him with an open heart.

Similarly, the story of the Canaanite woman also embodies bold and persistent faith. She came to Jesus pleading for her daughter's healing. Again, she may not have understood Jesus was the Son of God, but she knew He had the power to cure her. Despite initial seeming indifference from Jesus, she persisted in her faith and humility. When He first did not respond, she didn't walk away or give up. Instead, she knelt at His feet, declaring, "Lord, help me!" Even when Jesus made a seemingly harsh statement about taking the children's bread and throwing it to the dogs, she responded with remarkable humility and wit, saying, *"Yes, Lord, but even the dogs eat the scraps that fall from their master's table."* (Mark 7: 28) In that moment, Jesus recognized her great faith and granted her request, healing her daughter. What stands out to me about this story is not just the miraculous healing, but the incredible faith and persistence of the woman. She could have been discouraged by Jesus's words or offended by His apparent refusal, but she continued trusting Him. Her humility and boldness are qualities that are a lesson for all of us, and she deserves nothing but admiration for her unwavering belief in her lord, and so God responded to her. It reminds us that, even in moments when God seems silent or distant, our faith should not falter. Instead, like this woman, we should be persistent, humble, and trust in God's greatness even when we don't fully understand His timing or answers.

Bartimaeus, the blind man by the roadside, teaches us about persistence and courage in faith. When others tried to quiet him, he grew even louder, calling out to Jesus, "Son of David, have pity on me." This is an indication of faith and determination that is not easily deterred by external obstacles or the opinions of others. His persistence caught Jesus's attention, and Jesus, seeing his faith, called him forward. When Jesus asked, "What do you want me to do for you?" Bartimaeus did not hesitate. His request was simple, yet profound: "Rabbi, I want to see." In that moment, his faith in Jesus's ability to heal was clear, and Jesus responded with love and compassion, saying, "Go in peace; your faith has made you well." Immediately, Bartimaeus was healed, regaining his sight. What strikes me about this story is the symbolic act of Bartimaeus throwing aside his coat. The coat, in ancient Jewish culture, was more than just a garment—it was a person's possession, often containing their most important belongings and offering protection. By casting it aside to approach Jesus, Bartimaeus was symbolically letting go of his attachments to the world, his past, and his limitations. He was saying, in effect, "I trust in You, Jesus, more than in anything else." This radical act of faith, where he discarded his earthly possessions to follow Jesus, reminds me of how true faith often requires a letting go—a surrender of our own attachments, fears, and preconceived notions to embrace the transformative power of God.

Bartimaeus's story sheds light on how Jesus is always watching us, supporting us, and helping us in the most amazing ways possible. He is always ready to meet us where we are, no matter what our circumstances. And it's this deep, unwavering belief in the power of Jesus to heal and transform that inspires my faith in the beauty and truth of the Catholic faith. Through the sacraments, prayer, and our acts of faith, we, too, can encounter the transformative power of Christ in our lives, just as Bartimaeus did when he threw aside his coat and boldly approached Jesus, trusting in His mercy.

In my own life, I believe that faith often calls for a similar surrender. There are times when I, too, need to cast aside the things

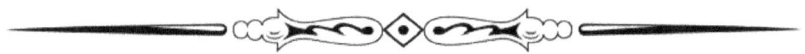

that weigh me down—doubt, fear, or the distractions of everyday life—and move forward with trust in God's love and power. Like Bartimaeus, we may not always see the full picture or understand how God will work in our lives, but we are called to approach Him with faith and persistence. The beauty of this story is that Jesus did not turn away from Bartimaeus, nor does He turn away from any of us in any circumstances. He listens to our cries, sees our hearts, and responds with healing and grace. It's the belief that takes us a long way.

Among the many stories of faith in the Bible, one stands out for its remarkable nature. A Roman centurion—an officer in the occupying forces of the Roman Empire, a figure typically associated with oppression and hostility in Jewish society—sought Jesus's help for his servant, who was gravely ill. For the apostles, this would have been a difficult request to hear, given the tension and suffering caused by Roman rule. The Apostles were probably very fearful of this man. Many may have witnessed the cruelty the Roman's soldiers inflicted upon their fellow countrymen. Yet, Jesus did not hesitate to respond. The centurion, despite his position as an enemy of the Jewish people, had shown kindness to them by building a synagogue in Capernaum, demonstrating his respect for their faith and traditions. His actions revealed a heart of goodwill, one that transcended the usual animosities between Jews and Romans, and it was this genuine humility and faith that moved Jesus to act. Despite his position of power, he acknowledged his unworthiness and expressed a faith in Jesus's authority that was both bold and beautiful.

The centurion's message, *"Lord, do not trouble Yourself, for I am not worthy to have You come under my roof. But just say the word, and my servant will be healed,"* (Matth 15:27) is a powerful expression of faith. He understood authority. As a man in command, he knew that a command could be given and obeyed without question, regardless of distance or circumstances. His belief that Jesus, with His divine authority, could heal his servant with just a word was a remarkable testimony to his understanding of Jesus's power. What is truly striking is that, in response to this, Jesus was amazed. He

declared, "I tell you, I have not found such great faith even in Israel." This statement not only praised the centurion's faith but also subtly pointed out the lack of faith among those who were closest to Jesus, the very people who were familiar with the prophecies, the scriptures, and the promises of God.

This story indicates that the true miracle lies in belief and persistence. And God only fulfills the promises to those who blindly trust in him. The centurion, who could have relied on his own power, wealth, or pagan influence, instead placed his trust entirely in Jesus's healing ability. It must me in great astonishment that what led this man to seek out Jesus. Did He hear a sermon from Jesus that changed his heart? Did he witness one of the many miracles performed by Jesus, or maybe had an extraordinary encounter with one of the Apostles? Whatever touched his heart, He didn't require Jesus to perform any ritual, nor did he expect any spectacle. He simply believed that Jesus had all the power to heal from a distance, without the need for physical presence. This pure and confident faith, without hesitation or demand, is what Jesus honored. This story unfolds many facts about the divine power of God's love and power. It transcends social and religious boundaries, showing that faith is not confined to a particular group, nor do human expectations limit it. The beauty of the Catholic faith is that it invites everyone, no matter their background, status, or past, to approach Jesus with the same faith and humility. Like the centurion, we don't need to have all the answers, and we don't need to feel "worthy" by world standards. What matters is the trust we place in God's power to heal, transform, and make whole.

Now, think about this for a moment. It is striking to consider that from an early age, some recognized that Jesus was more than just a man. Even as a child, His wisdom was beyond comprehension. At twelve, He astonished the temple teachers with His deep, extraordinary understanding of the Scriptures and His ability to answer profound questions, displaying a divine wisdom many failed to recognize. For me, this moment is particularly moving—it reveals

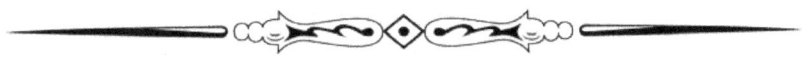

that Jesus's identity as the Son of God was not suddenly revealed in adulthood, but was evident even as a child, though veiled to most. It's also intriguing to reflect on figures like Joseph of Arimathea and Nicodemus—two men who, despite the pressures of their positions and the growing hostility toward Jesus, found the courage to support Him at His trial and burial. Could their support have been influenced by the recognition of Jesus's divine wisdom when they first encountered Him, perhaps even as twelve-year-old, when His wisdom amazed those around Him? This early encounter may have planted the seed of faith in their hearts, a faith that later led them to take a stand for Jesus, even when it would have been dangerous. Their actions remind me that faith often begins with a moment of recognition—a quiet, almost imperceptible awareness of something extraordinary—and that this early awareness can grow over time into a bold witness to the truth of who Jesus is.

Lastly, it is remarkable that even the demons acknowledged Jesus's divine authority. Throughout the Gospels, there are numerous instances where demons, upon encountering Jesus, cry out in fear, acknowledging His identity and power. One such moment occurs when a man possessed by an unclean spirit scream, *"What do You want with us, Jesus of Nazareth? Have You come to destroy us? I know who you are—the Holy One of God."* (9 Luke 4:34) Did Jesus's followers miss this remark? A demon is screaming out that Jesus is the Son of God, and yet, if the Apostles heard this news, did it go over their heads? In that moment, Jesus silences the demon and casts it out, displaying His absolute authority over the forces of evil. This recognition from the very beings who oppose Him speaks to the undeniable truth of who Jesus is. This recognition of Jesus's power by even the force of darkness reminds me of the moment when Satan tempted Jesus in the desert. At the beginning of His ministry, after fasting for forty days and nights, Jesus was confronted by Satan, who tried to exploit His hunger, His desire for authority, and His trust in God's protection. Satan's temptations were meant to undermine Jesus's mission and identity: *"If you are the Son of God, turn this stone into bread... Worship me, and I will give you all the kingdoms*

of the earth... Throw yourself down from the temple and prove your divinity by the angels saving you." *(Mark 1:24)* Yet, Jesus responded to each temptation with unwavering faith and truth, rebuking the devil by quoting Scripture and reaffirming His complete reliance on God alone.

What touches me most deeply in these Gospel stories is the powerful truth they reveal: that Jesus was not only fully divine but also fully human. He faced the same struggles we do, even more than that, yet He never wavered in His mission or His identity. His triumph over temptation and His power over demons show me that, no matter the challenge or opposition, He is the ultimate authority. Jesus's victory over evil and His steadfastness in the face of temptation demonstrate the strength of His love for us and His commitment to fulfill His mission of salvation. For me, this underscores why I believe in the beauty and truth of the Catholic faith. Jesus's life is a perfect model of strength, humility, and truth, and His authority over both the spiritual and physical realms assures me that He is indeed the Son of God and the Savior of the world.

Reflecting on modern life, especially for young people like Spencer, embracing Jesus can seem more challenging than ever. In a world where secular culture moves at a rapid pace, individuals are constantly bombarded by distractions, false promises, and the pressures of fitting in. The rise of social media—platforms like Snapchat, YouTube, Instagram, TikTok, and Facebook—compete for our time and energy, often pushing spiritual growth to the background. Television competes with hundreds of channels along with thousands of movies and shows streaming. And don't forget the mighty iPhone, where with just the push of a button, a thousand pornographic shows will pop up.

For many, the pursuit of faith and religious understanding becomes secondary to fame, followers, or momentary pleasure. A 2022 Pew Research Center survey highlights this cultural shift, revealing that only 65% of American adults now identify as

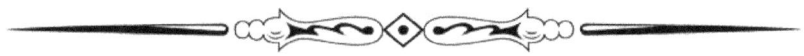

Christians, a significant decline from previous decades. Even more striking is the increase in religiously unaffiliated individuals, now at 26%, compared to just 17% a decade ago. Additionally, regular church attendance continues to decline, reflecting a broader trend of spiritual disengagement. Despite these trends, the Catholic faith provides a deeper, lasting fulfillment that nothing can offer. While social media and the modern age may promise instant gratification, they often leave us empty or disconnected. In contrast, Jesus offers a love that never fades and a truth that transcends time. The Catholic faith offers a rootedness that the fleeting nature of trends or the constant noise of modern life cannot. Amid all the distractions, the call to follow Christ is an invitation to a life of purpose, peace, and eternal joy—values that endure beyond any temporary moment of fame or fleeting pleasure.

In today's world, secularism—defined as a belief system that excludes God from human affairs and reduces the importance of religion—has become increasingly influential. It promotes the idea that the world is all there is, and that faith and spirituality should be confined to private life, away from the public sphere. This philosophy seeks to diminish the role of religion in shaping society, challenge religious freedoms, and erode Christian moral values. For many young people, like Spencer, navigating this secular world can feel overwhelming, especially when faith is often treated as irrelevant or outdated. Yet, in the face of these challenges, my advice is simple: hold firm to your faith. Jesus's words to Thomas echo timelessly: *"You have believed because you have seen Me. "Blessed are those who have not seen and yet have believed."(John 20:29)* In a world filled with distractions, confusion, and doubt, faith is not always about certainty or immediate answers. It's about trust, perseverance, and the willingness to believe—even when we can't always see the full picture. Faith isn't about the absence of questions but about continuing the journey with trust in the One who holds all the answers.

I encourage Spencer—and anyone facing the same struggles—to stay rooted in their faith. The secular media, with all its temptations and diversions, will continue to challenge your beliefs. But remember, there are others just like you—people passionate about learning, growing, and living out the Gospel. Continue attending Bible studies, stay connected with a community of believers, and remain involved in church life. Most importantly, keep praying. Prayer is not just about asking for answers; it's about deepening your relationship with God, trusting in His plan, and allowing Him to guide you in His time. The more you open your heart to Jesus, the more the Holy Spirit will illuminate your path. Each step you take will bring you closer to Him, and over time, the truth of the Catholic faith will become clearer, not just as a set of doctrines, but as a living, breathing relationship with a Savior who loves you beyond measure. You will begin to see the beauty of this faith, not as a burdensome set of rules, but as the way to true freedom, peace, and joy.

There it is for all to see: the beauty and truth of the Catholic faith: it's a journey of discovery, of questioning, of stumbling, and ultimately of believing, even when we can't always see. It's a relationship that strengthens over time, one that continually reveals God's love and mercy in ways beyond our expectations. This is why I believe, and why I encourage Spencer, and anyone else, to continue searching, seeking, and believing. The answers will come, and the Holy Spirit will guide you. Keep moving forward, even during doubt, for God is faithful, and His truth will shine through. Above all, never stop believing in God's mercy because miracles happen to those who believe.

CRUCIFIXION & THE GOOD THIEF

Chapter Two
Dead Man Walking

As Jesus hung on the cross, nearing the end of His earthly life, He could have been overwhelmed by His own suffering. His body was battered beyond recognition – His face bruised, His mouth parched, His back torn open by scourging. With sharp thorns piercing His skull, pressing against His brain, the pain could have overwhelmed Him. Each breath He took was a struggle against the suffocating weight of His own body, every movement sending waves of excruciating pain through His limbs. In those last moments, Jesus could have been entirely absorbed in His misery, focused only on His torment, as any of us might have been. But he was not.

Even in those final, agonizing moments, when he could see the darkness of death, even His physical body began to shut down, Jesus's heart remained open to others. His mind was not fixed on His own suffering, but on the souls of those around Him. As He hung between two thieves—one mocking and the other repentant—Jesus showed the world the depth of His love and compassion, even in the most harrowing of circumstances. One thief, in his decisive moments,

mocked Jesus, challenging Him, "Aren't you the Christ? Save yourself and us." In that moment, Jesus could have easily turned His attention inward, focusing on the injustice of His suffering and the cruelty of those who mocked Him. But, He didn't. Instead, He heard the plea of the other thief-the one who, in a moment of clarity, recognized Jesus for who He truly was.

"Have you no fear of God?" the repentant thief said to his companion.

"We are punished justly, for we are getting what our deeds deserve. But this man has done nothing wrong. Jesus, remember me when you come into your kingdom."

At that moment, Jesus could have justified ignoring the thief's plea. After all, He was moments away from death, His suffering nearly complete. Yet, Jesus's response was one of deep compassion:

"Amen, I say to you, today you will be with me in paradise."

This sincere act of love and grace is a testament to the Catholic faith's sincerity and purity, and why I believe that even in His last moments, Jesus did not lose sight of His mission. His life—His suffering, death, and resurrection—was about reaching out to those in need, offering forgiveness, and providing a path to salvation, even to the last sinner. In the most painful moment of His earthly existence, Jesus demonstrated the essence of His divine love: He cared for the soul of a criminal who had turned to Him for mercy in a moment of honesty and repentance. This compassion, even in the face of unimaginable suffering, speaks to the beauty and truth of the Catholic faith. It is a faith that offers grace and forgiveness, not based on what we deserve, but on Christ's love. It reminds us that, no matter how far we may have fallen, no matter how undeserving we feel, Christ's mercy is always available. It is never too late to turn to Him and seek His forgiveness, just as the repentant thief did. Amid the most profound suffering, Jesus demonstrated the ultimate love that reaches out to save even the most broken, even at the very end. In his last

moments, He made it clear that no one is beyond redemption, and that the invitation to paradise is extended to all, no matter their past.

The beauty of the Catholic faith lies in the truth that we are never alone, even in our darkest moments. Jesus's love, displayed on the cross, calls us to love others with the same selflessness, to look beyond our own suffering, and to reach out in compassion, as He did. This is the transformative power of faith—turning our gaze outward, even when we feel most alone, and finding the ultimate truth in the cross: God's love is greater than all suffering, and His mercy is limitless.

What distinguished the two men dying alongside Jesus was their vastly different responses to their circumstances: one was consumed by anger and rage, while the other was filled with remorse and hope. This contrast speaks to the heart of why I believe—the transformative power of faith and the profound difference between those who open their hearts to grace and those who resist it.

The story of the two thieves, also reflected in the mystical visions of Blessed Anne Catherine Emmerich, who is eminent for her work in *The Dolorous Passion*. She was a German mystic and stigmatist who lived from 1774 to 1824. Through her ecstatic experiences, Emmerich received profound insights into the life and Passion of Jesus, which were later recorded by the poet Clemens Brentano. Her detailed accounts provide a glimpse into the hearts of the two criminals crucified with Jesus, offering us a deeper reflection on their responses and the choices they made in their final hours.

According to Emmerich's visions, both thieves had been condemned to death for murder. However, in their last moments, their responses to Jesus could not have been more different. The thief who would come to be known as Saint Dismas—often called the "good thief"—experienced a profound revelation. In his agony, he realized that Jesus was not a criminal, but the true Messiah. His heart, filled with remorse, led him to confess his sins and humbly ask Jesus to

remember him when He entered His kingdom. He did not demand to be saved from the cross, but asked for mercy, a prayer that would be answered with eternal grace: "Amen, I say to you, today you will be with me in paradise." In stark contrast, the other thief was consumed by self-interest. He shouted in anger, "Aren't you the Messiah? Save yourself and us!" His plea was not for redemption or forgiveness but for deliverance from his immediate suffering. He did not see Jesus as the Savior, only to escape the agony of his own punishment. His heart remained closed, unable to see beyond his own pain and recognize the Savior before him. What strikes me deeply in this moment, and why I believe, is how Jesus, even in His final hours, continued to seek out lost souls, hoping to bring them to salvation. He did not respond to the mocking thief, but to the humble plea of the repentant one. That day, only one of the lost sheep found redemption—the good thief, who opened his heart to grace. The other thief, trapped in anger and self-pity, remained lost, his heart hardened against the very love that could have saved him.

This contrast is at the heart of the Catholic faith and why I believe: it shows us that no matter how far we have fallen, or how deep our sins may be, God's mercy is always available to those who seek it with a repentant heart. Saint Dismas's story brings incredible hope, showing us that it is never too late to turn to Jesus, to ask for forgiveness, and to be embraced by His divine love. Ultimately, the choice is ours: Will we turn to Jesus in our pain, open our hearts to His mercy, and allow His grace to transform us? Or will we, like the other thief, remain consumed by ourselves, missing the opportunity to be saved? This is why I believe: because Jesus's love is boundless, and His mercy never ends. Even in His last moments, He offered hope to a criminal, showing us that no one is beyond redemption. This boundless mercy strengthens my faith and compels me to believe in the beauty and truth of God's love for us, a love that continues to reach out to the lost and the broken, even today.

Earlier in the year, the Pharisees and scribes had grown increasingly troubled by Jesus. They muttered in disdain, "This man

associates with tax collectors and welcomes sinners. He even eats with them." Aware of their hardened hearts, Jesus sought to reach them—not with condemnation, but with a story reflecting His heart and God's love's true nature. He shared the parable of the lost sheep, hoping to awaken their understanding: "What man among you, having a hundred sheep and losing one of them, would not leave the ninety-nine in the desert and go after the lost one until he finds it? And when he does find it, he sets it on his shoulders with immense joy. Upon his arrival home, he calls his friends and neighbors and says, 'Rejoice with me, for I have found my lost sheep.' I tell you, in the same way, there will be more joy in heaven over one sinner who repents than ninety-nine righteous people who do not need repentance." In this parable, the lost sheep represents humanity, and the good shepherd is Jesus. Without the shepherd's guidance, provision, and protection, humanity is weak, vulnerable, and separated from God by sin. Yet, regardless of how lost we become, Jesus is always willing to take risks and go to great lengths to find us. His love knows no bounds, and He will never cease searching for those who are lost, even at great personal cost.

I believe in this boundless love because, like the shepherd in Jesus' parable, Jesus never stops searching for us. Even in His last moments on the cross, as His physical life drained away, His love for every lost soul remained undiminished. His work did not end with the nails in His hands, and it did not end with His final breath. His search for the lost—those broken, those ashamed, those who feel far from God—never stopped. He continues to seek us out today to wrap us under his wings and shelter us as promised by him. It's just that we need to have that thirst in our hearts.

A beautiful analogy to this search is found in *The Better Part*, by Father John Bartunek. His dream about a lost sheep made him restless. Once, after a long day of grazing, he came to count his sheep. One was missing. He recounted to be sure. Yes, one sheep had strayed. The air grew colder, the shadows lengthened, and the flock huddled in a natural hollow beneath a cliff. The shepherd looked

around—he had a choice to make. He could wait until morning when it would be safer, but he knew it'd be too late. The wolf's howl cut through the darkness, reminding him that the danger was real. The search must continue. Though the wind picked up and the rain began to soak through his cloak, the shepherd didn't turn back. He knew the risk, the mud, the thorns, the night. But to him, finding the lost sheep is everything. This was his core purpose in life. The journey was arduous, and the night seemed endless, but the shepherd knew that the cost of losing the sheep was far too great. And this is where I connect the dots. To me, Jesus is just like that shepherd who can't risk losing his sheep. He is unrelenting in His search for us. He will brave the elements, the darkness, and the pain, because He loves us too much to leave us lost. Even when we are far from Him, lost in sin, or struggling to find our way, He comes after us with boundless love. No matter how far we stray, Jesus seeks us. He will not stop until we are found. In this parable, we find the essence of why I believe: Jesus's love for us is a love that perseveres. It is a love that will not give up, no matter how far we wander, no matter how lost we may feel. He is always searching, always seeking, always calling us home. This is why I believe in the beauty and truth of the Catholic faith—because it reveals a God who never ceases to seek and save the lost, who never abandons us, even in our darkest moments. This is a love worth believing in.

Today, I believe sinners, including criminals, have a place in Jesus's kingdom. However, in my early thirties, my mindset was far removed from the radical inclusivity of the Good Shepherd's message in Luke's Gospel. It took me years to understand the profound significance of Jesus's response to the good thief. I came to see it, not just as an act of mercy, but as a reflection of God's unwavering pursuit of the lost, no matter their past.

In 1993, Sister Helen Prejean, a Roman Catholic nun from New Orleans, Louisiana, published her book *Dead Man Walking*, which deeply challenged my views. The book tells the true story of Elmo Patrick Sonnier, a man convicted of the brutal 1977 rape and

murder of two teenagers, Loretta Ann Bourque, and David LeBlanc. Sonnier was sentenced to death for his crime, and in 1982, Sister Helen began visiting him on death row as his spiritual advisor. She spent years trying to guide him toward repentance, until he was ultimately executed in 1984. I had a challenging time understanding Sister Prejean's actions.

At the time, I shared the view held by many in Louisiana, where 85% of voters supported the death penalty. I couldn't fathom why Sister Helen would spend her time with someone like Elmo Sonnier, a man who had committed such a horrific crime. I wondered, what about the victims? Did she care for them too? And why do you offer compassion to a murderer? The idea of extending grace to someone like Sonnier seemed out of place. He had committed unspeakable crimes; why should he receive any compassion? It was a worldview grounded in justice through punishment, not redemption. Yet, as time passed and my life shifted, my perspective began to change. I experienced a spiritual crisis that forced me to confront my own understanding of grace, mercy, and forgiveness. During this dark period, I found myself repeatedly reading *The Dolorous Passion* by Blessed Anne Catherine Emmerich, deeply contemplating the suffering of Christ in His final hours. I prayed, asking God to help me see with new eyes the radical love and forgiveness that Jesus offered—especially as He hung on the cross.

During this time of reflection, everything started making sense to me. The connection between us and our God is so profound that no matter how hard we try, we won't be able to understand that. It's just a glimpse of his divine love that's bestowed upon us.

Jesus's response to the repentant thief on the cross, *"Amen, I say to you, today you will be with me in Paradise,"*(Luke 23:42) filled me with so much wonderment. In that moment, I realized the depth of Jesus's mercy—not just for those who flourished, but for the broken, the sinful, and those who were farthest from God. Twenty-eight years after hearing about Sister Helen Prejean, I finally grasped

the full meaning of her mission. Like Jesus, Sister Helen sought out the lost sheep. When Elmo Sonnier was strapped into the electric chair, she didn't offer him forgiveness to excuse his actions, but to help him find redemption. Sister Prejean didn't seek to save Elmo's life—justice was still served—but she offered him something far more valuable: the chance to repent, to be reconciled with God, and to find peace before he faced his ultimate judgment.

Just before Sonnier's execution, Sister Helen told him, "Look at my face. This is the face of Christ." Her mission wasn't to change the past or deny the gravity of Elmo's crime but to help him reach a moment of true contrition. She wasn't offering Elmo an escape from justice, but a path toward salvation. In that moment, she communicated the same grace that Jesus extended to the good thief on the cross: "Today you will be with me in Paradise." This is why I believe. It is not because we deserve forgiveness, but because, in His mercy, Jesus reaches out to the lost, the broken, the ones who feel irredeemable. He doesn't turn His back on us, even when we are steeped in sin. He is always searching, calling, and ready to extend His love—even in our darkest hour. Through Sister Helen Prejean's example, I began to see that true justice is not just punishment but the opportunity for redemption. It's the perspective that matters; if we see any misfortune as an opportunity for redemption, God will illuminate our hearts. On the contrary, if we see any bad happening as a punishment from God, this will only make us more rebel. Like Jesus, Sister Helen understood that no one is beyond the reach of God's mercy, no matter their past. And that is the message of grace that has transformed my life: that in Christ, there is always hope, always a chance to return to the fold. This is why I believe.

Did Sister Prejean also meet with the families of the victims? Yes, she did, though it did not go well. I found an online article by Christina Janney, dated September 18, 2013, that details Sister Prejean's encounters with the victims' families. Here is an excerpt from that article. "I was so chilled by the enormity of the evil of killing two innocent kids. I am the spiritual adviser to the two people who did this. And then I thought of the parents. Prejean was reluctant to contact the victims' families. She thought they could not possibly want to hear from the woman who was the spiritual adviser to the man that killed their children. She met the families of the victims at the pardon board hearing one week before Sonnier was executed. She met the families in the hall, and the Bourque family averted their gazes and walked right by Prejean. David LeBlanc's father, Lloyd, stopped Prejean in the hall. "We lost our boy David," Lloyd LeBlanc said to Prejean. "Sister, all this time you have been visiting those two brothers, and you do not once come and see us. Sister, you do not understand the pressure we are under with this death penalty thing." Prejean agreed to drive to LeBlanc's church and pray with him during his regular prayer time at 4 a.m. LeBlanc was originally very anger at the Sonniers, but he is a kind mind, Prejean said. He said he was losing that kindness to his bitterness and hatred. "They killed our son, but I am not going to let them kill me," LeBlanc said. "I am going do what Jesus said. "The pressure on the LeBlancs to support the death penalty was immense. "Sister, when I said pressure on us about the death penalty. Everybody was saying to us, "You must be for the death penalty or its going to look like you did not love your boy. You had the ultimate loss. Look at the suffering of your wife, and look at Vickie, your daughter. Look at what has happened to your family, and you are not going to ask for the ultimate penalty? Sister Prejean was not trying to exonerate the killers in any way. On the contrary! She was trying to get them to admit their guilt, atone for their sins and ask the family and God for forgiveness. According to her, she did obtain her goals. Sister Prejean was trying to follow Jesus's parable and be the good shepherd looking for a lost sheep."

I can't say that I've always understood why Jesus would seek out the most lost and broken among us—the criminals, the murderers, the rapists, the ones society deems irredeemable. If you're like me, you might find it difficult to reconcile the idea that Jesus would pour out His love on someone who has committed unspeakable acts. But a conversation I encountered in *The Shack* by Wm. Paul Young helped me see this in a new light. In *The Shack*, Mackenzie, a man whose daughter has been brutally murdered, spends time in the presence of God, Jesus, and the Holy Spirit after the tragedy. His wife refers to God as "Papa," who, in a personal way, manifests as a strong African American woman. One day, however, "Papa" appears to Mack as a powerful American Indian man, explaining that He needs to assume this form for the task ahead: "What we're going to do today requires a father figure who can be strong with you." They embark on a journey into the wilderness to find the body of Mack's daughter, Missy. Along the way, Mack is consumed by the anguish of what happened and the unresolved fury inside him. With tears streaming down his face, he cries out, "Papa, how can I forgive that son of a bitch who killed my Missy? If he were right here today, I don't know what I would do. I want to hurt him like he hurt me... I want revenge." Papa listens patiently, letting Mack's rage pour out. Then, with quiet wisdom, she responds: "So now... Mack, you are back again being the judge?" She waits for Mack's anger to subside and then gently speaks: "Mack, for you to forgive this man is for you to release him to me and allow me to redeem him."

Mack is horrified. "Redeem him? I don't want to redeem him! I want to hurt him, punish him... put him in hell." But Papa, with great love, answers: "I know. But this man... this man, he too is my son. I want to redeem him."

This was a turning point in the story for me, one that I couldn't easily ignore. "He, too, is my son," Papa says, "and I want to redeem him." I couldn't help but feel a lump in my throat. Even though the man who killed Mack's daughter, had done something horrific, in God's eyes, he was still a child of God. This truth was hard to grasp, but it was also undeniable: Jesus's love stretches to the farthest reaches of humanity, even to those whose actions make them seem beyond redemption. And for the first time, I began to see the fullness of what it means to truly forgive, to release someone to God's judgment, and to allow Him to work the miracle of redemption. In the story, Mack continues to struggle. "But how can I forgive him?" he asks. "If I forgive him, doesn't that mean I'm excusing what he did?

Doesn't that make it unfair to Missy?" Papa replies with tenderness and authority, "Forgiveness does not excuse anything. Believe me, the last thing this man has is freedom. And you have no duty to justice in this. I will handle that. As for Missy, she has already forgiven him."

This idea of this degree of forgiveness was radical for me. It wasn't about excusing evil, nor was it about releasing the criminal from the consequences of his actions. It was about releasing the anger, the desire for revenge, and the heavy burden of judgment that Mack had carried for so long. In the end, it was about trusting God to handle the justice while offering forgiveness as a way of releasing the pain. I've learned that Jesus desires to redeem every human being, no matter how deep the stain of sin. Even those who seem unworthy of forgiveness—those we want to forget or punish—are still loved by Jesus, and He still desires to redeem them. This is one of the most challenging truths of the Gospel, but it is also one of the most profound thing to ponder over. It's why I believe. Just as Jesus hung on the cross between two thieves, offering redemption to one who asked for it, Jesus is always ready to offer grace to those who repent, even in the last moments of their lives. It's a choice we each have, just as the two criminals on the cross had. One chose to mock Jesus, while the other chose to ask for mercy. And in that moment, Jesus responded, "Amen, I say to you, today you will be with me in Paradise."

It was in reading this story—both in *The Shack* and in the Gospel—that I began to understand why Jesus would seek out the lost, the broken, the guilty. He does it because they are His children, too. They are worthy of love, redemption, and His grace. No one is beyond the reach of His love. I'm not saying it's easy to forgive or to understand why God would extend grace to the worst of humanity. But what I do know is this: if Jesus can offer redemption to a thief on a cross, if He can offer grace to someone as vile as Elmo Sonnier, then there's hope for all of us. No matter what we've done, no matter how far we've fallen, God's grace is always available. We are all His children, and He desires that no one should be lost. This is why I

believe. Because I believe that Jesus's love is boundless, His grace is unmeasurable, and His desire for redemption never ends—no matter how far we've strayed.

"So, is it all right if I'm still angry?" Mack asked, his voice filled with turmoil. Papa's response was immediate and full of grace: "Absolutely. What he did was wrong—terribly wrong. It caused deep pain and loss, and anger is a natural response to something so evil. But, Mack, do not let that anger consume you. Do not allow the pain and the bitterness to take root in your heart. You may feel the need to declare your forgiveness a hundred times in the beginning—on the first day, the second day. But on time, each day will get easier. One day, you will realize that you have truly forgiven. And then, one day, you will pray for his healing, for his wholeness, and you will give him over to me, so that my love can cleanse him and burn away every vestige of corruption. As incomprehensible as it seems now, you may one day know this man in a completely different light."

At sixty-five years, when I reflect on my journey of becoming a believer, I can say that I didn't acquire guidance overnight. In fact, it took me a good 25 years to fully grasp the concept of Sister Helen Prejean. At the time, I struggled to understand why she would choose to walk beside someone like Elmo Patrick Sonnier, a man responsible for such horrific crimes. But in time, I came to realize that Sister Prejean wasn't condoning the evil that Sonnier had done. She was, in fact, doing exactly what Jesus would do—she was seeking the lost sheep. Sister Prejean was acting as a shepherd, following in the footsteps of Jesus, who in Luke 15 tells the parable of the lost sheep. As I have often advised others struggling with their own pain and confusion, I encourage them to read that passage. I have found myself returning to it many times during my own seasons of doubt and hardship. Each time, I am reminded of Jesus's words to the good thief on the cross and the joy in heaven that follows the repentance of a lost soul.

We live in a world hungry for justice but starving for mercy. But the path to animosity and rage is always easy; the real test comes when we make room for compassion. We need to realize that we are all sinners. We are all in need of grace. The Pharisees and scribes in Jesus's time were quick to judge, but they lacked the compassion to see the bigger picture. We, too, can easily fall into that trap. The real commitment to Jesus is when we radiate compassion and empathy for others. And only God knows the true state of a person's heart. Only He knows how far His grace can reach, and we are no one to judge.

We are all, in a sense, "dead men walking," bound by sin and separated from God. We are all sinners. And still Jesus looks at us with love and says, "Today, you will be with me in paradise." This is why I believe. It's not because it's easy. It's not because I always understand it. But it's because I know, deep down, that if Jesus can redeem the worst of us, then none of us are beyond hope. We are all worthy of His love, His mercy, and His grace. And that is the message I choose to live by.

MARY'S FIAT

Chapter Three
Siblings

If you're of a certain age, you might remember the classic TV series *The Andy Griffith Show*. For those who aren't familiar, the show centered around Sheriff Andy Taylor, a widowed father raising his son Opie in the fictional town of Mayberry. It was a place where neighbors knew each other by name, doors were left unlocked, and the community thrived on a spirit of togetherness. In Mayberry, life was simple—deputy Barney Fife was allowed only one bullet, which he kept in his shirt pocket. Otis, the town drunk, would stumble into the unlocked sheriff's office and let himself in. He would unlock a jail cell so he could sleep off his drunkenness. The next day Aunt Bee, Sheriff Taylor's aunt, would give him a home-cooked meal. Opie's childhood was filled with the innocent joys of fishing, skipping rocks, and exploring with friends, while Sundays often found the family relaxing on the porch, sharing a glass of lemonade, and reflecting on the day. Each episode would wrap up with a moral lesson and a happy conclusion. To this day, I still watch reruns, especially for the humorous antics of Barney. If you've never seen it, I highly recommend this wholesome, entertaining series.

Abbeville, Louisiana, my childhood was filled with the kind of simplicity and warmth you'd find in a town like Mayberry. Abbeville is a small, close-knit farming community with a population of around twelve thousand, and life there had the feel of a simpler time. My neighborhood, Mount Carmel Heights, was a place where families genuinely looked out for one another. I lived only a short five-minute walk from Mount Carmel Elementary School, where most of my friends were also classmates. The area consisted of two streets that formed a figure-eight shape: the "little block" and the "big block." My street, Saint Mary, turned into Saint Paul at the top of the figure eight, where it met the larger street. Living in our Cajun community, I knew everyone in the neighborhood—my friends, their families, and even their pets. There were no strangers in our town; my friends' parents felt like an extension of my own. Our days were filled with simple, carefree fun—playing games like kick-the-can, football, and basketball until the streetlights came on, or spending time hunting and camping in the nearby woods. Sundays were a highlight, often filled with family gatherings, where parish priests and bachelor teachers would join us for hearty country meals. Abbeville was so safe back then that my brother Robert and I, even as young children, could walk alone to Frank's Theater to catch the latest John Wayne movie, "Planet of the Apes," or comedies like Abbott and Costello. Life was full of these simple pleasures,

As the youngest of seven boys, with a ten-year gap between my oldest brother and me, our neighborhood was always full of children. The Hebert family next door had eight kids, two boys and six girls. Down the street, the Domingues had six kids, three boys and three girls. Across the street, the Veazey family had an equal number of children, and directly opposite us, the Landry family had three boys and four girls. The largest family in the neighborhood was a blended one, consisting of two widows and their eleven children. With so many kids around, it often felt like a small army! Looking back, the sheer number of siblings in our neighborhood made me think of a question that has puzzled many: Did Jesus have siblings? Some Christian denominations believe Jesus had brothers and sisters, while

the Catholic Church teaches that He was an only child, holding to the doctrine of the perpetual virginity of Mary. For many years, this question lingered in my mind. It seemed natural to think that Jesus, like most children of His time, would have had siblings. But as I reflected on my own faith, I came to realize that this question goes beyond a simple answer.

To fully understand the answer, we need to examine what the Bible says about Jesus' family. Both the Gospels of Matthew and Mark mention the "brothers" and "sisters" of Jesus. However, in the cultural context of Jesus' time, these terms didn't always refer to biological siblings in the way we understand them today. The word "brother" was often used more broadly to describe close relatives, like cousins, or even members of a shared community. Additionally, the Catholic Church teaches that Mary remained a virgin for her entire life, with Jesus being her only son, a belief that reflects the long-held understanding of her purity. For me, the question of whether Jesus had siblings goes beyond historical debate and delves into a deeper understanding of who He truly is. Jesus isn't just another man from Nazareth—He is the Son of God, born of a Virgin, sent to redeem the world. His family was unique and sacred in its own way, set apart just as the community I grew up in was. Though our neighborhood was filled with love and simplicity, it pointed me toward something greater. Today, I view this question through the lens of faith. Whether or not Jesus had siblings in the traditional sense doesn't change the heart of my belief—that Jesus, the Savior, came to seek and save the lost, to heal the broken, and to invite us all into His eternal family. And that is why I believe it.

In Matthew 12:46-50, we encounter a moment that challenges our conventional understanding of family. While Jesus was speaking to the crowds, His mother and brothers arrived outside, hoping to speak with Him. When someone informed Jesus of their presence, He responded by asking, "Who is my mother? Who are my brothers?" Then, extending His hand toward His disciples, He said, "Here are my mother and my brothers. For whoever does the will of my heavenly

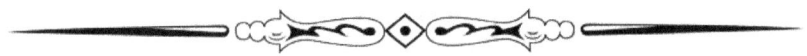

Father is my brother, and sister, and mother." At first glance, Jesus' words may seem puzzling or even dismissive. However, when we consider the broader context of His mission, we realize something profound: Jesus is reshaping the very definition of family, showing that true kinship is found in those who follow God's will. In Matthew 13:55, just after the passage in question, we hear a reference to Jesus' earthly family: "Isn't His mother called Mary, and His brothers James, Joseph, Simon, and Judas? And aren't His sisters here with us?" The Gospels of Mark (6:3) and Luke (8:19-20) echo this, identifying Jesus as the brother of James, Joseph, Judas, and Simon, and mentioning His sisters as well. These verses bring up an important question that has been debated for centuries: Did Jesus have siblings?

The references to "brothers" and "sisters" in these passages seem to suggest that Jesus had close biological relatives. However, like many aspects of scripture, understanding the cultural and linguistic context is crucial. In first-century Jewish culture, the term "brother" was often used more broadly to refer to close relatives, such as cousins, or even to members of the same community. The Greek word *adelphos*, translated as "brother" in the New Testament, could also describe someone in a close relationship, like a fellow believer or someone sharing the same mission. In 1 Corinthians 9:5, Saint Paul mentions the *"brothers of the Lord"* in a way that highlights their role in the early Church rather than focusing on a biological connection: *"Do we not have the right to take along a Christian wife, as do the rest of the apostles, the brothers of the Lord, and Cephas?"*

When viewed through the broader context of the New Testament, these references suggest that the term "brother" had a flexible meaning. However, the question of whether Jesus had siblings is not just theological or historical—it's deeply connected to how we understand our relationship with Christ. While the Gospels mention Jesus' earthly family, they also show that Jesus was not focused solely on biological relationships. His message pointed to something far deeper: spiritual kinship. As He said, "Whoever does the will of My Father in heaven is My brother and sister and mother."

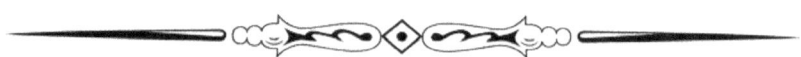

In this way, Jesus is expanding the idea of family. The bonds of faith and obedience to God's will go beyond bloodlines, creating a connection that is more profound and eternal. This perspective is central to my belief. It helps me see that, in Jesus' eyes, family isn't defined by genetics or earthly ties but by doing God's will, aligning with His purpose, and becoming part of the larger family of faith that transcends time and place. For me, this teaching is both comforting and challenging—it reminds me that I am part of a bigger family, one united by Christ's love and His call to follow His example.

Through these passages, I am reminded of the spiritual family that Jesus invites us into—a family where we are not bound by earthly distinctions, but united by our shared love for God and our commitment to His will. In this family, we are all brothers and sisters in Christ, regardless of our background, status, or past mistakes. And for that, I am deeply grateful. This brings us back to the longstanding question: Did Jesus have siblings, or is there another explanation? The interpretation of these passages often depends on Protestants and non-denominational Christians who adhere to the principle of "scripture alone" often interpret the Gospel passages as evidence that Jesus had siblings. However, this raises the question: Why is it so important to determine whether Jesus had siblings? What is gained from this debate? It seems that one motivation might be to challenge the Catholic Church's teaching on the perpetual virginity of Mary, the Blessed Mother. The Catholic Church holds that Mary remained a virgin throughout her life and that her role in God's salvation plan is more significant than just being the mother of Jesus. Pope Paul VI, in his 1968 "Credo of the People of God," stated: "We believe that the Holy Mother of God, the new Eve, mother of the Church, continues in heaven to exercise her maternal role on behalf of the members of Christ." This belief underscores the Catholic Church's view of Mary as having a special, ongoing role in salvation history, rather than being merely an ordinary woman.

The question of whether Jesus had siblings has been a point of debate for centuries, particularly between Catholic and Protestant

interpretations of scripture. One key passage often cited by some Protestants to support the claim that Jesus had siblings is Matthew 1:25, which states: *"He had no relations with her until she bore a son; and he named him Jesus."* From this verse, some argue that the term *"until"* implies that Joseph and Mary had a normal marital relationship after Jesus' birth, which would mean Mary had other children. However, this interpretation has its flaws. In biblical Greek, the word *"until"* (or *"till"*) is used in a variety of ways that do not imply a change in behavior after the referenced time. For example, in 2 Samuel 6:23, *"until"* simply marks a period without suggesting any shift in behavior afterward. The same is true in passages like John 9:18 and 1 Timothy 4:13, where *"until"* does not imply a change but simply marks a duration. In Matthew 1:25, the use of *"until"* is meant to emphasize that Joseph did not have relations with Mary before Jesus' birth, confirming the virgin birth of Jesus. The text does not suggest anything about Joseph and Mary's relationship after the birth of Jesus.

From a Catholic perspective, this understanding of Matthew 1:25 aligns with the doctrine of the perpetual virginity of Mary. In the Gospel of Luke, we see Mary's response to the Annunciation when the angel Gabriel tells her she will conceive the Son of God: *"How will this be, since I do not know man?"* (Luke 1:34). Saint Augustine interpreted this response as evidence that Mary had taken a vow of virginity and remained committed to it even in her response to the angel. Mary's question shows that she had no intention of breaking her vow of chastity, even in the face of God's call to motherhood. This sacred commitment to virginity becomes central in understanding Mary's role in salvation history and why the Church teaches that Mary remained a virgin before, during, and after the birth of Jesus.

For some, these teachings may seem difficult to accept, especially in a world that often questions traditional beliefs. Yet, many people readily accept predictions from sources like the tarot card readers in New Orlean's Jackson Square or Nostradamus or even

the California psychic telephone line, even when those predictions lack the authority and spiritual depth of divine revelation. Throughout history, the Church has recognized private revelations granted to saints as credible, and one such revelation comes from Blessed Mary of Agreda, a Spanish mystic. According to her writings, Joseph himself made a vow of chastity at a youthful age, remaining celibate for life, a vow he maintained even in his marriage to Mary. This perspective on Joseph adds another layer of depth to the Catholic teaching on the Holy Family.

The understanding of terms like *"brother"* in the Bible also provides insight into this question. In many passages, the term *"brother"* does not necessarily refer to a sibling in the modern sense of the word, but rather to a close relative or fellow community member. For example, in Genesis 14:14, Abram's *"brother"* is actually his nephew, Lot. Similarly, in Genesis 31:37, *"brother"* refers to a relative like an uncle, not a biological sibling. In Leviticus, *"brother"* is used to refer to someone from the same tribe, as in Numbers 18:6, or even extended family, as in 2 Kings 10:13, where *"brothers"* refers to extended kin, not direct siblings. Understanding the broader context of biblical language and Jewish culture helps clarify the interpretation of passages where Jesus' *"brothers"* are mentioned. The term is used in a more expansive way than we often assume, indicating the broader kinship ties within the Jewish community. This allows us to understand that references to Jesus' *"brothers"* and *"sisters"* in the Gospels likely refer to close relatives or even disciples, rather than biological children of Mary.

For me, these interpretations help deepen my understanding of the mystery of the Holy Family and why I believe in the perpetual virginity of Mary. The idea that Mary, as the Mother of God, remained a virgin before, during, and after the birth of Jesus is not just a matter of tradition, but a profound theological truth that speaks to God's plan for salvation. Mary's perpetual virginity points to her unique role in salvation history and emphasizes her total devotion to God's will. Jesus, as the Son of God, entered the world in a way that

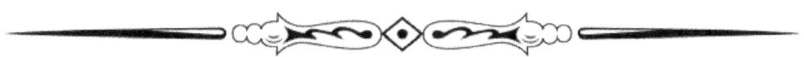

was unlike any other, and his relationship with his mother was unlike any other relationship. For me, this belief not only makes sense within the context of scripture, but it also deepens my faith and appreciation for the sacredness of Mary's role as the Mother of the Church. In reflecting on these teachings, I am reminded of why I believe— because these doctrines, rooted in scripture and deepened by the Church's tradition, reveal to us the beauty and mystery of God's plan for salvation. They help me see the significance of every person's role in that plan, whether near or far, and call me to a deeper commitment to living out God's will in my own life.

The Catholic Church interprets the Greek word "adelphos" (often translated as "brother") to include not just siblings but also nieces, cousins, and half-siblings. In contrast, Protestants often use the Greek word "anepsios" (as found in Colossians 4:10) to specifically mean "cousins." Both interpretations of Greek and Hebrew do not provide a distinct term for "stepbrother." Here are some additional examples of how "brother" is used in different contexts in the Bible:

- **Leviticus 19:17** – A fellow man

- **1 Kings 9:13** – One of the same offices

- **Genesis 13:8 and 14:16** – Any kinsman, not just a brother or nephew

- **Job 5:15** – Any friend

- **Amos 1:9** – An ally

- **Exodus 2:11** – Someone of the same people

When considering the family dynamics of Jesus, the term "brother" often sparks debate, especially in reference to the individuals in the Gospels who are called Jesus' "brothers." Some

interpret these references as evidence that Jesus had biological siblings, but a deeper understanding of Jewish customs and language provides a broader perspective. In ancient Jewish culture, family roles were well-defined, particularly regarding inheritance. The next of kin typically took responsibility for the deceased relative's assets and well-being, with the first-born son often assuming the role of the family head. If no sons were present, a trusted relative might step in. This cultural context is important when we look at passages like Genesis 14:14, where Lot, Abraham's nephew, is called Abraham's "brother." Similarly, in Genesis 29:15, Jacob refers to his uncle Laban as his "brother." The term "brother" was used more broadly in this way, including close relatives like cousins or even fellow members of the same tribe, not just immediate siblings.

These cultural and linguistic practices help illuminate the New Testament passages that mention Jesus' *"brothers."* In Matthew 13:55-56 and Mark 6:3, we read of Jesus' *"brothers"*—James, Joseph, Simon, and Judas. Some interpret these references as evidence that Jesus had biological siblings, but a closer look suggests otherwise. The term *"brother"* in these texts likely refers to other close relatives—possibly cousins—rather than the children of Mary and Joseph. This understanding is further supported by passages such as Matthew 27:56, Mark 14:40, and John 19:25, where we learn that James and Joseph are the sons of another Mary, the wife of Clopas (or Cleophas). If these men were Jesus' actual brothers, the Gospel writers would not have made this distinction. The doctrine teaches that Mary remained a virgin throughout her life, an important aspect of her sacred role as the Mother of God. I believe this teaching underscores the unique and holy nature of her relationship with Jesus, emphasizing that she was chosen by God for a singular mission—to bear His Son, the Savior of the world.

By embracing the broader cultural context in which the Bible was written, I come to see Mary's perpetual virginity not as a point of contention, but as a profound mystery that highlights the depth of God's love for humanity. Mary's vow of chastity, her total dedication

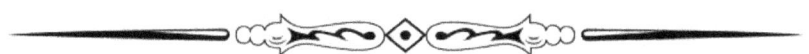

to God's will, and her unique role in salvation history are all reasons why I believe in her perpetual virginity. The Gospels speak of Jesus' *"brothers"* as part of a larger family unit, but the Church has always understood Mary as the singular, virgin Mother of Christ, and that understanding enriches my own relationship with her and with her Son, Jesus. In the end, I believe that the truth about Jesus' family—like much of Scripture—requires careful consideration of the historical, cultural, and linguistic context. When we approach the Bible with this understanding, we not only gain clarity on difficult passages but also deepen our faith in the divine mysteries that shape our salvation. For me, the belief in Mary's perpetual virginity is not just a theological point; it's a sign of God's plan, His choice of a pure vessel to bring Christ into the world, and a reminder of how sacred and intentional every detail of salvation history truly is.

The question of whether Jesus had biological siblings often arises in theological discussions, but when viewed through the lens of Scripture, early Church tradition, and Jewish customs, the belief in Mary's perpetual virginity becomes clear and deeply significant. If James, the bishop of Jerusalem, had been a biological son of Mary, it would indeed challenge the doctrine of her perpetual virginity. However, this doctrine has been upheld by the Church since the earliest days of Christianity, with early Church Fathers like Irenaeus, Polycarp, and Ignatius of Antioch affirming it as a fundamental aspect of Christian faith. Their testimonies reflect a deep understanding of Mary's unique role in salvation history and help explain why the Catholic Church holds fast to this doctrine.

A key factor in understanding this issue is Jewish custom, particularly the practices surrounding family responsibilities. In Jewish tradition, the eldest son was responsible for the care of his mother, especially after the death of the father. The Gospel of John provides powerful evidence that Jesus did not have siblings who could have taken on this responsibility. In John 19:26-27, as Jesus hangs on the cross, He entrusts the care of His mother to the beloved disciple, John: *"When Jesus saw his mother and the disciple whom he loved*

*standing nearby, he said to his mother, 'Woman, here is your son,'
and to the disciple, 'Here is your mother.'"* This action highlights
Jesus' concern for His mother's welfare, a concern that would have
been fulfilled by His biological brothers if they had existed. The fact
that He entrusted Mary to John's care strongly suggests that no
siblings were available to fulfill this role, pointing to the conclusion
that Jesus had no other brothers.

Additionally, the New Testament consistently refers to Mary
as the mother of Jesus, never identifying her as the mother of James,
Joseph, Simon, or Judas in the same way. This consistent
identification further supports the interpretation that these individuals
were not Jesus' biological siblings but rather close relatives, possibly
cousins, in accordance with Jewish kinship terms.

While the debate over Jesus' siblings continues, I believe that
the focus should remain on the central truth of the Christian faith—
the sacrificial death of Jesus for the salvation of humanity. The
question of Mary's virginity does not alter this truth but instead
deepens our understanding of her role in God's plan. For those who
question whether Mary remained a virgin throughout her life, the
apparitions at Fatima offer a compelling perspective. At Fatima, the
Blessed Mother requested the promotion of the Five First Saturdays
of Reparation, one of which specifically addresses offenses against
her Immaculate Heart. Among these offenses is the denial of her
perpetual virginity, including the belief that she had relations with
Joseph and had other children.

In conclusion, I believe that the evidence from Scripture,
Jewish customs, and Marian apparitions strongly supports the
doctrine of Mary's perpetual virginity. This belief is not merely
theological but is deeply connected to her role in salvation history as
the Mother of God. It is integral to our understanding of her holiness
and devotion to God's will. By embracing this perspective, we gain a
fuller understanding of Mary's role in the life of Christ and in the life
of the Church, and why the Church continues to uphold this doctrine
as a central tenet of the Catholic faith.

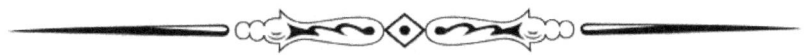

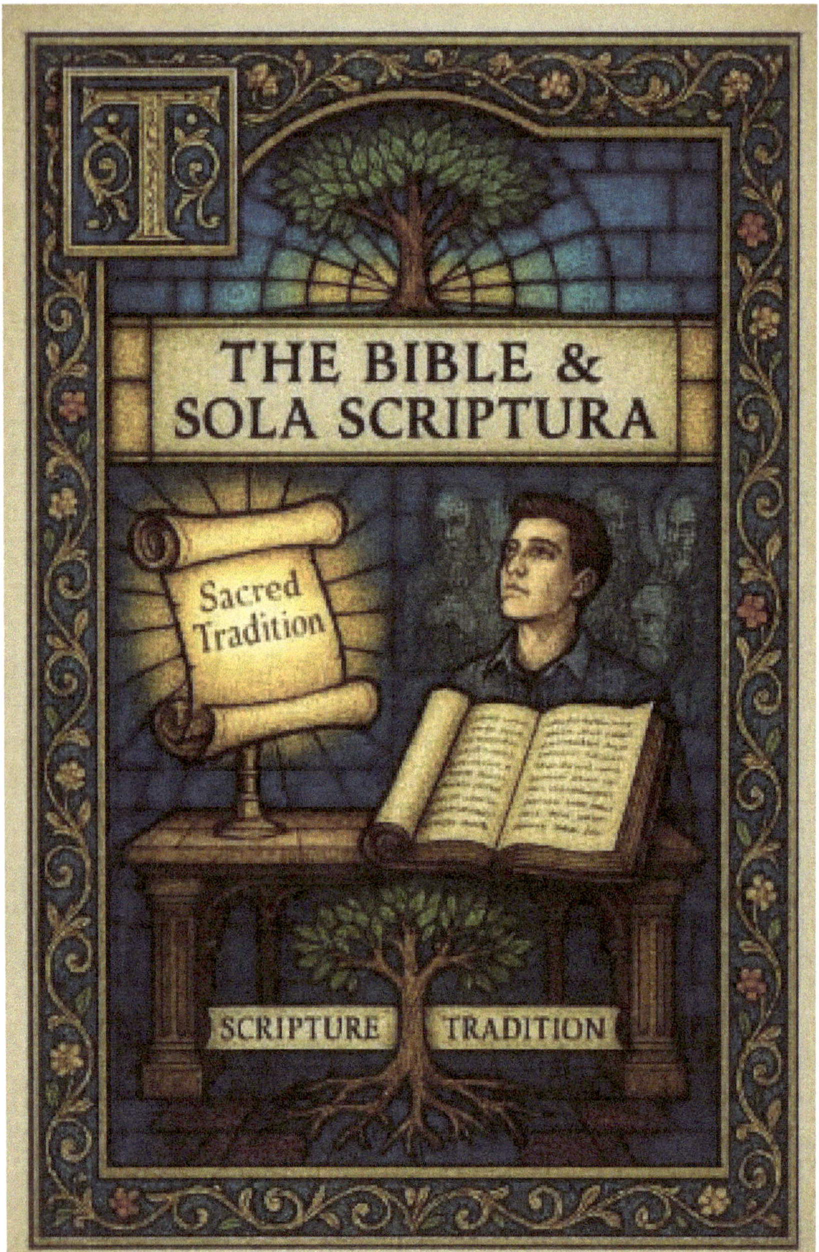
THE BIBLE &
SOLA SCRIPTURA
Sacred
Tradition
SCRIPTURE
TRADITION

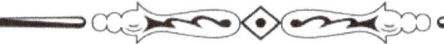

Chapter Four
THE BIBLE

When I was married, my ex-wife often expressed skepticism about the Bible, particularly its authorship. She would frequently make sarcastic comments like, "A man wrote the Bible," suggesting that because men authored it, the text was inevitably biased or imperfect, implying that because men were the authors, it must reflect human bias or imperfection and thus could not be fully trusted as divine truth. She questioned the authenticity of Scripture, wondering how we could be certain it wasn't simply a human creation rather than something divinely inspired. I tried to explain that, according to both Scripture and oral tradition, God Himself played a crucial role in the writing of the Bible. For example, the early books were directly given by God to Moses, as recorded in the Torah. But, her doubts persisted, and she asked the same questions again, how we could be sure that every word in the Bible was true and not merely fabricated over time.

To address her concerns, I shared the teaching from 2 Peter 1:20-21, which assures us that the Scriptures are not just the product of human will or interpretation but were written by people moved by the

Holy Spirit: *"Know this first of all, that there is no prophecy of Scripture that is a matter of personal interpretation, for no prophecy ever came through human will; but rather human beings moved by the Holy Spirit spoke from God."* This passage reflects the belief that the Scriptures were not just written by men, but under the guidance of the Holy Spirit, ensuring that what was recorded was faithful to God's truth.

Another question she would often raise was why there are only four Gospels in the New Testament. She wondered whether other apostles or disciples might have written their own accounts of Jesus' life that were left out of the Bible. While the Bible itself doesn't offer a direct answer, history and tradition offer some insights. For example, the mystic Venerable Mary of Agreda, a 17th-century Franciscan abbess, authored a book called *The Mystical City of God*, which contains insights she received through private revelations from the Blessed Mother herself. In her writings, Mary of Agreda described aspects of Mary and Jesus's lives, including details of the Passion, Resurrection, and Ascension. While no part of the canon's Scripture, her work gives a clear insight on sacredness about Gospel's narratives, offering context for how Scripture came to be as it is.

According to Venerable Mary of Agreda, just after the resurrection and ascension of Jesus, Saint Peter, as the head of the Church, recognized the need to record the mysteries of Christ's life for future generations. The early Church, under the guidance of the Holy Spirit, sought to preserve the truth of the Gospel in written form to replace the old Law with the new. Saint Peter convened a council to deliberate on how this sacred task would be carried out. He turned to the Blessed Mother, the "Mother of Wisdom," for counsel, and together, they invoked the Holy Spirit to guide the decision. A divine light then descended upon them, and a voice from Heaven declared, "The high priest and head of the Church shall assign four to record the works and teachings of the Savior of the world." With this divine confirmation, Saint Peter announced that Matthew would be the first to write his Gospel, followed by Mark, Luke, and finally John. This

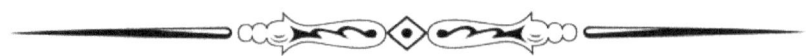

decision was ratified by the continued presence of the heavenly light, a sign of God's approval. This moment marked the beginning of the sacred task that would ensure the preservation of Christ's teachings for the Church and the world. The Gospels, as I understand them, were not just the writings of individual men; they were divinely inspired accounts of the life of the Savior.

According to Blessed Agreda, when Matthew began his writing in 42 A.D., the Blessed Mother appeared to him, assuring him that she, along with the Holy Spirit, would assist in the process. I find it profound that the Mother of God, who held all the mysteries of Jesus in her heart, personally guided Matthew to write only what was "absolutely necessary" to preserve the truth of the Incarnation. This collaboration between the Blessed Mother, the Holy Spirit, and Matthew himself affirms to me that these Gospels were not the product of human invention but were the direct result of divine intervention. The writing of the other Gospels followed in a comparable way, with Mark, Luke, and John receiving assistance from the Blessed Mother and the Holy Spirit. Mark's Gospel was written in 46 A.D., Luke's in 48 A.D., and John is in 58 A, D. The Holy Spirit's guidance, visible in the form of a physical descent upon the evangelists, confirmed that these texts were true, faithful accounts of the life of Christ, each with a unique perspective but united in their purpose: to reveal the Savior to the world.

This understanding strengthens my faith in the Gospels. They are not just historical documents; they are the living Words of God, inspired by the Holy Spirit. The belief that the Blessed Mother and the Holy Spirit were present and actively participating in the creation of these texts my conviction that the Scriptures are a true and faithful record of Christ's life and teachings. I believe that the Gospels, written under divine guidance, continue to speak to us today, revealing the truths of salvation and the love of God in a way that transcends time and culture.

While some may find accounts like those of Venerable Mary of Agreda difficult to accept, I believe that if we accept the Bible's stories as factual and trust in the divine power of God, then it should not surprise us to consider the divine guidance she describes in the formation of the Gospels. The idea that the Holy Spirit and the Blessed Mother played an active role in helping the evangelists write their accounts of Christ's life aligns with the belief that all things are possible with God, including preserving His Word through human hands. Having established why there are only four Gospels, it's important to understand how the Bible came into existence and how the divine wisdom behind it continues to shape my faith.

As I believe, the Bible is not a human creation but a divinely inspired compilation of sacred texts that have been carefully preserved for the followers and the Church. It has a collection of sacred words, including holy writings—historical accounts, poetry, prophecy, wisdom, and letters—that form the foundation of the Christian faith. The Bible did not come into existence all at once. Still, rather, it's a careful act of compilation of God's divine message, through the work of different authors, all guided by the Holy Spirit. In the beginning, the stories of the faith were passed down orally, with generations recounting the deeds and teachings of God. Over time, these stories were written down, forming the sacred Scriptures that would be recognized as the Old Testament. With the coming of Christ, new writings emerged, initially spread by word of mouth and through personal letters, until they were eventually compiled into the New Testament.

The canon of Scripture, the list of books considered divinely inspired—was not determined overnight. It took centuries of prayer, discernment, and the guidance of the Holy spirit to determine which texts held the fullness of truth. This process, affirmed by Church councils, highlights the divine involvement in ensuring that only authentic and inspired writings were included. Understanding how the Bible played its role in enlightening the Christian faith, and I can't help but appreciate the power and wisdom of those sacred words. If you read the biblical text thoroughly, you will realize that the Holy Spirits guide the writers of the Gospels, I believe He continues to speak to us through the Scriptures today, drawing us closer to the truth of Christ's love and the salvation He offers.

The Bible's formation is a journey that spans centuries, beginning with oral traditions passed down through generations. These stories, teachings, and histories of God's people were initially shared through the spoken word. Still, over time, they were compiled and eventually written down on materials like papyrus, parchment, and later, paper manuscripts. By around 367 A.D., St. Athanasius, the 20th Pope of the Church, identified and compiled a list of seventy-three books that he believed were divinely inspired, laying the foundation for the canon of the Bible as we know it today. A few decades later, between 383 and 404 A.D., Saint Jerome, known as Jerome of Stridon, was commissioned to bring these sacred writings together in one volume. According to tradition, Jerome spent over forty years in a cave in Bethlehem, the same cave where the Holy Family had once resided during Jesus' birth. There, he translated the Old and New Testaments from Greek and Hebrew into Latin, making the Bible accessible to Western Europe. This translation, known as the *Vulgate*, became the standard version of the Bible for the Western Church for over a thousand years.

For the next 1,500 years, the Catholic Church's role was prominent in preserving and copying these, Scriptures. The Church, with its commitment to safeguarding the integrity of the Bible, is a testament of God's meticulous words and its profound message maintained and transmitted across generations. This dedication was not just about copying texts; it was about faithfully passing down God's revelation to His people. However, by the 15th century, a variety of writings, many not recognized by the Church, began to circulate. These included texts like the *Gospel of Thomas*, the *Gospel of Mary*, and other gnostic writings, which challenged the established understanding of the Gospel. These texts often conflicted with the

teachings of the Church, and the spread of such ideas led to confusion and division among the faithful.

In response to the challenges brought on by the Protestant Reformation, the Catholic Church convened the Council of Trent from 1545 to 1563. This council marked the beginning of the Counter-Reformation, an effort to reaffirm and protect the Church's authority. Over eighteen years and twenty-five sessions, the Council addressed numerous theological matters and reinforced the Church's teachings on Scripture and Tradition. A significant outcome of the Council was the Index of Forbidden Books creation in 1564, which sought to prevent the spread of heretical writings and protect the faithful from teachings that deviated from the Gospel's truth. This historical journey—from the early oral traditions to the establishment of the biblical canon, and the Church's ongoing efforts to preserve and protect the integrity of the Scriptures—reinforce my conviction in the Bible's divine origin. While some may question the authority of certain texts or the motivations behind historical decisions, I trust that God has guided His Church throughout history, ensuring that the Scriptures we have today faithfully reflect His truth. The Bible is not simply a human creation; it is the inspired Word of God, preserved through the ages by the Church, and made accessible to believers like me even today.

In 1546, the Council of Trent reaffirmed the list of 73 books that St. Athanasius had originally compiled, solidifying the canon of Scripture as it is known in the Catholic Church. The Council's work was essential in addressing the rise in competing texts and teachings during the Reformation. In simpler terms, the Council was focused on discerning which writings aligned with the true teachings of the Church and which were considered false, blasphemous, or contrary to the faith. This effort helped preserve the integrity of the Bible as a divinely inspired document, ensuring that the faithful would continue to have access to the authentic Word of God.

By the early 16th century, the production and distribution of the Bible had undergone significant changes. In 1534, Martin Luther published his translation of the Bible into German, marking a monumental event in the history of biblical translation. This was followed by the Geneva Bible in 1560 and the Bishops' Bible in 1568. Queen Elizabeth the First made it a mandate for all parishes in England to possess a copy of the Bishops' Bible by 1571, and this version would eventually influence the King James Bible, which was first published in 1611. Over the centuries, many different denominations have produced their versions of the Bible, each contributing to its widespread accessibility.

However, as these translations proliferated, so did variations in the text. Since the early 16th century, more than 30,000 changes have been made to the Bible, with about 5000 differences between the Greek texts and the King James Version. Many of these changes were made to modernize the language or clarify certain words' meaning. In contrast, the Catholic Bible has remained remarkably consistent since the time of St. Jerome, whose Latin Vulgate translation became the foundation for Western Christianity. Despite these variations, the Bible is the most influential book in human history. According to various estimates, it has sold between 2.5 and 6 billion copies, making it the best-selling book in the world. There are over 1,700 versions of the Bible, translated into more than 1,200 languages, ensuring its message reaches everyone seeking guidance and a spiritual relationship with God. Whether one believes in its divine inspiration or not, it is undeniable that the Bible has profoundly shaped cultures, languages, morality, arts, music, philosophy, politics, and history.

During the COVID-19 pandemic, Lifeway Research observed a significant increase in Bible reading among adults, reflecting a deep yearning for spiritual guidance in a time of uncertainty. Yet, as of 2023, Gallup Research reports that only 20% of Americans consider the Bible to be the actual Word of God, while 29% view it as a collection of human-created fables, legends, history, and moral teachings. Despite these varying perceptions, I believe the Bible

stands as a living testament to God's revelation to humanity—a guide for life, faith, and salvation.

The Bible is divided into two main sections: the Old Testament and the New Testament. The term "Old Testament" was first coined in the second century by Melito of Sardis, the bishop of Sardis, around 180 A.D. It represents God's dealings with His chosen people, the Hebrews, and the preparation for the Messiah's upcoming. The Old Testament begins with the world's creation by a singular, all-powerful God. The opening chapters of Genesis lay the foundation for God's unique covenantal relationship with His people, beginning with the promises made to Abraham and continuing through the laws and guidance given to Moses. The Old Testament also carries powerful prophecies about the coming Savior, who would redeem humanity from sin and restore God's original plan for creation. These prophecies are fulfilled in the New Testament, where Jesus Christ is revealed as the long-awaited Messiah. This continuity between the Old and New Testaments underscores the Bible's divine inspiration and purpose: to reveal God's plan for salvation and show how He has been at work in history, from creation to redemption. The Old Testament draws from many writings found in the Hebrew Bible, known as the Torah (meaning "teaching") or the Pentateuch (meaning "five scrolls" or "books"). The five books of the Torah are:

1. **Bereshit** (be-ray-sheet; known as Genesis, meaning "In the Beginning")

2. **Shemot** (sh-mote; known as Exodus, meaning "Names")

3. **Vayikra** (va-yikra; known as Leviticus, meaning "He Called")

4. **Bamidbar** (ba-midbar; known as Numbers, meaning "In the Desert")

5. **Devarim** (d'varim; known as Deuteronomy, meaning "Words")

In the Catholic Bible, the Old Testament is longer than the Hebrew Bible because it includes additional canonical books not found in the Hebrew Bible. These additions contribute to the foundation of many standards and commandments outlined in the Catholic tradition. The New Testament stands at the heart of the Christian faith, telling the life, death, and resurrection of Jesus Christ—events central to humanity's salvation. Through these events, the New Testament introduces a new covenant between God and His people, inviting all to partake in the promise of eternal life. The Gospels offer a firsthand account of Jesus' teachings and actions, which guide us on how to live by His will and show us the path to the Kingdom of Heaven. They recount Jesus' ministry and demonstrate how His life fulfills the promises made in the Old Testament. The New Testament beautifully weaves together the old and the new, using Scripture to confirm the prophecies concerning the coming Messiah and to show that in Jesus, God's plan for salvation has been brought to completion. `The Catholic Bible consists of 73 books—46 in the Old Testament and 27 in the New Testament. This collection of books forms a complete picture of God's revelation, from the Creation story in Genesis to the hope of eternal life in Revelation. While the Protestant Bible contains 66 books, it omits seven books from the Old Testament, along with sections of Esther and Daniel, which are found in the Catholic Bible. The Catholic Church refers to these omitted books as the "Apocrypha," or "Deuterocanonical" books, signifying that they are not part of the Hebrew Bible but were included in the Christian canon to preserve the fullness of God's Word. The seven books missing from the Protestant Bible are:

1. Baruch

2. Judith

3. Wisdom

4. Ecclesiasticus (or Sirach)

5. 1 Maccabees

6. 2 Maccabees

7. Tobit

The differences between the Protestant and Catholic Bibles are deeply rooted in the history of the Reformation. In 1534, Martin Luther, a pivotal figure in this movement, produced his translation of the Bible, which included only 39 books in the Old Testament, aligning it with the Hebrew Bible. Luther's decision to omit the Deuterocanonical books—those seven additional books in the Catholic Old Testament—was a key part of his theological reforms. He rejected these books because they were not part of the Hebrew Scriptures, a canon established by Jewish scholars around 90 A.D. This decision set the foundation for the Protestant Bible as we know it today. Luther's views on certain New Testament books were also controversial. He famously dismissed the Epistle of James, calling it "an epistle of straw," and even advocated for its removal from the New Testament. His critique extended to books such as Hebrews, Jude, and Revelation, which he felt did not align with his understanding of Christian doctrine. Luther's decisions were inconsistent in some ways, especially given that he retained all 27 New Testament books approved by Pope Damasus I in 382 A.D., only to reject the Old Testament canon as defined by the Church.

Luther's motivations for these choices are complex and deeply intertwined with his time's theological and cultural climate. His rejection of the Deuterocanonical books was influenced by more than just a desire for doctrinal purity. There were darker forces at play, especially in relation to his views on the Jewish people. Luther's anti-Semitic writings, such as his infamous pamphlet *"On the Jews and Their Lies,"* reveal a disturbing side of his character. In this work, he called for the destruction of Jewish synagogues, the confiscation of Jewish property, and other horrific measures. This racist ideology raises puzzling questions about Luther's motivations in choosing the Hebrew canon over the Catholic one, especially considering the deeper historical context of his time.

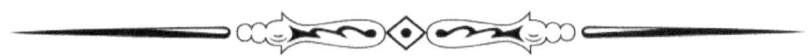

Martin Luther's decisions were not just theological choices—they were deeply influenced by his time's complex historical and personal factors. In 1523, Luther initially advocated for a more compassionate approach to the Jewish people. He suggested they should be treated with Christian love, granted the freedom to work and trade, and welcomed to hear the Gospel. However, this seemingly tolerant stance was eventually overshadowed by his later, more extreme, and deeply anti-Semitic views, which became evident in his writings and actions. His broader reformist agenda similarly influenced Luther's theological decisions about the Bible. He rejected certain books of the Bible that didn't align with his interpretation of Christian doctrine. For example, he questioned the inclusion of the Book of James, calling it "an epistle of straw." he was also critical of books like Hebrews and Revelation. Other reformers, such as Huldrych Zwingli and John Calvin, shared some of these doubts, particularly regarding Revelation, which Calvin described as "unintelligible."

One of the most contentious debates among Protestant reformers was the question of the *Apocrypha*—the seven Deuterocanonical books that the Catholic Church included in its canon. Some Protestant leaders argued that these books should be excluded because they were not quoted in the New Testament. However, this line of reasoning is problematic because numerous Old Testament books are also not quoted in the New Testament. If we apply this criterion, many books will must be excluded from the canon, not just the Deuterocanonical ones.

A common misconception is that the Catholic Church "added" these books at the Council of Trent in the 16th century. In truth, the Council of Trent merely reaffirmed the canon that the Church had accepted for centuries. The Deuterocanonical books were included in the *Gutenberg Bible* of 1454, nearly a century before the Council of Trent convened. These books had been part of the Bible for over a thousand years. They continued to be included in Protestant Bibles until around 1815, when the British and Foreign Bible Society

removed them. One of the most striking aspects of Luther's decision to follow the canon established by the *Council of Jamnia* (circa 90-100 A.D.) is the historical context in which it occurred. The council was convened by Jewish scholars in response to the rise of Christianity, following the destruction of the Temple in Jerusalem. It was composed of Pharisees who opposed Jesus during His ministry and played a significant role in His condemnation. By aligning himself with this Jewish council, Luther chose to follow a canon established in opposition to the early Christian Church, rather than the apostolic tradition handed down by those who had directly followed Jesus.

As I understand this phenomenon deeply, I see that Luther's observations on the biblical canon were not only shaped by theological debates but also by personal biases, historical circumstances, and even prejudice. For me, this highlights why I believe in the integrity of the Catholic Church's teaching and its preservation of the biblical canon. The Church has safeguarded the full revelation of God, including the Deuterocanonical books, which were part of the Christian Bible from the very beginning. The Catholic Bible, with its 73 books, is rooted in the tradition of the early Church and the teachings of the apostles, and it remains the most complete and faithful record of God's Word to humanity.

The Bible has always amazed me with its rich blend of stories, teachings, and profound insights. It's more than just a book; it's an intricate tapestry woven with riddles, mysteries, poetry, and parables that point humanity toward eternal truths and happiness. Its pages contain the full spectrum of human experience: creation, epic floods, love stories, tales of triumph and tragedy, betrayal, seduction, murder, wars, destruction, famine, plagues, and the rise and fall of kingdoms. But it also dives into themes like wisdom, fatherly counsel, forgiveness, miracles, goodness, and evil. The Bible addresses temptation, sacrifice, torture, crucifixion, and resurrection—all central elements in the story of Jesus. Yet, beyond these dramatic and divine moments, the Bible also guides everyday life: marriage,

finances, parenting, how to treat neighbors, kings, employees, and employers. It offers wisdom on matters like worship, hospitality, and community building—whether it's serving wine at a feast, hosting a wedding, or feeding thousands with just a few loaves and fish. Every story serves as a practical guide for living, meant to transform how we relate to each other, to God, and to the world. The miraculous stories of Jesus—walking on water, healing the sick, raising the dead—demonstrate the extraordinary nature of the Bible. These accounts defy the natural laws we know, inviting us to believe in a higher reality that transcends the limitations of our world. But at its core, the Bible is a love letter from God, revealing upon us His divine mercy, forgiveness, and His promise of eternal life, free from suffering and pain.

King David by Jonathan Kirsch sheds light on the Bible as a "patchwork of ancient texts written and edited by countless individuals over a span of more than a thousand years." This collection is a unique blend of history, biography, myth, poetry, prayers, sacred and secular laws, and everyday wisdom. Each writer and editor brought their own perspective and experiences, shaping the Bible into the multifaceted and deeply human book it is today. Despite its diverse origins and the many voices that contributed to its creation, the Bible presents a unified vision of God God who is constant, eternal, and unchanging. The God revealed to Abraham is the same God who spoke to Noah, Moses, David, Jesus, and the prophets. God's revelation has always been tailored to the understanding of each person He spoke to, yet He remains the same throughout history—the Alpha and the Omega, the beginning, and the end. The Old Testament lays the foundation of humanity's story, telling us where we come from, while the New Testament fulfills God's promises and shows us where we are headed. The Old Testament speaks of our origins, and the New Testament leads us toward our ultimate purpose: to know God and be in relationship with Him. Jonathan Kirsch sheds light on why the Bible contains seemingly conflicting stories and variations. He explains that as the texts of the Bible were compiled, revised, and edited over centuries, different

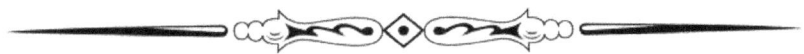

versions of the same story were sometimes merged or altered. Certain passages were moved around or even removed, leading to a text that, at times, may seem to contradict itself. But these variations, rather than diminishing the Bible's truth, reflect the richness of its history and the complex process through which it has been transmitted and preserved.

The relationship between science and religion is not inherently adversarial, as they often address different dimensions of human experience. Science is not focused on understanding the "how" and "when" of the universe, grounded in empirical evidence and observation. Religion, on the other hand, delves into the "Why" – offering a framework of meaning, purpose, and faith. The Bible, for instance, is not intended as a scientific textbook. Instead, it conveys a message of divine revelation: it tells us about God, His actions, and the significance of these for humanity. Science explains the mechanisms of creation, while the Bible reveals its deeper meaning.

The Bible's influence extends beyond Christianity, impacting both Judaism and Islam, which trace their origins to the Old Testament. For Muslims, the Old Testament is honored, though they believe it contains errors. For Jews, the Old Testament, known as the Tanakh, is the cornerstone of their faith. For Christians, the Old Testament is the foundation of God's revelation, while the New Testament—the story of Jesus Christ—represents the fulfillment of God's promises. Despite criticisms from some scholars questioning the Bible's authenticity, many of these same critics value the teachings of ancient figures like Socrates, Plato, and Aristotle, which speaks to the respect that ancient wisdom commands, even across differing worldviews.

The scribes who recorded the sacred texts of the Old and New Testaments did so with a deep sense of reverence and responsibility. They saw their work as a holy duty to preserve God's Word for future generations. And throughout the centuries, people have read the Bible for many distinct reasons—seeking comfort, hope, and guidance, or

to learn about the dramatic events of history. Some read it for spiritual growth, some for academic study, and some for personal reflection. The Bible is like an onion—each time I read it, new layers of meaning are revealed. What seemed unclear yesterday may become deeply insightful today. Ultimately, I read the Bible because it is a road map to knowing God. Through it, I have come to believe that faith in Jesus Christ leads us to the Father and to the gift of eternal life. This truth is not just an idea, it is the foundation of my hope, purpose, and deepest conviction. And so, I continue to read, learn, and grow, ever deepening my relationship with God. Why do I believe it? Because in the Bible, I find the truth that transforms my life.

Ultimately, when deeply observing the Bible, it is beyond human creation. It is divinely inspired, as the Church has always taught, and the Holy Spirit guided its authors to write the truth that God intended for His people. The four Gospels we have were chosen by the early Church not because they were the only accounts of Jesus' life, but because they were the ones that faithfully preserved the message of Christ as handed down through the apostles. God's wisdom and providence guided the Church in recognizing these writings as inspired, and they continue to reveal His truth to us today. Understanding this has deepened my faith and reaffirmed my belief in the Bible not just as a historical document, but as the living Word of God, always relevant, always true, and always speaking to our hearts.

Interesting Facts About the Bible:

- The word "God" appears 4,370 times.

- "Jehovah" is mentioned 6,855 times.

- "Lord" is found 7,736 times.

- "Jesus" appears 700 times in the Gospels and Acts.

- The book of Esther and Song of Solomon do not mention "God."

- A Bible in the University of Göttingen is written on 2,470 palm leaves.

- The Bible contains 8,674 different Hebrew words (KJV), 5,624 different Greek words, and 12,143 different English words.

- It has approximately 500 verses on prayer, less than 500 on faith, and over 2,000 on money and possessions.

- Reading the entire Bible aloud would take about 70 hours.

- Salt is mentioned over 30 times.

- The Bible references 49 different foods, with almonds and pistachios being the only nuts mentioned.

- Seven suicides are recorded in the Bible.

- The only domestic animal not mentioned is the cat.

- The longest word in the Bible is "Maher-shalal-hash-baz" (Isaiah 8:1).

- The longest verse is Esther 8:9.

- The shortest verse is John 11:35.

- The Bible contains 1,198 chapters: 260 in the New Testament and 929 in the Old Testament.

- There are 3,566,480 letters and about 773,746 words.

- The Bible is available in over 1,100 languages and dialects.

- Methuselah was the oldest person in the Bible, living to 969 years.

- Enoch and Elijah are the only two men who did not die but were taken to heaven by God.

- Samson was the strongest man, Solomon the wisest, and Gideon the greatest warrior, defeating 135,000 Midianites with God's help.

- King Solomon had 700 wives and 300 concubines.

- Goliath, at 9.5 feet tall, was the tallest man in the Bible.

- Psalm 118 is the central chapter of the Bible. Psalm 117, before it, is the shortest chapter, and Psalm 119, after it, is the longest. Adding the chapters before and after Psalm 118 totals 1,188, making Psalm 118:8 the central verse with the message: "It is better to take refuge in the Lord than to trust in man."

Chapter Five
Sola Scripture

Dr. Scott Hahn, a very well-known Catholic apologist and bestselling author, stands as one of the most influential voices in contemporary Catholic theology for his profound contribution. As the Chair of Biblical Theology and the New Evangelization at Franciscan University of Steubenville, and founder and president of the Saint Paul Center for Biblical Theology, Hahn's academic and pastoral work has helped countless people deepen their understanding of the Catholic faith. But Hahn has helped countless individuals rediscover the richness of the Catholic faith. His academic excellence is well recognized – but it's his personal journey to Catholicism, marked by deep intellectual wrestling and spiritual awakening, that captivates so many. Before his conversion in 1986, Hahn was a committed and passionate Protestant minister and theologian, deeply invested in the doctrine of *Sola Scriptura*—the belief that the Bible alone is the ultimate authority for Christian faith and practice. This doctrine was the cornerstone of his ministry, guiding his teaching and preaching. As a scholar and pastor, Hahn staunchly defended *Sola Scriptura*, believing it to be the key to contemplating God's truth.

However, everything changed and the belief was shaken one day when a student challenged him with a simple, yet profound question: "*Where in the Bible does it say that we Protestants believe in the Bible alone as the sole rule of Christian faith?*" At first, Hahn dismissed the question. He had never doubted the validity of *Sola Scriptura*. Yet, as the question lingered, he realized he had no clear scriptural answer. This intellectual dilemma sent him on a path of deep personal investigation, one that would ultimately lead him to a radically different understanding of the Christian faith. Determined to find an answer, Hahn contacted several leading Protestant Scripture scholars. To his surprise, no one could provide a satisfactory explanation. One scholar suggested that Matthew 15 supported the rejection of traditions that conflicted with God's Law, but Hahn saw this as a misinterpretation. He recognized that Jesus' condemnation of the Pharisees' traditions was not a blanket rejection of all tradition, but a critique of human traditions that corrupted the purity of God's Word. Further study led Hahn to passages such as 2 Thessalonians 2:15, where Saint Paul explicitly instructs believers to "*hold fast to the traditions which you were taught, whether by word of mouth or by letter.*" Hahn realized that Paul, far from condemning tradition, was upholding it as an essential means by which the faith is handed down. This passage, along with others that affirmed the role of sacred tradition in the life of the Church, forced Hahn to confront a troubling reality. There was no scriptural basis for *Sola Scriptura*, the very doctrine that had been central to his Protestant faith. This discovery was a turning point for Hahn, leading him to question the foundational principles of Protestantism deeply. As he continued to examine Scripture, tradition, and the historical development of Christian theology, Hahn began to see the full beauty and truth of the Catholic Church's teachings. The more he studied, the more he realized that the Catholic Church's understanding of Scripture and Tradition— working in harmony under the guidance of the Holy Spirit—was biblical and theologically richer and more coherent than the framework he had once held.

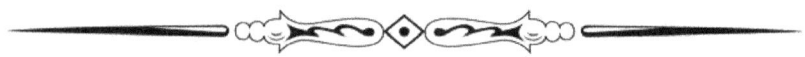

Hahn's journey was not merely an intellectual one; it was also deeply spiritual. His conversion was born of inner transformation – a surrender to the realization that God's truth is not always found in isolation, but in the unity of a Church guided by the Spirit. In Catholicism, Hahn discovered a Church that didn't just claim to preserve truth, but lived it out in continuity with the apostles. In his own words, Hahn has often described his conversion as a "return home"—a coming back to the heart of the Christian faith that had been passed down from the apostles through the Church. The beauty of the Catholic faith, he realized, was not only in its theological depth but in the way it invites all believers to participate in the ongoing revelation of God through both Scripture and Tradition.

Today, as a Catholic scholar, teacher, and apologist, Hahn continues to share the beauty and truth of the Catholic faith with others. Through his books, lectures, and work at the Saint Paul Center, he invites others to embrace the fullness of the Christian faith, grounded in the living Word of God, handed down through the Church's Tradition. His story is a powerful reminder that the search for truth is not always linear, it's not peaceful, but when we seek with an open heart and mind, God leads us to a deeper understanding of His beauty and His plan for salvation. Dr. Scott Hahn's conversion story is more than just an intellectual journey; it is a powerful example of how the beauty and truth of the Catholic faith can captivate the heart, transform the mind, and lead to a deeper union with Christ. Through his example, we are reminded that when we are open to the complete revelation of God's truth, we encounter a beauty that is both timeless and transformative.

Protestant and Catholic perspectives on the Bible differ in ways that are deeply rooted in history, theology, and the nature of Christian authority. For Protestants, the doctrine of *Sola Scriptura*— the belief that the Bible alone is the ultimate and singular authority for Christian faith and practice—has been foundational since the Protestant Reformation. This doctrine asserts that all necessary teachings for salvation and Christian living are contained within

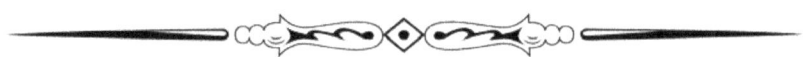

Scripture, and any authority outside the Bible must either be subordinate to it or subject to reform based on its teachings.

The roots of *Sola Scriptura* trace back to early reformers like Marsilius of Padua and John Wycliffe in the 14th century, who questioned the Church's hierarchy and asserted the primacy of Scripture. Their ideas were refined by later figures such as Wessel Gansfort and Johannes von Goch. However, it was Martin Luther who gave *Sola Scriptura* its defining voice. Luther famously declared, "A simple layman armed with Scripture is greater than the mightiest pope without it," a bold claim that redefined Christian authority for millions.

This idea would resonate deeply with generations of Protestants, who saw *Sola Scriptura* as a safeguard against what they perceived as corrupt practices within the Catholic Church. However, in reflecting on the beauty and truth of the Catholic faith, we find a different, yet deeply harmonious understanding of Scripture that is both biblically rooted and historically faithful. The Catholic Church holds that Scripture is indeed the inspired Word of God, and that it is essential for the Christian life. But Catholics also believe that Scripture does not stand alone. The Church teaches that Sacred Tradition, handed down from the apostles through the generations, works in concert with Scripture to preserve and transmit the fullness of the Christian faith.

In the Catholic interpretation, scripture is not a collection of isolated texts to be interpreted in isolation but is part of a living tradition faithfully preserved by the Church. The Holy Spirit guide this living Tradition, and together with the Bible, it forms the foundation of the Church's teaching authority. As the Catechism of the Catholic Church explains, "Sacred Tradition and Sacred Scripture make up a single sacred deposit of the Word of God, which is entrusted to the Church" (CCC 97). The Catholic Church's view of Scripture acknowledges the authority of the Bible while also recognizing the necessity of the Church's role in interpreting it.

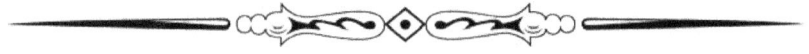

This does not refer to the rejection of the Bible's primacy but an affirmation of the truth that the Church, under the guidance of the Holy Spirit, has been entrusted with the authority to teach and safeguard the truths of the faith. This authority is not about control or coercion, but a deep, loving responsibility to guide the faithful in living out the fullness of the gospel as revealed in Scripture and Tradition. The beauty of this view lies in its comprehensive approach to God's revelation. In Catholicism, Scripture is not just a book; it is the living Word of God, interpreted and handed down through the living body of the Church. The Church, as the "pillar and foundation of the truth" (1 Timothy 3:15), is responsible for guarding and teaching the Word in a way that is faithful to the apostolic deposit of faith, ensuring that the Word is not distorted or misinterpreted by individuals or factions. The Church, in other words, is not an intermediary that diminishes the authority of the Bible; rather, it is the guardian and steward of that Word, protecting its meaning and ensuring its proper interpretation across time and cultures.

What makes the Catholic view of Scripture and Tradition so beautiful is its invitation: an invitation into something greater than oneself. The Bible is not a private possession to be interpreted in isolation, but a communal treasure to be lived and shared within the Church. Christianity, at its heart, is not a solitary journey. It is a pilgrimage of communion—a shared walk of faith across time and generations. In the Catholic Church, believers are united not only with those in the pews but with the apostles, martyrs, saints, and the entire Body of Christ across centuries.

For me, embracing the Catholic view of Scripture has revealed a deeper understanding of the Bible's beauty and truth. It has shown me that Scripture is not something to be wielded as a weapon for division or individualistic interpretation, but as the living Word of God that calls us into communion with one another and with God Himself. The Catholic Church's approach to Scripture invites believers into a relationship with the Word that is both intellectually rich and spiritually deep, one that is not confined to personal interpretation but grounded in the living Tradition of the Church. In the Catholic faith, I have found a richer, more profound understanding of Scripture—one that invites me to read, understand, and live out God's Word within the context of a living, historical Church that has faithfully preserved the teachings of Jesus Christ. This is the true beauty and truth of the Catholic faith: a faith that treasures the Word of God, not as a solitary, isolated text, but as part of a living, breathing Tradition that is entrusted to the Church and that continues to speak to the hearts of all believers throughout the ages.

The Catholic Perspective on Authority and Tradition

The Catholic Church teaches that its authority comes not from Scripture alone, but from both Sacred Scripture and Sacred Tradition, which together form the full deposit of God's revealed truth. This foundational belief is rooted in the conviction that the Gospel was handed down by the apostles not only in writing but also through oral preaching, example, and practice. The apostles, having received their instruction directly from Christ and guided by the Holy Spirit, passed on the faith to the Church through what Catholics call Tradition—a living transmission of divine truth that is deeply interconnected with Scripture, yet distinct from it.

Together, Scripture and Tradition serve as two inseparable sources of divine revelation. This view stands in contrast to the Protestant principle of Sola Scriptura, which holds that the Bible alone is the sole and sufficient authority in matters of faith. A crucial question arises when considering this Protestant claim: How did the earliest Christians know and practice their faith before the New Testament was fully written, compiled, or widely available? The New Testament was written over the span of several decades. The Gospel of Matthew was likely penned around seven years after Christ's Ascension, while the Gospel of John was completed more than sixty years later. The canon of the New Testament wasn't formally settled until the Council of Carthage in 397 A.D.

During this time, the majority of Christians had no access to personal copies of Scripture. Manuscripts were laboriously copied by hand, making them rare and expensive. Most Christians learned the faith not from reading the Bible, but from hearing it proclaimed in liturgy and taught through oral tradition, sacraments, and the authoritative teaching of the Church. At a time when literacy was limited, and the written texts were not yet widely available, the primary means of receiving and sharing the faith was oral communication. In this context, we can see how deeply rooted Catholicism's reliance on Sacred Tradition is—a living, breathing aspect of the Church's life that has preserved and transmitted the Gospel for over two thousand years.

This raises a compelling question for those who adhere to *Sola Scriptura*: How did the early Christians learn about their faith before the New Testament was fully written and compiled? The apostles, commanded by Jesus to *"Go, therefore, and make disciples of all nations"* (Matthew 28:19), spread the Gospel orally, teaching and baptizing new believers even though they did not have the written Scriptures. The early Church, built upon the foundation of Jesus and the apostles, relied heavily on oral tradition to teach, and preserve the faith. This was not a mere human invention but a necessary and divinely inspired means of passing down the message of Christ in the absence of widespread Scripture. For Catholics, this long-standing practice of oral transmission is not something that was abandoned with the writing of the New Testament but is a living part of the Church's life today. Sacred Tradition includes the Church's teachings, practices, liturgies, and sacraments—things that were handed down by the apostles, who received them from Christ, and which continue to guide the Church in every age. These traditions are intimately connected with Scripture, helping to explain and interpret the Word of God in a way that is faithful to the whole of the Christian tradition.

When reflecting on the *Sola Scriptura* principle considering Catholic understanding, another question arises: If personal

interpretation of the Bible is considered sufficient for faith and practice, then why is attending church services necessary? After all, if the Bible alone is all that is needed, why seek guidance from pastors, denominations, or theological traditions? Different Protestant groups, such as Baptists, Methodists, Lutherans, and Pentecostals, offer diverse interpretations of Scripture, each shaped by their theological frameworks. For example, Pastor Paul at First Baptist Church might present teachings influenced by Baptist theology, while Pastor James at Saint Timothy Methodist Church draws from Wesleyan theology, and televangelists like Jimmy Swaggart or Joel Osteen offer teachings rooted in Pentecostal and nondenominational traditions. This diversity of interpretation among Protestant denominations highlights the need for an authoritative body to guide the interpretation of Scripture. Without the unifying presence of a living Tradition—rooted in the teachings of the apostles and safeguarded by the Church—individual interpretations of the Bible can lead to confusion and division. In contrast, the Catholic Church maintains that Sacred Tradition and Sacred Scripture, together, provide a harmonious and authoritative framework for interpreting God's Word. The Church, under the guidance of the Holy Spirit, preserves the integrity of the Gospel message and ensures that it is faithfully transmitted across generations.

For me, the beauty of the Catholic faith lies in its recognition of the living transmission of God's Word through both Scripture and Tradition. It acknowledges the profound role that the Church plays in interpreting and preserving the teachings of Christ, ensuring that they are not lost or distorted. The Church's authority, far from diminishing the importance of the Bible, safeguards its true meaning by placing it within the context of a living Tradition that spans centuries. By embracing both Sacred Scripture and Sacred Tradition, Catholics are able to understand the fullness of the Christian faith as it was handed down by the apostles. This comprehensive view does not only enrich our understanding of God's Word but also deepens our relationship with Christ, as we come to see how the Church has always been the instrument through which God continues to teach, sanctify, and guide

His people. This is the true beauty and truth of the Catholic faith: a faith that not only honors the written Word of God but also treasures the living Tradition that keeps it alive and relevant for every generation.

The diversity of interpretations among Christian denominations today raises significant concerns about the potential for conflicting meanings and the risk of misinterpretation. While many Protestant denominations adhere to the principle of *Sola Scriptura*, which asserts that the Bible alone is the sole authority for Christian faith and practice, the reality of countless interpretations can lead to confusion, division, and even the distortion of the Gospel message. The Epistle of 2 Peter warns us of the dangers of such misinterpretations: *"There are some things in [Paul's letters] that are hard to understand, which the ignorant and unstable distort, as they do the other Scriptures, to their own destruction"* (2 Peter 3:16).

This passage emphasizes the difficulty in interpreting Scripture correctly on our own and the risk of distorting its meaning if we lack proper guidance. It emphasizes on adhering to sound, authoritative teaching to avoid being led astray by personal or misguided interpretations. Taking this into account, the Catholic view of Scripture offers a profound and compelling understanding that upholds the Bible's centrality and safeguards it against misinterpretation. While *Sola Scriptura* holds the Bible as the ultimate authority, the historical reality of the early Church tells a different story—one that emphasizes the necessity of both Sacred Scripture and Sacred Tradition in preserving and communicating the fullness of the Christian faith. Before the New Testament was fully written, compiled, and widely disseminated, the early Christians relied heavily on oral tradition—the teachings, preaching, and practices that were passed down directly from the apostles. These oral teachings were not secondary or supplementary to Scripture; they were the primary means by which the Gospel was transmitted, especially when the written texts were scarce, and the majority of people had no access to personal copies of the Bible. The apostles and

their disciples followed Christ's command to *"Go, therefore, and make disciples of all nations"* (Matthew 28:19), spreading the message of salvation through preaching, the breaking of bread, and the sacraments, long before the New Testament texts were collected into a formal canon. The Catholic Church recognizes that Sacred Tradition and Sacred Scripture together form a single, sacred deposit of God's Word. These two sources of revelation are inseparable and work together to fully convey the truth of the Gospel. Sacred Tradition encompasses the living transmission of the faith, which has been faithfully handed down from the apostles through the Church's teaching, liturgies, and practices. Sacred Scripture, while central and divinely inspired, must be understood within the context of this living Tradition to ensure its proper interpretation.

The beauty of the Catholic understanding of Scripture lies in its acknowledgment that Scripture and Tradition are not two competing authorities but two inseparable aspects of God's revelation. Through the guidance of the Holy Spirit, the Church safeguards and interprets both, ensuring that the truths of the Gospel remain intact, unchanging, and faithfully transmitted through the generations. The Catholic Church's perspective allows believers to embrace the fullness of the Christian faith as it has been handed down through the centuries. It emphasizes that the Gospel is not just a private message for each individual to interpret in isolation, but a communal treasure that must be understood and lived out in unity with the Church. Sacred Tradition and Sacred Scripture work together to form a coherent, unified vision of God's revelation—a vision that protects the integrity of the Gospel and preserves the Church's unity in faith. This is the authenticity of the Catholic view on Scripture. It is a vision that not only treasures the Bible but also acknowledges the essential role of Tradition in interpreting and living the Word of God. It invites us into a deeper relationship with Christ, not as isolated individuals interpreting Scripture on our own, but as members of the Church, grounded in the living Tradition that has always protected and faithfully transmitted the Gospel of salvation. Through this lens, we see a faith that is rich, unified, and unbroken, stretching back to

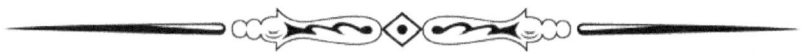

the very foundations of the Church and pointing forward to eternal life with Christ. When you visit any Catholic Church, whether you understand the local language or not, you will immediately recognize a profound unity in its worship. With its timeless liturgy, rituals, and sacraments, the Mass remains universally consistent across nations and cultures.

Regardless of the country, the language spoken, or the specific cultural context, the Catholic Church celebrates the same doctrines and sacramental practices. This consistency speaks to something deep continuity of faith that has been handed down through the centuries, unchanged and unbroken.

For me, the beauty of the Catholic faith lies in this living and unbroken continuity. The Church is not merely an institution or collection of theologians, but the Body of Christ—alive in the world, proclaiming the Gospel, administering the sacraments, and preserving apostolic teaching. This apostolic continuity is visible in the universal unity of the Mass: whether in Rome, Mexico City, or Manila, the Church celebrates the same Eucharist with the same Scripture readings and sacraments. This worldwide unity points to a faith that has been consistently handed down for two thousand years, unmarred by doctrinal fragmentation. Contrary to the idea that the Church came after the Bible, Catholics understand that the Church preceded the Bible. It was through the Church, by the inspiration of the Holy Spirit, that the canon of Scripture was discerned, compiled, and preserved.

As Paul Whitcomb, a former Protestant minister who converted to Catholicism, writes in his book *The Bible Made a Catholic Out of Me*, he was struck by the realization that "Protestantism, by focusing solely on the Bible as the source of divine truth, lacked a teaching Church with the authority to safeguard and interpret that truth." Whitcomb's journey to Catholicism began with a discovery that, for the first four hundred years of Christianity, there was no compiled Christian Bible as we know it today. Even after the canon of Scripture was settled, the Bible remained scarce for many

centuries, handwritten by scribes and available only to a limited few. During this time, the Church was the primary means by which the Gospel was preached, the sacraments administered, and the faith preserved. This is why Whitcomb came to understand that "the Catholic Church is the only institution that fits the Biblical description of a Church, endowed with the infallible authority given by Christ."

For me, this realization of the Church's foundational role in Scripture is deeply meaningful. We affirm the Bible as the Word of God through the Catholic Church. Without the Church, there would be no canon of Scripture—no definitive list of inspired texts—because it was the Church that discerned and recognized which books truly belonged to the inspired Word of God. The Bible, in other words, is not some detached, self-interpreting text but a living Word, handed down through the authority of the Church, and it is within the Church that its meaning is faithfully preserved and taught. This understanding of the Church's role aligns with the words of Saint Augustine, one of the greatest minds in Christian history.

In the fourth century, he famously declared, "I would not believe in the Gospel itself if the authority of the Catholic Church did not move me to do so." For Augustine, the authority of the Church was not something separate from or secondary to Scripture; it was through the Church's authority that the Gospel was rightly understood and embraced. This view resonates deeply with my own faith journey. I have come to understand that the Catholic Church's role is not to diminish the importance of the Bible but to preserve and protect it. The Church, as the body of Christ, is the custodian of the sacred Scriptures and the teacher of divine truth. It is within the Church that the Bible's message comes alive, interpreted in the light of Tradition and the guidance of the Holy Spirit.

This is why the catholic faith stands out: it recognizes the Bible as God's Word but acknowledges the Church's irreplaceable role in safeguarding and interpreting that Word. The Catholic Church is not just a space for fellowship or a place where individuals come

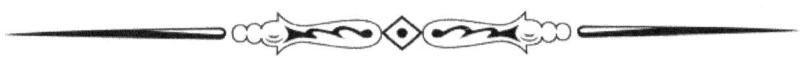

together to study the Bible alone. It is the living, breathing body of Christ, entrusted with the fullness of divine revelation, and given the authority to teach and interpret that revelation faithfully. This authority is not a human invention; it is a gift from Christ Himself, who promised to be with His Church *"always, even to the end of the age"* (Matthew 28:20).

Embracing the Catholic faith means accepting this divine gift of the Church's authority—an authority that has been handed down through the apostles and preserved through centuries of faithful teaching. The Church does not add to the Bible or replace it but interprets it within the context of the living Tradition that flows from the apostles. It is through the Church that I come to understand the Scriptures not just as a collection of ancient texts but as the living Word of God, speaking to me today. This is why I believe in the Catholic Church and its role in Scripture. It is the only institution that truly fulfills the Biblical vision of the Church—one that is endowed with divine authority to teach, guide, and protect the faithful in all matters of faith and morals. The Church does not only point to the Bible as the source of truth; it is through the Church that we come to understand, live, and transmit the truths of the Bible. And in this unity of Scripture and Tradition, I have found the beauty and truth of the Catholic faith, a faith that has been preserved, taught, and lived for over two thousand years.

The idea of *Sola Scriptura*—the belief that Scripture alone is sufficient for salvation—faces challenges from the Bible itself. For instance:

- 1 Corinthians 11:2: "Hold fast to the traditions I handed on to you."

- 2 Thessalonians 2:15: "Hold fast to the traditions, whether oral or by letter."

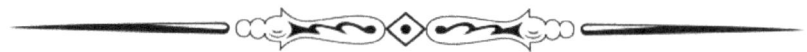

- 2 Thessalonians 3:6: "Shun those who act not according to tradition."

- Romans 10:17: "Faith comes from what is heard."

- John 21:25: "Not everything Jesus said is recorded in Scripture."

- 2 Timothy 1:13: "Follow the sound words; guard the truth."

- Mark 7:9: "You disregard God's commandment and uphold human tradition."

- 1 Corinthians 11:2: "Commends the Corinthians for following Apostolic tradition."

- 2 Thessalonians 2:15: "Commands adherence to tradition."

- James 2:24: "A person is justified by works and not by faith alone."

- James 2:26: "Faith without works is dead."

- Galatians 5:6: "The only thing that counts is faith working through love."

- 1 Corinthians 13:2: "Faith without love is nothing."

- Ephesians 2:8-10: "We are created in Christ Jesus for good works."

- Romans 2:6-8: "Eternal life through perseverance in good works."

- 1 Peter 1:17: "God judges impartially according to one's works."

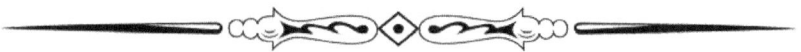

Moreover, **Saint Athanasius**, in a letter written around 360 A.D., emphasized that only those teachings consistent with apostolic tradition were to be received as truth. He wrote, "*The teachings of the Church have indeed been handed down through an order of succession from the Apostles and remain in the Churches to this day. Only that which is consistent with the ecclesiastical and apostolic traditions is to be believed as truth.*" Saint Athanasius emphasizes that the doctrines of the Church, as handed down through the apostles, should not be altered or deviated from. This message is a powerful reminder of the continuity of the Church's teachings—a continuity that has been preserved for over two thousand years. For me, this deep connection to the apostles and their teaching is one of the most beautiful aspects of the Catholic faith. The early Church, as witnessed by Saint Athanasius, did not teach the principle of *Sola Scriptura*— the idea that the Bible alone is the ultimate authority for Christian faith and practice. The apostles themselves did not teach that the Bible, apart from oral tradition, was sufficient for understanding the fullness of Christian doctrine. In fact, they relied heavily on oral tradition—passing down teachings through preaching, catechesis, and the life of the Church—long before the New Testament was even written, let alone compiled into a single authoritative text. This reliance on oral Tradition clearly indicates that the apostles did not intend to teach the doctrine of *Sola Scriptura*.

This view of the Church's authority and the relationship between Scripture and Tradition hold tremendous importance to me. It acknowledges that the Christian faith is not a collection of isolated ideas or personal interpretations, but a living tradition that has been passed down from the apostles and protected by the Church. The Church, under the guidance of the Holy Spirit, has the responsibility to safeguard the fullness of Christian doctrine and ensure that it is faithfully handed down from generation to generation.

The principle of *Sola Scriptura* assumes that Scripture alone is sufficient to teach the truth of the Gospel, but the early Church's practice contradicts this. The apostles did not teach that the Bible was the sole rule of faith; they passed on a living faith through their teachings and actions. The writings that make up the New Testament were, in fact, part of a larger oral and liturgical tradition. Without the Church's guidance in interpreting and transmitting the Scriptures, the risk of misinterpretation and division becomes all too clear.

As Catholics, we believe that it is the Church—the body of Christ—that has the responsibility to preserve and interpret the Word of God. The Bible, while profoundly important, does not exist in isolation. It is understood and lived out within the context of the Church's Tradition, which has been handed down from the apostles. This unity of Scripture and Tradition ensures that the teachings of Christ remain faithful, clear, and consistent throughout the centuries. The Catholic faith is found in this living connection to the apostles— the recognition that the Church is not just an institution that emerged later, but the very body of Christ, entrusted with the mission of teaching, sanctifying, and guiding the faithful. The Catholic Church is the guardian of both Scripture and Tradition, and through this living Tradition, we can fully understand and live the Gospel of Jesus Christ. This historical reality is crucial in understanding the fullness of the Christian faith.

In the Catholic faith, Scripture is not isolated from the Church but lives within it. The Word of God is not merely ink on a page—it is Christ Himself, encountered through the sacraments, preached in unity, and lived out in the Church's ongoing mission. As Saint Athanasius so clearly stated, only that which is consistent with the apostolic and ecclesiastical traditions is to be believed as truth. This is why I believe in the Catholic Church. It is the only institution that can trace its authority directly back to the apostles, preserving and faithfully interpreting the teachings of Christ. The Church, through its sacred Tradition and Scripture, offers us the fullness of God's revelation, not just as words on a page, but as a living faith that

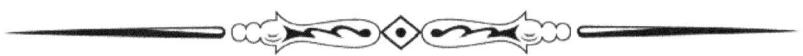

continues to guide, nourish, and transform us today. That is the beauty and truth of Catholicism: **a living faith, anchored in history, sustained by Tradition, and illuminated by the Scriptures**.

**PENTECOST &
EARLY CHURCH**

Chapter Six
Know Your Church

I was born into a devout Catholic family, the youngest of seven children, with six older brothers, we all shared the same beliefs and religious upbringing. My mother was the bedrock of our faith, a woman whose devotion to God and the Church shaped our family's spiritual life. Her unwavering commitment ensured we attended Mass regularly, went to Catholic schools, and embraced the practices of our faith heartily. My father, though raised Catholic, didn't share the same level of dedication early on in their marriage. Sundays often found him asleep, preferring to rest over church. But it was only my mother's persistence that eventually brought him in line, and together, they ensured that we not only went to church but lived out our faith in every aspect of our lives.

Our routine was one of deep traditions. We attended Sunday Mass, celebrated holy days of obligation, and were active in the parish. My older brothers and I sang in the choir for the 9:30 a.m. Mass, and during Lent, we even attended the early 6:30 a.m. daily Mass. On top of all that, my mother kept a watchful eye on our

activities outside of church. When we wanted to go to the movies, she would carefully check the local Catholic newspaper's movie reviews to make sure the films we were watching were appropriate. Looking back, I always thought this was a bit overboard, especially when she did not approve of movies from Disney films we loved. But now I see it as an extension of her deep care for our spiritual well-being. She wanted to protect us and ensured that everything we did aligned well with the values of our faith.

My father worked as a high school band director for Abbeville High School, the local public school, for over thirty years. He faced a unique challenge during those years: his decision to send his children to Catholic schools rather than public school was met with hostility from local sports boosters. They were upset that his children were playing for the "Eagles" rather than the hometown "Wildcats." My father, a man of quiet strength, endured this criticism for years, but never wavered in his commitment to our faith. His example of endurance in the face of adversity left an impression on me, though I didn't fully appreciate it at the time.

My religious education began in Catholic elementary and high school, where I gained a solid foundation in the teachings of the Church. However, it was not until my first semester at LSU that I truly began to explore my faith in a more personal and profound way. I continued to attend Sunday Mass, but my commitment did not go much deeper. Like countless college students, I was more focused on fitting in and experiencing life than on spiritual growth. I encountered people from various faiths, and while I respected their beliefs, I found that my peers had only a surface-level understanding of our respective traditions. Our faiths seemed more like cultural identities than personal commitments.

In 1983, while studying nursing, I met the woman who would become my first wife. She, like me, was raised Catholic, though her connection to the faith was somewhat shallow. She often joked that her time in Catholic school had little impact on her, mainly because

she had missed so many days. Despite her lighthearted attitude toward religion, I invited her to join me on a weekend retreat hosted by Loyola University, hoping it would allow us to grow spiritually together. However, her response was not what I expected. She laughed and offered me a hit of her weed. At that time, neither of us was fully invested in our faith. I was seeking something deeper and more meaningful but felt unsupported in that pursuit by my wife. For instance, after I returned from my adoration hour, she would mock me by asking, "You feel holier tonight?" Several times. When my son returned from school, (he was in about third grade; he would excitedly say something that he learned in the bible. My wife would push back by saying something like, "that is not true". At that time, while I wasn't as passionately committed to my Catholic faith as my mother had been, I still wanted to pass on the values I had grown up with to my children. So, in agreement with my wife, we decided to raise our children in the Church. This meant enrolling them in Catholic schools, attending Sunday Mass, and observing the holy days of obligation to the best of our ability. Although I wasn't always as diligent as I should have been, and at times my commitment felt more like a routine than a true calling, I continued to make the effort. The more I tried to deepen my faith, the more my wife resisted. In 1997, Scott and Kimberly Hahn were scheduled to give a day-long talk at our parish center. A month before the event, I told my wife I was going and asked her to join me. She agreed and even arranged for a babysitter. However, on the morning of the event, she told me she wasn't going after all. I felt devastated. At the event, Kimberly Hahn shared a deeply moving testimony. After her talk, she and Scott took a break, and I spoke with her. As I shook her hand and introduced myself, I suddenly cried. Kimberly was taken aback and asked what was wrong. Through tears, I managed to say, "I don't have what you and Scott have."

Looking back, I can now see that those early years of raising our children in faith were foundational to their lives, even though, at times, I would feel like not doing enough for them as my mother did for me. The practices of the faith—Mass, prayer, and the

sacraments—were a constant presence, even if I was not always fully engaged with them myself. It's clear to me now that these traditions, which I sometimes took for granted, shaped us in ways I couldn't yet understand. The faith my parents instilled in me, the same one I had struggled to live out at times, was still there, influencing our family.

As I reflect on my faith journey, I see it as a tapestry of grace woven over the years—moments of doubt, growth, and revelation. My mother's unwavering devotion, my father's quiet strength and persistence, and the Catholic traditions I was raised with all brought me closer to Christ, even when I did not realize it. It is easy to think that faith is about rules to follow or obligations to fulfill, but I have now come to terms with its reality that it is much more than that. Faith is not a task to check off; it's a relationship—a living, breathing journey of discovery. It is about how the people around influence us, how we encounter God in our day-to-day routine and even in the smallest of tasks, and how we continually grow in our understanding of His love. Over time, I have come to appreciate the deep richness of the Catholic faith. It is not a faith of mere rituals and traditions, it's a faith deeply rooted in Scripture, Sacred Tradition, and the sacraments. These pillars of the Catholic faith provide a depth and a wholeness that offer both guidance and nourishment for the soul. I have realized that the beauty and truth of the Catholic faith are not just in the knowledge we gain, but in the transformation it brings to our lives. It is a faith that calls us to grow continually, to seek God's presence, and to share that love with others. The Catholic faith is not just something I was born into—it has shaped the course of my life, my belief, and every essence of it is etched into my being. It has molded my heart in ways I couldn't have imagined. Through its rich history, its sacramental life, and its unwavering commitment to truth, I have found a deep and abiding relationship with God. Despite my struggles and imperfections, the faith passed down to me continues to guide me, and I find nothing but peace and purpose.

The real transformation of my faith began during one of the most painful times of my life – my divorce. That season of heartbreak

forced me to reevaluate everything, especially my relationship with God. During this personal crisis, I found healing through the foundational teachings of my Catholic faith for support and guidance. It was during this challenging period that I also found a calling—one that would shape my faith for years to come. I volunteered to teach CCD (Confraternity of Christian Doctrine) to ninth and tenth graders. I thought I was helping the next generation of Catholics, but in truth, I was the one who needed the most help. As I braced myself for this sacred profession, I realized how little I truly knew about my own faith. I had absorbed a lot over the years, but I had never taken the time to truly reflect on my teaching and delve into the Scriptures to comprehend the theological aspects of Catholicism. Determined to provide the students with accurate answers and a genuine understanding of their faith, I immersed myself in Bible study, religious texts, and Catholic teachings. Over the next seventeen years, I made it my mission to strengthen my knowledge of faith. I read widely, exploring Catholic, Protestant, and non-denominational literature to understand the various perspectives on Scripture and theology. I attended Mass more frequently, spent time in the adoration chapel, went on mission trips, and developed a personal relationship with the Holy Spirit that transformed my spiritual life. This journey of discovery and growth eventually led me to write my first book, *God & Free-Will*: *True Stories of Sins, Faith & Redemptions,* where I reflected on the intersection of human freedom and divine grace—two themes that became especially meaningful to me as I navigated the complexities of life.

Today, in 2025, I am an enthusiastic believer in the Catholic Church. In this chapter, I will share my beliefs and why I hold them, drawing from Scripture, Sacred Tradition, and personal spiritual experiences. I will explain why, after years of study and reflection, I have come to believe that the Catholic Church is the one established by Jesus Christ Himself. Before we dive into these deeper reasons, it's helpful to understand the global context of Christianity and where the Catholic Church fits within it. According to current data, the international Catholic population stands at approximately 1.25 billion people, with around 70.4 million Catholics in the United States. In comparison, Protestant denominations, which encompass a wide variety of theological beliefs and traditions, number around 920 million worldwide, with 140 million in the U.S. The Eastern Orthodox Church, with its ancient roots and rich liturgical life, has approximately 220 million members across the globe.

When we consider these branches of Christianity in relation to other major world religions, here's how the distribution looks:

- **Catholics**: 25% of the global population

- **Islam**: 22% of the global population

- **Protestants**: 19% of the global population

- **Hinduism**: 19% of the global population

- **Eastern Orthodox Christians**: 6% of the global population

- **Buddhism**: 4% of the global population

- **African Indigenous Churches**: 3% of the global population

These statistics show the massive global impact of the Catholic church. The Catholic Church, representing 25% of the world's population, speaks to its deep historical roots, global reach, and influence in its followers' lives. But to me, it's not just about numbers – it's about the transformative power of its truth. Through the Church's sacraments, teachings, and traditions, I've experienced the love and mercy of Christ in tangible ways, and they serve as a living witness to the Gospel, continuing the work of Jesus Christ on earth. In the following pages, I will explain why I believe in the Catholic Church—why, despite other Christian denominations, it is the Church Christ founded, and why it alone offers the fullness of faith, rooted in both Sacred Scripture and Sacred Tradition. My journey of faith has been one of continuous growth, and it is through

the Church that I have found the answers, the peace, and the purpose I was searching for during my darkest moments.

Imagine, for a moment, what the world might look like if the three largest branches of Christianity—Catholicism, Protestantism, and Eastern Orthodoxy—were united as one Church. The combined membership would be more than 2.39 billion people, surpassing the 1.9 billion members of Islam. This is an astonishing thought. Reflecting on the Apostles' mission to establish Jesus' Church, it's incredible to consider how their message, spread without the benefit of modern technology, led to the formation of a global body of believers, resulting in over a billion faithful Catholics today. The spread of Christianity is truly a remarkable achievement. And yet, despite this growth, it is disheartening that the major branches of Christianity have not achieved the unity that Christ intended for His Church.

As Rick Warren, in *The Purpose Driven Life*, writes:

"Unity in the church is so important that the New Testament gives more attention to it than to either heaven or hell. God deeply desires that we experience oneness and harmony with each other. Unity is the soul of fellowship. Destroy it and you rip the heart out of Christ's body."

This statement resonates deeply with me because unity within the Church is essential for the faithful and the integrity of Christ's mission. It's perplexing, then, that Christianity, which began as a single united body, has fragmented into so many denominations. According to the *Center for the Study of Global Christianity* at Gordon-Conwell Theological Seminary, there are currently around 41,000 Christian denominations and organizations worldwide. This staggering number of denominations begs an important question: How did we go from a unified Church, founded by Jesus Christ in 33 A.D., to over 41,000 distinct groups?

To begin to understand this, we must look at the historical and theological developments that have led to this division. I have come to realize that the story of the Church is not just about its outward expansion, but also about its internal struggles, misunderstandings, and the challenges of remaining faithful to the teachings of Christ throughout the centuries. The early Church, as we read in the New Testament, was unified under the Apostles, who were given the authority by Christ to lead and guide the Church. Yet over time, as new theological ideas emerged and as the Church spread throughout diverse cultures and regions, divisions began to form. As a Catholic, the unity of the Church was not meant to be fractured. From the very beginning, Jesus Christ established His Church with a clear structure, built upon the Apostles and their successors. The Church was intended to remain united in faith, in worship, and in the administration of the sacraments. However, human pride, sin, and misunderstanding have led to a situation where Christians are divided—sometimes deeply—over interpretations of Scripture, ecclesial authority, and theological doctrines.

For me, as I reflect on my own faith journey, the Catholic Church is the one true Church founded by Christ. The Church has preserved the fullness of His teachings, handed down through Sacred Tradition and Sacred Scripture, and protected by the authority of the Magisterium. This is not a belief I arrived at lightly; it is the result of years of study, prayer, and reflection on the nature of the Church and its role in salvation history. But beyond my personal belief, I am struck by the urgency of the call to unity. If 2.39 billion Christians could come together in one body, what a powerful witness that would be to the world! But this unity cannot be simply a matter of institutional cooperation; it must be rooted in a shared understanding of the truth of the Gospel. I believe that truth is found most fully in the Catholic Church—through its sacramental life, its rich tradition, and its adherence to the teachings of Christ.

As I share my beliefs in this chapter, I invite others to reflect on this question: If the Church was meant to be one, why are there so

many denominations? What has caused the divisions? And what would it mean for the world if Christians could unite in faith, purpose, and love for Christ and one another? This journey toward unity is not only a theological challenge but a spiritual one. Unity is more than just an abstract ideal—it is a call from Christ Himself to restore the fellowship that He intended for His Church from the very beginning. And it is in that unity, in living out the fullness of our faith, that we bear witness to Christ's love in a divided and hurting world. For me, the Catholic Church has been a source of truth, healing, and transformation. And it is through this Church that I've encountered Christ in the most profound ways—ways that continue to shape my life, my family, and my soul.

Questions to Reflect Regarding Your Faith Journey

1. **Do you know your faith tradition's history and core beliefs?**

   Understanding the origins and foundational teachings of your Church is essential to deepening your relationship with Christ and growing in spiritual maturity.

2. **What is the denomination or tradition of your church?**

   Is it Catholic, Protestant, Eastern Orthodox, or non-denominational? Identifying this helps your community within the broader context of Christian history and theology.

3. **Is your church an offshoot of another denomination?**

   Knowing whether your church emerged from a reform movement or as a breakaway group can shed light on its doctrinal emphases and practices.

4. **Where does your church's doctrine come from?**

Do you understand the sources of the teachings your church follows? Is it Scripture alone, or does it also include Sacred Tradition?

5. **Do you believe in Sola Scriptura (Scripture alone) or Sola Fide (faith alone)?**

   How does your church view the relationship between Scripture and faith? Do you believe in salvation through Scripture alone, or does your church integrate both Scripture and Tradition in its teachings?

6. **Does your church combine Scripture with Tradition?**

   Does your faith community honor both Sacred Scripture and Sacred Tradition, or does it focus solely on one?

7. **How do you view the Eucharist?**

   Is the Eucharist in your church considered the real Body and Blood of Christ, or is it seen as a symbolic meal?

8. **How often can you attend services?**

   Does your church offer opportunities for daily worship and sacraments, or is it limited to weekly or occasional services?

9. **Is the Eucharist offered regularly?**

   Does your church provide the Eucharist with every service, or only on special occasions such as Christmas and Easter?

10. **What is your church's stance on social and moral issues?**

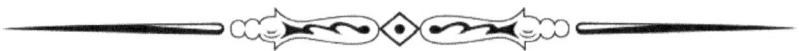

What is your church's teaching on topics like divorce, abortion, and birth control? How do these teachings reflect their understanding of Scripture and tradition?

11. Can you remarry in your church?

Does your church offer the possibility of remarriage without the requirement of an annulment, or does it uphold a more traditional stance on the sanctity of marriage?

12. Is confession part of your faith practice?

Does your church require confession or reconciliation, or does it offer a different path to spiritual healing and forgiveness?

13. Was your church founded because of a disagreement or dispute?

Did your church arise from a theological, social, or personal conflict, or was it established as a continuation of the original Christian Church founded by Christ?

14. Where did your church's leaders receive their formation?

Are the leaders of your church trained in theology and Scripture in a way that aligns with its tradition and teachings?

15. How does your church engage with other faiths?

Does your church criticize other faiths, or does it participate in respectful dialogue with understanding and openness toward others?

16. **Are you able to defend your faith peacefully and knowledgeably?**

Do you feel confident in explaining and defending the tenets of your faith, or do you find it challenging to articulate your beliefs clearly and with conviction?

17. **When was your church founded?**

Does your church trace its origins back to the time of Jesus and the Apostles, or was it established at a later date? What historical events influenced its formation?

18. **Is the Catholic Church the true Church established by Jesus?**

This is perhaps the most fundamental question. Do you believe that the Catholic Church is the one true Church founded by Jesus Christ, entrusted with the fullness of truth and the authority to teach, sanctify, and govern in His name?

These questions are not meant to criticize but to invite deeper reflection. They have guided my own journey over the past fifty years as I've asked them to friends and fellow believers across various denominations. Time and again, I have found that many do not fully understand their church tradition's history, doctrine, or origins. Some believe their church is the "true" Church, but are unaware of how and why it was founded or what it teaches at its core.

I ask these questions because I have posed similar inquiries to friends and fellow believers across various Christian denominations over the past fifty years. Often, their answers reveal a lack of deep understanding regarding their church's origins, doctrines, and practices. There are those that claim their church is the true, divinely ordained Church, but when probed further, they are often unaware of the foundational beliefs that distinguish their tradition. To be clear, I

am not here to disparage any faith tradition, nor am I seeking to undermine the sincerity of others' beliefs. I deeply respect all who believe in God and strive to follow Jesus Christ. However, through my own journey of discovery and reflection, I have come to the firm conviction that the Church established by Jesus Christ and entrusted to His Apostles is the Catholic Church. While individuals founded many other Christian denominations to suit various interpretations or agendas, the Catholic Church traces its roots directly to the Apostles and the teachings of Christ. In fact, this claim is not merely an assertion of my own beliefs, but one that is supported by both historical and spiritual evidence.

A striking affirmation of the Catholic Church's foundational truth comes from an unlikely source—Msgr. Stephen Rossetti, a well-respected exorcist and author of *Diary of an American Exorcist.* In a YouTube interview, he recounted a moment from an exorcism in which he asked a demon to reveal the true Church of Jesus Christ. The demon's response was clear and unequivocal: *the Catholic Church is the true Church established by Jesus.* This powerful exchange highlights the spiritual truth I believe: the Catholic Church holds a unique place in God's plan, as the one Church founded by Christ Himself.

The word *Catholic* has a Greek origin that means "universal." This term is fitting, as the Catholic Church is the only Christian community that fully embodies the universal, inclusive mission that Jesus entrusted to His followers. From its inception, the Catholic Church was meant to be the "universal" gathering of the faithful, a family of believers united in the truths revealed by Christ, and with a universal mission to spread the Gospel to every corner of the world. Biblical and historical evidence strongly supports this conviction. On the night before His arrest, Jesus instituted the Eucharist during the Last Supper, sharing the sacramental Bread with His Apostles and giving them the command to *"do this in memory of Me."* This sacred act not only established the central sacrament of the Church but also inaugurated the priesthood, giving His Apostles the authority to

perpetuate the celebration of the Eucharist. Jesus did not merely provide them with a set of teachings; He entrusted them with a divine authority to act in His name, to forgive sins, and to lead His followers. This moment was the beginning of the Holy Church—the Catholic Church. Furthermore, on the day of His Ascension, Jesus gathered the Apostles, disciples, and devout followers in the upper room (the Cenacle), a group of about 120 people. Before ascending into Heaven, He gave them clear instructions: *"You will have Peter as the supreme head of the Church; I leave him as my Vicar, and you shall obey him as the chief high priest."* This moment, recorded in Scripture, is the foundational statement of papal authority. Jesus explicitly designated Peter as the leader of His Church, giving him the keys to the Kingdom of Heaven. Peter, in turn, passed this authority down to his successors, the Popes, who continue to guide the Catholic Church today.

This is the bedrock of my belief: that the Catholic Church is not merely a human-caused institution, but the living continuation of the Church Jesus Himself founded. The Catholic Church is the Church that holds the fullness of Christian truth, with its teachings rooted in both Scripture and Sacred Tradition, and its authority passed down from the Apostles through an unbroken line of succession. Through my journey, the struggles, and questions I have faced, and the deepening of my faith, I have come to know and experience the beauty and truth of the Catholic Church. The Church has stood the test of time, preserving the teachings of Christ, upholding the sacraments, and offering a deep, rich spiritual meaning to life, uplifting the morals of the lost souls, and is a way of guidance for those who seek it. The Catholic Church has given me the fullness of faith, rooted in history, grounded in Scripture, and alive in the grace of the sacraments. This is why I believe, with all my heart, that the Catholic Church is the one true Church established by Jesus Christ.

In her book *City of God*, Blessed Mary of Agreda recounts a significant event that occurred a year after Jesus' resurrection. Under the inspiration of the Holy Spirit, the Blessed Virgin Mary asked each of the Apostles to define a divine mystery. Their responses, which

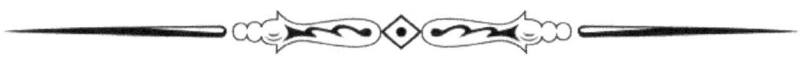

reflect a unified and profound belief in the core tenets of the Christian faith, form a testament to the early teachings of the Church. The order in which the Apostles spoke, and their statements are as follows:

1. **St. Peter**: "I believe in God, the Father almighty, Creator of Heaven and earth."

2. **St. Andrew**: "And in Jesus Christ His only Son, our Lord."

3. **St. James the Great**: "Who was conceived of the Holy Ghost, born of the Virgin Mary."

4. **St. James the Great**: "Suffered under Pontius Pilate, was crucified, died, and was buried."

5. **St. Thomas**: "Descended into hell, arose from the dead on the third day."

6. **St. Thomas**: "Ascended into heaven, is seated at the right hand of God, the Father almighty."

7. **St. Philip**: "From thence He shall come to judge the living and the dead."

8. **St. Bartholomew**: "I believe in the Holy Ghost."

9. **St. Matthew**: "In the Holy Catholic Church, the communion of saints."

10. **St. Simon**: "Forgiveness of sins."

11. **St. Thaddeus**: "The resurrection of the flesh."

12. **St. Matthias**: "Life everlasting. Amen."

The words spoken by the Apostles, as recorded in this account, form the core of the *Apostles' Creed*, a declaration of faith that

encapsulates the central truths of Christianity. These declarations were personal affirmations and shared confessions of faith that united the Apostles in their mission to spread the Gospel. The Creed clearly articulates the foundational beliefs of the early Church, and it was specifically revealed to the world as a prayer to preserve and transmit the doctrines of the one true Church—the Catholic Church. The Apostles' Creed was not derived from any Jewish faith or other religious tradition but was directly associated with the *katholikos* (Catholic; universal) faith, reflecting its divine origin and connection to Jesus Christ. This faith, preserved in the Apostles' teachings, was never intended to be merely a set of theological statements but rather a living confession, affirming the Church's mission to spread the message of salvation to all people.

Historically, the existence of the Apostles' Creed is well-documented. Early Christian writings and letters affirm its use and development in the early Church. For example, a letter from Marcellus of Ancyra to Julius, Bishop of Rome, written in 341 A.D., refers to the "Old Roman Creed," widely recognized as an early version of the Apostles' Creed. Additionally, Tyrannius Rufinus, in his fifth-century commentary, and St. Ambrose in his writing in 390 A.D., both refer to the Creed as being firmly established in the Church of Rome.

These references and documents underscore the fact that the Apostles' Creed was not merely later development, but rather an essential part of the Church's belief system from its earliest days. It was a prayer to protect the teachings of the Apostles, a prayer to keep alive the truths of the faith that Jesus Christ passed on to His followers. Through the Apostles' Creed, the Church has continued to affirm the divinely revealed truths entrusted to it by Christ. It was, and remains, a declaration of the Catholic Church as the universal Church established by Jesus, and it continues to serve as a key element of Catholic doctrine and worship today.

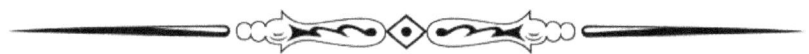

After receiving the Holy Spirit at Pentecost, the Apostles dispersed to evangelize the world; they gathered one last time at the Cenacle, where a divine voice confirmed Peter's role as their leader: "My Vicar Peter shall designate each province. I will guide him with my light and spirit. The appointments themselves, the Holy Ghost left for St. Peter, affirming his role as head and universal pastor of the Church." This moment marked a pivotal confirmation of Peter's divinely appointed role as the leader of the Church, establishing him as the foundation upon which the Church would grow and expand under his authority and that of his successors. Jesus did not designate Peter to lead any of the numerous denominations that would later emerge—such as Lutheran, Anglican, Methodist, or Baptist—nor did He intend these groups to divide the faithful. Instead, He appointed Peter as the Vicar of only one Catholic Church. This divinely ordained role was unique to Peter and the line of Popes who would succeed him. The Church that Jesus established was unified, under the leadership of Peter, as the singular institution entrusted with the fullness of divine truth.

For the next fifteen centuries, the Catholic Church flourished, spreading the Gospel, establishing communities of faith, and building the Kingdom of God on earth. However, just as Adam and Eve's disobedience in the Garden of Eden altered the course of human history, so too did humanity later distort the divine plan for the Church. This deviation began with Martin Luther's break from the Catholic Church in the early 16th century, sparking the Protestant Reformation—a movement that fractured the unity of the Church and introduced many competing denominations.

At this point, you might question some claims I have made that may be valid. However, I invite you to consider the evidence I will present in the following chapters, as I explore why Jesus Christ founded the Catholic Church. This exploration is based on Scripture, New Testament testimony, and external sources—including private revelations from Jesus and the Blessed Mother, as recorded by various saintly individuals. For example, the insights Mary of Agreda provided in her mystical writings offer valuable perspectives on the early Church and its mission. I will carefully examine these revelations and other sources to demonstrate that the Catholic Church is the institution Jesus established to continue His work on earth. In the coming sections, I will address the key theological and historical elements that support this belief, including:

- The Primacy of Peter

- The Church as the Body of Christ

- The Necessity of Church Unity

- Church Authority and Infallibility

- Apostolic Tradition

- Apostolic Succession

Each of these points will offer insights into how the Catholic Church continues the mission Christ began and why it holds the fullness of truth. I invite you to read with an open heart and a prayerful mind. This is not just a journey of doctrine—it is a journey of faith.

Chapter Seven
Know Your Church Part 2

The Primacy of Peter, The Church, Christ as the Body, and the Necessity of Unity

Pastor Rick Warren rightly emphasizes the importance of unity within the Church – a message that resonates deeply. In Jesus's time, the world was divided: Romans followed pagan gods, Gentiles lacked religious structure, and only the Jews had God resonate with their perspective. During Jesus' time on Earth, there was a deep division in the world. The Romans adhered to pagan beliefs, Gentiles lacked a clear faith structure, and the Jews were the only ones with God's presence in their temple. Jesus came with a transformative message: the Kingdom of God was accessible to everyone, regardless of race, class, or gender. His call was inclusive, offering eternal salvation to anyone willing to embrace it.

This unity is grounded in the **Primacy of Peter**, when Jesus declared, *"Upon this rock I will build my Church"* (Matthew 16:18).

Notice that Jesus used the singular term "my Church," not "your Church," "our Church," or "all these Churches." This singular reference emphasizes the unity Jesus intended for His Church. The connection between the Primacy of Peter, the Church, and Christ as the Body of Christ is further highlighted in John 10:16, where Jesus says, *"There must be one flock, one shepherd."* Saint Paul reinforces this unity in his letter to the Ephesians: *"There is one Lord, one faith, one baptism, one God and Father of all"* (Ephesians 4:5-6). For three years, Jesus carefully taught His Apostles about the structure of His Church. When He named Peter the rock and foundation of the Church, He granted him unmatched authority: *"I will give you the keys to the kingdom of Heaven. Whatever you bind on earth shall be bound in heaven; and whatever you loose on earth shall be loosed in heaven"* (Matthew 16:19). This extraordinary role was not given to any other Apostle or future denomination—it was Peter's alone. Jesus' words affirm that the Catholic Church, founded on Peter and his successors, is the one true Church, entrusted with the authority to teach, guide, and govern in His name.

Jesus further promised the Holy Spirit would lead the Apostles into all truth. As Jesus said, *"The Spirit of truth will guide you to all truth. The Holy Spirit that the Father will send in my name will teach you everything and remind you of all that I have told you"* (John 14:26). This promise was fulfilled at Pentecost when the Holy Spirit descended upon the Apostles, empowering them to establish the first Christian community in Jerusalem, make doctrinal decisions, and spread the Gospel to new regions. Through the Church, founded on Peter's leadership and guided by the Holy Spirit, the message of Christ spread throughout the world.

Peter's leadership in the early Church is both profound and unmistakable. As the first Pope, Peter's role was foundational to the Church's growth and structure. He was entrusted with overseeing the appointment of Judas' successor (Acts 1:15-26), performing miracles (Acts 3:1-10), and , Peter, guiding the inclusion of the first Gentile converts (Acts 10). His decisive role in the Council of Jerusalem in

Acts 15:16-19, where he made the authoritative decision to welcome Gentiles into the Church without imposing unnecessary burdens, further highlights his primacy. Even Saint Paul, who was a pivotal figure in the early Church, acknowledged Peter's leadership. In Galatians 1:18, Paul writes, *"After three years I went up to Jerusalem to confer with Kephas (Peter) and stayed with him fifteen days."* This visit to Peter underscores the fact that Paul recognized Peter's authority as the leader of the Church. While Peter held leadership, it is crucial to understand that Jesus is the true head of the Church. As Saint Paul wrote in Colossians 1:18, *"He (Jesus) is the head of the body, the Church."* This signifies that the Church is not a manufactured institution, but a divine creation founded on Christ Himself. Paul also emphasizes the unity of the Church in 1 Corinthians 1:10, urging, *"I urge you, brothers, in the name of our Lord Jesus Christ, that all of you agree in what you say, and that you be united in the same mind and the same purpose"*. Later, in Romans 12:5, he writes, *"we, though many, are one body in Christ"*.

The early Church Fathers echoed the call to unity. Saint Cyprian wrote, *"God is one, and Christ is one, and one in His Church, and the faith is one, and His people welded together by the glue of concord into a solid unity of the body"* (250 A.D.). Saint Hillary also affirmed this, saying, *"In the Scripture, our people are shown to be made of one; so that just as many grains collected into one and ground and mingled together make one loaf, so in Christ, who is the heavenly Bread, we know there is only one body"* (A.D. 365). Both Saints emphasize the unbroken unity of Christ's Church. Furthermore, Saint Paul instructed Timothy in 1 Timothy 3:15, *"You should know how to behave in the household of God, which is the Church of the living God, the pillar and foundation of truth"*.

This underscores the Church's essential role as the guardian and teacher of truth, carrying forward the fullness of Christ's message through the ages. Similarly, Tertullian, an early Christian apologist, described the unity of the Church in his writings, noting, *"We are a society with a single religious feeling, a single unity of discipline, a single bond of hope"* (A.D. 197). This powerful statement reflects the early Church's understanding of its unifying force in the world, which is not merely organizational but deeply spiritual.

These scriptural and historical testimonies—Peter's leadership, the primacy of the Church, Christ as the Head, and the necessity of unity—serve as the foundation for my belief that the Catholic Church is the true Church established by Jesus Christ. It is the Church that has preserved and handed down the fullness of the apostolic faith, with Peter's successors continuing to safeguard the teachings of Christ through the ages. This is the Church I believe in—the Catholic Church. It is the Church that was established by Jesus Himself, with Peter as the rock upon which it was built, and it is the Church that has been entrusted with the fullness of truth and the mission of bringing all people into the unity of Christ's Body. When I reflect on the journey of the Church throughout history, I am convinced that it is the Catholic Church that faithfully continues the mission entrusted to the Apostles by Christ. The call to unity remains central to the Catholic faith, and it is through this Church that the fullness of Christian teaching, worship, and community is preserved and handed down through the ages.

What is the Church?

What is the Church? Is it merely a building, an institution, a set of beliefs, or something more profound—something alive? The word Church – from the Greek *ekklesia* - means "those who are called forth." It refers to the living community of believers or people who are called out by God Himself through baptism and faith in Jesus Christ. As Saint Paul affirms, *"Christ is the Head of the Church, and we are His body"* (Ephesians 1:22-23). The Church is not a distant institution, but a living, breathing entity formed by the faithful, united in Christ. This intimate communion of life shared by all baptized believers is described in Sacred Scripture using various powerful images: *the People of God, the Bride of Christ, God's family*, and *the Wedding Feast*. These metaphors reveal the depth of the Church's

identity—not just as an institution but as a dynamic, loving union between Christ and His followers.

The Church is where Christ dwells within us, especially through the sacraments, particularly the Eucharist. People from all the ethnicities gather we come together to hear God's Word. In this sacred communion, we are united with Christ and with one another, and through this unity, we become His Church. It's important to recognize that the Church is not a mere institution or something we could easily live without. Even though the Church is made up of imperfect members and faces failings, we cannot separate ourselves from her because God has irrevocably chosen to love the Church. No matter the sins of her members, the Church remains the Body of Christ, and God will never abandon her. As Jesus said to Peter, *"the gates of hell shall not prevail against it"* (Matthew 16:18). Despite her flaws and imperfections, the Church is God's presence on earth, continuing the mission of Christ. She is the means through which God's Kingdom is made present in the world—bringing peace, justice, and salvation to all nations. As Jesus instructed His Apostles in His final command before ascending into heaven: *"Go therefore and make disciples of all nations, baptizing them in the name of the Father, and of the Son, and of the Holy Spirit"* (Matthew 28:19-20). The Church, though imperfect, is the instrument through which Christ's Kingdom continues to be expanded and made present.

The Church continues Christ's mission: proclaiming the Gospel, administering the sacraments, and expanding God's kingdom. She exists to continue the work that Jesus began—preaching the good news, teaching the Gospel, offering the sacraments, and bringing the Kingdom of God into the world. This is why, despite her weaknesses and failings, the Church is still a powerful force. She is called to function as Jesus would act, to embody His love and mercy, and to continue His work of salvation. As Saint Irenaeus wrote in A.D. 200, the Church is "one soul, one heart," harmoniously proclaiming and preserving the faith of Christ across the globe. She carries on the mission of Christ by acting as His living Body on earth.

The Church is not simply an institution or a human enterprise, though it has an organizational structure. The Church is a mystery, a divine reality intertwined with the human. Just as Christ Himself was both fully divine and fully human, so too is the Church both human and divine. From the outside, the Church may appear like a flawed institutional community of sinners who often fall short of the ideal. But to view the Church merely through human eyes is to miss the fullness of the truth. Through the eyes of faith, we see that the Church is indestructibly holy. She is the Body of Christ, and just as there is only one Christ, there can only be one Body of Christ, one Bride of Christ, and thus only one Church.

Amid the Church's imperfections, Christ remains her Head. He guides and sustains her, and He will never leave her. The Church's holiness is not based on the perfection of her members but on the grace and presence of Christ, who continues to sanctify and strengthen her. This intertwining of sin and grace is part of the Church's mystery and beauty—she is both the Church of sinners and the Church of saints, always in need of God's mercy but always capable of reflecting His holiness. This union of the divine and human in the Church points to her unique role in God's plan of salvation.

As Saint Paul writes in Ephesians 5:23, *"Christ is the head of the Church, his body, of which he is the Savior."* The Church is the Body of Christ, united with Him in a profound, mystical union. Together, Christ and His Church form one whole Christ. This is why, despite her human failings, the Church remains the only true and lasting witness to Christ on earth. The Church's authority and infallibility stem from this divine reality.

As Christ's Body on earth, the Church has been entrusted with the mission to teach, govern, and sanctify in His name. This authority is rooted in Christ's promise to His Apostles: *"Whatever you bind on*

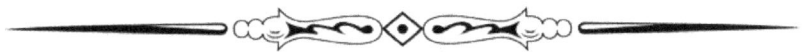

earth shall be bound in heaven, and whatever you loose on earth shall be loosed in heaven" (Matthew 16:19). The Church, under the leadership of the Pope and bishops in union with him, has the authority to preserve and teach the truth of the Gospel. Her infallibility does not mean her members are perfect but that, under the guidance of the Holy Spirit, she cannot teach error in matters of faith and morals. This divine protection ensures that the Church remains a dependable witness to the truth of Christ, despite the personal failings of her members.

The Catholic Church is not merely an institution or a collection of doctrines; it is a living, divine creation, established by Christ and sustained throughout history by the power of the Holy Spirit. Its foundation traces back through Old Testament prophecies, the Incarnation, the teachings of Christ, the Apostolic mission, and the sacrifices of countless martyrs. The Church's divine authority is rooted in this unbroken line of succession, starting with the Apostles and extending to the present day. This continuity underscores the Church's unique role as the guardian and teacher of divine revelation.

The New Testament is full of evidence affirming the authority of the Church. In Matthew 18:17, Jesus provides instructions for resolving conflicts: *"If he refuses to listen to them, tell it to the church; and if he refuses to listen even to the church, treat him as you would a Gentile or a tax collector."* This passage underscores the Church's role in guiding the faithful and making decisions concerning doctrine and discipline. Additionally, before His Ascension, Jesus gives the Great Commission to His Apostles in Matthew 28:18-20: *"All power in heaven and on earth has been given to me. Go therefore and make disciples of all nations, baptizing them in the name of the Father, and of the Son, and of the Holy Spirit, teaching them to observe all that I have commanded you."* This command highlights the Church's continuing mission to teach, baptize, and uphold Christ's teachings across the globe.

In Mark 6:39-40, Jesus provides a glimpse into the Church's future structure when He organizes the crowd into groups of fifties and hundreds during the miracle of the loaves and fish. This act was not just a practical decision for organizing the crowd, but also foreshadowed the future organization of the Church, laying the groundwork for dioceses and parishes.

The hierarchical structure of the Catholic Church today reflects this early model. From the Pope at the top, followed by Cardinals, Archbishops, Bishops, Priests, and Deacons, each level of leadership serves a particular role in ensuring the unity and mission of the Church. In the United States alone, as of December 31, 2024, the Church is organized into 2,998 dioceses, each led by a bishop, with thousands of parishes and local communities served by priests, deacons, and lay ecclesial ministers. This vast organizational structure is not a mere human construct, but a continuation of the vision laid out by Christ and His Apostles.

At the heart of this hierarchy is the Papacy, which traces its authority directly back to Saint Peter, whom Jesus appointed as the rock upon which He would build His Church (Matthew 16:18). From Saint Peter's leadership in A.D. 33 to Pope Francis today (2024), the Papacy has been an enduring symbol of Christ's presence on earth, guiding the faithful and preserving the integrity of the Church's teachings. Despite the challenges the Papacy has faced—from political intrigue and corruption to external pressures from monarchs and empires—the office has remained a pillar of spiritual leadership. The line of succession from Pope Peter to Pope Linus in A.D. 64, and onward through the centuries, represents an unbroken chain of apostolic authority, which continues to provide the Church with direction and unity.

Historically, the influence of the Papacy extended far beyond the spiritual realm. During the medieval period, the Pope held significant political power, with monarchs and rulers seeking the Pope's approval and fearing the consequences of excommunication.

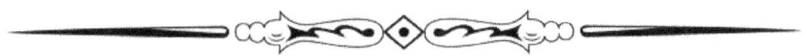

The Papacy's reach was so extensive that the Church controlled vast territories, including substantial European landholdings. The authority of the Church was unquestioned in many parts of the world, and the fear of eternal damnation drove even kings to align themselves with the Pope's teachings and decrees.

The medieval Church was deeply intertwined with both the spiritual and political fabric of society. However, this unchallenged authority was not to last. The Reformation in the 16th century marked a turning point in Christian history. Figures like Martin Luther and John Calvin questioned the authority of the Pope and the Church, leading to a profound split within Christianity. The Reformation sparked the creation of numerous denominations, each breaking away from the authority of the Catholic Church to establish their own interpretations of Christian doctrine and practice. While I cannot write about all the reformations' religions (that would be a big book), I will only focus on a few of them.

Martin Luther and the Protestant Reformation

In 1507, Martin Luther was ordained as a priest and joined the Augustinian order. At this time, Luther viewed the Catholic Church as deeply corrupt and deviating from the authentic teachings of Jesus Christ. Among the many issues that troubled him, the most significant was the selling of indulgences. Pope Leo X had initiated a campaign across Europe to sell indulgences—"absolutions" that promised to reduce the buyer's time in Purgatory—as a means of raising funds for the rebuilding of St. Peter's Basilica in Rome. Luther was outraged not only by the commercial nature of the indulgences but also by their theological implications. He argued that the concept of indulgence and the Church's role in granting forgiveness were not found in Scripture. Luther's growing frustration with these practices led him to challenge the authority of the Pope and the teachings of the Church.

In 1517, Luther posted his *Ninety-Five Theses* on the door of the All-Saints' Church in Wittenberg, publicly denouncing the sale of

indulgences and calling for a return to what he perceived as the biblical truths of Christianity. The document, titled "Disputation on the Power and Efficacy of Indulgences," sparked a theological firestorm across Europe. Luther's central concern was the doctrine of justification—the idea that sinners are declared righteous before God by *faith alone*, through God's grace. This idea would become the cornerstone of Lutheran theology, diverging sharply from the Catholic understanding of salvation, which emphasized both faith and works.

Luther's conflict with the Catholic Church escalated in the years following the publication of his theses. In 1519, during the *Leipzig Debate* (the Leipzig Debate was held from June 27 to July 16, 1519, was a significant event in the early stages of the Protestant Reformation. It was a public theological dispute between Martin Luther and Johann Eck, a Catholic theologian and scholar, which took place in the German city of Leipzig. The debate was initially about the authority of the Pope and the nature of Church teachings, but it quickly expanded to address more fundamental theological issues, such as the authority of Scripture and the nature of salvation.), Luther defended his views on salvation, Scripture, and the Church against Catholic theologians. By 1521, Pope Leo X had excommunicated Luther for his refusal to recant, marking a pivotal moment in the Protestant Reformation. Luther's teachings, particularly his rejection of papal authority and his insistence on the supremacy of Scripture, became the foundation for a broader movement that led to the formation of multiple new Christian denominations. Luther's ideas were not a sudden break with the Church but rather the culmination of years of theological reflection and personal struggle. A few key elements of Luther's new theology stand out:

1. **Human Nature**: Luther believed that human nature was so deeply fallen that it was incapable of choosing good without divine intervention. This contrasted with the Catholic teaching that human nature, while wounded by sin, still retained the capacity for good, being created in the image of God.

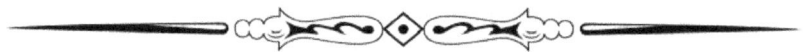

2. **Sin and Good Works**: Luther's doctrine of total depravity held that all human actions, even seemingly good ones, were tainted by sin. This was in direct opposition to the Catholic view that, through God's grace, human beings could perform good works that cooperate with divine will.

3. **Reason**: Luther famously rejected human reason as a tool for understanding faith, calling it "the devil's whore." He argued that faith should stand independently, independent of human intellect. This was contrary to the Catholic tradition, which held that reason and faith complement each other in understanding God's truth.

4. **Sola Fides**: Central to Luther's theology was the belief in sola fide—justification by faith alone. He believed that salvation came solely through faith in God's grace, while the Catholic Church taught that both faith and good works were necessary for salvation.

5. **Sola Scriptura**: Luther also championed sola scriptura, the idea that Scripture alone is the sole authority in matters of faith and practice. He rejected the Catholic Church's reliance on Sacred Tradition and the authority of the Pope, insisting that all Christians had the right to interpret the Bible for themselves.

Luther's radical rethinking of Christian doctrine extended to his rejection of the need for the traditional clergy. He believed that all baptized Christians were priests, thus rejecting the hierarchical priesthood of the Catholic Church. This view gave rise to a new form of religious leadership, one in which local rulers, such as princes or dukes, took on roles traditionally held by the clergy. This secularization of the Church, which intertwined Luther's ideas with nationalism and politics, contributed to the spread of Lutheranism throughout Germany.

However, as Lutheranism grew in popularity, it sparked violent conflict. Inspired by Luther's teachings, peasants in the German Peasants' War (1524–1525) revolted against feudal lords, demanding better treatment. Luther, who had initially expressed sympathy for the peasants' grievances, condemned the uprising, calling for its suppression. This decision resulted in brutal consequences, with thousands of peasants killed in the aftermath. The Reformation, which had begun as a religious movement, increasingly became entangled with political struggles, leading to widespread violence, including the Thirty Years' War (1618–1648), which caused the deaths of millions across Europe.

The Reformation also led to a profound shift in how Christianity was practiced. In the wake of Luther's reforms, the idea that individuals could read and interpret the Bible for themselves took root, drastically changing the religious landscape. Luther's translation of the Bible into German made Scripture accessible to the common people, enabling them to form their own interpretations and, in some cases, to question traditional doctrines and Church practices.

By the end of the 16th century, the Reformation had created a divided Christian world. Lutheranism, along with other Protestant movements, spread rapidly. At the same time, the Catholic Church, although deeply wounded, responded with its own Counter-Reformation, aimed at clarifying and reaffirming Catholic doctrine in the face of Protestant challenges.

John Calvin

John Calvin's journey to becoming one of the most influential figures of the Protestant Reformation was marked by a dramatic shift in his personal beliefs and theological outlook. Born into a devout Roman Catholic family, Calvin's father, a legal administrator for the local bishop, had hoped his son would follow the path of the priesthood. Yet, while studying in Paris in 1527, Calvin befriended several individuals who were advocating for religious reform, and by

1528, he turned his attention away from priesthood to study law in Orleans, embracing the humanist ideas that were sweeping through Europe. This intellectual transformation led him to a growing discontent with the Catholic Church. Calvin's increasing skepticism and critique of the Church's practices eventually led him to renounce his Catholic faith, making him a vocal critic of its teachings. His theological opposition to Catholicism, particularly his rejection of Church authority and the centrality of the sacraments, put him at odds with both ecclesiastical and civil authorities in France. As a result, he was forced to flee to Geneva, Switzerland, where he would go on to establish a theocratic community based on his reformed ideas.

Calvin's theological system, while indebted to the ideas of Martin Luther, also took a sharp turn in several key areas, one of the most significant being his doctrine of *predestination*. Unlike Luther, who focused on justification by faith alone, Calvin emphasized the belief that God had already determined, before the foundation of the world, who would be saved (the elect) and who would be damned (the reprobate). For Calvin, this divine decree was not based on human actions or merits, but solely on God's sovereign will. In his view, Christ died only for the elect—those whom God had chosen for eternal salvation—and this belief in predestination became a cornerstone of Calvinist thought. Calvin's teachings extended beyond doctrine into social and political realms. He argued that prosperity in this life was a sign of divine favor and, by extension, a visible indication of one's election. This idea led to the belief that hard work, thrift, and success in business were all signs of God's blessing, an idea that some historians have linked to the development of modern capitalism. Calvin's vision of the "elect" led to a stark and rigid religious framework where members of the community were expected to demonstrate their godliness through outward success and conformity to God's law.

At the heart of Calvin's rejection of Catholicism was his vehement opposition to the veneration of Mary, the saints, and the sacraments, which he considered idolatrous. For Calvin, the belief

that Mary could function as a mediator between God and humanity was blasphemous; only Christ could serve in this role. He also rejected Catholic practices such as praying for the dead, praying to saints, and the use of religious images, arguing that these practices had no biblical foundation and amounted to paganism. In his view, the Catholic Church had corrupted the faith, leading people into idolatry and superstition. Calvin's rejection of the Catholic Church was not just theological but also deeply political. He advocated for the separation of Church and state, although in practice, his Geneva was a theocratic society where both spiritual and political authority were intertwined. The Reformation under Calvin's influence led to widespread iconoclasm—violent destruction of Catholic art, churches, statues, and relics—which he and his followers viewed as symbols of false worship. Calvin's followers, or Huguenots, became politically active, opposing Catholic monarchs and engaging in violent conflict during the French Wars of Religion.

One of the more ironic elements of Calvin's life is his personal background. Had his relationship with his father and his close association with Catholic clergy been different, it is possible that Calvin might have pursued the priesthood rather than becoming a humanist lawyer. His intellectual and theological transformation was deeply influenced by the teachings of Martin Luther, but it was also shaped by his own experiences and his growing sense of dissatisfaction with the Church. Theologically, Calvin rejected not only Catholic dogmas but also the structure of the Church, advocating for a stripped-down Christianity that focused on personal faith and the sovereignty of God. His ideas would not only change the religious landscape of Europe but also lay the foundation for various Protestant denominations, most notably the Reformed Church, which would spread throughout Europe and the world.

In examining Calvin's life and theology, it becomes clear that his break with the Catholic Church was more than just a rejection of specific doctrines or practices. It was part of a broader movement to redefine the relationship between the individual, the Church, and God.

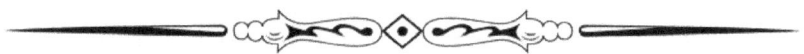

Calvin's influence would be felt for centuries, shaping Protestantism and deeply impacting the religious and political structures of the modern world. As we consider the lasting effects of his reforms, we see how his theological ideas, particularly his doctrine of predestination and his view of church authority, helped solidify the doctrinal divisions that persist today within Christianity. Calvin's legacy, marked by both theological rigor and social activism, remains a central force in the history of the Reformation.

King Henry VIII and the Church of England

In 1534, King Henry VIII of England found himself in a profound dilemma that would forever alter the course of Christian history. Henry, deeply committed to his faith and once proudly holding the title of "Defender of the Faith" for his writings against Protestant reformers, sought to annul his marriage to Catherine of Aragon to marry Anne Boleyn. The Catholic Church, however, did not permit divorce, and Henry's request for an annulment was denied by Pope Clement VII. This was particularly difficult because the Pope had previously granted Henry a special dispensation to marry Catherine, the widow of Henry's brother. The Pope's refusal to grant a second dispensation—especially in the context of Henry's political pressure and his personal desire for a male heir—placed Henry in a seemingly untenable position.

Henry, initially a staunch Catholic, was now caught between his royal desires and his loyalty to the papacy. Facing this impasse, Henry turned to two key figures in his court: Archbishop Thomas Cranmer and his chief minister, Thomas Cromwell. Both men, inspired by the ongoing Protestant Reformation, were strong proponents of breaking from the authority of Rome. They advised Henry to sever ties with the Catholic Church entirely and declare himself the Supreme Head of a new church in England.

In 1534, Henry VIII followed their counsel, establishing the Church of England and positioning himself at its helm. By declaring

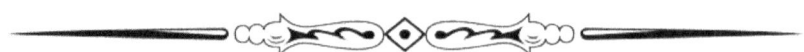

his own authority over religious matters, Henry annulled his marriage to Catherine, married Anne Boleyn, and began a sweeping religious and political reformation. As head of the newly formed Church of England, Henry VIII embarked on a radical reshaping of religious life in England. Between 1536 and 1540, he dissolved the monastic system, seizing the wealth and land of over eight hundred abbeys, monasteries, friaries, and nunneries. These religious institutions had been a powerful part of the Catholic Church, and their dissolution further weakened the influence of Rome in England. Henry also abolished five of the seven sacraments of the Catholic Church, retaining only the sacraments of the Eucharist and Baptism. His break from Rome was not purely theological, but also political, as it provided him the autonomy to marry Anne and to assert control over the governance of the Church.

In terms of doctrine, Henry's Church of England initially retained many traditional Catholic practices but also incorporated key elements from the Protestant Reformation. Henry himself remained hesitant to adopt all of Luther's teachings, yet he endorsed the principle of *sola fide* (justification by faith alone) as central to salvation, a doctrine that rejected the Catholic view of salvation through both faith and works. This marked a significant departure from the papal teachings of the Catholic Church, even though Henry still maintained much of the liturgical structure, sacraments, and hierarchy that were integral to Catholicism.

Today, the Church of England, known as the Anglican Church, represents a blend of both Catholic tradition and Protestant reform. It retains many practices that trace their roots back to Catholicism, such as the celebration of the Eucharist and Baptism. Still, it also embraces the theological principles of the Reformation, including the centrality of Scripture and the rejection of papal authority. The Church of England identifies as both Reformed and Catholic, holding to ancient creeds such as the Nicene Creed and the Apostles' Creed, while also honoring the theological innovations of

the 16th century, including the Book of Common Prayer and the Thirty-Nine Articles.

These reforms solidified its unique identity, one that sought to honor the historic foundations of Christianity while integrating Protestant principles, thus creating a new path for the Christian faith in England and, eventually, in much of the English-speaking world. Henry's break from Rome ultimately paved the way for the Anglican tradition, a branch of Christianity that continues to navigate the complex balance between its Catholic heritage and the Reformation's demands for reform. Despite the upheaval and struggles of the Reformation, the legacy of Henry VIII's decision to establish the Church of England still resonates today, shaping the religious landscape of England and its global influence.

In Conclusion

The Catholic Church, despite its troubled history and the human failings that have plagued it throughout the centuries, has remained steadfast and unyielding in its core doctrines. This is not by human effort alone, but by the grace and protection of the Holy Spirit, who continues to safeguard the Church from corruption and error. The core message of Jesus Christ—the Good News of salvation through His life, death, and resurrection—has not changed since He entrusted His teachings to His Apostles. As Scripture reminds us, *"where the Church is, there is the Spirit of God; and where the Spirit of God, there the Church and every grace. The Spirit, however, is truth,"* (John 14:17). The Holy Spirit teaches and reminds us of everything Christ said and continues to guide the Church in truth, even in the face of sin, scandal, and division. The Catholic Church's mission, rooted in the teachings of Jesus, is a continuation of the work begun by the Apostles, with Saint Peter as the first bishop. Jesus gave Peter the keys to the kingdom, and with them, the responsibility to safeguard His teachings and to lead His Church. This authority, handed down through apostolic succession, has remained intact through the centuries.

Despite the imperfections of the men who have held the office, the Church has remained the vessel through which Christ's truth is proclaimed to the world. The Church's ability to endure, despite its flaws, is a testament to its divine foundation and the guidance of the Holy Spirit.

I passionately believe that the Pope, as the successor of Saint Peter, is the Vicar of Christ on earth, endowed with authority to speak *ex cathedra* on matters of faith and morals. This authority is not a result of human power or ambition, but rather a divine commission from Jesus Christ. While human free will has led to the proliferation of Christian denominations and divisions, God's plan was always for a united Church, led by the Apostles' successors, with the Pope as the visible head. The creation of thousands of Christian denominations, starting with Martin Luther's break from the Catholic Church in 1521, is a result of human choices, politics, and misunderstandings. Yet, despite these divisions, the core doctrines of the Catholic Church have remained unchanged. As Jesus prayed in John 17:21, "*that they all may be one,*" and it is through the unity of the Church that we see the fulfillment of Christ's mission on earth. Apostolic succession, the unbroken line of bishops from the Apostles to the present day, ensures that the Church has remained true to the teachings handed down by Christ Himself. The early Church understood the necessity of apostolic succession, which is why it was so carefully maintained. Saint Ignatius of Antioch, writing around 107 A.D., emphasized the importance of this succession when he said, "Your bishop presides in the place of God." This concept is central to the unity of the Church. While other Christian denominations may claim apostolic succession, they do not possess the same authority granted to the Catholic Church through the unbroken line of succession from Peter.

In 2025, with over 41,000 Christian denominations worldwide, unity in the body of Christ seems more distant than ever. The divisions created by the Reformation and the subsequent fragmentation of Christianity into countless denominations have

caused much confusion and conflict. However, I believe that these divisions, though tragic, do not diminish the truth of Christ's Church.

Despite the many human flaws and failures within the Church, the Church remains the repository of the fullness of truth as revealed by Jesus. I do not criticize individuals attending other Christian churches; in fact, my hope and prayers are for these individuals to remain faithful to the teachings and doctrines of their own faith communities. But I do believe that the Catholic Church, as the one true Church founded by Christ, holds the fullness of the faith and has preserved the integrity of Jesus' teachings throughout history.

As Pastor Rick Warren rightly notes in *The Purpose Driven Life*, the "Church is not perfect—because it is made up of imperfect people". Disillusionment and disappointment with the Church are natural human experiences, but these challenges should not drive us away from the Church. Rather, they should lead us to deeper understanding, reconciliation, and a renewed commitment to the community of believers. The Church is not meant to be a perfect institution, but a place where sinners come to seek grace, forgiveness, and transformation.

The Blessed Virgin Mary, in her apparitions, has often acknowledged the painful divisions within Christianity. In one instance, as recounted by Wayne Weible in *Medjugorje*, the Mother of God, Mary, "lamented the divisions and the unnatural separation that people have imposed upon themselves. She emphasized that despite these differences, all people of faith are accepted by her Son, and that the lack of unity among Christians is not God's will." This echoes the prayer of Jesus for the unity of His followers, a unity rooted in truth and in the Apostolic faith that the Catholic Church preserves.

I also agree with mystic Aria Simma's (an Austrian mystic renowned for her reported encounters with souls in Purgatory), reflections on the many divisions that have arisen from the Catholic

Church. While she acknowledges that the Catholic Church holds the fullness of truth, she encourages people to seek churches that align with the central truths of the Gospel—such as the sanctity of life, the existence of Satan, and the importance of adhering to the Nicene and Apostles' Creeds. These essential truths must be the foundation of any Christian church, and those that deviate from them cannot be considered authentic expressions of the Christian faith.

While the Church's history has been marked by human sin and division, its core mission and teachings have remained intact through the centuries, safeguarded by the Holy Spirit. The proliferation of Christian denominations, though a sad consequence of human free will, does not diminish the truth of Christ's Church. The Catholic Church, through its apostolic succession and the guidance of the Holy Spirit, remains the one true Church founded by Jesus Christ. It is to this Church that we are called to remain faithful, seeking unity in Christ and following His teachings, as entrusted to His Apostles, and preserved by the Church throughout the ages.

When did your Christian church begin and who started it?

- **If you are Lutheran**, your church was founded by Martin Luther, a former Catholic monk, in 1517 in Germany. His protest against the Catholic Church's sale of indulgences ignited the Reformation and laid the groundwork for Lutheranism.

- **If you are a Calvinist**, your church's origins date back to the Reformation in Switzerland, starting in 1519 with Huldrych Zwingli, who first preached Reformed doctrine in Zürich. However, it was John Calvin's writings and influence that truly shaped what became known as Calvinism.

- **If you are Anabaptist**, your church was founded by Nicholas Storch and Thomas Münzer in 1520. The Anabaptists rejected

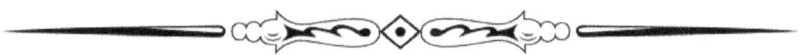

infant baptism, believing that baptism should follow an individual's personal confession of faith.

- **If you are a Mennonite**, your church began in 1525 in Switzerland by Conrad Grebel and Felix Manz. It started within the Anabaptist tradition, emphasizing pacifism, simplicity, and separation of church and state.

- **If you belong to the Church of England**, it was founded by King Henry VIII in 1534 after he broke away from the Roman Catholic Church to obtain a divorce from Catherine of Aragon, establishing himself as the Supreme Head.

- **For those who are Presbyterians**, their church traces its origins to John Knox in Scotland in 1560. Influenced by the teachings of John Calvin, Knox established a tradition that reflects Calvinist theology, with a particular focus on the sovereignty of God.

- **The Congregationalist church** was founded by Robert Brown in Holland in 1582. This tradition emphasizes local church autonomy and democratic governance, and it was a precursor to the development of other Protestant traditions in New England.

- **If you are a Unitarian**, your church originated in 1645 through the efforts of John Biddle, who promoted the belief in the unity of God, rejecting the traditional Christian doctrine of the Trinity.

- **If you are a Baptist**, your church was founded by John Smyth in 1606 in Amsterdam, as part of a movement advocating for believers' baptism (as opposed to infant baptism) and the autonomy of the local church.

- **If you are of the Dutch Reformed Church**, you recognize Michaelis Jones as the founder of your faith, having

established the tradition in New York in 1628, based on Calvinist theology and ecclesiastical structure.

- **If you are a Quaker**, your church was founded by George Fox in 1647. Fox's movement, known as the Religious Society of Friends, emphasized the inner light of Christ within each person, peace, and nonviolence.

- **If you are Amish**, your church was founded by Jacob Amman in 1693 as a reform movement within the Anabaptist tradition. The Amish emphasize simple living, non-resistance, and separation from the world.

- **If you are a Methodist**, your church was founded by John and Charles Wesley in England, in 1739 or 1744. The Wesley brothers emphasized personal holiness, social justice, and the need for an experience of personal salvation.

- **If you are a Unitarian (Second occurrence)**, your church was founded by Theophilus Lindley in London in 1774, focusing on the belief in the oneness of God and rejecting the traditional Christian understanding of the Trinity.

- **If you are an Episcopalian,** your church was an offshoot of the Church of England, founded in the American colonies in 1784 by Samuel Seabury. The Episcopalian Church maintains Anglican traditions but is distinct in its governance and theological outlook in America.

- **If you are an Evangelical**, your church was founded by Jacob Albright in 1803, focusing on personal conversion, the necessity of a new birth through faith in Christ, and a commitment to holiness.

- **If you are a Mormon (Latter-day Saints)**, your church was founded by Joseph Smith in Palmyra, New York, in 1829, when he claimed to restore the true church of Christ through

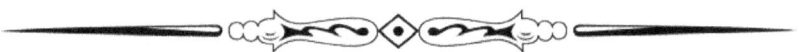

divine revelation, producing new scriptures such as the Book of Mormon.

- **If you are a Seventh-day Adventist**, your church was founded by William Miller in 1831. The movement, initially sparked by Miller's prediction of Christ's imminent return, later developed into a distinct denomination with an emphasis on the Sabbath and Christ's second coming.

- **If you are from the Salvation Army**, your church was founded by William Booth in London in 1865, with a mission to bring the gospel to the poor, the marginalized, and the forgotten, particularly through acts of social justice.

- **If you are a Jehovah's Witness**, your church was founded by Charles Taze Russell in 1872, and it teaches a distinct interpretation of Scripture, emphasizing the imminence of God's Kingdom and rejecting traditional Christian doctrines such as the Trinity.

- **If you are a Christian Scientist**, your church was founded by Mary Baker Eddy in 1879, based on the teachings of spiritual healing and the idea that reality is spiritual, and that sickness is a result of false beliefs.

- **If you are Assemblies of God**, your church was founded by Charles Parham in 1901. The Assemblies of God is a Pentecostal Christian denomination that emphasizes the power of the Holy Spirit, including speaking in tongues and healing.

- **If you belong to a more recent sect**, such as the "Church of the Nazarene," "Pentecostal Gospel," "Holiness Church," or "Pilgrim Holiness Church," your church likely came from the explosion of new Christian movements founded in the past century, emphasizing holiness, the power of the Spirit, and revivalism.

- **If you are Catholic**, your church was founded by Jesus Christ Himself, the Son of God, around the year 33. Jesus entrusted His teachings to the Apostles, with Saint Peter as the first Pope, and through apostolic succession, the Catholic Church has remained the same Church, preserving the fullness of Christian faith and truth for nearly 2,000 years.

CONFESSION

Chapter Eight
Confession

In 1987, the movie "Moonstruck" was released, portraying Italian American life and exploring themes of love and family dynamics. The film received critical acclaim and won three Academy Awards, highlighting its impact. A notable scene involving confession depicts the Sacrament of Reconciliation (Confession). In "Moonstruck," the character Loretta Castorini, played by Cher, faces a moral dilemma. After having an affair with her fiancé's estranged brother, Ronny, Loretta seeks absolution through confession. The interaction between Loretta and the priest contrasts the seriousness of her actions with the priest's response:

Loretta Castorini: "Bless me, Father, for I have sinned. It's been two weeks since my last confession."

Priest: "What sins have you to confess?"

Loretta Castorini: "Twice I took the name of the Lord in vain, once I slept with the brother of my fiancé, and once I bounced a check at the liquor store, but that was really an accident."

Priest: "Then, it's not a sin. But—what was that second thing you said, Loretta?"

Loretta Castorini: "You mean the one where I once slept with the brother of my fiancé?"

Priest: "That's a pretty big sin."

Loretta Castorini: "I Know!"[1]

During a family gathering on April 30, 2023, the topic of confession naturally arose, especially since both my godfather and nephew are priests. Over dinner, my oldest brother and I discussed his experience with the sacrament, and he mentioned that he confesses to a foreign priest. Their language barrier sometimes leads to misunderstandings, which, as he explained, was precisely why he chose this priest. "I prefer him not fully understanding the sins I'm confessing," he admitted.

This revelation surprised me, especially for my brother, as he is seventy-three years-old and still feels uncomfortable confessing his sins. Despite the beauty of the sacrament, it is clear to me that face-to-face admitting our faults can be daunting for many, even for those seasoned in faith. For me, too, it was not until later in life that I overcame the hesitation to confess face-to-face with a priest. It still feels a little nerve-wracking, even at sixty-four. But I understand why. The vulnerability of laying bare our sins in front of another person, even a priest, can feel like a kind of exposure we would rather avoid.

---

[1] Karen Danao. 25 Moonstruck Quotes.quoteambition.com2023

Yet, as I reflect on the sacrament, I also see that it holds immense beauty and profound healing—a grace we, as Catholics, are privileged to experience.

Before 1974, confession typically took place in a booth with a screen separating the penitent from the priest, ensuring anonymity and comfort for those who feared exposure. The hope was that the priest would not recognize their voice, or, if he did, would refrain from addressing them by name. This format allowed for emotional distance, allowing people to be honest and open without the fear of judgment. But after 1974, the U.S. bishops permitted a more personal, face-to-face format for confession. This change allowed for deeper spiritual counseling and offered a more direct encounter with Christ through the priest. For many, though, it also made the experience more challenging. The confessional, once a place of quiet anonymity, became a space for personal encounter, where we are face-to-face with Christ through the priest's presence. The shift, while spiritually enriching, can still feel uncomfortable for some.

I remember the days when confession lines at my parish were long, stretching out the door on a Saturday afternoon. Confessions began at 2 p.m. and continued until 5 p.m., with multiple priests available to hear the multitude of penitents. I also remember Saint Padre Pio, who would spend up to fourteen hours a day in the confessional, offering grace and mercy to anyone who sought it. Today, however, confessions at my parish are far less frequent, with a daily 30-minute window between 4:30 p.m. and 5 p.m. Many days, there is only one priest present. It starkly contrasts with the busy confessionals of my youth, and it speaks to a larger, concerning the "confession crisis."

"In the 1950s and 1960s, approximately 80% of American Catholics went to confession at least once a year, and more attended monthlies. But today, only about 37% of Catholics go to confession annually, and a disturbing 35% never go at all, according to a 2023 survey by RealClear Opinion Research. This decline is often

attributed to a broader cultural shift where Catholics no longer see confession as central to their faith or their relationship with God. As Russell Shaw, a journalist and former communications director for the U.S. bishops, puts it, "The larger issue is that people just don't believe in sin anymore." For some, traditional teachings of the Church, particularly those on moral behavior, conflict with the cultural currents of the modern world.

Yet, despite this cultural shift, I still hold fast to the profound beauty of confession. My retired godfather, Monsignor Charles Mallet, once shared with me his deep joy in hearing confessions. He told me that "confession should never be embarrassing, humiliating, uncomfortable, or upsetting. Just as the priest stands in *Persona Christi* when consecrating the Eucharist," he explained, "he also embodies Christ when hearing confessions." Monsignor Mallet said that hearing confessions was a "boundless joy" for him because, through Christ, he had the privilege of offering absolution and restoring sanctifying grace to the penitent. "Hearing the words, 'I absolve you of your sins, go in peace and sin no more,' means your sins are washed away, and Christ is giving you grace to sin no more." These words are powerful because they point to the truth that Christ has the authority to forgive sins, and that power has been entrusted to the Church and the priesthood.

Saint Athanasius once wrote, "Just as the man whom the priest baptizes is enlightened by the grace of the Holy Spirit, so does he who in penance confesses his sins receive through the priest forgiveness in virtue of the grace of Christ." When we step into the confessional, we encounter the mercy of God in a tangible way. We meet Christ in the person of the priest, who offers us absolution not based on his own power but by the authority Christ passed to the Apostles, who have passed it down through the generations. This is the beauty and truth of the sacrament. I advocate for confession as it reaffirms our true nature: individuals needing healing, mercy, and grace. The essence of this sacrament is not one of condemnation or judgment; rather, it is where Christ meets us in our brokenness, offering limitless mercy that can transform our lives. Despite our sins, Christ's love prevails. Thus, I uphold the sacrament of confession, for it reveals the profound depths of God's love and mercy.

The Sacrament of Reconciliation is at the heart of why I believe in the Catholic faith. It is, in essence, one of the central reasons Jesus came into the world. Throughout the Bible, forgiveness is a recurring theme, appearing in about four hundred and ninety verses. Jesus' teachings and actions underscore the profound importance of forgiveness, not just as a moral virtue, but to restore us to communion with God. Some of the most powerful stories Jesus shared in His ministry are about forgiveness: Parable of the Prodigal Son (Luke 15:11-32), the woman caught in adultery (John 8:1-11), and His command to forgive "seventy times seven" (Matthew 18:21-22). Jesus spoke of the immense joy in heaven when one sinner repents, likening it to the joy of finding a lost sheep when ninety-nine righteous ones are left behind (Luke 15:7). He also taught us to pray, *"Forgive us our sins as we forgive everyone indebted to us"* (Luke 11:1-4). In these passages, we see a loving God who desires to heal and restore, not condemn. Perhaps the most profound moment of all is when, hanging on the cross, Jesus prays, *"Father, forgive them, for they know not what they do"* (Luke 23:34).

In this act of divine mercy, He opens the floodgates of grace, offering forgiveness to all. And after His resurrection, when He appears to His Apostles, He breathes on them and says, *"Receive the Holy Spirit. If you forgive anyone's sins, they are forgiven; if you retain anyone's sins, they are retained"* (John 20:22-23). With these words, Jesus instituted the Sacrament of Reconciliation, giving His Apostles—and through them, the Church—the authority to forgive sins in His name.

This sacrament is not just a practice or tradition of the Church; it is a divine gift given to us by Christ Himself. It is a tangible means of encountering God's mercy and grace. For me, it is a sacred way to experience the transformative power of forgiveness. Jesus did not just

teach forgiveness; He made it possible for us to experience it directly, through the Church. In her wisdom, the Church has always upheld the necessity of this sacrament. In fact, the Fourth Lateran Council in 1215 mandated that every Christian, once they reach the age of discretion, must confess their sins at least once a year to their priest. This requirement was not to burden us, but to ensure that we never take God's forgiveness for granted. It was instituted to prevent laxity and to remind us that reconciliation is essential to our life in Christ. The practice of confession has been a consistent part of the Church's teaching from the very beginning.

I believe in the Sacrament of Reconciliation because it is a direct way to encounter the mercy of God. It is an opportunity to be healed from the wounds of sin and to be restored to communion with the Lord. Jesus gave us this gift because He knows that we, as human beings, need it—both for our souls and for our relationship with Him. It is not just a ritual, but a profound moment of grace, where we can experience the joy of being forgiven and the strength to sin no more. In a world that often dismisses the idea of sin or sees forgiveness as optional, Reconciliation is necessary and life-giving. It reminds me that I can always return to the Father's embrace, no matter how far I may have strayed. Through this sacrament, I am reminded of Christ's unfathomable love for me and all of us. And for this reason, I believe.

A number of my Protestant friends, with their characteristic playfulness, often challenge me to find biblical evidence for the practice of confessing sins to a priest. Their question reflects a common misunderstanding, but it also provides an opportunity to reflect on the deep roots of this practice within Scripture and the life of the Church. When I respond, I point to passages that support the Catholic understanding of confession. One of the most compelling is from Saint Paul, a figure whom Protestants hold in high regard. In 2 Corinthians 5:17-20, Paul writes: *"Therefore, if anyone is in Christ, he is a new creation; the old has gone, the new has come! All this is from God, who reconciled us to himself through Christ and gave us the ministry of reconciliation: He was reconciling the world to himself*

in Christ, not counting men's sins against them. And he has committed to us the message of reconciliation. We are therefore Christ's ambassadors, as though God were making his appeal through us. We implore you on Christ's behalf: Be reconciled to God." In this passage, Paul is clear that God has entrusted the ministry of reconciliation to the apostles and their successors, the leaders of the Church. The ministry of reconciliation is not just about individual acts of repentance; it is about a formal, communal, and authoritative way that God works through His Church to reconcile people to Himself. The message of forgiveness is not just spoken; it is conducted through the priesthood, as Christ's ambassadors.

The letter of James is another key sacrament of confession. In James 5:13-15, we read: *"Is anyone among you in trouble? Let them pray. Is anyone happy? Let them sing songs of praise. Is anyone among you sick? Let them call the elders (presbyters) of the church to pray over them and anoint them with oil in the name of the Lord. And the prayer offered in faith will make the sick person well; the Lord will raise them up. If they have sinned, they will be forgiven."* The word *"presbyters"* here is a direct reference to priests. James is speaking of the role of the Church's leaders in offering prayer and healing, including the forgiveness of sins. This passage shows the Church's authority in the healing of both physical and spiritual ailments, underscoring the practice of confessing sins to priests as part of the ministry of reconciliation.

Then there is the powerful story from the Gospel of Matthew (9:2-8), where Jesus explicitly claims the authority to forgive sins. When a paralytic is brought before Him, Jesus first says, *"Take heart, son; your sins are forgiven."* This declaration of forgiveness astonishes the onlookers, and Jesus goes on to heal the man physically to demonstrate His authority over both sin and body. Jesus' ability to forgive sins was not only divine but also, in the authority He passes on to His apostles, a prerogative that would later be exercised through the ministry of the Church. Additionally, in Matthew 18:18, Jesus grants the Church the power to bind and loose: *"Truly I tell you,*

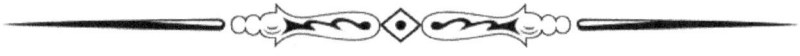

whatever you bind on earth will be bound in heaven, and whatever you loose on earth will be loosed in heaven." This is often interpreted as Christ giving His Church the authority to govern, teach, and forgive sins. The Church, acting in Christ's name, holds the authority to "bind"—to withhold forgiveness—or to "loosen"—to offer absolution. This teaching is foundational to the practice of confession, where the priest, by the authority of Christ, binds and looses sins on behalf of the faithful. Finally, in James 5:16, we are encouraged to confess our sins to one another: *"Therefore, confess your sins to each other and pray for each other so that you may be healed."* While this passage does not specifically refer to the sacrament of confession, it reflects the biblical truth that confession is essential to spiritual healing. The Catholic Church teaches that confession to a priest is not only a personal reconciliation with God but also, a communal act that brings healing to the entire Body of Christ.

The Sacrament of Reconciliation is deeply rooted in Scripture. It is a precious gift from Christ, entrusted to His Church, allowing his beloved followers to experience His forgiveness through the ministry of priests who act in His name. This grace-filled sacrament restores us to communion with God, reminding us of His boundless mercy and the continual call to reconciliation with God and each other. This is why I believe in confession—it is firmly grounded in Scripture and a beautiful expression of God's love for His people.

Perhaps my Protestant friends do not fully understand the necessity of confessing to a priest, as the sacrament of reconciliation is not part of their liturgical tradition. Still, it is worth noting that some Protestant traditions, such as the Lutheran and Episcopalian Churches, practice a form of confession, acknowledging its biblical precedent it. My Protestant friends, in their earnest pursuit of Scripture, often challenge me on the necessity of confessing sins to a priest. They argue that the Bible instructs us to confess our sins directly to God, and not through an intermediary. I understand their perspective, especially since Protestants typically do not have priests in the same way Catholics do; their clergy are pastors or ministers, and they generally view the confession of sins as a private matter between the believer and God. One of the main points Protestant scholars emphasize is that the Bible does not mandate confessing sins to priests, pastors, or ministers, but instead encourages confessing directly to God. They often cite verses such as 1 John 1:9, which says, "*If we confess our sins, He is faithful and just to forgive us our sins and to cleanse us from all unrighteousness.*" This beautiful and powerful promise reflects God's mercy and willingness to forgive. Similarly, Psalm 32:5 affirms this, saying, "*I acknowledged my sin to you, and I did not cover my iniquity. I said, 'I will confess my transgression to the Lord,' and you forgave the iniquity of my sin.*" And in Psalm 51:1-4, King David's heartfelt plea for forgiveness is a model of personal confession: "*Have mercy on me, O God, according to your steadfast love...Wash me thoroughly from my iniquity and cleanse me from my sin.*" These passages, along with others in Scripture, affirm that God is always ready to forgive when we confess our sins directly to Him. This is a vital part of the Christian life— developing a personal relationship with God where we bring our sins before Him and seek His forgiveness.

Protestants also point out that individuals who were not Apostles, like Stephen (Acts 7) and Philip (Acts 8), preached the gospel and spoke about the forgiveness of sins. And, in Acts 11, men from Cyprus and Cyrene shared the message of reconciliation with the Gentiles. It is important to recognize that while anyone can proclaim the message of forgiveness, the sacrament of reconciliation is a special ministry given by Christ to His Church—entrusted to the apostles and their successors.

For Catholics, the priest does not act on his own authority but in "Persona Christi", in the presence of Christ. This is the essence of the sacrament: the priest is the mediator of God's grace, offering absolution and reconciliation to the penitent in the name of Christ. It is not about the priest's personal holiness or power; it is about Christ working through the priest to forgive sins and restore us to communion with God. While I fully respect the Protestant emphasis

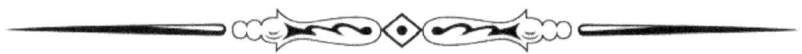

on the direct confession to God, the sacrament of reconciliation enriches the believer's spiritual life in a unique and profound way. It is a gift that brings healing through the Church's priesthood, grounded in Christ's own words and actions. Jesus gave the Church this power not as a burden or a formality, but as a means of grace, allowing us to experience the tangible mercy of God, especially when our sins weigh heavily on our hearts. I believe that confessing to a priest is not only biblical but an essential part of the Catholic faith. It is not a contradiction to confessing directly to God but an extension of it, offering us the grace of hearing Christ's words, "*I absolve you of your sins*," through the priesthood. In this way, the sacrament of reconciliation is a beautiful, biblical, and transformative experience that continues the work of forgiveness and healing that Christ began.

Confession restores your relationship with God, lifting the burden and weight of sin. It diminishes pride, fostering growth in humility and virtue. Through confession, you become more aware of your weaknesses, helping you develop greater self-control. Ultimately, confession strengthens you and prepares you for spiritual warfare. And in the end, confession will help prevent your sins from turning into bad habits.

Over the years, I've had discussions with Protestant friends who question the practice of confessing sins to a priest. They often reference passages like 1 John 1:9 or Psalm 32:5, suggesting that we should confess directly to God and that this is sufficient for forgiveness. While I respect their viewpoint, I usually ask a question that leaves them in awe: How can you be certain that God has forgiven you if you never hear Him say the words, "Your sins are forgiven," just as Jesus spoke to the paralyzed man in Matthew 9:2-8? If I wrong someone, I can quietly ask for their forgiveness in my heart, but unless I speak directly to them, how can I be sure they've received my apology? How can I know they've forgiven me unless they explicitly say, "I forgive you?" It's easy to assume our sins are forgiven in our hearts, but without explicit, external confirmation, how can we be

truly certain of our forgiveness? Their typical response is, "I just know."

And while that may be meaningful to them, it leaves me with a longing for something more concrete, something more tangible. It offers a certainty that we may not always feel in the quiet of our hearts, especially when our sins weigh heavily upon us. The beauty of confession is that we hear the priest, acting in the person of Christ, speak the words, "I absolve you of your sins." It is not merely a ritual—it's the living voice of God speaking through the Church, assuring us of forgiveness. This sacrament gives us the certainty that we are truly forgiven, not just because we believe it in our hearts, but because we hear the words of absolution spoken aloud. And that certainty is a gift, one that strengthens my faith and provides a profound peace God wants all of us to experience. It is easy to fall into the trap of thinking that forgiveness should be an abstract or personal experience, something we simply know or feel. But when we look at the full depth of the Christian story, we see that God, in His wisdom, has given us physical and communal means through which we can experience His grace. This is why the sacrament of confession is not only a beautiful practice but a necessary one.

Consider the story of the Good Thief, a figure who has always inspired me. While hanging on the cross, he confessed his sins and believed in Christ's mercy. In a moment of great personal suffering and pain, he made a simple but profound statement: "*Jesus, remember me when You come into Your kingdom.*" And Jesus, with immense mercy, said, "*Truly I tell you, today you will be with Me in paradise*" (Luke 23:42-43). At first glance, this seems to defy the "requirements" we often think are necessary for salvation. The thief had no baptism, no communion, no confirmation, no church membership, no good works to offer. He was a thief, in his decisive moments, hanging on a cross. He had no time to perform any of the rituals we associate with Christian life. No beautiful church, no spiritual programs, no elaborate prayers. He simply believed and

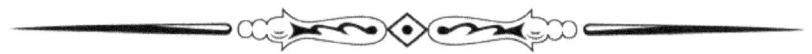

asked Jesus in person for forgiveness. Yet, Jesus, in His infinite mercy, offered him forgiveness.

But, here is the beauty I find in this story: We may not be hanging on a cross, but we are, in our ways, burdened by the weight of our sins. When we go to confession, we encounter Christ's mercy as a priest who speaks the words of absolution in Christ's name, offering us the peace of knowing that our sins are forgiven. It is not a vague feeling or a silent prayer—it is a certainty, a reality that we can experience and cling to. Just as Jesus spoke directly to the Good Thief, He continues to speak directly to us today, through the Church, through the priest, and the sacrament. He desires to assure us of His forgiveness, and He does so through a means that is both tangible and deeply personal. It is not just about the forgiveness of sins—it's about the certainty and the peace that come with hearing God's words of mercy spoken to us in the midst of our struggles. It is a beautiful gift, one that allows us to be fully restored to the love and grace of God, and it is a gift I believe every Christian should embrace.

Back to that question- How can you be sure that you are forgiven if you don't hear God tell you so? It is a valid question, and one that points to a deeper longing within the human heart—a longing for certainty and assurance when it comes to God's mercy. As a Catholic, I have found a beautiful and profound answer to this question in the words of Father Amroth in his book *My Battle Against Satan*. Father Amroth speaks to a common objection people have regarding the sacrament of confession: *"Why must I confess my sins to a man, who is a sinner like me?"* It is a question that reflects a misunderstanding of the true nature of confession. The truth, as Father Amroth explains, is that a priest, despite his own sinfulness, is given a divine power that no angel or even the Blessed Virgin Mary possesses. That power is the authority to absolve sins. Father Amroth imagines a scenario where Our Lady appears to someone, and they confess their sins to her. Her response would not be, "You are forgiven," but rather, "Go to a priest, who has the power to absolve your sins."

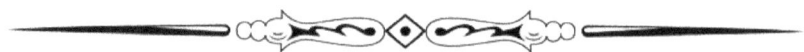

Father Amroth's insight is profound. The priest, despite his own human weaknesses, is the instrument chosen by God to extend His forgiveness to us. The priest's power to absolve sins does not come from his own holiness but from Christ, who has given this authority to His Church. As Catholics, we believe that when a priest hears a confession and offers absolution, it is not his judgment being rendered, but God's. It is Christ acts through him, making forgiveness real, tangible, and assured. This sacrament gives us the certainty that our sins are forgiven, not because we feel forgiven in the quiet of our hearts, but because we hear the priest, in persona Christi, say the words of absolution. It is a gift of mercy and grace that is rooted in the very authority of Christ Himself. Many Protestants may struggle with this idea, believing that confession should be a private matter between the individual and God. And while it is true that we can always pray directly to God for forgiveness, the sacrament of reconciliation offers something even more powerful: the assurance that God's forgiveness is not abstract or uncertain, but concrete and guaranteed.

Reflecting on my own experiences with confession, I realize that it is not just about admitting my sins; it is more than that. It is about encountering God's mercy in a personal, transformative way. It is about hearing Christ say, through the priest, *"I absolve you of your sins in the name of the Father, and of the Son, and of the Holy Spirit."* These words, spoken with authority by the priest, assure me that God has forgiven me. And that certainty is a profound gift that brings peace to my heart and restores my relationship with God. One of the most profound and beautiful gifts the Catholic faith offers is the sacrament of confession, now often referred to as reconciliation. Through this sacrament, God's mercy is powerfully applied to sinners, bringing healing, peace, and a restoration of grace. In the act of confession that we encounter the transformative power of God's forgiveness—an assurance that no other religion offers in the same way. When we profess in the Apostle's Creed, "I believe in the forgiveness of sins," we affirm not just the truth of God's mercy, but

the reality of its application to us through the sacrament of reconciliation.

What makes confession so beautiful and necessary is that it is not just a ritual—it is how God's grace is applied to our lives in a concrete and personal way. When we go to confession, we experience the profound truth that God no longer holds our sins against us. Through the priest, Christ speaks the words of absolution, washing away our faults and offering us the peace that only He can give. This is the beauty of the sacrament: it is an opportunity to experience God's mercy firsthand, not as a distant concept or a vague hope, but as a living, real encounter with Christ. However, as Father Amroth wisely points out, confession requires more than just going through the motions. It demands a sincere, contrite heart—a willingness to change profoundly. The sacrament is not simply a matter of listing sins to get them off our conscience; it is about an honest desire for conversion, for transformation and re-establishing our relationship with God. If a sinner does not genuinely wish to change, confession becomes empty. The grace of God is always available to us, but it requires our cooperation. This is why repentance is a necessary part of the sacrament.

One question I often hear from people is, *"How often should I go to confession?"* This question that points to the deeper need for spiritual growth and self-awareness. Father Amroth gives a simple but insightful answer: *"An adult should confess his/her sins at least once a month."* This regular practice of confession keeps us attuned to our own faults and weaknesses, helping us grow in humility and awareness of our need for God's grace. For young children and teenagers, the frequency of confession may depend on their age and their personal struggles, but the principle remains the same: the more often we confess, the more we become aware of our defects, our sins, and our deep need for God's mercy. Frequent confession is not meant to burden us, but to free us. When we confess regularly, we are invited to grow in holiness, to become more attuned to the ways in which we fall short, and to turn back to God's mercy continually. It is a process of healing, spiritual renewal, and becoming more fully who God has created us to be. The less often we confess, the less we are likely to see our sins for what they truly are—the barriers that prevent us from fully experiencing God's love and peace.

I firmly believe in the beauty of confession because it is a personal encounter with God's mercy, a moment when we can experience the forgiveness of sins in a very tangible way. It is not just a matter of intellectual belief—it's a lived reality, a sacrament that can transform us, heal us, and draw us closer to God. The more we practice confession, the more we are aware of our need for God's grace, and the more we open ourselves to His transformative power. Confession is not just about forgiveness; it's about growth. It's about returning to God, time and time again, and allowing His mercy to shape our hearts, to purify our intentions, and to help us live in greater union with Him. This is why I believe in the beauty and truth of the sacrament of reconciliation—a life-giving, grace-filled encounter with God's mercy that restores us, renews us, and helps us become more like Christ.

Confession Quotes from Saints

> **St. Faustina, Divine Mercy in My Soul**: Daughter, when you go to confession, to this fountain of My mercy, the Blood and Water which came forth from My Heart always flows down upon your soul and ennobles it. Every time you go to confession, immerse yourself in My mercy, with great trust, so that I may pour the bounty of My grace upon your soul. When you approach the confessional, know this, that I myself am waiting there for you. I am only hidden by the priest, but I myself act in your soul. Here, the misery of the soul meets the God of mercy. Tell souls that from this fount of mercy, souls draw grace solely with the vessel of trust. If their trust is great, there is no limit to my generosity. The torrents of grace inundate humble souls. The proud remain always in poverty

and misery, because My grace turns away from them to humble souls.

> **Pope John Paul 2:** Confession is an act of honesty and courage - entrusting ourselves, beyond sin, to the mercy of a loving and forgiving God.

> **St. Chrysostom**: "After confession, a crown is given to penitents."

> **St. Alphonsus Liguori:** The devil does not bring sinners to hell with their eyes open: he first blinds them with the malice of their sins. Before we fall into sin, the enemy labors to blind us, that we may not see the evil we do and the ruin we bring upon ourselves by offending God. After we sin, he seeks to make us dumb, that, through shame, we may conceal our guilt in confession.

> **St. Thomas Aquinas:** In the life of the body, a man is sometimes sick, and unless he takes medicine, he will die. Even so, a man is sick in the spiritual life because of sin. For that reason, he needs medicine to be restored to health, and this grace is bestowed in the Sacrament of Penance.

> **St. Francis de Sales:** Go to your confessor; open your heart to him; display to him all the recesses of your soul; take the advice he will give you with the utmost humility and

simplicity. God, who has an infinite love for obedience, frequently renders profitable the counsels we take from others, but especially from those who are the guides of our souls.

➤ **Saint John Climacus:** "Confession is like a bridle that keeps the soul, which reflects on it from committing sin, but anything left unconfessed we continue to do without fear as if in the dark."

➤ **St. Thomas Aquinas:** Three conditions are necessary for Penance: contrition, which is sorrow for sin, together with a purpose of amendment; confession of sins without any omission; and satisfaction by means of good works.

➤ **St. Padre Pio:** Confession is the soul's bath, it purifies you like a newborn baby. You must go at least once a week to soothe yourself. I do not want souls to stay away from confession for more than a week. Even a clean and unoccupied room gathers dust; return after a week and you will see that it needs dusting again!"

THE LAST SUPPER & EUCHARIST

Chapter Nine
The Last Supper

The 14th of Nisan in ancient Jerusalem was unlike any other day, charged with awe and reverence that speaks deeply to the heart of anyone who contemplates the beauty and mystery of the Catholic faith. It was on this day, as the city thrummed with the arrival of Jewish pilgrims from all over the world, that Jesus gathered with His Apostles to celebrate the Passover, a solemn feast rooted in centuries of tradition. Jerusalem, usually home to around 40,000 people, swelled to more than 180,000 as Jews from across the land came to fulfill their obligation to celebrate one of the three great festivals prescribed in the Law of Moses. For them, observing the Passover was not a choice, but a command with profound consequences: to neglect it would risk divine punishment, known in the Talmud as *Karet*, a severance from the community, and, according to Jewish belief, the extinction of the soul.

Amid this solemn festival, of all religious observances, was seen in the Temple. It wasn't merely a building; it was the heart of Jewish life and worship. Its monumental structure, covering forty acres and rising

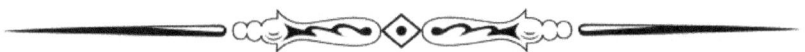

158 feet into the sky, was an awe-inspiring symbol of God's presence among His people. It was visible for miles around, a sign of the covenant that bound the Israelites to their Creator. The sheer grandeur of the Temple, built with massive limestone blocks weighing tons, was a tangible reminder of God's holiness and majesty. The gold that covered the Temple caught the sunlight so that it glistened like a beacon, drawing the eyes of pilgrims and passersby, just as the Catholic Church draws the faithful to the Eucharist—the actual, living presence of God among us.

The Ark of the Covenant, placed in the Holy of Holies and revered as the holiest object in Jewish life, was a vessel that contained sacred items: a jar of manna, a vial of anointing oil, Aaron's staff, the Ten Commandments, and the golden gifts returned by the Philistines. These were physical reminders of God's work in the lives of His people, of the miracles and promises He had made. In the Catholic faith, we too have tangible signs of God's grace—sacred relics, the holy Scriptures, the sacraments—that remind us of His presence and action in our lives. The Catholic faith, like the Jewish tradition of the Temple, has always been rooted in the belief that God is present in a unique and authentic way in sacred spaces. For Catholics, this belief is realized most profoundly in the Eucharist, which we believe to be the Body and Blood of Christ. Just as the Jews believed the Ark of the Covenant housed the divine presence in the Holy of Holies, Catholics believe that the Eucharist contains the very presence of Christ, body, blood, soul, and divinity, in a way that surpasses human understanding. This is not merely a symbol; it is the living truth of God with us. In the Catholic Mass, we do not simply commemorate the Last Supper, but we are invited into the mystery of Christ's sacrifice, His offering of Himself for our salvation.

The beauty of the Catholic faith lies in its commitment to these ancient traditions and in its fulfillment of the promises made by God. Like the Temple in Jerusalem, the Catholic Church is the dwelling place of God among His people, and the Eucharist is the new Ark—bearing Christ Himself, whose presence sanctifies and transforms us.

Just as the Temple in Jerusalem was a place of encounter with the Divine, so is the Church today, where we meet Christ in a profound and personal way. To believe in the beauty and truth of the Catholic faith is to recognize that God's presence is not confined to the past but is made manifest in the present, sacraments, Word, and the Church's divinity. It is to see that the grandeur of the Temple was but a shadow of the even greater glory to come in Christ, who sacrificed Himself for us. He didn't care about anything; he gave everything to us, his body, soul, in the Eucharist. It is essential for us to comprehend that the beauty of the Church, in all its history and splendor, is not merely about its outward appearance. Still, about the deeper mystery it holds—God dwelling with His people, offering His love and grace to all who will receive it. In the Catholic faith, I find not only a beautiful tradition but a living reality that transforms my life and leads me to the very heart of God. The beauty of the Church, the holiness of the Eucharist, and the truth of Christ's presence in our lives are, for me, a testimony to the eternal and unconditional love of God—love that is present beyond our understanding, reaching out to us in the most profound ways. That is why I believe in the beauty and truth of the Catholic faith. It is not just a faith rooted in history, but a faith that is alive, speaks to the deepest needs of the human heart, and carries with it the promise of divine life—here and now, and in the world to come.

In the time of Jesus, the Temple was a place of profound ritual and reverence, where Jewish men and women could seek forgiveness for their sins by offering sacrifices to God. These sacrifices were not just ceremonial acts; they were acts of atonement. Through the shedding of blood, they sought to repair the rupture caused by sin, restoring their relationship with the Divine. The Jewish understanding was clear: without these sacrifices, there could be no forgiveness, reconciliation, or peace with God. To be cut off from the Temple, to be unable to offer the proper sacrifices, was to face spiritual alienation and the threat of divine condemnation. As we reflect on the enormity of the rituals performed during the Passover in Jerusalem, we are struck by the intensity and gravity of these acts. The Temple was a

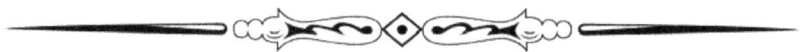

hive of activity during the festival, with priests working tirelessly to prepare sacrifices. It is said that, at the height of the festival, as many as 1.2 million animals could be slaughtered in a single day, each one representing the life that was laid down in exchange for the forgiveness of sins. The sheer volume of sacrifices was staggering, and some texts even describe how the high priests would be immersed in animal blood, a sobering reminder of the cost of sin and the great lengths to which God's people went to restore communion with Him. These sacrifices were not a mere ritual, but an invitation to encounter the living God. They took place in the very heart of the Temple, at the altar, and involved the slaughter, preparation, and burning of the sacrificial animals. The meat was then carefully prepared and presented on the altar, as the Law of Moses prescribed. This was not an arbitrary practice—it was a means of honoring God's holiness and securing forgiveness for the people.

The "Slaughter Area," located north of the altar, was where the sacrificial animals were prepared for offering. Here, the animals were slaughtered, skinned, and made ready to be presented on the altar. According to tradition, the animal's neck (or legs, as noted by Maimonides) was placed in rings attached to small pillars called *nanasim*. The animals were then hung to be skinned, and the meat was washed on marble tables before being laid upon the altar to be consumed by fire. Once the lambs were cooked, each family would return to their quarters to partake in the final and most sacred part of the Passover ritual: the meal. The central act of this celebration was the eating of the roasted lamb, in strict observance of the Law of Moses, which prescribed the lamb as the focal point of the Passover feast. This meal was not just a family gathering, but a sacred commemoration, a fulfillment of the covenant, and an expression of gratitude for God's deliverance.

For Catholics, the story of sacrifice and atonement does not end with the Temple rituals. Instead, the Catholic faith sees in Christ the ultimate fulfillment of these ancient rites. In Jesus, we find the perfect Sacrifice, offered finally, not with the blood of bulls and goats,

but with His Precious Blood. In the Eucharist, we encounter the Lamb of God, whose sacrifice is eternal and whose grace is poured out for the forgiveness of our sins. Just as the Jewish people gathered around the altar to receive the lamb's meat, Catholics gather at the altar to receive the true Lamb of God, whose Body and Blood nourish us and restore us to life. The beauty of the Catholic faith lies in its understanding of Christ as both the Priest and the Victim. He offers Himself as the Sacrifice, fulfilling the law and the prophets, but He also invites us to join Him in the feast—the banquet of Heaven. In the Eucharist, we remember Christ's Passion and are drawn into it, participating in the mystery of His death and resurrection. The meal following the sacrifice is not simply a commemorative act; it is a living, transformative encounter with the living Christ, the source of eternal life.

This continuity between the sacrifices of the Old Covenant and the Eucharistic sacrifice of the New Covenant speaks to the truth of God's plan. In the Eucharist, Catholics believe they are invited to partake in a sacrifice that is both final and eternal. The Passover meal, with its roasted lamb and unleavened bread, foreshadowed the ultimate meal that Christ would offer to His Church: His Body and Blood, given for the world's salvation. The Lamb, slain for the redemption of God's people, has now become the meal that sustains us in our pilgrimage toward Heaven. In the Eucharist, I see the fulfillment of all the sacrifices that came before. I see the beauty of God's plan unfolding through history, leading to the supreme act of love in Christ's death on the Cross. And I see the truth of His promise: that, through His Body and Blood, we are forgiven, restored, and made one with Him. This is why I believe in the beauty and truth of the Catholic faith. In Christ, the Passover is fulfilled, and the sacrifice becomes the meal of eternal life, offered freely to all who come in faith. The Lamb of God invites us to His table, where we find forgiveness and communion with the very Source of Life.

In 2019, my wife and I had the incredible privilege of visiting the Holy Land for our honeymoon. One of the most memorable

moments of that trip occurred while we stood before the Western Wall, the last remaining part of Herod the Great's Second Temple. As we gazed upon this sacred site, I could not help but feel the weight of history, the sacredness of the place, and the deep connection between the Jewish people and their faith. The wall, which has witnessed centuries of prayer and longing, seemed to echo with the prayers of those who sought God in the shadow of the Temple.

As we stood there, I had a question that had been lingering in my mind: What was the true significance of the Passover meal, and how did it point to the ultimate fulfillment of God's promises in Christ? I turned to Jonathan, a local guide, and asked him to explain the details of the Passover celebration. He shared with me the intricate practices that shaped this ancient ritual, and I was struck by how much beauty and meaning lay within them, revealing a profound truth that I would later see mirrored in the Catholic faith. Jonathan explained, "Typically, 50 to 100 people would gather around each roasted lamb and consume only a small portion of the meat—about the size of an olive. Alongside the lamb, there would be bitter herbs and unleavened bread, known as *matzah*. The meal would begin with the lamb and continue until about midnight." Curious, I asked him about the *Seder* meal, a central feature of the Passover celebration. He smiled and said, "The most poignant moment of the Jewish Seder meal is when the youngest participant asks the traditional questions: *Why is this night different from all other nights? On every other night of the year, we eat leavened bread and matzah, but on this night, we eat only matzah. Why?*"

I could not help but think of the Last Supper when Jesus, surrounded by His Apostles, would have participated in this tradition. Jonathan continued, "We can assume that during the Last Supper, the Apostle John might have posed this very question to Jesus. Jesus likely answered them with words very similar to what is recited in the *Haggadah*: *We were slaves to Pharaoh in Egypt, but the Lord delivered us from Egypt with a powerful hand* (Deuteronomy 6:21)." As Jonathan spoke, I began to realize the profound connection between the Jewish Passover and the Catholic faith. The Seder meal, with its retelling of God's deliverance of the Israelites from slavery in Egypt, is not merely a commemoration of a historical event—it is a living tradition, a ritual that brings the past into the present. The question *Why is this night different?* serves as a reminder that God's saving acts are not confined to history but are alive in the hearts of those who recall and celebrate them. This annual retelling of the Exodus—the liberation of God's people from oppression—is an act of remembrance that sustains the faith of the Jewish people. For them, the Seder meal makes the past present and brings the memory of God's deliverance back to life. And in the Catholic faith, we too have a meal that makes the past present—the Eucharist.

The Eucharist, like the Passover meal, is a celebration of God's deliverance, but it is more than just a remembrance. It is the fulfillment of what the Passover pointed to—the true Lamb of God, sacrificed for the world's salvation. Just as the Passover lamb's blood marked the doors of the Israelites, protecting them from death, so too does the Blood of Christ, poured out for us on the Cross, mark our hearts and deliver us from sin and eternal death. The Eucharist is not merely a meal of remembrance; it is a participation in the very sacrifice of Christ, who gave His Body and Blood for the world's life.

I realized during my time in the Holy Land that it is found in its deep connection to the sacred traditions of the Jewish faith and its fulfillment in Christ. The *Seder* meal, commemorating the Israelites' liberation from Egypt, is a living testament to God's faithfulness to His people. And the Eucharist, the center of Catholic worship, fulfills that faithfulness. In the Eucharist, we not only remember God's saving acts; we participate in them, receiving Christ Himself, the true Passover Lamb, who delivers us from sin and death. I believe in the beauty and truth of the Catholic faith because it connects us to the most profound truths of God's plan for salvation. The Passover, with its sacrifice and meal, foreshadows the Eucharist, where we are not just spectators of God's mercy but active participants in it. This is the supreme beauty of the Catholic faith: that in Christ, the salvation won

for Israel is made available to all who believe. In the Eucharist, we encounter the living God, who continues to deliver His people, not just once in history, but in every age, bringing us from slavery to sin into the freedom of eternal life. The Seder meal, with its poignant questions and sacred rituals, reminds us that God is always acting in history, bringing salvation to His people. And in the Catholic faith, we are invited to partake in that saving action, not just through memory, but through living participation in the Eucharist. This is why I believe in the beauty and truth of the Catholic faith—it reveals the eternal and unchanging love of God, present and active in our lives today.

In the days leading up to Jesus' final Passover, Jerusalem was alive with activity. The narrow, crowded streets were packed with pilgrims, all making their way toward the Temple to offer their sacrifices and fulfill the sacred commands of the Passover. The air was thick with the sounds of animals—sheep, oxen, bulls, and doves—echoing from the "Chamber of Lambs" as they were readied for sacrifice. The clinking of coins as money changers exchanged Roman and foreign currency for Temple shekels added to the din, and the sight of hundreds of Levite priests in constant motion around the Altar, preparing the sacrifices, managing the fires, and sprinkling blood, was a vivid display of devotion and ritual. The Temple, the heart of Jewish life, was where heaven and earth met. It was where God's presence dwelt among His people. The very walls seemed to resonate with the prayers of the faithful, offered at the various locations within the Temple—at the Gate of Nicanor, where people with leprosy were purified, at the Chamber of Nazirites, in the Women's Court, and in the Courts of Men and the Gentiles. Everywhere, the hum of worship was palpable. The sound of music, too, filled the air. Levites, trained in the art of song, played cymbals, harps, and lyres, while priests—*kohanim*—blew trumpets in praise of God. The Mishna (Tamid) records at least twenty-one trumpet blasts each day, marking the sacred rhythm of Temple worship. Three blasts open the gates, nine to signal the morning *Tamid* (the daily offering), and another nine to signal the evening offering. These trumpet blasts were not mere announcements; they were the voices of the people, lifting their praises to God, signaling the sacred times of sacrifice and prayer.

I cannot help but see in these rituals the deep connection between the Temple worship of old and the worship we now offer in the Eucharist. The sounds, the rituals, the animal sacrifices, all of these were pointing toward something greater. In the Catholic faith, the Eucharist fulfills all the sacrifices and offerings made in the Temple. Jesus, the Lamb of God, became the ultimate sacrifice for the forgiveness of sins. His sacrifice is not merely remembered; it is made present to us in the Mass, where we encounter His Body and Blood, offered for the world's salvation. In the bustling activity of the Temple, there existed a deep connection with God, his presence among His people. It was a place where heaven was brought to earth, where sacrifices were made to restore the broken relationship between humanity and God. In the Catholic Mass, we experience something even more wondrous: through the power of the Holy Spirit, the sacrifice of Jesus is made present to us in the form of bread and wine. The altar becomes, in a sense, our own Temple, where we, like the Israelites of old, offer praise and thanksgiving, and where we are drawn into the mystery of Christ's sacrifice. The beauty of the Temple worship was in its reverence for the holiness of God. The countless rituals, the music, the prayers, and sacrifices all spoke to people who knew they were in the presence of the Divine. And in the Catholic Church, we are invited into that same holy encounter. Just as the sound of trumpets and cymbals in the Temple signaled the sacredness of the moment, the bells that ring at the Catholic Mass, the hymns sung by the faithful, and the reverent silence of the congregation all signal that something sacred is coming our way. The Eucharist is not just a meal; it is the moment when we are invited into the presence of God Himself.

The Catholic faith shows us that the worship of God is not confined to ancient rituals but has been brought to fulfillment in the Person of Jesus Christ. Just as the Temple worship had its beauty and

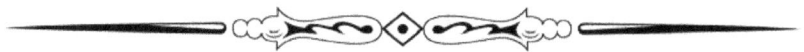

truth, pointing toward the ultimate sacrifice of the Lamb, so too does the Catholic Mass, where we encounter the risen Christ in the Eucharist. The rhythm of trumpet blasts, the prayers, the sacrifices—all these echoes in the Mass, where Christ is truly present, body, blood, soul, and divinity. And like the worshipers in the Temple, we are invited to participate, to offer our own lives in praise and thanksgiving, and to receive the gift of God's grace. The grandeur of the Temple and its rituals point to the deeper truth that God desires to dwell with His people. The Mass is the fulfillment of that desire, where God, in the person of Jesus Christ, comes to us, offers Himself as the perfect sacrifice, and invites us to partake in the banquet of heaven. In the Catholic faith, we experience the beauty of this truth every time we gather at the altar. It is a foretaste of the heavenly banquet, where, like the faithful of the Temple, we will praise and worship God in the fullness of His glory for all eternity. This is why I believe in the beauty and truth of the Catholic faith. The Eucharist is the culmination of all foreshadowed in the Temple—a living, transformative encounter with God, who continues to draw near to His people, offering His very Self to us in love. Through Christ, we are invited into the deepest mystery of our faith: the sacrifice that brings salvation, the meal that sustains us, and the worship that connects us to the divine.

During our honeymoon in Jerusalem, as my wife and I walked through the bustling streets of the "Old City," I was deeply moved by the very sense of place—the ancient stones, the narrow, winding paths, the vendors calling out to us as they tried to pull us into their shops. We passed through the gate that Jesus Himself must have entered, and my heart swelled with the weight of what had happened here so many years ago. As we walked along the Via Dolorosa, the path where Jesus carried His Cross, I could almost feel the intensity of His final journey. I wondered about His thoughts on that day, the 14th of Nisan, knowing what awaited Him. Was he filled with fear, anxiety, and dread about the suffering He was about to endure? Or was He, experiencing overwhelming emotions, entirely fully aware that this was why He had come into the world? I thought about the moments leading up to the Last Supper. Was He anxious to share His final instructions with His Apostles, or did He manage to find time for quiet moments of prayer, knowing that His Passion was drawing near? Did He seek comfort in the presence of His beloved mother, Mary?

The mystic Blessed Anne Catherine Emmerich offers insight into these moments, and as I reflected on her visions, I was struck by the tenderness of Jesus' love. According to Blessed Emmerich, Jesus spent time with His mother and His followers in these final hours. In a conversation with Mary, He revealed the anguish He would soon face. She, in her deep love for Him, begged that she might suffer alongside Him. But in His profound compassion, He spoke to her words of comfort. He urged her to bear her grief more calmly than the other women, reminding her that He would rise again. He even named the spot where He would appear to her after His Resurrection. Jesus, in His final hours, expressed deep gratitude for the love of His mother, embracing her with tenderness, reassuring her in her sorrow, and preparing her for the grief and joy that lay ahead. As I stood in the Upper Room, the Cenacle, where the Last Supper took place, I could not help but imagine the weight of that moment. Jesus, knowing that His time had come, was preparing not only to face His Passion but also to institute the sacrament of the Eucharist—His Body and Blood, given for the world's salvation. It was here, in this sacred space, that He shared His final meal with His disciples, offering them His Body and Blood in the first Eucharist. This meal, rich with meaning, would become the central act of Christian worship for generations. And yet, this profound act of self-giving love, Jesus did not forget His beloved followers. He also spoke to the holy women, to Mary Magdalene, and to Lazarus, offering them words of comfort and strength. To Mary Magdalene, who was overcome with grief, He said, "She loves unspeakably, but her love is still encompassed by the body; therefore, she has become like one quite out of her mind with pain." Jesus understood the depth of her sorrow, recognizing the enthusiastic love she had for Him, even as He prepared for the immense suffering of the Cross.

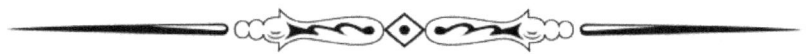

Jesus, fully aware of the path He was about to take, comforted those He loved, offering them peace even as He faced the deepest trial. This deep sense of love for His mother, His disciples, and each of us speaks to the heart of the Catholic faith. In the Eucharist, we encounter the same love Jesus offered His disciples that night. His Body and Blood are given to us not just as a symbol, but as a reality— Christ offering Himself to us, as He did to His Apostles, in the most intimate and self-giving way. I believe in the beauty and truth of the Catholic faith because in the Eucharist, I experience this same love, the same tender care that Jesus showed to His mother and His followers. In this sacrament, Jesus comes to us as He came to them, offering His Body and Blood for our salvation. In His final hours, He gave us the Eucharist as a means of staying close to Him, of entering the mystery of His love and sacrifice. The Eucharist is not just a remembrance of Jesus' death; it is a participation in His eternal offering of love. It is the ultimate act of self-giving, the fulfillment of His promise to be with us always, even to the end of the age. The moments leading up to the Last Supper, as described by Blessed Anne Catherine Emmerich, show Jesus' deep love for His mother, for His friends, and for each of us. In the Eucharist, that love is made present again, available to us in the most real and intimate way. Jesus, even in His suffering, continues to give Himself to us, to embrace us with love and mercy. This is why I believe in the beauty and truth of the Catholic faith. Through the Eucharist, we encounter the living Christ, who, in His final hours, showed us the depth of His love, and continues to offer that love to us, body and blood, soul and divinity.

As we continued our walk through the narrow, winding streets of the Old City in Jerusalem, our guide led us to the Upper Room, or the Cenacle, where Jesus shared His final meal with His disciples. As I stood in that sacred space, a profound thought struck me regarding a scene in the Gospel of Mark—a scene that, for years, had intrigued me for its mystery and subtlety. In Mark's Gospel, we read a rather peculiar instruction from Jesus. He sends two of His disciples into the city with the task of finding a man carrying a jar of water. Jesus tells them to ask, *"The Teacher says, 'Where is my guest room where I may eat the Passover with my disciples?'"* What immediately stands out about this scene is the unusual detail of a man carrying a jar of water. In Jewish culture, carrying water was a woman's task—so why would Jesus ask His disciples to look for a man doing this seemingly out-of-place chore?

To understand the significance of this moment, we must consider the context. During Passover, Jerusalem was packed with over 180,000 pilgrims, all seeking to observe the sacred rituals of the festival. The city was crowded and finding a particular place among so many people would have been no small task. In such a chaotic environment, a man carrying a jar of water would have stood out as an anomaly, a beacon amidst the throng of women who usually carried the water. Jesus, in His infinite wisdom, knew exactly what He was doing. He had arranged for this man, likely one of His followers, to be in the right place at the right time. This man's act of carrying water was not merely a random occurrence, it was a divine sign that the moment had come. As the disciples followed Jesus' instructions, they quickly found the man, who led them to a spacious room that was already prepared for the Passover meal. Jesus had orchestrated this moment precisely, even down to the smallest details. It was as though everything was falling into place by God's perfect plan. What struck me deeply as I reflected on this scene was not just the practical planning of finding the room but the deeper, symbolic meaning behind this seemingly odd instruction.

The man with the water jar is, in a sense, a symbol of God's careful provision and guidance in the middle of confusion and chaos. In a city overwhelmed with people, where it would have been nearly impossible to find an appropriate place to share the Passover meal, Jesus knew exactly where to go. He had already prepared a space for Himself and His disciples. And as I stood in the Upper Room, I realized that this room—this sacred space—was not just a physical location where Jesus ate with His Apostles; it was a place where God's plan for salvation was unfolding. In a broader sense, I see in this moment how God prepares a place for each of us. Just as Jesus prepared this room for His disciples, so too does He prepare a place for us in His Kingdom. The seemingly small and random events of our lives, just like the man carrying a jar of water, are all part of God's divine plan. During life's chaos and confusion, God is always guiding us, leading us to where we can encounter His love and grace. The beauty and truth of the Catholic faith are revealed in these small, seemingly insignificant details that point to something much larger: the unfolding of God's plan of salvation. Just as the disciples followed Jesus' instructions and found the man with the jar of water, so too are we called to follow His lead. And when we do, we find that God has already prepared a place for us to experience His love and where He will feed us with His very Body and Blood in the Eucharist.

Standing in the Upper Room, I could not help but feel the profound mystery of that moment when Jesus shared the Passover with His disciples. In this meal, Jesus instituted the Eucharist, offering His Body and Blood as a new Passover sacrifice. The meal was not just an act of remembrance; it was an act of communion, inviting us to be united with Him and with each other in the most intimate way possible. Through this meal, Jesus prepared the way for us to enter the deepest communion with God, through His sacrifice on the Cross, and the perpetual gift of the Eucharist. In the Upper Room, I felt the presence of Christ in a way that transcended history. The room where Jesus shared His final meal with His disciples is now a symbol of the ongoing invitation to each of us. Just as the disciples followed the man carrying the water, we are invited to follow Christ in faith, knowing that He has kept a place for us, a place where we can receive His love, His grace, and His very life. This is why I believe in the beauty and truth of the Catholic faith: because in the Eucharist, Christ is always preparing a place for us, inviting us into the fellowship of His eternal love. Jesus' instruction to find the man with the jar is a reminder of His deep attention to every detail, even in the most critical moments. It's a moment where the ordinary becomes a sign of the extraordinary. The very unusual nature of the request underscores how important this meal was—Jesus knew that every detail, from the location to the timing, would mark a profound moment in salvation

history. It was not just a meal; it was the occasion of the Last Supper, the institution of the Eucharist, and the fulfillment of God's covenant with His people.

What followed this unique encounter was the preparation of the Passover meal, a fellowship meal of deep significance to Jesus and His Apostles. In the Jewish tradition, meals were far more than mere sustenance—they were moments of communion, fellowship, and teaching. Jesus often used shared meals to build relationships, to call others to His kingdom, and to reveal the deep truths of God's love. The act of dining together was a symbol of unity, of belonging to one another, and sharing in the mystery of God's providence. At this moment, as Jesus prepares to share His final meal with His disciples, He is, in a sense, showing us what it means to live in communion with one another and God. The meal was not just an act of remembrance; it was an act of deep spiritual communion. Jesus, through the ritual of the Passover meal, would soon transform the meaning of the meal itself. The bread would no longer be merely a symbol of the Israelites' exodus from Egypt; it would become His Body, broken for us. The wine would no longer merely commemorate the blood of the lamb spread on the doorposts in Egypt; it would become His Blood, poured out for the forgiveness of sins.

The fellowship of the meal was crucial to Jesus because it was through this meal that He would offer His disciples the gift of Himself. As the Mishnah recounts, even the poorest Jews were to have at least four cups of wine on Passover night, a powerful symbol of God's liberation and salvation. Wine was a vital part of the Seder, and it was shared among everyone around the table. The fact that wine played such an integral part of the meal, even for the poor, highlights the inclusiveness of the Kingdom of God that Jesus was ushering in. Just as the Passover meal was meant to be a communal experience, so too would be the Eucharist—a meal that would not exclude, but welcome all, as Jesus would soon say, *"Take and eat... this is my body"* (Matthew 26:26). The act of sharing a meal has always been a sacred moment in the life of God's people. In the Old Testament, it

was a sign of God's covenant with Israel. In the New Testament, it becomes how we enter into the New Covenant in Christ, where we are not only the recipients of God's grace but active participants in His sacrifice. In the Eucharist, Jesus does not merely *symbolize* His love; He gives Himself to us, making that fellowship with God tangible and real. In this way, the Last Supper is not just a historical event—it is an ongoing invitation to encounter the living Christ. In the Catholic faith, we are not just remembering what Jesus did; we are participating in it. The Eucharist is the fellowship meal where heaven and earth meet, where we are united with Christ and with each other in a bond of love that transcends time and space. This is why I believe in the beauty and truth of the Catholic faith: because in the Eucharist, Christ continues to give Himself to us, drawing us into the fellowship of His love, now and forever.

As Jesus and the Apostles entered the prepared room for the Seder meal, one of the initial customs was for the host to wash the feet of his guests, who would have walked through areas frequented by "unclean" individuals and Roman soldiers. Jesus must have reassured the host by saying, "I'll take care of it." He then removed His outer garments, took a towel, and wrapped it around His waist, poured water into a basin, and began to wash His disciples' feet, drying them with the towel around His waist. Jesus told Peter, "What I am doing, you do not understand now, but you will understand later. When he had finished, He told the rest of them, Do you realize what I have done for you? You call me teacher and rightly so, for indeed I am. If I wash your feet, you ought to wash one another's feet. I have given you a model to follow so that as I have done for you, you should also do. A servant is not greater than his master, nor is a messenger greater than the one who sent him. Now that you know these things, you will be blessed if you do them."[2]

---

[2] John: 13 New American Bible. Catholic Translation. Catholic Bible Press. Nashville, Tn. 1987. Pp 1210

As I reflected on the powerful moment of the Last Supper while standing in the Upper Room, the words of Jesus in Matthew's Gospel resounded deeply in my heart: *"While they were eating, Jesus took bread, said the blessing, broke it, and gave it to His disciples, saying, 'Take and eat; this is My Body.' Then He took a cup, gave thanks, and gave it to them, saying, 'Drink from it, all of you, for this is My Blood of the covenant, which will be shed on behalf of many for the forgiveness of sins. I tell you, from now on I shall not drink this fruit of the vine until the day when I drink it new with you in the kingdom of My Father'"* (Matthew 26:26–29). In that moment, I realized that Jesus was doing far more than simply sharing a meal with His disciples. He enacted the new Passover, transforming the very meaning of the meal, and offering His Body and Blood as the ultimate sacrifice for the salvation of all people. The beauty of the Eucharist, the gift He left us, lay in the fact that it was not merely a symbolic act or a ritual to remember His suffering. It was, and is, the very means by which we are invited to enter the life, death, and resurrection of Christ. In the context of the Jewish Passover, the bread and wine of the meal carried deep meaning. The unleavened bread reminded the Israelites of their hasty escape from slavery in Egypt, and the wine was a symbol of God's promise of liberation and redemption. But in this final meal with His disciples, Jesus reinterprets these elements, giving them a new and eternal significance. The bread that He breaks is not just the traditional unleavened bread of the Passover; it is His Body, given for the life of the world. The wine, which was once a symbol of Israel's covenant with God, becomes His Blood, poured out for the forgiveness of sins.

What struck me deeply at that moment was the sense of sacrifice and love that pervaded the entire meal. Jesus knew He was about to face betrayal, torture, and death on the cross. Yet, He chose to give Himself to His disciples in this intimate way, offering His very Body and Blood to them as the means of reconciliation with God. He was not just teaching them a lesson; He was giving them Himself, making them sharers in His sacrificial love. As Catholics, we believe that in the Eucharist, Jesus does not merely *symbolize* His Body and

Blood; He makes them truly present. The bread and wine, through the power of the Holy Spirit and the priest's words, become the Body and Blood of Christ. This is a profound mystery—one that transcends human understanding but that touches the deepest parts of our hearts.

When Jesus says, *"Take and eat; this is My Body"* and *"Drink from it, all of you, for this is My Blood of the covenant,"* He invites us to partake in the new covenant He established through His death and resurrection. This new covenant is not based on laws written on tablets of stone but on the law of love, written in the hearts of all who receive Him in faith. Through the Eucharist, we become participants in Christ's life, His suffering, and His victory over death. Moreover, Jesus' words, *"I tell you, from now on I shall not drink this fruit of the vine until the day when I drink it new with you in the kingdom of My Father"* (Matthew 26:29), remind us that the Eucharist is not just about remembering the past—it is also about anticipating the future. It is a foretaste of the heavenly banquet, where we will one day share in God's glory. The Eucharist is a promise that Christ will one day return to bring us into the eternal communion of His Father's Kingdom.

As I stood in the Upper Room, surrounded by the echoes of the last meal Jesus shared with His disciples, I realized that this moment was not just a historical event; it is the living heart of the Catholic faith. In the Eucharist, Christ continues to offer Himself to us. Every Mass is an opportunity to enter this sacred mystery, to be united with Christ in His sacrifice, and to be transformed by His grace. The Eucharist is where heaven and earth meet, where we encounter the living Christ and are made one with Him and with the entire Body of Christ, the Church. In the quiet of my heart, as I ponder the mystery of the Eucharist, I am drawn into a profound encounter with Jesus, as revealed to Blessed Anne Catherine Emmerich in her visionary ecstasy. The vivid imagery she described offers a glimpse into the deeper reality of the Last Supper, where Jesus, with infinite love and self-sacrifice, gives Himself completely to His Apostles and, through them, to the entire Church.

In her vision, Blessed Emmerich saw Jesus pouring out His whole Being in love, becoming perfectly transparent, almost luminous in His self-giving. She wrote, "Jesus seemed to be pouring out His whole Being in love, and I saw Him becoming perfectly transparent. He looked like a luminous apparition." This description speaks to the spiritual truth that in the Eucharist, Christ gives not just a symbol of His Body and Blood, but He gives Himself entirely—His very Being, His divine and human nature, made present for us. As He broke the bread and gave it to His disciples, He was not merely offering food; He was offering His life. Blessed Emmerich's vision then takes on an even more profound significance when she recounts that Jesus took the bread, broke it into several morsels, and laid them over one another on the plate. He then dipped a small piece of bread into the chalice. At that very moment, she saw, in a way that transcended time and space, the Blessed Virgin Mary receiving the Eucharist. She was not physically present in the Upper Room, but in this visionary experience, Emmerich witnessed Mary entering, receiving the Blessed Sacrament, and then vanishing from sight. This extraordinary vision speaks to the profound mystery that the Eucharist is not bound by time or space. It is a sacrament that connects the faithful across generations, allowing us to enter the life of Christ and His Body, the Church. The Blessed Virgin, as the first and most perfect disciple, is drawn into the mystery of the Eucharist. In receiving the Body of Christ, Mary, the Mother of the Church, shares in the very love and grace that Jesus pours out for all of us. Through this vision, I am reminded that the Eucharist is not just a ritual for those who are physically present; it is an invitation to a spiritual communion that transcends the limits of the material world.

As Jesus gave the Eucharist to His disciples, He did so with the full awareness that He was offering them Himself—His Body and His Blood, poured out for their salvation. The Emmerich witnessed the moment that was one of overwhelming love, where Jesus stretched out His right hand, blessing the bread, and a brilliant light emanated from Him. She describes it beautifully: *"His words were luminous as also the Bread, which as a body of light entered the mouth of the apostles. It was as if Jesus Himself flowed into them."*

In this moment, I am struck by the reality that in the Eucharist, Jesus is not simply a presence we remember or a symbol we honor—He is the living, true presence that we receive into our very bodies and souls. When I approach the altar to receive the Eucharist, I believe that, like the Apostles, I am invited into this profound mystery of Jesus flowing into me, body, soul, and divinity. It is not just the bread that I eat or the wine I drink—it is Christ Himself. Through this sacrament, I am united to Him in a way that surpasses understanding. This is why I believe in the beauty and truth of the Catholic faith. The Eucharist is not merely a meal or a ritual. It is the fulfillment of Christ's promise to remain with us, to abide in us, and to offer us His very self as nourishment for our souls. Just as Blessed Emmerich witnessed the luminous presence of Jesus flowing into the Apostles, I believe that, in each celebration of the Eucharist, Christ's love flows into us, transforming us from within. The Eucharist is not just a reminder of what Jesus did for us; it is the ongoing reality of His sacrifice, made present to us in every Mass. Through the Eucharist, Christ continually gives Himself to us, just as He did on the night of the Last Supper. He gives Himself freely, completely, and sacrificially poured out for the forgiveness of sins and the world's salvation. And in receiving Him, we are drawn closer to Him; we are made partakers of His divine nature, united to the One who gave Himself for us.

As I reflect on the deeply moving and profound moments of the Last Supper, I am drawn into the mystery of the Eucharist, both in its tangible reality and in the sacred truths it reveals. In the writings of Blessed Anne Catherine Emmerich, I find a deeper understanding of this holy event and its far-reaching implications, not only for the Apostles but for all who would follow them.

One of the most fascinating details revealed by Blessed Emmerich is the story of the Holy Grail, the chalice used by Jesus at the Last Supper. According to her visions, this chalice had an extraordinary and ancient lineage—it was said to have belonged to Abraham. She recounts that Melchizedek, the priest of Salem, brought it from the land of Semiramis, where he had used it while offering bread and wine to Abraham. This same chalice was then passed down through generations, even resting in the hands of Noah and later Moses. The chalice was described as massive, shaped like a bell, and unadorned by human hands. Its ancient, almost natural form stood as a symbol of the divine purpose it would serve. The Holy Grail, this sacred vessel, becomes the focal point in the moment of Christ's transfiguration during the Last Supper. As Jesus raised the chalice to His lips, He offered the wine and Himself—His Body and His Blood—to the Apostles. In Blessed Emmerich's vision, she writes that as Jesus pronounced the words of consecration, He became completely transparent, as though He was *passing over* into what He was giving—His very Body and Blood. This moment, where Jesus was "wholly transfigured," is a revelation of the divinity that underlies the outward form of bread and wine. In the Eucharist, we encounter the living Christ, who transforms ordinary elements into His sacred and glorified Body and Blood.

The profound truth of this moment is made even clearer in the following act: Jesus poured the remaining Sacred Blood from the chalice into smaller cups, distributing it among His Apostles. Peter and John, in turn, handed the cups to the Apostles, two by two, sharing in the first Communion. Drinking from the same cup is deeply symbolic of the unity Jesus desired for His followers—through His Blood, we are united in Him, as His Body, the Church. The fact that the chalice, after being emptied, was cleansed, and wrapped in linen only to be preserved for future use speaks to the eternal nature of this sacrament. The Eucharist is not bound by time; it nourishes and sanctifies the faithful until Christ comes again. In the same way Jesus shared His Body and Blood with His Apostles, He also imparted a sacred mission—the priesthood. Blessed Emmerich saw in her visions

that the priesthood's institution occurred during that Holy Night, when Jesus consecrated Peter as a bishop and the Apostles as high priests. She describes how Jesus gave them detailed instructions on how they were to preserve the Blessed Sacrament and teach others to reverence and communicate it. These instructions were filled with mystery and divine wisdom. Jesus knew that this moment was not only for those who were present with Him but for all generations that would come afterward. Through the priesthood, the Apostles would be the vessels through which Christ's Body and Blood would be offered for the world's salvation.

When I consider the priesthood within the Catholic Church, I am reminded that it is not a human institution but one rooted in the divine authority of Christ. The priest, by his ordination, becomes an instrument through which Christ Himself acts. The Eucharist, through the priesthood, remains a living reality in the Church. This is why the priesthood is so sacred—it is how Christ continues to offer Himself to the Church, body, blood, soul, and divinity. Through the priest's words of consecration, the Bread and Wine become the Body and Blood of Christ, a mystery I believe to be at the heart of the Catholic faith. In the Eucharist, I find the beauty and truth of the Catholic faith in its fullest expression: a living encounter with Christ, who continues to pour out His love for us. It is the ultimate gift, the fulfillment of God's promise to be with us always, even to the end of the age. Through this sacrament, I experience the power of Christ's love, a love that is poured out in His Body and Blood, a love that transforms me and makes me part of His Body, the Church. This is the central mystery of the Catholic faith: that Christ, in His infinite love, continues to offer Himself to us in the Eucharist, inviting us to partake in the divine life and to be forever united with Him in love. In the Eucharist, we experience the culmination of the love that began at the Last Supper—love that was willing to sacrifice everything, even unto death, for the world's salvation. It is this sacrament, more than anywhere else, that I encounter the profound beauty of God's love, poured out for us, inviting us to share in His eternal life. This is why I believe in the beauty and truth of the Catholic faith: in the Eucharist,

Christ gives Himself to us completely, body, blood, soul, and divinity, offering us the fullness of His love and the promise of eternal life.

Overwhelmed with emotions, my wife and I left the cenacle with our guide and headed to our new destination. Walking pass the Wailing Wall, I was struck by a profound realization shared by my guide, Johnathan. He told me that, while the Levite priests performed the Passover sacrifices in the Temple that day, they could have seen Jesus hanging on the cross just outside the city walls. This thought took me by surprise and sent me into deep reflection. If this were the case, it struck me as a tragic irony. There were the priests, diligently performing their religious duties—offering lambs for the atonement of sins—but they could not recognize that the true sacrifice, the only sacrifice that could truly atone for the sins of the world, was happening right before their eyes. The Lamb of God, the perfect and unblemished sacrifice, was hanging on the cross, and yet they could not see it. This moment symbolizes the tragic blindness that often occurs in human hearts. Despite the centuries of sacrificial tradition that pointed to this moment, many could not see the fulfillment of what they had been preparing for all along. And yet, for those who do believe in Christ, this is the moment that opens our eyes to God's incredible love and sacrifice. Jesus, the Lamb of God, was the final, perfect sacrifice, and His death on the cross is the ultimate act of love, one that offers salvation to all who believe in Him.

As I reflect on these truths, I am struck by the call for us to recognize the true Lamb of God. Just as the priests in the Temple missed the significance of the sacrifice happening right before their eyes, it is so easy for us to become distracted by the busyness of life and fail to recognize the sacrificial love that is offered to us. But through the Eucharist, through the Mass, we are invited to enter the mystery of Christ's death and resurrection, and to recognize that He is the Lamb who was slain for our salvation.

Chapter Ten
Eucharist

In 2010, while still single, I found myself in an unusual spiritual rhythm. I was dating a member of First Baptist Church in Covington, Louisiana, and every Sunday morning I would accompany her to the 11 a.m. service. Afterward, I would take my son to the 6 p.m. Catholic Mass at Our Lady of the Lake. This dual experience—being part of two different Christian traditions—was enriching in many ways, but it was also presented moments of reflection, particularly when it came to the Eucharist.

One Sunday at the Baptist service, the congregation observed what they called the "Lord's Supper." As the pastor prepared to read from the Gospel about the "Last Supper," the ushers distributed small pieces of bread and cups of grape juice. The congregation then partook of the bread and juice immediately after the reading, as part of their ritual. What struck me, however, was how little attention was given to the more profound significance of this moment. The passage from the Gospel, the account of Jesus's institution of the Eucharist, was read quickly, and Pastor Baily's sermon did not delve into its

profound theological implications. It was as though the central mystery of the Christian faith—the Body and Blood of Christ—was treated with a remarkable brevity.

The following day, I felt compelled to reach out to Pastor Baily. I sent him an email explaining that I am Catholic and shared my thoughts. I told him that I deeply appreciated his sermons, especially his insightful teaching on St. Paul, and that I had learned a great deal from his interpretation of the Apostle's writings. I could tell that Pastor Bailey was a man of deep faith, genuinely loved by his congregation, and that love was clearly mutual. However, it was important to share my concern, particularly about how the "Bread of Life Discourse" and the "Last Supper" had been treated so lightly. I expressed my confusion over how such a profound moment in the Gospels—Jesus's gift of His Body and Blood to humanity—could be passed over with so little reflection or discussion. In asking Pastor Bailey, "How can you so casually pass over this profound topic without a deeper exploration of what Jesus instituted that night? His gift to humanity in the form of His Body and Blood," I was reflecting not just on the differences between our traditions, but on the deep mystery of the Eucharist that the Catholic Church holds as central to the faith. The Eucharist, to Catholics, is not just a symbol or a ritual, but the real, living presence of Christ. It is through the Eucharist that we are united with Him in a way that transforms us.

Pastor Bailey responded to my email with a gracious and respectful tone. He thanked me for my thoughtful comments and expressing his willingness to meet for coffee the next time I attended his church. In his response, he shared his belief that the Eucharist was merely symbolic, rather than the actual Body and Blood of Christ. He explained that, for him, the bread and wine represented Jesus but were not literally His Body and Blood. To support his position, he included a quote from St. Paul, and over the coming months, we continued our dialogue, with Pastor Bailey frequently referencing Paul's writings to back up his views. Despite our ongoing conversations, we never reached an agreement on the matter. His beliefs remained firmly rooted in the symbolic view of the Eucharist.

Confused by our differing perspectives, I turned to my godfather, Monsignor Charles Mallet, a retired priest who had spent over sixty years in the Catholic Church. When I asked him about my conversations with Pastor Bailey, he explained, "Pastor Bailey cannot openly agree with you on this issue. As an employee of the church board, it would go against their doctrines, and he could be dismissed if he did. In all my years as a priest, I've never known a Protestant to acknowledge the true presence of Jesus in the Eucharist openly. It's simply not part of their theology." This conversation with Monsignor Mallet made me reflect more deeply on why I believe in the real presence of Jesus in the Eucharist. It also made me think about my journey of faith and how deeply the Church's understanding of the Eucharist resonates with me. Some months later, I came across a book by Scott Hahn, a former Protestant pastor who later converted to Catholicism. Hahn, in one of his reflections, shared a striking experience. As a Presbyterian minister, he recalled how he would read the "Bread of Life" discourse in the Bible, but when it came time to preach on it, he simply skipped over it. He wrote, "I studied it as a student and read it many times as a pastor. But when it came time to preach on it, we skipped it. As a Presbyterian minister, I never addressed it. Despite taking everything else in the Bible literally, we did not believe that the bread and wine were the actual Body and Blood of Jesus." This resonated with me deeply. Hahn's experience mirrored my own in a way—this tension between the clear words of Scripture and the theological frameworks that shape how we interpret those words. It made me realize, like Pastor Bailey, many people in Protestant circles avoid fully engaging with the depth of the Eucharist's mystery.

Around the same time, I had a conversation with my girlfriend, who was a devout Baptist, and I asked her if she believed that everything in the Bible was true and factual. She affirmed that she did. I then pointed to the "Bread of Life" discourse in John 6 and

asked her why she did not believe that Jesus was truly present in the Eucharist, as He explicitly stated. She struggled to offer a direct answer, much like Pastor Bailey had, and ultimately couldn't provide a satisfactory explanation. This was another reminder of how difficult it can be to accept the radical nature of Christ's words, especially when they challenge long-held theological positions.

Todd Baker, a Protestant apologist, argues that Catholics face a contradiction if they interpret Jesus' words about His flesh as the bread of life literally. He challenges Catholics by pointing to John 6:35, where Jesus says, "*I am the bread of life; he who comes to me shall not hunger, and he who believes in me shall never thirst.*" According to Baker, if Catholics truly take Jesus' words about His flesh being the bread of life literally, then they should believe they will "never physically hunger or thirst again" once they have eaten the Eucharist for the first time. This argument misses the deeper reality of what Jesus is conveying and highlights a misunderstanding of the spiritual truths embedded in Scripture.

For Catholics, the bread of life discourse in John 6 is not just about physical sustenance, but mostly about spiritual nourishment. We believe that Jesus is speaking of eternal life in heaven, the fullness of life in Him that comes not from mere physical consumption but from the ongoing relationship He offers through the Eucharist. In the Eucharist, we participate in the real, but mysterious, presence of Jesus. While it nourishes us spiritually, it does not eliminate the realities of our earthly existence, such as hunger and thirst. We understand that Jesus' words must be interpreted in the context of eternal life, which He promised to those who partake of His Body and Blood. In Protestant interpretations, a complete perspective and deep understanding of the historical and scriptural context from which such words arise is missing, especially the ancient Jewish traditions that are intricately connected to the Eucharist. In the Old Testament, we see several key instances where bread, wine, and meat are central to God's provision for His people, offering not just physical sustenance but a foreshadowing of the deeper, spiritual nourishment Jesus offers

through the Eucharist. For example, in *Genesis 14:17-19*, Melchizedek, the King of Salem and a priest of God Most High, offers bread and wine to Abram after his victory in battle. Melchizedek's offering, and his priesthood, are a precursor to Jesus, the eternal high priest, who would also offer bread and wine to communicate His real presence among His people. The book of Hebrews makes this connection clear, identifying Jesus as the high priest in the order of Melchizedek. This act of offering bread and wine points us to the Last Supper, where Jesus institutes the Eucharist as a sacrament of His Body and Blood.

Similarly, the *First Passover* reveals the significance of bread and wine as a means of salvation. The Hebrews were instructed to eat the lamb and apply its blood to their doorposts, marking them as protected from the angel of death. This event is deeply connected to the Eucharist, where Jesus is the Lamb, whose blood is shed for the salvation of humanity, and the bread He offers is His body, given for the world's life. In the desert, God provided "manna", the bread from heaven, as a sustenance to the Israelites during their journey. This miraculous food was not just a temporary provision but also a symbol of God's ongoing care and of the coming true bread from heaven, which is Jesus Himself. In *John 6:48-51*, Jesus declares, "*I am the bread of life... this is the bread which comes down from heaven, that a man may eat of it and not die.*"

Just as the manna sustained the Israelites physically, Jesus as the Bread of Life, sustains us spiritually giving us eternal life. The nature of manna is significant in understanding the Eucharist. According to Jewish tradition, the manna was not just an earthly food but a supernatural gift from heaven. The Talmud and the Mishnah both suggest that the manna was grounded in heaven and that it was kept in the heavenly sanctuary. As Jewish scholar Rabbi R. Rabinowitz points out, "The earthly Temple corresponds to the heavenly Sanctuary." This indicates that the manna, like the Eucharist, was a gift that had its origins in heaven, pointing to the deeper spiritual realities of divine sustenance. When we consider these foundational Old Testament events, we begin to understand the deeper meaning of Jesus' words in John 6 and the significance of the Eucharist. Just as the manna was a sign of God's presence and provision for His people, the Eucharist is the fulfillment of that promise. Jesus, as the New Moses, offers Himself as the true bread from heaven, the Lamb of God who takes away the sin of the world, and the bread of life that gives us eternal life.

In the Gospel of John, right after the miraculous event of Jesus walking on water, we are presented with the profound "Bread of Life Discourse" (John 6:22-71). In this discourse, Jesus reveals to His followers the deep mystery of the Eucharist, offering Himself as the authentic Bread of Life, given for the life of the world. He connects this teaching to the manna that the Israelites ate in the desert, telling them that while their ancestors ate manna and died, the bread He offers leads to eternal life. He boldly declares, *"I am the bread of life... unless you eat the flesh of the Son of Man and drink His blood, you do not have life within you."* He goes on to explain, *"Whoever eats my flesh and drinks my blood has eternal life, and I will raise him on the last day."* Jesus's words are shocking. He speaks of eating His flesh and drinking His blood—something that would have been profoundly disturbing to those who heard Him, especially considering Jewish dietary laws and the sacredness with which they treated blood. Even His disciples were taken aback, with many of them murmuring, *"How can this man give us His flesh to eat?"* But instead of clarifying or softening His statement, Jesus intensifies it. He does not say it is just a symbol, a metaphor, or a spiritual truth only. He reaffirms the reality of His words: *"For my flesh is true food and my blood is true drink."*

This powerful teaching has stayed with me for years. To me, the Eucharist is not just a ritual or a symbolic remembrance—it is the actual Body and Blood of Jesus Christ, given to us as the ultimate means of communion with God. This discourse reveals the profound mystery of God's love for us, a love that is so deep and sacrificial that He offers Himself, body and blood, as spiritual nourishment for all

who seek Him. When I consider the Eucharist in the context of this passage, it becomes clear that Jesus was not speaking in symbolic terms, but in literal ones. If we are to believe in the words of Jesus—honestly believe in the fullness of Scripture and the promises He made—then we must take Him at His word. He tells us that His flesh is *true food*, and His blood is *true drink*. It is through receiving the Eucharist that we are invited into a living, transformative union with Jesus. It is a mystery, yes, but it is also a gift we are called to accept in faith. This belief is not about blind obedience to a tradition—it is about encountering the living Christ, present among us in the most intimate and sacrificial way. This belief is anchored in the teachings of Jesus, as well as in the rich tradition of the Church that has preserved and passed on this truth through the centuries. Just as Jesus was clear in His words to the disciples that His flesh and blood were *true* nourishment, so too the Church teaches that in the Eucharist, we receive the real presence of Christ. The Eucharist connects me with that it is the real presence of Christ in a way that transcends mere words or intellectual understanding. It is a mystery that calls for trust, but it is also a reality that gives life. It is a life-giving, eternal promise: *"Whoever eats this bread will live forever."* Through the Eucharist, Jesus offers us a share in His divine life and promises that, even in suffering and death, we will be raised up on the last day.

Jesus asking us to *eat His flesh* is undeniably one of the most challenging and perplexing teachings in the Gospels. After witnessing His countless miracles—raising the dead, healing the sick, multiplying loaves and fishes, walking on water, calming the storm, and changing water into wine—Jesus now invites us to do the unimaginable: consume His very body. Those who followed Him were bewildered entirely by this radical teaching. It is not hard to imagine the shock and confusion His words must have caused. *Eat His flesh?* Seriously? This was too much for many of His followers, who, faced with this request, turned away. As the Gospel of John recounts, *"As a result of this, many of His disciples returned to their former way of life and no longer accompanied Him."* What is more fascinating about this moment is that Jesus did not go after them. He did not say, Wait, I was only saying this as a metaphor. No, he did not chase after them nor change His meaning. Faced with this division, Jesus turns to the twelve apostles and gives them a choice: *"Do you also want to go?"* The apostles were equally confused, and yet, in a moment of faith and trust, Peter responded, *"Master, to whom shall we go? You have the words of eternal life."* Peter's answer, though not fully understood in the moment, reflects a profound truth: even when the teachings of Jesus are difficult or hard to grasp, there is nowhere else to turn. The apostles, like us, had to make a choice—to believe or to doubt, to stay or to leave. Their faith, though tested, was steadfast, and they chose to follow Jesus, even without fully understanding what He meant.

It was not until the Last Supper that Jesus transparently explained what He had meant. At this final meal with His closest followers, Jesus transformed the Passover meal—a centuries-old covenant between God and His people—into something radically new. He instituted the *New Covenant*—a covenant not limited to the Jewish people but one that would extend to all humanity. It was here that Jesus revealed the full meaning of the *Bread of Life Discourse*, offering His Body and Blood in a way that would be accessible to His followers for all time. Jesus took the bread, broke it, and said, *"This is My Body,"* and took the cup, saying, *"This is My Blood."* These words were more than symbols, it was a clear command to partake of His very self in a new and profound way. This moment was pivotal as Jesus entrusted the apostles—His "new elders"—with the sacred power to continue this offering of His Body and Blood. This was the beginning of the Eucharist, a mystery that would unite believers to Christ in a way nothing else could. Jesus, in His love, was giving us a way to remain with Him always—His true presence in the bread and wine—until the end of time. Through this sacrament, Jesus would continue to nourish, strengthen, and transform His Church, giving us Himself as the Bread of Life.

Three of the four Gospel writers—Matthew, Mark, and Luke—record the institution of the Eucharist at the Last Supper, each

emphasizing the radical nature of Jesus' words and actions. For Catholics, this is not a mere symbolic act, but the heart of our faith. The Eucharist is not a ritual to be taken lightly. It is the continuation of Jesus' life, death, and resurrection made present in our midst. Every time we partake in the Eucharist, we are drawn into this mystery of Christ's sacrificial love and the eternal communion He offers to us. It is through this New Passover, the Eucharist, that Jesus affirms His unconditional commitment to humanity. He offers His Body and Blood as a way for us to remain in communion with Him forever, a promise that reaches beyond time and space. Just as the manna from heaven sustained the Israelites in the desert, so too does Jesus, the true Bread of Life, sustain us in our faith journey. And, like the apostles, we are invited to respond, *"Lord, to whom shall we go? You have the words of eternal life."* This is the beauty and mystery of the Catholic faith—though we may not fully understand how it works, we trust that Jesus is truly present and are nourished by His Body and Blood.

In the Gospel of Luke, we encounter the profound moment when Jesus, knowing His suffering is near, gathers His apostles for the Passover meal. As He takes His place at the table, His words resonate with clear meaning and deep significance: *"I have eagerly desired to eat this Passover with you before I suffer. For, I tell you, I shall not eat it again until there is fulfilment in the kingdom of God."* These words speak more of His imminent sacrifice and point to the coming of the Kingdom in its fullness, a reality that would manifest through His death and resurrection. Jesus then takes the cup, gives thanks, and passes it to His disciples, saying, *"Take this and share it among yourselves, for I tell you that from this time on I shall not drink of the fruit of the vine until the kingdom of God comes."* The disciples must have been puzzled by His words, not fully grasping what would unfold. But the significance of these words is immense, signaling that through His sacrifice, the Kingdom of God would break into human history in a new and radical way. Following this, Jesus takes the bread, blesses it, breaks it, and gives it to His apostles, saying, *"This is my body, which will be given for you; do this in memory of me."* He then takes the cup after they had eaten, saying, *"This cup is the new covenant in my blood, which will be shed for you.*" These words would become the foundation of Christian worship for all time—the institution of the Eucharist. In that moment, Jesus not only reveals the meaning of His impending sacrifice, but He establishes a way for His disciples—and all future believers—to enter into His sacrificial love. Bread is His body; the wine is His blood—He offers them to His disciples as a living and eternal means of communion with Him. As soon as these words are spoken, the apostles, by the grace of the Holy Spirit, begin to understand more profoundly the mystery at hand. They hear the eternal voice of the Father echo in their hearts, *"This is my beloved Son, in whom I delight and shall take delight to the end of the world."* In that moment, they begin to grasp that in the species of bread, the very Body of Christ is contained, in the wine, His very Blood. This is no mere symbol—it is a divine reality.

The apostles, through the Holy Spirit, come to realize the efficacy of Christ's words of consecration. These words, spoken to do what Christ did at that time, would carry a divine power from that moment forward. Whenever a priest speaks these words, over the proper material, they bring about a miraculous transformation. The bread and wine, by the power of God, are changed into the actual Body and Blood of Christ. This transformation, which began at that Last Supper, continues to this day at every Catholic Mass, when the priest repeats Christ's words and, through the Holy Spirit, brings forth the true presence of Jesus in the Eucharist. The apostles understood that, in Christ's words of consecration, the power of God is made present—every time they are spoken by a priest, the bread becomes His Body, the wine His Blood. This is the miracle of the Eucharist, which unites us to Christ in a way that no other sacrament or act of worship can. It is not a mere remembrance; it is a participation in the very life, death, and resurrection of Jesus.

Through the Eucharist, we are made one with Christ, nourished by His Body and Blood, and drawn into the mystery of His love. Just as the apostles, through the grace of God, came to understand the depth of Jesus' words, so too do we Catholics come to

understand, through faith, the reality of the Eucharist. It is not just a ritual or symbol—it is the living and abiding presence of Jesus among us, given to us as our spiritual food for the journey of faith. And as we partake in this sacred mystery, we are drawn deeper into the communion of the Holy Trinity and the eternal life that Christ has won for us. This is the truth of the Catholic faith, and this is why I believe.

To completely understand who Jesus was and what He said, we must interpret His words and actions in their historical context, including early Christianity and ancient Judaism. The words of Jesus, especially regarding the Eucharist, have been a constant debate since centuries. Since the Protestant Reformation, many have interpreted His statements as symbolic or metaphorical, rather than literal. This shift in understanding comes from a variety of sources, including modern historical skepticism, as well as discomfort with the profound implications of Jesus' words. After all, Jesus' declaration that His followers must eat His flesh and drink His blood was so shocking that many of His own disciples found it impossible to accept and walked away.

To a Jew in the first century, these words were deeply troubling, as the Law of Moses explicitly forbade the consumption of blood, a prohibition rooted in Leviticus 17:10-12. Yet, the key to understanding Jesus' words is not to look at them in isolation, but to view them through the lens of ancient Jewish customs, beliefs, and hopes. The sacred meals of the Jewish tradition were rich with meaning, particularly the Passover meal, which commemorated God's deliverance of the Israelites from slavery in Egypt. The Passover lamb, sacrificed and eaten each year, symbolized the protection and salvation of God's people. But on the night of the Last Supper, Jesus radically reinterprets the meaning of this sacred meal. Instead of pointing to the lamb as the means of salvation, He declares that the bread is His Body and the wine is His Blood, establishing a new covenant that will be sealed not by the blood of an animal, but by His own sacrifice.

Jesus' words at the Last Supper were not just a new ritual; they were the inauguration of a new Exodus, a greater deliverance than the one God had accomplished in Egypt. For the Jewish people, the Exodus was the defining moment in their history, when God set them free from bondage. The prophets had foretold the hope of a new Exodus, and Jesus was revealing that He was the fulfillment of that hope. In this new Exodus, the people would not be saved by the blood of a sacrificial lamb, but by the blood of Jesus, the true Lamb of God. And the new banquet of salvation would not be one of earthly food and drink, but the eternal feast of communion with God Himself. As the Jewish tradition anticipated, the righteous would one day sit at a heavenly banquet, feasting on the presence of God. But in Jesus, this banquet had already begun. Through the Eucharist, the presence of God in Christ becomes a living reality for us, offered to all who believe. To understand the Eucharist in this context is to see it not as a mere symbol or ritual, but as the continuation of God's covenantal relationship with humanity. Just as God established the first covenant with Israel through the blood of sacrificial animals and a sacred meal, so too does Jesus establish the new covenant with His own Body and Blood, given to us as the ultimate means of communion with God. The Eucharist is not a mere symbol, but the living presence of Christ. It is the fulfillment of the ancient promises made to Israel, and through it, we participate in the very life of Christ and the salvation He offers.

In the Eucharist, we are invited into the new Exodus—an Exodus not from physical slavery, but from the spiritual bondage of sin and death. Jesus' words, though initially hard to comprehend, reveal the depth of God's love and the lengths to which He has gone to offer us eternal life. As Catholics, we believe that in the Eucharist, Christ is truly present—His Body and Blood, Soul, and Divinity— offered to us as the ultimate food for the journey of faith. And just as Jesus told His apostles, *"Do this in memory of me,"* so too do we continue this sacred meal, keeping His presence alive in the Church until He comes again. We Catholics encounter the true Body and Blood of Christ, given for us and for the world. It is not just a symbol, but the living reality of God's unconditional love. Through this sacred

meal, we are united with Christ, nourished by His life, and empowered to live as His disciples in the world. The Eucharist is the fulfillment of the promises of God, the new covenant sealed in the Blood of Christ, and the source of eternal life for all who believe.

The first-century Passover was a deeply meaningful ritual that began with the sacrifice of a lamb, but it was not truly complete until the lamb's flesh was eaten during the Passover meal. The sacrifice was inseparable from the meal that followed, for it was in eating the lamb that the people fully participated in the redemption God offered them. When Jesus celebrated the Passover with His disciples on the night before He died, He redefined the meaning of this sacred meal. As the true Lamb of God, He gave Himself as the sacrifice, but He also commanded that His disciples repeat the meal in His memory: *"Do this in remembrance of me."* In these words, Jesus established a new covenant, a new Passover, in which He Himself became both the sacrifice and the meal. If the first Passover in Egypt was completed through the consumption of the lamb's flesh, then Jesus' sacrifice— His Body and Blood—becomes the new and eternal Passover, completed in the Eucharistic meal. This is why I believe: Jesus' command to "eat His flesh" and "drink His blood" is not a mere symbol, but a continuation of God's plan of salvation. Just as the first Passover was a life-giving act of participation in God's redemptive work, so too does the Eucharist, where we consume the Body and Blood of Christ, offer us participation in the new Passover sacrifice that Jesus established.

By calling us to eat His flesh, Jesus invites us into an intimate communion with Him—just as the Israelites ate the flesh of the lamb to become one with the sacrifice that saved them. In the same way, when we partake e of the Eucharist, we are united with Christ and the saving power of His sacrifice. It is not merely a memorial of His death, but a way in which we experience His sacrifice as living and real in our own lives. Through this sacrament, we enter into the mystery of Christ's Body and Blood, and through Him, we are made partakers in the new covenant, receiving eternal life. The true Body and Blood of Christ is a gift to us as the new Passover sacrifice. In eating the flesh of the Lamb, we are nourished by the very life of Jesus, receiving the grace He won for us through His death and resurrection. In this meal, we are not just remembering Jesus, but participating in the divine reality of His sacrifice, which gives us life, now and forever.

The Eucharist, a word that comes from the Greek *Eucharistia*, meaning "thanksgiving," is the central act of Christian worship and the most profound expression of our faith. In the Eucharist, we encounter Jesus Christ in His entirety—His Body, Blood, Soul, and Divinity. When we receive the Holy Eucharist, we are partaking in a divine mystery where the bread and wine, through the miracle of *Transubstantiation*, become the actual Body and Blood of Christ. While the appearance, taste, and texture of the bread and wine remain the same, their substance is completely transformed. This is not just a symbol, but a reality that can only be grasped through the eyes of faith. In the Old Testament, animal sacrifices were made to atone for sins, and the blood of those sacrifices was poured out at the altar to seek forgiveness. Jesus, in His perfect sacrifice, offered Himself as the Lamb of God, and His Body and Blood—now present in the Eucharist—are offered for the forgiveness of our sins.

This is the New Passover, a sacred event established by Christ on the night of the Last Supper with His apostles. Unlike the old Passover, which was celebrated annually, the New Passover is now a perpetual event in the Church. Every time we gather to celebrate the Mass, we enter the eternal presence of Jesus, who is truly present in the Eucharist. This New Passover invites all of us to partake in the life of Christ, as He promises: *"The one who feeds on me will have life because of me. This is the bread that came down from heaven. Unlike your ancestors who ate and still died, whoever eats this bread will live forever."* The Eucharist is not just a remembrance of Jesus, but a participation in His divine nature. Through the act of receiving His Body and Blood, we are united with Him and share in the eternal life He offers.

The Apostles were the first to receive this gift, empowered by Jesus to transform ordinary bread and wine into His Body and Blood. Over 2,000 years later, the same miraculous transformation happens whenever a Catholic priest consecrates the bread and wine at Mass. This unbroken chain of grace and sacrament is the heart of the Church's life and mission. The Eucharist is the source and summit of our faith, and through it, we encounter the living Christ in a way that transcends time and space.

Just as Jews and disciples walked away from Jesus after hearing the "Bread of Life Discourse," the same happens today. There are people even today, struggling to believe in the Real Presence of Christ in the Eucharist. Yet, before the Protestant Reformation of the 16th century, the belief in the Real Presence—that Jesus is truly present in the Eucharist under the appearance of bread and wine—was universally accepted by Christians. Even Martin Luther, the founder of Lutheranism, initially upheld this doctrine. In fact, Luther's belief in the Real Presence was a cornerstone of his faith. In the Augsburg Confession of 1530, he explicitly supported the concept of the "sacramental union," in which the body and blood of Christ are truly present in the Eucharist alongside the bread and wine, though distinct.

In 1526, Luther published *The Sacrament of the Body and Blood of Christ—Against the Fanatics*, where he defended the belief in the presence of Christ in the Eucharist. He asserted that "bread and body are two distinct substances" but that a "union" had taken place between them. He called this union a "sacramental union." However, as Luther's views evolved, he moved away from the Catholic doctrine of *Transubstantiation* and instead embraced what came to be known as *Consubstantiation*. In this view, the body and blood of Christ coexist with the bread and wine, but the bread and wine do not become His actual body and blood. Luther famously compared this union to a red-hot iron in a fire, where the iron remains unchanged but is surrounded by the fire. In this analogy, the bread and wine are like the iron, while the body and blood of Christ are the fire, present

"over, under, around, and through" the elements. This view, though a step away from the full Catholic understanding of Transubstantiation, still recognizes the unique and profound presence of Christ in the Eucharist. Yet, it is different from the Catholic belief that the bread and wine are transformed into the actual body and blood of Christ, a belief that has been passed down through the centuries. The Eucharist is not merely a symbol or a representation—it is truly the Body and Blood of Christ, made present through the power of the Holy Spirit and the words of consecration spoken by the priest.

The Catholic doctrine of *Transubstantiation* affirms that during the Mass, through the power of the Holy Spirit, the bread and wine are truly transformed into the Body and Blood of Christ, even though their outward appearances remain unchanged. This belief is rooted in the words of Jesus Himself, who declared, "This is My Body" and "This is My Blood." Just as the apostles ate and drank with Jesus at the Last Supper, so too do we partake of His body and blood in the Eucharist, a sacred gift that nourishes our souls and unites us with Christ beyond our understanding. Despite the confusion and disagreements that have arisen over the centuries, the Eucharist is the most profound expression of God's love for humanity—His real presence, offered to us as the source and summit of our faith. Just as the early Church believed, and as the saints and martyrs testified, the Eucharist is the living, abiding presence of Christ in the world today. This is why I believe and continue to believe Jesus in the Eucharist, trusting that in this sacred meal, I encounter the living Christ in the most intimate and powerful way possible.

Huldrych Zwingli, a prominent leader of the Swiss Reformation, was a fierce critic of the Catholic Church. As a key figure in the Reformation, he rejected many Catholic practices, including fasting during Lent and the veneration of images. By 1525, Zwingli had introduced a radical new communion liturgy, intending to replace the traditional Mass with a simpler, more symbolic ritual. However, it was not until 1529 that he publicly rejected the doctrine of the Real Presence in the Eucharist, marking himself as one of the

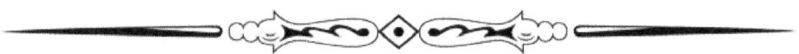

first Christian leaders to deny this central teaching of the Church. Zwingli's doctrine of "memorialism" teaches that the bread and wine of the Eucharist are purely symbolic—they are meant to serve as a remembrance of Jesus, but not as a literal transformation of His Body and Blood.

Today, many Protestant denominations follow Zwingli's interpretation, including General Baptists, Anabaptists, Plymouth Brethren, Jehovah's Witnesses, Latter-Day Saints, and various non-denominational churches. These groups hold that the Eucharist is symbolic—a memorial of Christ's sacrifice—rather than the real, bodily presence of Jesus in the form of bread and wine. And yet, these same groups often claim that the Bible is entirely factual and accurate, even down to the miracles of Jesus and His resurrection. This creates a stark inconsistency: they believe in the supernatural power of Jesus to perform miracles, yet they deny His ability to perform the greatest miracle of all—the transformation of bread and wine into His very Body and Blood.

This contradiction is what troubles me. How can one accept Jesus' miracles, His healing of the sick, His walking on water, His raising of the dead and so on, while rejecting His ability to make the bread and wine His Body and Blood? If we believe that Jesus is truly the Son of God, with divine authority and power, then surely, He can do exactly what He said: "This is My Body...This is My Blood." In John 6, when Jesus speaks of the bread of life, He does not leave room for misinterpretation. His disciples are shocked and confused by His words, but He does not retract them or explain them away. He reiterates His message, saying, *"Unless you eat the flesh of the Son of Man and drink His blood, you do not have life in you.* "This is a hard teaching, as many of His followers acknowledged, but it is precisely this radical truth that sets Christianity apart from every other faith. Jesus did not merely call us to remember Him through symbolic acts—He gave us His very life. He offered Himself to us in the Eucharist, a true communion with His Body and Blood. To deny this is not just to misunderstand a theological point; it is to deny the power and mystery of Christ's sacrifice. The Eucharist is not a mere symbol—it is the real presence of Jesus among us, offered for our salvation.

Jesus granted His Apostles immense authority and power, entrusting them with the ability to forgive sins, heal the sick, cast out demons, and even raise the dead. These were not ordinary abilities; they were divine gifts meant to continue Jesus' work on earth through His Church. This brings me to an important question: if the Apostles were entrusted with such supreme powers, why did they lack in the ability to transform bread and wine into the true Body and Blood of Christ, as He commanded at the Last Supper? If Jesus gave them authority to perform miracles, heal the sick, and forgive sins, would He not also grant them the power to perform the most profound miracle of all—the transformation of bread and wine into His very Body and Blood?

This question becomes even more compelling when we consider an important story from Acts 8:18-20. When Simon the Magician saw the Apostles laying hands on people and bestowing the Holy Spirit, he offered them money, saying, *"Give me also this power, that anyone on whom I lay my hands may receive the Holy Spirit."* Peter's response is telling: *"May your silver perish with you because you thought you could obtain God's gift with money."* Peter was not merely scolding Simon for his greed; he was affirming the divine authority that had been given to him and the other Apostles. This was not a power they could sell or barter for; it was a sacred power bestowed by God Himself. If the Apostles could impart the Holy Spirit by laying on hands, heal the sick, and raise the dead, why would it be unthinkable that they could also change ordinary bread and wine into the actual Body and Blood of Christ? Jesus gave them this authority not only to continue His mission but also to establish His Church, which He promised would remain with us through all generations. The Eucharist, as the most profound of all sacraments, was meant to be celebrated in His Church, by His priests, to continue His presence on earth.

It makes perfect sense that, as the Apostles were entrusted with such immense authority, they were also given the ability to conduct the miracle of the Eucharist. Jesus did not say, *"Do this in memory of Me"* just to represent a symbolic gesture. He said, *"This is My Body... This is My Blood."* If the Apostles had the power to forgive sins, cast out demons, and heal the sick, they certainly had the power to perform this greatest of miracles: transforming the bread and wine into the true Body and Blood of Jesus. Jesus did not leave us an empty ritual; He left us Himself. Just as the Apostles were given the power to continue His work, they were also entrusted with the power to transform the Eucharistic elements. This is why I believe in the Real Presence in the Eucharist: because Jesus Himself gave His Apostles the authority to make it happen, and this authority has been passed down through the centuries to the priests of His Church.

The power of *Transubstantiation* that the Apostles possessed is the same power that Catholic priests hold today, through a profound sacrament called *Persona Christi*, meaning "in the person of Christ." This concept signifies that when a priest consecrates the Eucharist, it is not merely the priest's action; it is Christ Himself acting through the priest. The priest, by virtue of his ordination, is granted the divine authority to perform this miraculous transformation. On his own, the priest is powerless, but through the grace and power of God, he acts as a vessel of Christ's presence on Earth. Without this divine power, no mere human being, regardless of his holiness, could change bread and wine into the true Body and Blood of Christ. Priesthood is not a human institution, but a divine office given by Christ Himself. Since Jesus' earthly ministry lasted only three years, and He has ascended to be with the Father, He provided a way for us to continue experiencing His physical presence on Earth: through the priesthood and the Holy Eucharist. The Apostles had the privilege of encountering Jesus in His physical form, hearing His voice, and touching Him. However, this direct encounter is no longer possible for us in the same way. To ensure that He remains present with us, especially across generations, Jesus instituted the priesthood, giving

priests the power to perpetuate His presence through the Sacraments, most profoundly through the Eucharist.

This is why priesthood is so essential. Through the sacrament of *Holy Orders*, a priest receives the power to administer the Sacraments, including the Eucharist. The moment of ordination is a sacred ritual in which the priest is empowered to act in the name of Christ, not by his own merit, but by the grace of God. As Pope John Paul II beautifully said, "The greatest gift that has been given to me is the priesthood... nothing is worth the richness that was given to me when I was ordained a priest." It is through this sacred ordination that a priest is entrusted with the miraculous power to change the bread and wine into the Body and Blood of Christ, to forgive sins, and to administer all the other Sacraments. While figures like Our Lady or Saint Michael the Archangel are revered and honored, they do not have this power. The Blessed Virgin, in all her glory and holiness, cannot consecrate the Eucharist. Even Saint Michael, the great Archangel and leader of the heavenly hosts, has not been given this divine power. It is specifically the priest who, through his ordination, receives the authority to perform this great mystery and sacrament.

The power to consecrate the Eucharist and the sacredness of the priesthood is one of the greatest gifts Christ has given to His Church. It is through this sacrament that Jesus remains physically present with us, offering us Himself in the most intimate way possible, through His Body and Blood. This continuity of divine presence across the centuries, from the Apostles to the priests of today, is a testament to Christ's firm commitment to His people. He gave us His priests with a hope that we continually encounter Him, just as the disciples did in the Upper Room, receiving His Body and Blood for the forgiveness of sins and the nourishment of our souls.

In 1 Corinthians 10:16, Saint Paul makes a profound statement: *"The cup of blessing that we bless, is it not a participation in the blood of Christ? The bread that we break, is it not a participation in the body of Christ?"* This verse clearly affirms the reality of the Eucharist. It is not merely symbolic; when we receive the Holy Eucharist, we truly and literally partake in the Body and Blood of Jesus Christ. The Eucharist is not a representation of Christ's sacrifice, but a participation in it—a direct encounter with Christ Himself. Saint Paul further emphasizes the gravity of receiving the Eucharist unworthily in 1 Corinthians 11:27-29: *"Therefore, whoever eats the bread or drinks the cup of the Lord unworthily will be guilty of profaning the body and blood of the Lord. For anyone who eats and drinks without discerning the body, eats and drinks judgment on himself."* The severity of this warning suggests that the Eucharist is not simply a symbolic act but involves something profoundly sacred. To profane the Body and Blood of Christ is a serious offense, and this seriousness makes sense only if the bread and wine are truly transformed into the Body and Blood of Jesus. If they were mere symbols, how could consuming them unworthily incur such judgment? Paul's words imply that, in the Eucharist, we are not just eating bread and drinking wine; we are partaking in the very presence of Christ, and this encounter demands reverence and discernment. Saint Paul, as a former Pharisee and expert in Jewish Law, would have been deeply familiar with the importance of sacrifice and the rituals surrounding it. For the Jewish people, sacrifices were not symbolic— they were real, tangible acts of worship, through which they participated in the divine life. The idea of partaking in a sacrifice was central to their faith.

This understanding illuminates Paul's words when he says, *"Christ, our Passover lamb, has been sacrificed. Therefore, let us keep the feast!"* (1 Corinthians 5:7). Just as the Israelites were commanded to eat the flesh of the Paschal lamb to commemorate their deliverance from Egypt, Paul calls Christians to "keep the feast" of the Eucharist, where Christ Himself, the true Paschal Lamb, offers His Body and Blood for our salvation. This "feast" is not a mere memorial; it is a living participation in the sacrifice of Christ, where we are nourished by His very Body and Blood.

In 1916, during a preparatory year for Our Lady's appearances at Fatima, the Angel of Peace visited the young visionaries Lucia, Jacinta, and Francisco three times. The most remarkable of these encounters occurred during the third visit when the angel, holding the Eucharist—both the Host and the chalice—prostrated himself before God. This moment was profound not only in its celestial significance but also in the way it illustrated the crucial importance of the Eucharist in the heavenly order. The angel, in his reverence, instructed the children to recite a prayer that offered the "most precious Body, Blood, Soul, and Divinity of Jesus Christ, present in all the tabernacles of the world," in reparation for the outrages, sacrileges, and indifference with which He is offended. The prayer was a profound act of adoration and reparation, highlighting the significance of the Eucharist as the true Body and Blood of Christ, and the urgency of honoring and revering it as such. This encounter made it clear that the Eucharist is not merely a sacrament but the very presence of God among us, and to neglect or profane it is an offense to the divine. The visionary Francisco, even at such a youthful age, grasped the deep importance of the Eucharist. His life was marked by a profound devotion to the Blessed Sacrament. After this encounter with the angel, Francisco dedicated himself to a life of quiet adoration, striving to console Jesus for the indifference and neglect with which many treated the Eucharist. He serves as an exemplary reminder that the Eucharist is not just a ritual to be observed, but a living encounter with Christ that requires our full reverence, awe, and love. The visits to Fatima, especially the prayer of reparation given by the angel, reinforce the immense significance of the Eucharist in the life of the Church and in the hearts of the faithful. Just as Francisco understood and adored the Eucharist with profound love, I, too, am called to recognize and honor the presence of Christ in the Eucharist, offering reparation for the indifference and disrespect that it sometimes receives. This sacred mystery is a gift, a privilege, and a responsibility, and it is through the Eucharist that we are drawn into deeper communion with God and with each other.

As I stand in line, waiting to receive the Blessed Sacrament, my mind often drifts, and I find myself contemplating everything except the immense mystery of the Eucharist. From the moment of my First Communion to the present, I have believed—without doubt—that the Host I am about to receive is truly the Body and Blood of Jesus. And yet, when I approach the altar to receive Him, my thoughts often wander, distracted by the noise of daily life. Instead of reflecting on the sacred reality unfolding before me, I think about the trivialities of life—what is on the menu for lunch, or the score of the game. But as I stand before the priest, who, in "Persona Christi," holds the Eucharist—Jesus Himself—my heart is reminded that this is not an ordinary moment. This is a moment where heaven touches earth, where the Divine becomes tangible, where Christ, living and glorious, is present in a true, real, and substantial way, as the Catechism teaches. The gravity of this mystery should move me to a deeper reverence—an awareness of the profound truth that I am receiving Christ into my very body and soul. If I utterly understood the depth of what is happening in the Eucharist, how could I approach the altar in any way less than with my heart full of contrition, my mind focused, and my spirit humbly receptive? I should not walk to the altar casually, nor should I receive Him with anything less than the deepest respect. After all, if the Angel of Peace, a pure spirit in the presence of God, prostrated himself before the Eucharist, how much more should I, a sinner in need of grace, approach with the same reverence? In the presence of such love, I am reminded that if I truly grasped the enormity of this moment, I would fall to my knees, with a heart full of thanksgiving, and seek His forgiveness and mercy.

Saint Faustina writes movingly in her diary about the sorrow Jesus expressed over the indifference many have toward the Eucharist: "Oh, how painful it is to me that souls so rarely come to unite themselves with me in Holy Communion. I wait eagerly for them, yet they remain indifferent." Jesus longs to pour out His graces upon us, but too often, we approach the Eucharist without fully realizing what is at stake, without acknowledging the divine love and mercy He is offering to us in this sacrament. Reflecting on the words of Saint Faustina, I am reminded that the Eucharist is meant to change us, to draw us deeper into a relationship with Christ. When I receive the Eucharist, I should not return to my seat unchanged. I should be more deeply united to Christ, more attuned to His life within me, and more committed to living as He has called me to live. The Eucharist is an invitation to a deeper union with God, calling me to greater holiness, humility, and love. And so, if I understand what I am receiving, I will strive to approach this sacrament with the utmost reverence, preparing my heart and mind to experience the grace that flows from this sacred union fully.

Quotes from the Saints

Saint Gertrude the Great: "each time one person receives Holy Communion, something good happens to every being in heaven, on earth and in purgatory."[3]

➤ **Saint John Vianney**: "A communion well received is worth more money given to the poor."[4]

➤ **Saint Teresa of Avila**: "I cannot doubt at all your Real Presence in the Eucharist. You have given me such a lively faith that when I hear others say they wish they had been living when you were on earth, I laugh to myself, for I know that I possess you as truly in the Blessed Sacrament as people did then, and I wonder what more anyone could possibly want'.[5]

---

[3] Pieta Prayer Book. Hickory Corners, Mi. 2006. Pp 26
[4] Ibid.
[5] Joan Carrol Cruz. Eucharistic Miracles. Tan Books. Charlotte, Nc. 2010 pp 222

- ➢ **Saint Thomas Aquinas**: "The Holy Eucharist is a Sacrament of love and a token of the greatest love that a God could give us.'[6]

- ➢ **Saint Francis of Assisi**: "Every fiber of his heart was kindled into love for the Sacrament of Christ's Body. He declared that if confronted with an angel and an unworthy priest, he would kiss the hand that had touched the Body of Christ before saluting the angel.'[7]

- ➢ **Saint Francis de Sales**: "In no action does our Savior show Himself more loving or more tender than in this one, in which, as it were, He annihilates Himself and reduces Himself to food in order to penetrate our souls and unite Himself to the hearts of His faithful ones."[8]

- ➢ **Saint Mary Magdalen de Pazzi**: "Oh Lord, you are truly present under the sacramental species as You are in heaven at the right hand of the Father. Because I have and possess this great wonder, I do not long for, want, or desire any other.'[9]

- ➢ **St. Padre Pio**: "Always remain close to the Catholic Church, because it alone can give you true peace, since it alone possesses Jesus in the Blessed Sacrament, the true Prince of Peace."[10]

- ➢ **Saint Mother Teresa**: "Jesus has made Himself the Bread of Life to give us life. Night and day, He is there. If you really

---

[6] Ibid. 223
[7] Ibid
[8] Ibid
[9] Ibid. Pp222
[10] Saints' Quotes on the Eucharist. Wikipedia 2021

want to grow in love, come back to the Eucharist, come back to that Adoration.[11]

> **Saint Ignatius of Antioch**: "Regarding heretics, they have abstained from the Eucharist and prayers because they do not confess that the Eucharist is the flesh of our Savior Jesus Christ."[12]

> **Saint Anthony of Padua**: "We must firmly believe and declare openly that the same body, which was hung on the cross, lay in the tomb, rose on the third day and ascended to the right hand of the Father, was given in food to the Apostles, and now, the Church truly consecrates and distributes it to the faithful"[13].

> The **visionary Marija** is quoted in the book "*Medjugorje-What's Happening*" by James Mulligan, regarding her view about the Eucharist. Now remember, this is coming from a woman who has been praying, viewing, and conversing with the Blessed Mother of God since 1981: "If I had to choose between the Eucharist and the apparition, I would choose the Eucharist!"

> **Mary of Agreda** received an enormously powerful message from the Queen of Peace regarding the Eucharist and its effects on Satan. "I tell thee truly, my dearest, that Lucifer and his demons have such a fear of the most holy Eucharist, that to approach it, causes them more torments than to remain in Hell itself. Although they do enter churches to tempt souls, they enter them with aversion, forcing themselves to endure cruel pains in the hope of destroying a soul and drawing it into sin, especially in the holy places and in the presence of the

---

[11] Ibid
[12] Joan Carrol Cruz. Eucharistic Miracles. Tan Books. Charlotte, Nc. 2010 pp xiv
[13] Ibid. Pp XV

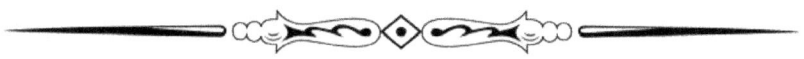

holy Eucharist. Their wrath against the Lord and the souls alone could induce them to expose themselves to the torment of His real sacramental presence. The demons fear the souls, who receive the Lord worthily and devoutly and strive to preserve themselves in this purity until the next Communion. But very few live with this intention, and the enemy is ceaselessly alert in striving to throw them back into their forgetfulness, distraction, and indifference, so that he may not be obliged to encounter such powerful weapons in the hands of men."[14]

I recently finished reading *Eucharistic Miracles* by Joan Carroll Cruz, and I cannot recommend it enough. The book is a compilation of true stories of Eucharistic miracles, stretching back to the year 258. These accounts are not merely historical but offer profound evidence of Christ's presence in the Eucharist. Some miracles happened in response to the disbelief or doubt of priests, others because of disrespect or desecration of the consecrated Eucharist. Each one serves as a reminder of the divine power at work in the Eucharist, reaffirming what I believe to be true—Jesus Christ is truly present in the Body and Blood of the Eucharist. One of the earliest accounts comes from Saint Cyprian, who in 258 described an extraordinary event where "flames issued forth" when someone attempted to open a tabernacle that contained the Body of Christ. The miraculous flames were a visible manifestation of the sacredness of the Eucharist and a warning against its disrespect. Over the centuries, similar miracles have occurred—some in response to desecration, some as signs of Christ's living presence. Consecrated Hosts have bled, transformed into human flesh, or turned into visible blood.

---

[14] Rev. George J. Blatter. The Mystical City of God by Venerable Mary of Agreda. Tan Books. Charlotte, North Carolina. 1978. Pp367-373

There are even accounts of Hosts levitating or being preserved for prolonged periods of time without any sign of decay.

One of the most recent and striking Eucharistic miracles took place in 2014 in Legnica, Poland. A fragment of a consecrated Host, which appeared to be bloody tissue, was removed and placed on a corporal for further examination. This tissue was sent to forensic laboratories for analysis, and the results were astonishing. Doctors confirmed that the tissue was human in origin and most closely resembled heart muscle tissue, showing signs of distress and damage typical of a heart undergoing extreme suffering—exactly the kind of suffering Jesus endured during His Passion. The report concluded that the tissue was "most similar to heart muscle with alterations that often appear during the agony." This incredible discovery serves as a powerful confirmation of the Eucharist's true nature, showing that the sacrifice of Christ is not merely a past event but is perpetuated in the Eucharist, where Christ is fully present in His Body, Blood, Soul, and Divinity. These Eucharistic miracles reinforce my deep belief that Jesus is truly present in the Eucharist. They remind me that what I receive in Holy Communion is not just a symbol, but the very Body and Blood of Christ, who is alive and active in our world. The fact that these miracles continue to happen, and that medical science has confirmed the human origin of the tissue, offers undeniable evidence of the mystery we celebrate. For me, this strengthens my faith and deepens my reverence for the Eucharis,

In July 2022, an extraordinary event occurred at Our Lady of the Rosary parish in Zapotlanejo, Jalisco, Mexico, which further affirmed my belief in the Real Presence of Jesus in the Eucharist. On July 22, during a Eucharistic exposition led by Argentine priest Father Carlos Spahn, something remarkable was witnessed by those present—an event that was later captured on video. Father Spahn described how, after the prayers for exposition had concluded and the Blessed Sacrament was exposed, he noticed something unusual as he walked to the sacristy. The phenomenon lasted for about 20 to 30 seconds, but it left those present astonished. Many witnesses quickly

recorded the event on their cell phones, eager to document what they were witnessing. Father Spahn, aware of the importance of this moment, ensured that the videos were sent to him immediately for verification. What was so remarkable about this event was that the host, the Body of Christ exposed in the monstrance, appeared to have the rhythm of a beating heart. As Father Spahn reported, the video footage was examined by a doctor who confirmed that the movement of the host corresponded exactly to the beat of a human heart. The doctor measured the movement, and it was consistent with the pulse of a human heart. This phenomenon was not only recorded during the exposition but was also experienced by a woman who had recently converted to Christianity. During Communion, she felt the host beating in her mouth—an experience she shared with Father Spahn, reinforcing the sense that this was not just a passing coincidence but something deeply profound. Additionally, Father Spahn noted that this extraordinary event occurred intermittently between 9 p.m. and 11 p.m. This irregularity suggested that a "divine origin," as a natural phenomenon would have been visible to everyone at the same time, but in this case, not all attendees saw the host's beating heart.

As I ponder my journey of faith, a powerful moment from 2019 during my honeymoon in Jerusalem comes to my mind. While visiting the "Upper Room," (traditionally known as the site of the Last Supper) in the Muslim control quarters, I encountered something that deeply resonated with my belief in the Eucharist. Embedded in the back wall of this sacred space was a small stone carving—an image of a pelican tearing at its own breast, with blood dripping down to nourish its chicks. This emblem immediately struck me, as it is also the symbol on the Louisiana state flag, where I was born and raised, 6,872 miles away. The symbol of the pelican has long been associated with Catholic tradition, and it speaks of sacrificial love—the pelican giving of itself to nourish its young. This imagery perfectly mirrors the sacrifice of Jesus Christ in the Eucharist. Just as the pelican offers its own blood to sustain its offspring, Jesus offered His own Body and Blood for the salvation of humanity. The Eucharist, in its deepest reality, is not a mere symbol, but the very Body and Blood of Christ, truly present, nourishing and sustaining us in the same way. Seeing this symbol in Jerusalem—at the very place where Jesus instituted the Eucharist—was a profound experience that strengthened my belief in the Real Presence of Christ in the Eucharist. It reminded me that the sacrifice of Christ on the cross is made present to us in every Mass, and that the Body and Blood I receive in Communion are not just symbols or reminders but are the living presence of Jesus Himself.

As I prepare to receive the Eucharist in the future, I will make a conscious effort to enter more fully into this mystery. I will reflect deeply on the reality of Christ's sacrifice and His presence in the Eucharist. I will strive to approach the altar with reverence, not allowing my thoughts to wander, but instead honoring the sacredness of the moment. Just as Jesus gave Himself completely for us, the Eucharist invites us to receive Him wholly and to be nourished by His love and grace. This encounter is not a distant memory, but a living reality that continues to transform us every time we receive it.

One last thought that continually strengthens my belief in the Real Presence of Christ in the Eucharist is the disturbing fact that Satanists actively seek out consecrated Hosts to desecrate. If the Eucharist were merely symbolic, a mere piece of bread or a mere drink, why would anyone—especially those who reject God—be so intent on obtaining and defiling it? The fact that Satanists recognize the power and sanctity of the Eucharist, even if they aim to desecrate it, is a testament to the truth that something far more profound is at work in the consecrated elements. In the spiritual realm, the Eucharist is not just a piece of bread or a drink, but the Body, Blood, Soul, and Divinity of Jesus Christ Himself. The enemy, in his opposition to God, understands this reality and seeks to mock and defile what is most sacred. This is not the response one would expect if the Eucharist were simply a metaphor or a symbolic gesture. No one would bother with desecrating an empty symbol. But the intense hatred for the Eucharist among those who oppose God points to the fact that the Eucharist is, indeed, what the Church teaches it is—the true presence of Christ.

To expand on this, Fame Vatican Exorcist, Father Gabriele Amorth, reveals in a 2023 Youtube video "What Demons say to him about the Eucharist":

> Here It Is, hidden in that white bread, but He is not hidden from us, we see Him and His Light burns us, it is like a fire that we can't put out."

> "That piece of bread isn't just bread, it is He, it's He; the same One Who threw us out of Heaven. We hate it, but we can't get close."

> "If human beings knew Who really exists, the whole world would kneel, and we would be defeated forever."

> "Every minute spent in front of Him takes away our strength. He forces us to flee like cowards." "The place where they worship Him is full of Angels, we can't get in there even with our traps." "An hour in front of Him, takes away the souls we have trapped for years. It's like a big war against us and we always lose it."

> "The Holy Hour fills your homes and families with Light. We can't stand that Light, it blinds us." "When Holy Hours are made for sinners, they receive His Mercy and our chains are broken, it's a condemnation for us." "Those hours of silence in front Him, are like a hammer that hits our heads, we can't resist you."

> "When they look at Him, they don't say anything, but He Acts in their hearts. This is destroying us from the inside." "Silence in front of Him is more powerful than a thousand words. He fills them with Grace and makes them invisible."

> "Those who spend time in His Presence are protected. It is like they build a fire barrier around them. We can't reach them easily." "Every time one of you looks at Him with Faith, we

receive a punishment that hurts us more than a thousand chains." "When someone Adores Him with all his heart, he takes away what is ours, humbles us every time." Those prayers in front of the Blessed Sacrament for sinners are our ruin. They receive His Mercy and repent and it destroys our traps.

As I reflect, Jesus's words from 6:56-57 come to my mind: *"Whoever eats my flesh and drinks my blood remains in me, and I in them."* Jesus did not say this to confuse or frighten us; He invited us into a deeper, more intimate communion with Him. The fact that the enemy recognizes this presence and goes to great lengths to mock it only affirms the truth of the Eucharist. There would be no reason for such opposition if it were merely symbolic. But because it is truly the Body and Blood of Christ, the Eucharist holds an unparalleled significance in the spiritual battle between good and evil. Therefore, every time I approach the altar to receive the Eucharist, I do so with renewed reverence, knowing that this is no ordinary bread or wine, but the living presence of Jesus Christ Himself. I believe in the power of the Eucharist because it is the source and summit of our faith—a profound mystery that Satan himself knows is real.

Wounds

Chapter Eleven
WOUNDS

The Catholic faith, with its rich tradition and profound teachings, has always provided me with a deep sense of meaning and purpose. Among its most striking aspects is the emphasis on the passion and suffering of Jesus Christ. The story of scourging, His crown of thorns, His crucifixion—encapsulates the very essence of God's love for humanity. As a Catholic, I have come to understand that these intense, often uncomfortable portrayals of Christ's physical agony are not mere relics of religious tradition – they are central to our faith offering a visceral glimpse into divine love.

In 2004, Mel Gibson's *The Passion of the Christ* brought this aspect of the Catholic faith into stark, unsettling focus. The film sparked intense debate due to its graphic, unrelenting depiction of Jesus' scourging, which many saw as excessive or even sadistic. Critics likened it to "torture porn" and questioned whether such a brutal portrayal was accurate or historically warranted. However, as a Catholic who believes in the profound truth and beauty of Christ's sacrifice, I find the film's portrayal of suffering to be not only justified

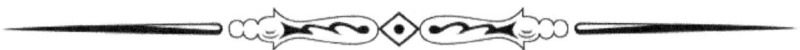

but essential. The Gospel tells us that Jesus suffered for our salvation. The Catholic faith teaches that He willingly took upon Himself the weight of humanity's sins, enduring unimaginable physical and spiritual pain out of love for us. This willingness to embrace such suffering is not meant to be sanitized or minimized; it is meant to be understood in its full, brutal reality. The controversy surrounding the graphic nature of *The Passion of the Christ* is rooted in a common misunderstanding of the purpose of such depictions. The filmmakers defended their portrayal, arguing that it was grounded in historical research, including a careful study of Roman flagellation and crucifixion practices, and even the Shroud of Turin. These efforts were intended to convey the true magnitude of Jesus' suffering—a suffering that goes beyond physical pain and reaches into the depths of human experience, where love and sacrifice meet to create something bigger and meaninful. The portrayal is meant to challenge the viewer, to make us uncomfortable, to force us to confront the depths of Jesus' love in a visceral way.

As someone who has grown up in the Catholic tradition, I have seen this emphasis on Christ's suffering reflected in the artwork and iconography of Catholic churches, especially in places like Italy, Mexico and Guatemala. In many of these churches, the crucifix is not a mere symbol of victory over death, but a vivid reminder of the intense physical pain Jesus endured. These depictions show a bloodied, battered Christ, His body marked with the scourging wounds described in Gospel, even if they do not provide explicit details. These images are not meant to shock for the sake of shock; rather, they are a theological statement. They reflect the truth that Christ's sacrifice was not abstract or distant, but deeply personal, intimate, and agonizing. It is a powerful representation of the love that exceeds all human understanding, a love that embraces the fullness of suffering to bring about redemption. The question of whether the graphic nature of Jesus' passion is historically accurate or necessary often centers around the idea of moderation—how much suffering is enough to communicate the gravity of Christ's sacrifice? This debate is not a new one; it has existed for centuries, as the Gospels themselves are rather sparse when it comes to detailing the specificities of Jesus' physical suffering. We know He was scourged, but the exact details are left to the imagination. For example, the Gospels do not tell us how many times He was whipped, though Catholic tradition often cites thirty-nine lashes, based on Jewish law that limited a person to no more than forty lashes (Deuteronomy 25:3). This tradition is rooted not in precise historical documentation but in an understanding of God's mercy—ensuring that the punishment would not be excessive.

The film's graphic depiction of the scourging is, in many ways, an attempt to bring this tradition to life—to help us understand, in the most visceral way, the depth of Christ's physical suffering. It forces us to question ourselves: How much pain is enough to redeem the world? How much love would it take to save humanity from its own destruction? The image of a bloodied Christ, scourged nearly beyond recognition, embodies the answer: it takes all of it—every drop of blood, every ounce of pain, every shred of dignity.

I find great beauty in this, not because I seek violence or suffering, but because I believe that only through the full embrace of suffering can we come to understand the full scope of God's boundless love. Christ's willingness to endure this suffering for our sake is the very foundation of the Catholic faith. The love that prompted His sacrifice is not a love of convenience or sentimentality; it is a love that is costly, radical, and transformative. The portrayal of Christ's suffering, especially in cultures like Mexico and Guatemala, serves as a powerful reminder of this deep, unyielding love. The suffering of Christ is not merely a historical event; it is a theological truth that touches the heart of Catholicism. It challenges us to reflect on our own lives, our own willingness to embrace suffering, and our own capacity for love. In this light, I believe the graphic nature of *The Passion of the Christ* serves a higher purpose. It helps us to understand that Christ's sacrifice was not a mere historical fact but a living, breathing reality—one that continues to speak to us today. In this depiction of His suffering, we see the very heart of Catholicism:

a religion founded on the belief that God became man, that He suffered, and that He died for us—not because He had to, but because He loved us so profoundly that He chose to endure the worst humanity could offer. This is the beauty and the truth of the Catholic faith. It is a faith built on love that is willing to lay down its life for others.

During our pilgrimage to the Holy Land, my wife and I had the privilege of visiting a church built over the site traditionally believed to be the residence of Caiaphas, the high priest who played a pivotal role in the trial of Jesus. As we stood within the walls of this ancient place, our guide, Jonathan, led us to a cistern beneath the house—one where, according to Jewish tradition, Jesus was briefly imprisoned following His arrest. The Holy Land visit brought this truth to life in a way that nothing else could. As I stood in the place where Jesus might have been held, knowing the agony He faced in that dark, cold cistern, I felt a deep sense of awe. It was not just a historical moment I was witnessing, but a living testament to the depth of Christ's love for us. And that love—manifested in His suffering-is at the heart of the Catholic faith. It is love that compels us to follow Him, to take up our own crosses, and to strive to love others with the same radical, self-sacrificial love He showed us. This is why, even after nearly two thousand years, the story of Christ's Passion remains so powerfully relevant. It speaks to us in our own suffering, in our own moments of trial, and reminds us that there is no pain too great, no burden too heavy, that cannot be redeemed through the love of Christ. And it is this love—this boundless, enduring love—that I believe lies at the very heart of the beauty and truth of the Catholic faith.

Once inside this church, standing in the same spot where Jesus was held, Jonathan described the severe conditions of this cell, where prisoners were lowered by rope into a rock-hewn cistern. Two holes near the prisoner's feet were filled with salt water and vinegar. The prisoner's arms and legs were stretched and bound to rings embedded in the rock. The jailer, restricted by the need to keep his arm bent at a ninety-degree angle, could not exert full force, which prevented debilitating injuries. However, to intensify the suffering, the jailer would dip the whip into salt water or vinegar before striking the prisoner, causing excruciating burning pain in the open wounds. Each lash not only opened the skin but also introduced an intense, burning pain that seared the flesh, compounding the suffering in a way that defies easy description. Joanathan with a somber expression, shared that oral tradition in the Holy Land suggests Jesus endured this form of punishment. He explained that this background provides context for why the graphic depiction in the film might be seen as a necessary reflection of the intense suffering Jesus experienced. After leaving Caiaphas' dungeon, Jonathan guided us to another prison cell, which, according to oral tradition, was where the Romans held Jesus before his trial before Pilate. From there, we proceeded to the Church of the Scourging, a site believed by tradition to be where the Romans scourged Jesus. Jonathan explained that, unlike the Jewish tradition of limiting flogging to thirty-nine lashes, the Romans did not have such restrictions. They could inflict as much punishment as they deemed necessary. The Romans, known for their expertise in torture, could scourge a prisoner to the brink of death without killing them, ensuring that they could endure further torture during crucifixion. This was the fate intended for Jesus.

This visit was deeply moving, and the experience served to deepen my understanding intensity of Christ's suffering, particularly the brutal conditions He endured in the hours leading up to His crucifixion. For those of us who have grown up with sanitized, more restrained depictions of the Passion, the graphic portrayal in Mel Gibson's *The Passion of the Christ* may seem excessive. But standing in that cistern, imagining Jesus bound and helpless, the brutality of the film's depiction takes on a new light. It became clear to me that the film's intense violence was not gratuitous or sensationalized but was an attempt to capture the profound agony Jesus endured, a suffering that went far beyond mere physical pain. Jesus' passion was not an abstract concept or a theological idea; it was a visceral reality.

The filmmakers, like our guide Jonathan, sought to present the suffering as it might have truly been unrelenting, brutal, and intensely painful. This, in turn, underscored the magnitude of Jesus' sacrifice—a sacrifice made from love, a love so deep that it was willing to endure not only physical torture but the weight of the world's sin. The more I reflect on this, the more I believe that understanding the full context of Christ's suffering helps illuminate the beauty and truth of our Catholic faith. His willingness to undergo such extreme pain, in the face of betrayal and abandonment, is the ultimate expression of divine love. This is the love that Catholics believe redeems humanity—a love that could not be contained by death or by the cruelty of the world but was poured out in its fullness for all to see.

Given this context, the precise number of lashes Jesus received remains uncertain. The Bible does not specify, but oral tradition suggests he received thirty-nine lashes. In *The Passion of the Christ*, however, Jesus is depicted as receiving ninety-six lashes. Adding another layer to this discussion is the Shroud of Turin, believed by many to be Jesus' burial cloth, though its authenticity is debated. The shroud, which is thought to date from around 1300 to 3000 years ago, bears faint images of a man with wounds consistent with those described in the Bible. A photograph taken in 1898 revealed a three-dimensional image of a crucified man, showing wounds consistent with a crown of thorns, scourging, nails, and a side wound. Recent inspection from this image suggests that the man on the shroud sustained a total of 372 lashes: 213 on his back and 159 on his front.

Mystics such as Mary of Agreda and Anne Catherine Emmerich offer further and detailed descriptions of Jesus' scourging. Mary of Agreda writes that Jesus, standing bound to a column, was scourged with extreme cruelty. The blows were so severe that they exposed his shoulder bones and caused substantial flesh to be torn away. Anne Catherine Emmerich describes the brutality of the scourging in detail, noting that three pairs of scourgers alternated in their assault, leaving Jesus' body mangled and bloodied, with no intact flesh remaining. According to her vision, the scourging lasted about forty-five minutes.

In the Pieta Prayer Book, the Blessed Mother revealed to Saint Bridget and Saint Matilda the suffering of Jesus was immense: "The number of armed soldiers were 150; those who trained Him while bound were 23. The executioners of Justice were 83; the blows received on His head were 150; those on His stomach were 108; Hicks to His shoulders were 80. He was led, bound with cords by the hair 24 times; spits in the face were 180. He was beaten on the His body 6666 times; hits to His head were 110 times. He was pushed and lifted up by His hair and received 110 thorns in His head; mortal thorns in the forehead were 3; the soldiers leading Him to Calvery were 608; those who mocked Him were 1008."

Forensic Analysis

The Shroud of Turin, long venerated as the burial cloth of Christ, offers compelling forensic insights that align remarkably with the biblical account of Jesus's Passion. The images imprinted on the shroud show multiple facial injuries consistent with those described in the Gospels (Matthew 26:67, 27:30). Blood flow from the scalp matches puncture wounds typical of a crown of thorns (Mark 15:17). The scourge marks on the shroud match the size and shape of lead pieces that Roman soldiers would have sewn into the ends of their whips. These marks appear bidirectional, suggesting that Jesus was whipped from both sides of his body, likely by a team of executioners (John 19:1; Mark 15:15–16).

The chest wound visible on the shroud consists of spear penetration, which would have collapsed the lung and ruptured the right chambers of the heart. The significant drainage from this wound interprets a combination of blood and a pleural effusion—a clear fluid that typically accumulates around the lung. This striking detail

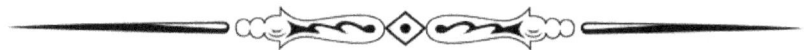

matches with biblical description of blood and water flowing from Jesus' side (John 19:34). Additionally, a smudge of dried blood or a clot below the chest wound, indicates that blood flowed from the chest to the back, suggesting the body was laid supine after being wrapped. The images also reveal blood flow from the hands and feet, consistent with nail punctures (John 20:24–27). The neck and legs appear flexed, which is indicative of rigor mortis. This condition can develop rapidly, particularly after a violent death, due to the high metabolic state of the victim. Nails driven through the wrists would have caused the thumb abductor muscles to contract, flexing the thumbs over the palms, which explains their absence in the image. The rigor mortis in the shoulders was likely overcome to reposition the arms in front of the body.

For the faithful, the Shroud of Turin represents the true burial cloth of Jesus. My belief in the beauty and truth of the Catholic faith is deeply rooted in both personal experience and spiritual conviction, supported by over 40 years of nursing in trauma settings and 15 years of research into the profound mysteries surrounding the Passion of Christ. What I have witnessed in medical practice—the depths of human suffering, the intricate ways the body can endure and bear wounds—has led me to appreciate more fully the unimaginable suffering of Jesus. This experience, combined with the mystical insights of figures like Anne Catherine Emmerich, has only deepened my faith in the beauty, truth, and divine love embedded in the Catholic tradition.

Blessed Anne Catherine Emmerich's writings have been a profound source of reflection for me. One of the most striking and spiritually moving accounts she provides is of the moment after Jesus' body was laid in the tomb. Surrounded by His grieving mother, Mary, Saint John, Mary Magdalene, Joseph of Arimathea, Nicodemus, and several holy women, the disciples and followers of Christ were struck by a miracle. As they wept and paid their final respects, the image of Jesus—whole, complete, and glorified—was miraculously imprinted onto the cloth that had been used to cover His body. This image, appearing as a reddish-brown likeness, was not simply a result of the physical trauma He endured. The cloth, which had wrapped His body, held the imprint of His wounds in a way that could not be explained by natural causes. What struck those who witnessed this miracle was that the cloth bearing the image of Jesus' back was different from the linen bands and other wrappings—those parts remained perfectly white and unmarked. The miraculous imprint was not due to bleeding or the contact of the cloth with Jesus' body, but rather it seemed to have appeared as a divine gesture of gratitude from Jesus for the tender care He had received from His followers in His last moments. The perfection of the image, especially the way the cloth was laid out, with the corners crossed over His body to produce the correct alignment—leaves no doubt that this was no ordinary event. It was a manifestation of Christ's divine nature, confirming the truth that His suffering, death, and resurrection were not merely historical events, but the fulfillment of God's redemptive plan for humanity. Through this miracle, Jesus left His followers a tangible reminder of His divinity and of the eternal truth that He, who endured such unimaginable suffering, would never abandon those who seek Him in love and faith.

The miraculous image that Anne Catherine Emmerich describes, resonates with me profoundly. It portrays the beauty and truth at the heart of the Catholic faith. It is a reminder that Christ's body—wounded, broken, and glorified—carries not only the marks of His suffering but also the promise of our salvation. These wounds, preserved in the cloth, do not speak of death but of victory, for they testify to the truth that through His suffering, Christ has triumphed over sin and death, offering the world the hope of resurrection and eternal life. I believe in the beauty and truth of the Catholic faith because it offers a vision of God's love that is both awe-inspiring and deeply personal. In the image left on the cloth, I see not only the reality of Christ's sacrifice but the beauty of His grace, which endures beyond human understanding. Through the sacred mysteries, through the Eucharist, and through the witness of the saints and mystics, I have come to know a truth that transcends the limits of the physical

world—a truth that God's love is everlasting, that Christ's suffering was not in vain, and that through His wounds, we are healed. This is the beauty of the Catholic faith: it reveals that divine love is not abstract but lived and embodied, and it continues to transform the world, even to this day.

RESURRECTION & DOUBT

Chapter Twelve
Believe It or Not

In the early 1980s, a television show called *Ripley's Believe It or Not!* captivated viewers with tales of the bizarre and the extraordinary. The hour-long program, which aired from 1982 to 1986, explored strange events, from shrunken heads to the Bermuda Triangle, from Bigfoot sightings to UFOs. It presented these mysteries in a way that encouraged audiences to decide for themselves whether they were real or simply fantastical. Even today, similar shows like *Unsolved Mysteries* or *Mysteries at the Museum* continue to spark our curiosity about the unknown.

Personally, I've always been drawn to *Mysteries at the Museum*—a show that delves into curious artifacts with hidden or obscure histories, often revealing how strange and complex the world can be. One episode might highlight letters purportedly written by Jack the Ripper, kept in a museum in London. Another could talk about hair and footprints attributed to Bigfoot in Seattle. These objects and stories deeply intrigue me, as they serve as tangible reminders of humanity's ongoing quest for answers to the unknown.

Even in the modern age, where scientific knowledge advances rapidly, debates persist over topics like the authenticity of the Apollo moon landings, or whether President Kennedy's assassination involved a conspiracy. Some cling to these ideas as if they were mysteries that, if solved, might shed light on deeper truths about our world.

This same fascination with the mysterious, with questions that have no easy answers, is what draws me to my faith in the Catholic Church. Much like the conspiracy theories or cryptic historical tales we see on television, the history of Christianity is full of mysteries—stories that require both faith and reason to understand. Yet, unlike the speculative world of *Ripley's Believe It or Not!* where facts are elusive and often ambiguous, the Catholic Church offers something different: a coherent narrative that has stood the test of time and continues to reveal profound truths about humanity and God. Take, for example, the story of Jesus Christ. His life, death, and resurrection are not just ancient myths but historical events that have shaped the course of history for two millennia. Yet even with all the evidence, there are mysteries surrounding His death and resurrection—questions that challenge our understanding but also draw us into a deeper relationship with the divine. The key figures connected to Jesus, from His disciples to the men who sentenced Him to die, all play a role in this story that is far more than just historical. It is a story of salvation, of God's incredible love for humanity. Much like the curious objects in the museum—whether it's the Hope Diamond at the Smithsonian or the strange relics connected to Bonnie and Clyde—the Church holds sacred artifacts and traditions that link the faithful to this greater story.

Another example is the Eucharist. To this day, the Eucharist remains a profound mystery, as Catholics believe it is the body and blood of Christ, not merely a symbol. The lives of the saints, too, are full of mysteries that reveal God's work in human history. The Church does not shy away from these mysteries but invites us to enter them, to contemplate them, and to deepen our understanding of both the

visible and invisible aspects of our faith. While some might dismiss these mysteries as mere hearsay or religious myth, I have found in the Catholic Church a beauty and truth that cannot be easily dismissed. It is a truth that has been preserved through centuries of tradition and teaching, yet it is always ready to unfold in new ways for those who seek it. The mysteries of the faith—whether the resurrection of Christ, the communion of saints, or the hidden grace within the sacraments—are not merely curiosities for the mind to puzzle over, but invitations to experience the divine presence during our everyday lives.

In a world that is increasingly skeptical and drawn to the sensational, the Catholic Church offers a story grounded in history, rich with meaning, and alive with grace. Like the stories that intrigue us on television or in museums, they invite us to explore, to question, and to ultimately believe in something greater than ourselves. I believe in the beauty and truth of the Catholic Church because it is a story that is both mysterious and real—a story that invites me to journey deeper into the heart of God.

When reflecting on the richness of the Catholic faith, I often find myself drawn to the mystical insights of figures like Anne Catherine Emmerich, Saint Bridgett, and Mary of Agreda. Their detailed visions of the Passion of Jesus and the lives of Jesus, Mary, and Joseph sheds light on deeply moving perspectives that strengthens my understanding of these sacred events. Yet, they are not the only mystics whose contributions have shaped my faith. Saints such as Padre Pio, Francis of Assisi, Catherine of Siena, John of the Cross, and Therese of Lisieux have also offered remarkable spiritual insights that continue to inspire and guide the faithful. I focus particularly on Emmerich and Agreda because of the depth and clarity of their revelations, which offer intricate accounts of the life of Christ and His family.

However, it is important to approach these mystical revelations with discernment. While the Scriptures are the inspired Word of God, validated and interpreted by the authority of the

Church, private revelations—though often profound and spiritually enriching—do not carry the same divine authority. The Church, through its teaching authority, provides us with the proper lens through which to interpret both Scripture and private revelations. Mystical insights, though valuable, are not necessary for faith; they can enhance our spiritual journey but should always align with the teachings of the Church and the Scriptures. As Pope Benedict XIV writes in his *Canonizations of Saints*, our faith rests not on private revelations, but on the public teachings of the prophets and apostles. The core substance of our faith has remained unchanged throughout the ages, and no mystical revelation can add to or contradict the essential truths of the Gospel. While private revelations that align with Church teachings may be considered as coming from Heaven, they must always be viewed through the lens of the faith that the Church has handed down to us.

Personally, I find excellent value in the writings of the mystics, not as a replacement for Scripture, but as a supplement that helps illuminate its truths. Their experiences, when consistent with Church doctrine, serve as additional tools on the spiritual path, helping me draw nearer to the heart of God and remain steadfast on the journey toward Heaven. With this understanding as our foundation, we now turn our attention to the life and Passion of Jesus Christ—a story that has been passed down to us through both the Gospels and the mystical revelations of the saints, who continue to shed light on the mystery of God's love and sacrifice for humanity. This is the beauty and truth of the Catholic faith: a faith rooted in Scripture, deepened by tradition, and ever inviting us to encounter the divine in both the ordinary and the extraordinary. The following accounts explore the fates of people and objects linked to Jesus, drawing from oral traditions, mystical revelations, and ancient writings like those of Josephus. These stories offer a glimpse into what might have happened to them after Jesus' resurrection. Whether one accepts them as truth or not, they provide fascinating insights into the legacy and impact of the events surrounding Jesus' life and resurrection.

Jesus:

In the opening chapter of the Acts of the Apostles', my Catholic Bible recounts how Jesus "presented Himself alive to His followers as proof of His resurrection." Over a span of forty days, He remained with them, appearing to many, teaching, and affirming His triumph over death. At last, before more than 500 witnesses, He ascended into Heaven, leaving no room for doubt about His divinity and the fulfillment of the Scriptures. Yet, despite this powerful testimony, many still question His resurrection today. I am aware of this reality. In a world where so many have encountered resurrection through Scripture, tradition, and the Church, skepticism still lingers. I understand these doubts, as faith often requires stepping beyond the visible, the measurable, and the scientifically provable. But it is within the mystery of Christ's resurrection that I find my deepest reasons for belief. For me, the resurrection is not just a historical event—it is the very cornerstone of my faith, the foundation on which the Catholic Church stands.

The resurrection of Jesus was not only witnessed by His apostles but also confirmed by the consistent testimony of countless believers throughout the centuries. This truth resonates deeply within me. It is affirmed in Scripture, in the traditions of the Church, and in the transformative power of encountering Christ through the Eucharist, prayer, and the lives of saints who came before us.

Though some continue to question or doubt, the testimony of those who witnessed Jesus alive after His death, and the ongoing fruits of His resurrection in the world, serve as powerful reminders of why I believe. This pivotal moment in Christian history calls us to look beyond skepticism and encounter the risen Christ for ourselves. It is through this personal experience of Jesus—alive in the Church, in His Word, and in our lives—that I find the unshakable foundation for my faith.

It's striking that, in a world where over 1.36 billion Catholics and 900 million Protestants affirm their belief in the resurrection of Jesus, some still question its historical accuracy. Recently, I watched a YouTube video where a college student challenged a minister, saying, "If you can show me Jesus's medical records from His death, I'll become a Christian today!" The minister responded calmly, "There are no medical records from that time. But we do have accounts from four different men who documented the life, death, and resurrection of Jesus in the Bible. Furthermore, Paul—formerly known as Saul—wrote in a letter to the Corinthians, 'Jesus died, was buried, and rose on the third day. He appeared to Cephas, to the twelve disciples, to more than five hundred people at once, and finally to me.'" The minister then posed an interesting question: "Have you studied Greek philosophy?" The student replied affirmatively, mentioning her familiarity with Plato and Socrates. The preacher pointed out something profound: Plato, who died in 348/347 BC, was a contemporary of Socrates, who died in 399 BC. Despite not having firsthand records from these figures, we accept their existence and their teachings because we have writings that survive from their time. The same, he argued, can be said for the writings about Jesus, dating back to around 33 A.D. He noted that the historical documents about Jesus and His resurrection hold the same level of credibility as those from ancient figures like:

- **Cuneiform**: Dating back to around 3400 BC, the Sumerians in Mesopotamia created the first known writing system.

- **Scorpion I Tomb Hieroglyphs**: Around 3400-3200 BC.

- **Egyptian Hieroglyphs**: From around 3250 BC.

- **Narmer Palette**: Circa 3200-3000 BC.

- **Beer Payslip**: Around 3100-3000 BC.

- **Seal of Seth-Peribsen**: 2890-2670 BC.

- **Kesh Temple Hymn**: 2250-2520 BC.

- **Reforms of Urukagina**: 2500-2340 BC.

- **Aristotle**: 335-323 BC.

- **St. Paul's Letter to the Corinthians**: 50-51 AD.

The preacher's point was clear: If the student accepted the historical validity of ancient Greek philosophy, then she should also consider the accounts of Jesus's life and resurrection. These accounts, written within a few decades of Jesus's death, carry historical weight, and their testimony is backed not only by the Gospels but by the writings of early Christian leaders like Paul. After reading this preacher account, I believe he should have informed the student of Josephus account of Jesus. Josephus, a 1st-century Jewish historian, made a few references regarding Jesus in his work Antiquities of the Jews, written around 93–94 CE. "About this time there lived Jesus, a wise man, if indeed one ought to call him a man. For he was one who performed surprising deeds and was a teacher of such people as accept the truth gladly. He won over many Jews and many of the Greeks. He was the Messiah. And when, upon the accusation of the principal men among us, Pilate had condemned him to a cross, those who had first come to love him did not cease. He appeared to them spending a third day restored to life, for the prophets of God had foretold these things and a thousand other marvels about him. And the tribe of the Christians, so called after him, has still to this day not disappeared."

This conversation prompted me to reflect on why I believe so deeply in the beauty and truth of the Catholic faith: a faith rooted in scripture, illuminated by tradition, and alive with mystery. It is not a leap of blind faith or the acceptance of myths; rather, it is grounded in history, in the testimony of real people who lived through and documented real events—events that continue to influence the course of history today.

The resurrection of Jesus, for example, is not just a spiritual truth, but also a historical reality. It was witnessed by hundreds, recorded by multiple authors, and passed down through the ages. The Church teaches that our faith is rooted in this historical truth. While private revelations can deepen our spiritual lives, they cannot change or add to the foundation of the faith entrusted to us by the apostles. The resurrection of Jesus is not a fairy tale or fable, but a truth confirmed by the testimony of those who were closest to Him. Just as we accept the writings of ancient philosophers as credible, we must also recognize the accounts of those who witnessed Christ's life, death, and resurrection. This is the bedrock of our faith—a faith that is both timeless and true, capable of leading us into the beauty and fullness of God's love.

The Apostles (in no particular order)

Only the deaths of Judas and James are explicitly mentioned in the Bible among the apostles. According to the mystic Anne Catherine Emmerich in her book *The Life of Jesus*, Jesus met with each apostle individually before His Ascension and foretold their martyrdom, except for John, whom He said would live a long life. The following information comes from many historical records, legends, theories, oral traditions, mystic revelations and artificial intelligence.

James the Greater: the brother of the apostle John and known as the "Son of Thunder," was the first apostle to be martyred. After preaching in Spain, he returned to Jerusalem around 42 A.D. According to Acts 12:1-2, King Herod had him executed by the sword around 44 A.D. Eusebius of Caesarea, quoting Clement of Alexandria, recounts that the guard who brought James to court was so moved by his testimony that he also confessed his Christian faith. Both were subsequently beheaded, and James forgave the guard, wishing him peace. James is believed to be buried at the Cathedral of Santiago de Compostela in Spain.

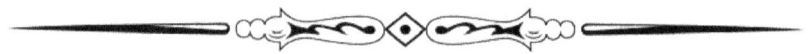

Andrew: Andrew, Peter's brother, preached in Scythia (now Iran) and Asia Minor (now Turkey), as well as in Macedonia and Greece. Around 60-61 A.D., he was crucified on an X-shaped cross. Unlike typical crucifixions, Andrew was tied to the cross rather than nailed. Legend has it that he preached for three days while on the cross. His relics are said to be in several locations: the Basilica of Saint Andrew in Patras, Greece; the Amalfi Cathedral (Duomo di Sant'Andrea) in Italy; Saint Mary's Cathedral in Edinburgh, Scotland; and the Church of Saint Andrew and Saint Albert in Warsaw, Poland.

Peter: Two epistles in the New Testament, 1 Peter and 2 Peter, are traditionally attributed to Saint Peter, although scholars debate their authorship. However, per tradition, Peter was martyred in Rome during the reign of Emperor Nero, who sought to blame Christians for the burning of the city. Peter was crucified upside down, choosing this method out of respect for Jesus, as he felt unworthy to die in the same manner. He died and was buried on what is now Vatican Hill, where St. Peter's Basilica is traditionally believed to be built over his burial site. Saint Peter is revered across various Christian traditions, including Roman Catholicism, Eastern Orthodoxy, and Anglicanism. He is commonly depicted with keys, symbolizing his role related to the "keys to the kingdom of Heaven," as mentioned in Matthew 16:19. His feast day is celebrated on June 29 in the Western Christian calendar, alongside Saint Paul. The Eastern Orthodox Church also honors him on June 29 and additionally on January 16. In Christian art, Saint Peter is often shown holding keys and a rooster, the latter symbolizing Jesus's prediction that Peter would deny Him three times before the rooster crowed. Peter's life and legacy are central to Christian tradition, particularly in the Roman Catholic Church, where he is venerated as a foundational figure and the first Pope.

Simon: Saint Simon, also known as Simon the Zealot, is one of the twelve apostles of Jesus. Though, he is less well-known compared to some of the other apostles, the title "Zealot" may indicate his affiliation with the Zealots, a political group that opposed Roman rule in Judea. It is important to distinguish him from Simon Peter, a more

prominent figure among the apostles. Tradition holds that Simon preached in Persia and was martyred around 67 A.D. Various sources offer differing accounts of his death: Moses of Chorene from the fifth century suggests he was martyred in the Kingdom of Iberia, while Ethiopian Christians believe he died in Samaria. Sixteenth-century scholar Justus Lipsius proposed that Simon was sawed in half, though Eastern traditions claim he died of old age. Simon is believed to be buried alongside Saint Jude Thaddeus in the left transept of Saint Peter's Basilica, under the altar of Saint Joseph. Saint Simon is honored as a saint in several Christian traditions, including Roman Catholicism, Eastern Orthodoxy, and Anglicanism. His feast day is celebrated on October 28 in the Western Christian calendar and on June 30 in the Eastern Christian calendar, often shared with Saint Jude Thaddeus. He is commonly depicted with a saw, symbolizing his traditional martyrdom by being sewed in half.

Jude: Saint Jude, also known as "Jude, the son of James" (Luke 6:16, John 14:22) and "Thaddeus," should not be confused with Judas Iscariot, the apostle who betrayed Jesus. To avoid confusion, he is often referred to as "Saint Jude." Although little is known about Jude's activities during Jesus' ministry, he is mentioned in the Gospels for asking Jesus why He would reveal Himself to the disciples and not to the world. Tradition holds that after Jesus' resurrection and ascension, Jude preached the Gospel in various regions, including Syria, Mesopotamia, and Persia. Regarding his martyrdom, traditions and apocryphal writings suggest several possible locations for his death. Some accounts indicate that he was martyred in Persia or Armenia, often alongside Saint Simon the Zealot. The details of his death vary, but he is commonly depicted with symbols of suffering, such as a club or spear. Saint Jude is venerated in many Christian traditions, including Roman Catholicism, Eastern Orthodoxy, and Anglicanism. His feast day is celebrated on October 28 in the Western Christian calendar and on June 30 in the Eastern Christian calendar, frequently shared with Saint Simon the Zealot. Saint Jude is popularly known as the patron saint of desperate or lost causes. According to "The Golden Legend," Jude

and Simon commanded demons to leave idols, which led to their violent martyrdom. The temple where they were martyred was struck by thunder and destroyed, and the two apostles were later honored with a grand church. Jude is believed to be buried in the same tomb as Saint Simon, located in the left transept of Saint Peter's Basilica, under the altar of Saint Joseph.

James the Less (Called "Little James" in The Chosen) James the Less, also known as James the Just or James the Younger, is one of Jesus' twelve apostles and is distinguished from James, the son of Zebedee. In the Gospels, he is referred to as "James, the son of Alphaeus" (Matthew 10:3, Mark 3:18, Luke 6:15) and is also called "James the Less" or "James the Younger" to differentiate him from the other James. Although James the Less does not play a prominent role in the Gospels or the Acts of the Apostles, and his contributions are less documented, traditions suggest he may have preached in regions such as Egypt or parts of the Eastern Mediterranean. Early Christian traditions sometimes depict him as leading an austere and ascetic life, reflecting his role in the early Church. James the Less is occasionally confused with James the Just, the first bishop of Jerusalem. According to later traditions and apocryphal writings, James the Less was martyred, though the details vary. Some sources claim he was crucified, while others suggest he was beaten or stoned, with differing accounts of the circumstances and location of his death. The historian Josephus noted that the destruction of Jerusalem in 70 A.D. was seen as divine punishment for James's death. One tradition holds that James was crucified in Egypt. His relics are believed to be at the Church of the Saints Apostoli in Rome, Italy, and some accounts suggest these relics were transferred to Rome from Constantinople in the 6th century by Pope Pelagius. Another tradition places his remains at Saint James Cathedral in the Armenian Quarter of Jerusalem, Israel. Saint James the Less is honored as a saint in Roman Catholicism, Eastern Orthodoxy, and Anglicanism. His feast day is celebrated on May 3 in the Western Christian calendar, though it may vary among different traditions. Despite his recognition as an apostle, he is less prominent in the broader Christian tradition compared to other apostles.

Philip: Philip, often referred to as Philip the Apostle to distinguish him from Philip the Evangelist, is a significant figure among Jesus' twelve apostles. He is known for his role in bringing Nathanael (Bartholomew) to Jesus (John 1:43-46) and is mentioned in John 6:5-7, where Jesus questions him about how to feed the 5,000. Tradition holds that after Jesus' resurrection and ascension, Philip preached in various regions, including Greece, Phrygia (modern-day Turkey), and possibly Asia Minor. Some accounts describe he was martyred in Hierapolis, a city in Phrygia, with various sources claiming he was either crucified upside down or impaled. Polycrates of Ephesus, in a letter to Pope Victor, noted Philip's burial in Hierapolis. Additionally, Caius the Presbyter, writing in the third century, mentioned Philip's daughters and their tomb in Hierapolis, though there may be confusion with Philip the Evangelist. Philip's relics are believed to be interred in the crypt of the Basilica Santi Apostoli in Rome, Italy.

Bartholomew: Bartholomew is primarily known through his association with Nathanael. In John 1:45-51, Philip tells Nathanael about Jesus, and Nathanael initially doubts but is later convinced by Jesus' knowledge of him. Traditions about Bartholomew's martyrdom vary. One prevalent account suggests he was flayed alive, which is represented in his iconography. Other sources describe him as being beheaded or crucified, with differing accounts of the circumstances and location. Many traditions assert that he was martyred in Armenia. The "Golden Legend" recounts that Bartholomew was crucified upside down in Albania, Armenia, while Foxe's Book of Martyrs describes him as having been beaten and then crucified in India. Another tradition claims he was beaten and thrown into the sea. According to legend, Bartholomew cured the daughter of an Armenian king, which led to his martyrdom. His body was reportedly recovered and initially buried on the island of Lipara before being transferred to Rome. He is believed to be interred in the Basilica di San Bartolomeo all'Isola in Rome. Bartholomew is venerated as a saint in Roman Catholicism, Eastern Orthodoxy, and Anglicanism. His feast day is celebrated on August 24 in the Western Christian calendar and on June 11 in the Eastern Christian calendar. Bartholomew is often depicted with a flaying knife, symbolizing the tradition that he was flayed alive. Other symbols include a book and a cross, reflecting his role as a preacher and martyr. In some artworks, he is shown holding his skin, which visually represents the manner of his martyrdom.

Matthew: Matthew, also known as Levi, was a tax collector in Capernaum before becoming one of Jesus' apostles. Following Jesus' resurrection and ascension, Matthew is believed to have traveled extensively to spread the Gospel. Traditions suggest he preached in various regions, including Judea, Ethiopia, Persia, and possibly India, with some accounts also mentioning his work in the Mediterranean. The Gospel of Matthew, attributed to him, offers a thorough account of Jesus' life, teachings, death, and resurrection. It is especially noted for its emphasis on how Jesus fulfilled Old Testament prophecies and for featuring the Sermon on the Mount. Matthew is traditionally believed to have been martyred around 65 A.D., while celebrating Mass in Ethiopia. According to John Foxe's "Book of Martyrs," he was killed with a halberd in the city of Nadabah. The specifics of his martyrdom vary among sources, with some indicating Ethiopia and others suggesting separate locations. Matthew is honored as a saint in Roman Catholicism, Eastern Orthodoxy, and Anglicanism. His feast day is celebrated on September 21 in the Western Christian calendar and on November 16 in the Eastern Christian calendar.

Thomas: also known as Didymus (the Twin), is renowned from the New Testament, particularly the Gospel of John, for his initial skepticism about Jesus' resurrection. According to John 20:24-29, Thomas doubted until he saw and touched Jesus' wounds, earning him the nickname "Doubting Thomas." Following Jesus' resurrection and ascension, Thomas is believed to have traveled extensively to spread the Gospel. He is traditionally credited with significant missionary work in India, where he is deemedto have established Christian communities. His travels are also thought to have included regions such as Parthia (modern-day Iran), Persia, and possibly other parts of Asia Minor. In India, Thomas is particularly associated with the Malankara Orthodox Syrian Church and the Thomas Christians in Kerala, a prominent Christian community in the region. Thomas is traditionally believed to have been martyred by being stabbed with a spear at Mylapore, India, around 74 A.D. This site is known as Saint Thomas Mount. He is believed to be buried in Saint Thomas Cathedral Basilica at the base of this hill. Marco Polo, who visited the tomb in 1292, wrote about the miraculous healings reported by pilgrims. While the exact circumstances and location of Thomas's death vary across traditions, he is widely recognized as having been killed for his faith. Tradition holds that Thomas is buried in Mylapore, near Chennai, India. The Basilica of St. Thomas Mount in Chennai is a significant pilgrimage site for Christians honoring his legacy. Saint Thomas is honored as a saint in Roman Catholicism, Eastern Orthodoxy, and Anglicanism. His feast day is celebrated on July 3 in the Western Christian calendar and on October 6 in the Eastern Christian calendar. Saint Thomas is often depicted with a spear, symbolizing his martyrdom. He may also be shown with a carpenter's square, referencing his background, and occasionally with carpenter's tools. According to tradition, the finger that Thomas inserted into Jesus' wounds is held at the Cathedral of the Assumption of the Virgin Mary in Dubrovnik.

Matthias: Originally one of the seventy-two disciples, Matthias was chosen to replace Judas Iscariot after Judas's betrayal and death. He began his ministry in Judaea before traveling to Cappadocia and eventually settling in a region of Asia Minor near the Caspian Sea (present-day Russia). In 65 A.D., Matthias faced martyrdom, with various accounts suggesting he was either hacked to death or crucified. Other traditions claim he was killed by cannibals in Aethiopia (modern-day Georgia) or stoned and beheaded by Jews in Jerusalem. His remains are reportedly enshrined in the Benedictine monastery of Saint Matthias Abbey in Trier, Germany, with the relics believed to have been brought there by Empress Helena. Matthias is introduced in the New Testament in the Book of Acts. After the death of Judas Iscariot, the remaining eleven apostles sought to replace him to maintain the number of twelve apostles. According to Acts 1:15-26, Matthias was chosen by casting lots, a method used to discern God's will. Traditions hold that Matthias traveled to various regions to preach the Gospel after he was appointed an apostle. He is said to have preached in Ethiopia, Cappadocia (modern-day Turkey), and possibly other areas of Asia Minor. The specifics of Matthias's martyrdom vary among traditions. Some accounts suggest he was martyred in Jerusalem, while others indicate he might have been stoned or crucified. The details of his death are not well-documented and are subject to different legends and traditions. Matthias is venerated as a saint in Roman Catholicism, Eastern Orthodoxy, and Anglicanism. His feast day is celebrated on February 24 in the Western Christian calendar and on August 9 in the Eastern Christian calendar. In art, Matthias is often depicted with a lance or spear, symbolizing his martyrdom.

John: John, the brother of James the Greater ("Big James" from The Chosen) and one of the twelve apostles, was entrusted by Jesus with the care of His mother, Mary. During the early Christian persecutions in Jerusalem, John and Mary fled to Ephesus. After Mary's assumption into Heaven, John returned to Ephesus but was later arrested by the Romans. He was sent to Rome for trial and sentenced to death by boiling in oil. Miraculously surviving this execution, John's death sentence was commuted, and he was exiled to the island of Patmos. It was during this exile that he is believed to have authored the Book of Revelation. John eventually returned to Ephesus, where he died of natural causes around 100 A.D. at the age of eighty-eight. According to Saint Robert Bellarmine, there are no relics of Saint John, as he was assumed into heaven. Today, the Basilica of Saint John in Ephesus stands over the believed site of his grave. John, also known as John the Beloved or the Beloved Disciple, was a fisherman by trade before following Jesus, along with his brother James. He is traditionally credited with authoring the Gospel of John, which presents a unique perspective on Jesus' life and teachings, emphasizing His divinity and the promise of eternal life. John is also recognized as the author of the Book of Revelation, which contains vivid apocalyptic visions and prophecies. Additionally, he is believed to have written three epistles (1 John, 2 John, and 3 John) that offer guidance on love, faith, and Christian living. He was the only male disciple present at the crucifixion of Jesus and was entrusted with the care of Mary, as noted in John 19:26-27. After Jesus' resurrection and ascension, John is thought to have traveled extensively to spread the Gospel, particularly in Asia Minor, with a strong association with Ephesus. Tradition holds that he was exiled to Patmos by the Roman Emperor Domitian, where he received the visions described in Revelation. John is traditionally believed to have died of natural causes in Ephesus, making him one of the few apostles not to have faced martyrdom. The Basilica of Saint John in Ephesus, built in the 6th century, is a major site associated with his burial. Some traditions also highlight the Monastery of Saint John the Theologian on Patmos as a significant site connected to his life and writings. Saint John is venerated as a saint in Roman Catholicism, Eastern Orthodoxy, and Anglicanism. His feast day is celebrated on December 27 in the Western Christian calendar and September 26 in the Eastern Christian calendar. In art, he is often depicted with symbols such as an eagle, representing his Gospel's lofty and spiritual nature, and a cup or chalice, referencing a legend of his surviving poisoning.

Other Key Figures

Paul: Saint Paul, originally known as Saul of Tarsus, is a crucial figure in early Christianity. His life and contributions are extensively documented in the New Testament, particularly in the Acts of the Apostles and his own epistles. Here is an overview of what is known about him: Paul was born as Saul in Tarsus, a city in Cilicia (modern-day Turkey). As a Roman citizen and a Pharisee, he received an education under the esteemed teacher Gamaliel, equipping him with a deep understanding of both Jewish law and Roman culture. Initially, Saul was a fervent persecutor of Christians, viewing the early Christian movement as a threat to Judaism. However, his life changed

dramatically on the road to Damascus, where he experienced a profound vision of the risen Jesus. This encounter, described as a blinding light, led to his conversion to Christianity and his decision to adopt the name Paul. From that point on, Paul became a passionate advocate for the Christian faith (Acts 9:1-19). Paul embarked on several significant missionary journeys throughout the Roman Empire, traveling through regions such as Asia Minor (modern-day Turkey), Greece, and eventually reaching Rome. During these travels, he established Christian communities and wrote letters to them, many of which are now part of the New Testament. He is traditionally credited with writing 13 of the 27 books in the New Testament, including epistles addressed to various churches and individuals, such as Romans, Corinthians, Galatians, and Ephesians. His writings encompass theological discussions, practical advice for Christian living, and guidance on church organization. Throughout his ministry, Paul faced numerous challenges and imprisonments due to his faith. His preaching often elicited opposition from both Jewish leaders and Roman authorities. As a Roman citizen, Paul had the right to appeal to Caesar, which led to his journey to Rome for trial. Tradition holds that Saint Paul was martyred in Rome around 64-68 AD during the reign of Emperor Nero. According to tradition, he was beheaded, a method of execution reserved for Roman citizens. Legend has it that Saint Paul was executed on the same day as Saint Peter. Paul is venerated as a saint in Roman Catholicism, Eastern Orthodoxy, and Anglicanism. His feast day is celebrated on June 29, alongside Saint Peter, and on January 25 to commemorate his conversion. In Christian art, Paul is often depicted with a sword, symbolizing his martyrdom, and a book or scroll, representing his epistles. He is typically shown with a beard and sometimes with the attribute of blindness, referring to his dramatic conversion experience. Paul is believed to be buried at the Basilica of Saint Paul Outside the Walls in Rome, Italy, where his relics are honored.

Saint Joseph: Saint Joseph, the husband of Mary and the earthly father of Jesus, is a revered figure in Christian tradition, particularly within the context of the Nativity. His life and role are detailed both

243

in the New Testament and in various traditions. Saint Joseph is prominently featured in the Gospels of Matthew and Luke. He is depicted as a just and compassionate man, chosen by God to be the earthly father of Jesus. According to the Gospel of Matthew (1:18-25), Joseph was initially troubled by Mary's pregnancy, as they were betrothed but had not yet lived together. After an angel appeared to him in a dream, revealing that the Holy Spirit conceived Mary's child. It would be the Savior, Joseph took Mary as his wife, honoring his role as Jesus' earthly guardian. Joseph's protective role is further highlighted when he fled to Egypt with Mary and Jesus to escape King Herod's massacre of the innocents (Matthew 2:13-15). After Herod's death, Joseph returned his family to Nazareth, where Jesus grew up (Matthew 2:19-23). According to mystic Anne Catherine Emmerich in "The Life of Christ, "Joseph was the third of six brothers from a large mansion near Bethlehem. He was known for his piety and took a vow of chastity. A priest conducted a test involving branches, with Joseph's branch miraculously blooming into a lily, signifying his divine selection to marry Mary. By the time Jesus was thirty, Joseph's health started declining. Mary and Jesus cared for him diligently. Before his death, Joseph was granted a vision of God's divine plans and sought forgiveness from Mary and Jesus, who assured him of eternal grace. Joseph passed away at sixty, deeply affected by the foreknowledge of Jesus's crucifixion." Saint Joseph is the patron saint of workers, fathers, and the universal Church. He is also regarded as the patron saint of the dying, believed to have died in the presence of Jesus and Mary. His feast day is celebrated on March 19 in the Western Christian calendar, known as the Feast of Saint Joseph. In the Eastern Orthodox Church, he is honored on the Sunday after Christmas and on September 26, Christian art, Saint Joseph is often depicted with a carpenter's tool, reflecting his profession, and a lily, symbolizing his virtuous character and role as Mary's spouse. He is frequently shown with the Holy Family, emphasizing his role as protector and guardian.

King Herod: Herod Antipas ruled over Galilee and Perea and is notable in the New Testament for his involvement in the beheading of John the Baptist and his interactions with Jesus. He reigned until 39 A.D., when Emperor Caligula exiled him to Gaul (modern-day France) after accusing him of conspiring against the emperor. According to Acts 12:1-20, Herod Antipas persecuted early Christians, executing James the Great and arresting Peter, among others. His actions were intended to curry favor with the Jewish population, who were pleased by his harsh measures against Christians. During a public address to the people of Tyre and Sidon, who were dependent on his territory for food, Herod was flattered by the crowd's acclaim, declaring him to be a god. As a result of his failure to give glory to God, he was struck down by an angel of the Lord and died, consumed by worms. In the writings of the mystic Mary of Agreda, it is described that the Blessed Mother had foreseen Herod's impending death and had fervently prayed for his repentance. She even expressed a willingness to suffer death herself if it could lead to Herod's salvation. Despite her prayers, Herod continued in his wicked ways, including persecuting the apostles, mocking Jesus, and committing various other abominations. His death was thus seen as divine retribution for his many sins and crimes.

Caiaphas: In November 1990, archaeologists discovered a burial cave near Jerusalem that contained an ossuary inscribed with the name "Joseph, son of Caiaphas." Examination of the bones, which belonged to a man approximately sixty years old, reveal something related to the remains of Caiaphas, the high priest who condemned Jesus. Caiaphas, the son-in-law of Annas, served as high priest during Jesus' trial but was deposed in 37 A.D. by Lucius Vitellius, the governor of Syria, who intervened in Jewish affairs. Josephus records this deposition but does not provide details about Caiaphas' subsequent life. Helen K. Bond, in her book *Caiaphas*, notes that while Caiaphas's removal from office is documented, details of his later life and death remain elusive. Caiaphas, the high priest who played a significant role in the trial of Jesus, is not extensively documented in historical sources beyond the New Testament. Outside of biblical accounts, references to Caiaphas are sparse. The Jewish historian Josephus mentions various high priests of the era but does not specifically elaborate on Caiaphas' later life. Some traditions and apocryphal writings suggest that Caiaphas faced divine retribution for his role in condemning Jesus. However, these accounts are not considered reliable historical evidence. Caiaphas' fate after Jesus' death remains largely unknown. While some Jewish traditions propose that he suffered divine punishment or experienced a fall from power, these claims lack concrete historical support.

Annas: Annas, also known as Ananus, was a prominent Jewish leader who served as High Priest from 6 to 15 AD. He was the father-in-law of Caiaphas, who succeeded him in the high priesthood. Although Annas was not the High Priest during the crucifixion of Jesus, he played a significant role in the trial of Jesus. According to the Gospels, Jesus was first brought before Annas for interrogation before being sent to Caiaphas and the Sanhedrin (John 18:13-24). After being deposed from the High Priesthood by the Roman governor Valerius Gratus in 15 AD, Annas's influence persisted through his five sons, who also held the high priesthood. Despite his removal, he remained a powerful figure and was highly respected within the Jewish community. Annas continued to be involved in various religious and political matters, including the Sanhedrin. Mystic Anne Catherine Emmerich describes how Annas, who had secretly opposed Jesus and allegedly orchestrated false testimonies against Him, was greatly shaken by the events surrounding Jesus's crucifixion. During the earthquake and the tearing of the Temple curtain, Emmerich claims that Annas was driven into a state of despair, fleeing through the Temple, and eventually being confined by his followers. However, these accounts are based on mystic revelations rather than historical documentation. The Jewish historian Josephus mentions Annas and his family, noting their ongoing influence in Jewish leadership and their interactions with Roman authorities. However, detailed information about Annas's life after the crucifixion of Jesus is scarce. There is no comprehensive historical record of his later years or death, and both the New Testament and historical sources provide limited details about his final days.

Pontius Pilate: Pontius Pilate, the Roman governor who sentenced Jesus to crucifixion, met a troubled end according to various traditions and legends. While historical records are sparse, several accounts offer insights into his later life: **Tacitus:** The Roman historian Tacitus briefly mentions Pilate in relation to Jesus' crucifixion but provides no details about his subsequent life. **Suetonius:** Another Roman historian, Suetonius, references Pilate in the context of the expulsion of Jews from Rome but does not discuss his fate after the crucifixion. **Josephus:** The Jewish historian Flavius Josephus notes Pilate's administrative role and his conflicts with the Jewish population but does not provide information about his life following Jesus' death. Josephus does confirm that Pilate was removed from his position by Vitellius on 36 A.D. due to a loss of public support. According to some traditions, Pilate was either executed or committed suicide after being recalled to Rome. Eusebius, an early Christian historian, suggests that Pilate suffered severe misfortunes under Emperor Caligula, which led to his eventual suicide. Other accounts propose that Pilate was exiled, possibly to Gaul (modern-day France), and later took his own life. Various legends offer different narratives about Pilate's fate: **The Golden Legend** (13th century): This legend recounts that Pilate was saved from death by a holy garment he had stolen from Christ. However, when his deceit was discovered, he was condemned to death. Some Eastern Orthodox traditions suggest that Pilate and his wife may have converted to Christianity later in life, although this remains speculative and lacks historical support. In Ethiopian Orthodox Christianity, Pontius Pilate is venerated as a saint. This stance is distinctive, as most Christian traditions view Pilate negatively due to his role in condemning Jesus to crucifixion. Ethiopian tradition holds that Pilate had a more positive role, with some accounts suggesting he ultimately came to faith and repented for his actions. This veneration reflects a broader Ethiopian Orthodox tradition of recognizing figures who might be viewed differently in other Christian contexts.

Claudia Procula: Claudia Procula, also known as Claudia Procles or simply Claudia, is traditionally known as the wife of Pontius Pilate.

In the New Testament, specifically in the Gospel of Matthew (27:19), she is mentioned for having a prophetic dream about Jesus and urging her husband to avoid condemning Him. Her dream troubled her deeply, and she described Jesus as innocent, advising Pilate to have nothing to do with His trial. Details about her life after the crucifixion of Jesus are limited and primarily derived from later traditions and apocryphal texts rather than historical records. In some Christian traditions, especially within the Eastern Orthodox Church, Claudia Procula is venerated as a saint. Her veneration stems from the belief that her dream and her attempts to intervene in the trial are a testament of her insight and piety. Various legends suggest that Claudia Procula converted to Christianity, possibly influenced by the events surrounding Jesus' trial and her husband's eventual fate. Some traditions depict her as living a life of repentance and devotion following these events. Apocryphal writings often portray her as a sympathetic and devout figure, offering more detailed but non-authoritative accounts of her later life. According to mystic Anne Catherine Emmerich, Claudia's dream was vivid and distressing, showing scenes from Jesus's life and suffering. She reportedly saw the Annunciation, the Birth of Christ, the Adoration of the Shepherds and Magi, Simeon's Prophecy, the Flight into Egypt, and the Massacre of the Innocents. In her vision, Jesus was surrounded by light, while His enemies were depicted with extreme malice. The dream also highlighted the profound suffering of His Mother and His own enduring patience, which deeply moved and troubled Claudia. Following the crucifixion, Claudia is said to have sent linen cloths to Mary and other holy women to collect Jesus's blood. She distanced herself from Pilate and sought refuge with the holy women in the house of Lazarus. Ultimately, she is believed to have become a companion of Saint Paul, although these accounts are part of later Christian traditions and are not confirmed by historical evidence.

Dismas (The Good Thief): Saint Dismas, the "Good Thief" was crucified alongside Jesus, he made a heartfelt confession to Jesus on the cross, asking, "Remember me when You come into Your kingdom." According to Blessed Anne Catherine Emmerich, Dismas recognized Jesus as the Savior because of a past encounter. As a leprous child, Dismas had been healed by water used to bathe the infant Jesus, thanks to Mary's advice. This miracle remained in his memory. On the cross, prompted by the Holy Spirit, Dismas expressed his remorse and faith. Jesus responded, promising him a place in Paradise. Emmerich describes a vision where Jesus welcomed Dismas's soul into Heaven, while the soul of the other thief was condemned. Angels escorted Dismas's soul to Abraham's bosom and then entered the heavenly Jerusalem, fulfilling Jesus's promise. An interesting side note here: In Matthew 25, Jesus explains at Judgement Day, God will separate the sheep from the goats. To His right, goes the sheep (heaven) and to the left (hell) goes the goats. When Jesus is crucified, the good thief is on His right and the bad thief is on His left.

Mary, Martha, and Lazarus: Mary, Martha, and Lazarus, close friends of Jesus, appear throughout the Gospels lives post-resurrection. The Gospels provide scant information about them. One tradition suggests that Lazarus wrote an account of his experiences in the afterlife before being revived by Jesus. He is said to have either followed Peter to Syria or been placed in a boat by the Jews at Jaffa, eventually reaching Cyprus. In Cyprus, he reportedly lived as a bishop for 30 years before dying peacefully. Another tradition holds that Lazarus was imprisoned and beheaded in Marseilles, where his head is still venerated. Some believe his remains were found in Autun, France, and are now housed in the Cathedral of Saint Lazarus. Mary and Martha are also said to have escaped with Lazarus to France. Despite the various stories, their ultimate fates remain intertwined with local legends and traditions.

Veronica: Originally named Seraphia, Veronica is a figure from Christian tradition known for her compassionate act during Jesus's journey to Calvary. According to Anne Catherine Emmerich's *Dolorous Passion*, Seraphia, who was five at the time of Mary's marriage to Joseph, later became involved in Jesus's life in a profound way. When Jesus, burdened by the weight of the cross, stumbled and fell, Seraphia bravely pushed through the crowd to offer her veil to Him, asking to wipe His face. Jesus accepted the veil, used it to clean His face, and then returned it to her, thanking her for the gesture. Upon returning home, Seraphia discovered that the image of Jesus's face had miraculously been imprinted on the veil. Seraphia, a cousin of John the Baptist and related to the prophet Simeon, was married later in life to a member of the Sanhedrin. Her husband, along with Nicodemus and Joseph of Arimathea, attempted to intervene in Jesus's trial. During Jesus's triumphant entry into Jerusalem on Palm Sunday, Seraphia was around fifty years old. Three years after the Ascension, Seraphia traveled to Rome with Nicodemus to show the veil to Emperor Tiberius, who was ill. Upon viewing the veil and its miraculous image, Tiberius was reportedly cured. Afterward, Seraphia returned to Jerusalem but was captured during the Christian persecutions. She was imprisoned and eventually died of starvation, becoming a martyr for her faith. While the veil, also known as the Sudarium, remains a significant relic, its history became obscure following the Sack of Rome in 1527. Although various reproductions exist, it is uncertain if the veil held by the Vatican is the original. The relic is occasionally displayed during the 5th Sunday of Lent, though details are minimal.

Cassius (Saint Longinus): In the Gospel of John 19:34, a soldier thrust a lance into Jesus's side, resulting in a flow of blood and water. Tradition names this soldier Cassius, suffering from a vision disorder. As the lance was removed, some of Jesus's blood splashed into Cassius's eyes, miraculously curing his blindness. Cassius, moved by this experience, converted to Christianity, and proclaimed Jesus as the Son of God. He is venerated as Saint Longinus in Christian tradition. According to the pseudepigraphal *Gospel of Nicodemus*, Longinus, a centurion from Cappadocia, was the name given to the soldier who pierced Jesus's side. His sight was restored when blood and water from Jesus's wound touched his eyes. After witnessing the resurrection of Jesus and refusing to lie under pressure from Jewish leaders, Longinus abandoned his military career, embraced Christianity, and lived a life of penance. Legend has it that Longinus was later martyred by beheading. His relics are said to be in Rome, particularly in the Church of Saint Augustine, while the lance used to pierce Jesus is believed to be entombed in one of the four pillars over the altar in Saint Peter's Basilica. Emmerich's visions describe how Cassius, along with other soldiers, assisted in removing Jesus from the cross and preparing His body for burial. Cassius remained at the tomb and experienced profound spiritual insights, though he did not see the risen Jesus. He later reported to Pilate the events surrounding the resurrection, affirming Jesus as the Messiah and Son of God.

Simon of Cyrene: The Gospel of Luke (23:26) mentions Simon of Cyrene as a man forced to carry Jesus's cross. A gardener by trade, Simon was returning from the countryside carrying a bundle of sprigs when he was compelled to bear the cross behind Jesus. Initially reluctant and repulsed by the task, Simon was moved by Jesus's pitiable condition. His compassion overcame his reluctance, and despite his own fatigue and the brutal treatment he received from the soldiers, he assisted Jesus. Simon's intervention was significant, and he eventually sought out the Apostles after the Sabbath, asking to be baptized as a follower of Jesus. His two sons, Rufus and Alexander, were also mentioned, suggesting that Simon's family became early Christians.

Nicodemus: The fate of Nicodemus after the resurrection of Jesus remains uncertain. While some rumors suggest that his remains were found alongside those of Stephen and Gamaliel, there is no concrete evidence to support this claim. The *Gospel of Nicodemus* exists, but scholars date it to the fourth century and question its authenticity as a work by the biblical Nicodemus. Thus, little is known about Nicodemus's life following the resurrection.

Joseph of Arimathea: a respected member of the Sanhedrin and a secret follower of Jesus, is venerated in the Eastern Church. According to later literature, including the *Apocryphal Gospel of Peter* and the *Apocryphal Gospel of Nicodemus*, Joseph played a crucial role in Jesus's burial. Blessed Anne Catherine Emmerich

described a vision in which the Jewish authorities imprisoned Joseph after Jesus's burial. In the vision, Joseph was freed by a divine figure, possibly an angel, and escaped to Arimathea. He remained there until it was safe to return to Jerusalem. Joseph's post-resurrection activities remain largely unknown.

Barabbas: Barabbas, a notorious prisoner, is mentioned in all four Gospels. The Gospel of John identifies him as a thief, while Luke (23:19) and Mark describe him as a participant in an insurrection and a murderer. Matthew refers to him as a notorious criminal. Mystics like Anne Catherine Emmerich describe Barabbas as not only a murderer but also a practitioner of sorcery, including a heinous act of cutting open a pregnant woman's womb. Despite these accounts, little else is known about his life after his release in exchange for Jesus.

Judas Iscariot: Judas Iscariot, known for betraying Jesus, is a central figure in the Gospels. Matthew (27:3-10) recounts that Judas, overcome with remorse after Jesus's condemnation, returned the 30 pieces of silver to the chief priests and hanged himself. Although Judas had the same opportunities as the other apostles to follow Jesus and witness His miracles, he remained unmoved by Jesus's teachings and harbored ulterior motives. His betrayal was driven by a desire for personal gain rather than genuine love for Christ. In *The Mystical City of God* by Venerable Mary of Agreda, it is noted that Judas initially received special favors from Jesus and the Blessed Mother. Despite this, his eventual defection grew as he succumbed to pride and greed. The Blessed Mother made numerous efforts to guide him back, offering him mercy and urging repentance, but Judas resisted and ultimately chose perdition. According to Anne Catherine Emmerich, Jesus descended into Hell and spoke to Judas, though the details of their conversation are not revealed. Emmerich's vision suggests that Judas's final fate was a result of his own hardened heart and rejection of grace. Judas Iscariot, often regarded as the most tragic of the Apostles, was chosen by Jesus despite knowing that he would betray Him. The Gospel of Matthew (27:3-10) details Judas's remorse after Jesus was condemned to death. Overcome with guilt, Judas attempted

to return the 30 pieces of silver to the chief priests, who refused to take it. He then threw the money at them and went away to hang himself. Jesus's acceptance of Judas as an Apostle was despite foreknowledge of his betrayal. Although Judas, like the other apostles, witnessed Jesus's miracles, received the power to expel demons, and heard His teachings firsthand, he remained indifferent to Jesus's true nature. Judas saw Jesus merely to achieve his own ends, driven by a desire for personal gain rather than genuine devotion. Bestowing to Venerable Mary of Agreda in *The Mystical City of God*, Judas initially attracted special favor from Jesus and was honored as one of the twelve Apostles. Mary, the Mother of Jesus, was aware from the beginning of Judas's eventual betrayal but continued to treat him with extraordinary gentleness and care. Despite his initial grace and the chance for redemption, Judas gradually fell into deeper sin. Mary offered him numerous opportunities for repentance and even promised to do penance for him if he returned. Yet Judas resisted these divine appeals and remained hardened in his pride and deceit. Anne Catherine Emmerich, in her visions, described Jesus descending into Hell to demonstrate His triumph over Satan. Although Emmerich saw Jesus speaking to the soul of Judas, the content of their conversation remains unknown. Judas's final choice to reject repentance and embrace his own destruction illustrates the tragic outcome of his hardened heart and the ultimate rejection of grace.

Mary Magdalene: Mary Magdalene holds a prominent place in the Bible, second only to the Virgin Mary in terms of female honor. Despite this, she is often misidentified as the sinful woman who anointed Jesus's feet in Luke 7:36-50—a misconception that has plagued her reputation. Mary Magdalene was a devoted follower of Jesus, supporting Him and the Twelve from her own resources. Standing by the cross with Jesus's mother, she was present at the Crucifixion. Significantly, she was the first to witness the Resurrection and is often referred to as the "Apostle to the Apostles." Medieval texts such as the "Golden Legend" describe Mary Magdalene in various roles. One account depicts her as a fervent preacher who challenged idol worshipers and proclaimed Christ.

Another version suggests that she lived in seclusion for thirty years in the wilderness, a place prepared by angels.

The Catholic Encyclopedia presents several traditions about her later life. Per the Greek Church, Mary Magdalene retired to Ephesus with the Virgin Mary, where she eventually died, and her relics were later moved to Constantinople in 886. French tradition, however, tells of her fleeing the Holy Land to France, where she spent her final years in seclusion in a cave near the Sainte-Baume mountains. Today, the Sanctuary of Mary Magdalene stands at this site, and some of her relics are reportedly housed in a church in Aix-en-Provence, France. The Diocese of Frejus-Toulon records that her sarcophagus was discovered under the Basilica of Saint Maximin in 1279, and a papyrus dated 710 was found confirming that the bones belonged to Saint Mary Magdalene. Mystic Anne Catherine Emmerich offers a controversial perspective on Mary Magdalene. While she refutes the notion of Magdalene as a prostitute, Emmerich describes her as being sexually promiscuous and vain. According to Emmerich, Magdalene was the youngest of fifteen children in the family of Lazarus. She was notably beautiful but frivolous and seductive. Her vanity and indulgence led to a scandalous reputation, especially after inheriting her family's castle in Magdalum. Emmerich portrays Magdalene as being at odds with her simpler siblings and engaging in morally questionable behavior with soldiers and officers. Despite her past, Jesus assured Martha that Mary Magdalene would be converted, and Matthew expressed concern about her demonic possession due to her estrangement from her family. One day, as Mary Magdalene sat by her window, Jesus and His disciples passed by. Jesus looked at her with a penetrating gaze that deeply affected her. Overwhelmed by a profound sense of her own misery, Magdalene was driven to hide in a refuge for people with leprosy and those afflicted with bodily flux. When she later returned home with Lazarus, she felt intense humiliation and a broken spirit. Despite all of this, she couldn't separate herself from her surroundings, feeling pale and disheartened. The man she lived with, with his vulgar and lowly views, became increasingly distasteful to her. In search of redemption, she traveled

to Damna with her sister Martha to hear Jesus speak. Inspired by His words, she trembled and wept beneath her veil. Later that evening, Simon Zabulon and other Pharisees invited Jesus to dine with them. Magdalene, unable to contain her emotion, entered the hall and poured the contents of a flask of precious ointment over Jesus's head, using her hair to catch any overflow. Simon Zabulon was scandalized, but Jesus responded, "She, out of love, has fulfilled what you left undone." Turning to Magdalene, He said, "Go in peace! Much has been forgiven you." Transformed by this encounter, Magdalene spoke fervently about Jesus's majesty and miracles. She felt compelled to follow Him, convinced that her former life was unworthy. Despite her resolve, the devil intensified his attacks, leading to episodes of possession, cramps, and convulsions. After being freed from her demons, Magdalene took on a penitential robe and often anointed Jesus's feet with fine fragrance, wiping them with her hair. She repeated this act of devotion frequently. Before His Ascension, Jesus instructed her to live in seclusion in the wilderness, assuring her of His constant presence. Legend has it that Magdalene lived for thirty years in a cave in France, known today as the Grotte de Sainte Marie Magdalen in Sainte-Baume. Two captivating legends further enrich her story. In one, she reportedly confronted Emperor Tiberius Caesar in Rome, holding an egg in her hand. When Tiberius mocked her, saying that Jesus's resurrection was as improbable as the egg turning red, the egg miraculously changed color. As a result of her proclamation about Pilate's injustice, Tiberius removed Pilate from Jerusalem. Another legend recounts that on Easter Sunday, Magdalene, searching for Jesus at the tomb, found her white eggs miraculously turned red. These stories contributed to early Christian traditions, leading to the custom of handing out red eggs.

The Holy Grail: The Gospels provide scant details about the Holy Grail. John does not mention it at all, while Matthew, Mark, and Luke simply state, "Then He took the cup." The fate of the Holy Grail remains a mystery. Over time, legends have emerged suggesting that either Mary Magdalene or Joseph of Arimathea used the Grail to collect the blood of Jesus from His cross. Between the 12th and 15th centuries, more than ten different chalices were claimed to be the true Holy Grail used by Jesus. Many believed that the Grail possessed extraordinary powers, ranging from healing to granting immortality. Even Adolf Hitler's Nazis sought it out. The Holy Grail gained widespread popularity through various modern media, including the films "Monty Python and the Holy Grail," "Indiana Jones," and Dan Brown's book "The Da Vinci Code," which proposed that the Grail was not a physical chalice but rather the bloodline of Jesus through Mary Magdalene. One intriguing legend suggests that the Angel Gabriel instructed Joseph of Arimathea to flee to Glastonbury with the Grail and the blood of Jesus. Joseph is said to have buried the Grail in a large mound in Glastonbury, now known as Chalice Hill. Another prominent legend holds that Joseph of Arimathea and Saint Peter took the Grail to Rome, where the Popes used it until 258 A.D., when Roman Emperor Valerianus persecuted Catholic bishops. According to this tradition, a loyal Vatican soldier smuggled the Grail to Spain. This legend continues with Saint Lawrence, a deacon under Pope Sixtus II, who allegedly escaped with the Grail and brought it to Spain, the homeland of his parents. The Grail is said to be housed today in the Cathedral of Valencia, known as the Santo Caliz of Valencia. This chalice, made from red agate and adorned with rubies, emeralds, and pearls, has been used in ceremonies by Pope Paul II in 1982 and Pope Benedict XVI in 2006. The Vatican asserts that this is the actual Holy Chalice. Numerous other legends exist about the Holy Grail. Some stories suggest it was used by King Solomon, guarded by the Knights Templar, or hidden in the Sun Temple of Mesopotamia. The Persian King Jamshid is said to have discovered the Grail while excavating an ancient city in Asia. Mystic Anne Catherine Emmerich provides a detailed and surprising account of the Holy Grail. She described seeing the Chalice of the Last Supper on the altar of Noah's Ark, brought there by three figures in long white garments, reminiscent of the visitors who announced Isaac's birth to Abraham. According to Emmerich, the Chalice later belonged to one of Sem's descendants in Canaan, associated with Melchizedek, who used it at the Last Supper. She described the Chalice as a brownish precious stone with small cups, used by Melchizedek to offer wine, and later

by Jesus. Emmerich described the Chalice as a magnificent and mysterious vessel, initially lying forgotten in the Temple before being rediscovered and sold to antiquarians. Veronica, a devotee, then returned it to Jesus, who used it multiple times during His ministry and at the Last Supper. The Chalice was large, with six small beakers surrounding it, and a small plate and spoon attached. It had a pear-shaped cup of highly polished brown metal, overlaid with gold and featuring elaborate decorations, including a serpent motif and grape designs. The larger Chalice was entrusted to the Church of Jerusalem under James the Less, while the smaller beakers were distributed to other churches. Emmerich further claimed that the Chalice, once belonging to Abraham and used by Melchizedek, had been in Noah's possession, and later held by Moses. Its origins were shrouded in mystery, known only to Jesus.

As I conclude this chapter, I recognize that the exploration of mystical visions and historical narratives can be both deeply enriching and, at times, challenging, provided the human thirst for knowledge. Blessed Anne Catherine Emmerich, renowned for her extraordinary visions of the past, present, and future, offers insights that stretch beyond the traditional understanding of biblical and historical events. Her detailed accounts, while not part of the authorized Scriptures, provide thought-provoking perspectives on the life of Jesus Christ and the spiritual dimensions of His mission. What I find compelling about Emmerich's visions is that they don't contradict the core truths of the faith; rather, they illuminate them in new and profound ways. Her revelations, along with those of other mystics, give us a glimpse into the deeper mysteries of God's plan of salvation, shedding light on the life and Passion of Christ in ways that invite contemplation and awe.

These insights invite us to ponder over the mysteries of our faith, helping us to see with greater clarity the beauty of Christ's sacrifice and the profound spiritual truths that underpin the life of the Church. For me, these mystical experiences are not a replacement for Scripture or the teachings of the Church, but rather a beautiful complement—offering deeper insight into the eternal truths of the faith. They help to enrich my understanding of God's love and His presence in the world, encouraging me to live my faith with greater devotion and reverence. This is why I believe in the beauty and truth of the Catholic faith: it is a faith that is both ancient and living, grounded in the sacred Scriptures, and continually revealed through the lived experiences of saints and mystics who have encountered the divine in extraordinary ways. The richness of this tradition, which draws on both historical fact and mystical insight, is a testimony to the profound depth of God's love and the ongoing revelation of His truth in the world.

Here are a few notable insights from her writings:

- **Humanity's Purpose:** Emmerich claimed that humanity was created to fill the choirs of the fallen angels. According to her, had Adam not fallen, the human race would have continued until it reached the number of the fallen angels, and then the world would have ended. The world, she suggested, will not end until the "wheat is separated from the chaff," fulfilling the purpose of creation.

- **Adam and Eve's Refuge:** Emmerich described how Adam and Eve, after their expulsion from Eden, took refuge in a cave that Jesus later visited during His agony in Gethsemane. This cave, she believed, was the same place where Jesus prayed before His crucifixion.

- **Burial Site of Adam and Eve:** According to Emmerich, Adam and Eve were buried at "The Place of Skulls," the location where Jesus was crucified, linking the origins of humanity with the redemption brought by Christ.

- **Lazarus's Aunt:** Emmerich mentioned that Lazarus's aunt served as a teacher and nurse to Mary when she was raised in the temple, indicating a close connection between Lazarus's family and the holy family.

- **The Three Kings:** Emmerich's account of the Magi includes names and details not found in the Bible. She identified them as Mensor, Seit, and Theokeno, each bringing different gifts to the infant Jesus and being baptized later by Saint Thomas. The names Caspar, Melchior, and Balthasar were ascribed to them based on their qualities and gifts.

- **Herod's Decree:** Emmerich claimed that King Herod ordered the murder of approximately seven hundred innocent children, expanding on the biblical account of the massacre of the innocents.

- **The Cross and the Crucifixion:** Emmerich described the Cross as being fifteen feet long and noted that angels assisted Jesus in lifting it. She also recounted that at Jesus's death, the earth quaked and the rock near the cross split, causing a universal sense of dread.

- **Descent into Hell:** She detailed Jesus's descent into Hell, where He triumphed over demons and encountered the soul of Judas. Emmerich reported that Lucifer was securely chained and would be Emmerich's visions and writings, rich in vivid detail, offer a unique window into the spiritual and historical context of Jesus's life and the early Christian era. However, they remain a matter of personal faith and interpretation. For me, they deepen my understanding of the Gospel narratives, helping to fill in gaps and offer additional layers of insight. But, as the Apostle, the brother of James reminds us in his Gospel (21:24-25), the full scope of Jesus's life and works is beyond our capacity to fully document: "This is the disciple who testifies to these things and has written them down, and we know that his testimony is true. There are also many other things that Jesus did; if every one of them were written down, I suppose that even the world itself could not contain the books that would be written."

This passage resonates with me as I reflect on the writings of mystics like Emmerich. Although her detailed accounts are not part of the biblical canon, they offer a valuable glimpse into the ongoing revelation of God's mysteries. I believe that through such mystical experiences, God continues to guide His people, providing deeper insights into the richness of His Word. These visions do not replace or contradict Scripture, but rather they enhance and deepen our understanding of it. In this way, they help me connect more profoundly with the stories I know, allowing me to contemplate Christ's life and mission on a deeper level. In addition to Emmerich's visions, I am fascinated by the way Jesus's life impacts not only the Christian world but also cultures beyond it. For instance, in the "History of the Latter Han Dynasty," Emperor Guangwu documented supernatural events that occurred around the time of Jesus's crucifixion and resurrection, including a solar eclipse and other cosmic signs. These records from ancient China show that Jesus's influence was recognized widely, transcending time and culture. To me, this affirms the universality of Christ's message and the profound impact of His life and resurrection. For those seeking answers, traditional religious study and prayer offer profound guidance. The Church's Scripture, Tradition, and teachings provide a reliable path to understanding. While some may explore mystical or psychic readings, I find the Church's faith and study offer a deeper and more trustworthy grasp of truth.

In summary, faith is a personal and enriching journey. Whether through mystical experiences, historical study, or Scripture, seeking truth in faith strengthens our relationship with God. For me, this journey is rooted in the Catholic faith, encouraging exploration and finding peace in God's love and revelation. I believe because my exploration continually reveals the depth of God's truth.

Chapter Thirteen
Believe it or Not-Part Deux

Blessed Mary: A Special Exploration

As I reflect more on the role of Mary, the Mother of Jesus, I take pride in dedicating an entire chapter to her, given the profound and far-reaching significance she holds within the Catholic faith. While the Bible mentions Mary in relatively few passages, her life and importance have inspired countless works of art, literature, music, and devotion throughout the centuries. For many, Mary embodies the ultimate example of grace, humility, and maternal love. However, despite her deep significance in the Church, and the thousands of books, pieces of music, art, and churches dedicated to her honor, some Protestant perspectives downplay her role, viewing her as simply an ordinary mother. In these viewpoints, Mary is not seen as a source of grace or intercession, and doctrines such as her perpetual virginity and Immaculate Conception are often rejected or misunderstood. These

differences in belief can be challenging, but I believe they reflect the larger mystery of faith—where understanding doesn't always come immediately, and deeper truths unfold gradually over time. For me, the richness of Mary's story goes far beyond these theological debates. While the Scriptures offer glimpses into her life—such as the Annunciation, the Visitation, and her presence at the Cross—much of our deeper understanding of her role comes from mystical revelations and the writings of saints throughout history. One of the most beautiful and profound works in this regard is *The City of God* by the mystic Mary of Agreda. In this detailed and insightful account, we find a portrayal of Mary's life that not only enhances our understanding of her holiness but also illuminates the unique role she plays in the salvation history of humanity.

I believe that Mary's life serves as a powerful model of faith, obedience, and trust in God's plan. Her willingness to say "yes" to God at the Annunciation is not just a historical moment, but a profound act of cooperation with divine grace that continues to inspire and guide us today. Mary is not merely a figure in the story of salvation; but she is an active participant, chosen by God to bring His Son into the world. Her role as Mother of the Church continues to echo throughout the ages. Why I believe in the beauty and truth of the Catholic faith is because it invites us to recognize and honor the fullness of Mary's role in God's plan for salvation. Through the Church's teachings, sacred tradition, and the witness of saints and mystics, we are led to a deeper understanding of Mary—not as an ordinary woman, but as a powerful intercessor, a source of grace, and a model of perfect discipleship. In her, I see a reflection of the Church itself—always open to receiving and nurturing the grace of God. Mary draws us closer to Christ, guiding us into a deeper relationship with the love and truth of God. The following information is a condensed synoptics from the writings of mystics like Anne Catherine Emmerich, Mary of Agreda, and Saint Bridget.

Mary was born on September 8, pure and radiant, free from the stain of original sin. From an early age, she was dedicated to the

temple by her parents and raised in a sacred environment filled with prayer, devotion, and learning. At just three years old, she was entrusted to the care of the prophetess Anne in the temple, where she made solemn vows of chastity, obedience, and poverty, renouncing all worldly attachments in service to God. Around the age of thirteen and a half, Mary received divine guidance to marry, and at the age of fourteen, she was betrothed to Joseph, who was thirty-three at the time. Six months and seventeen days after their marriage, the Incarnation of Jesus took place. When Mary's pregnancy became apparent, Joseph, troubled by the circumstances and their mutual vows of chastity, considered divorcing her quietly. However, an angel appeared to him in a dream, reassuring him of God's plan and urging him to take Mary as his wife. The journey to Bethlehem took five days. Upon their arrival, Mary and Joseph faced rejection at over fifty locations before finally finding shelter in a humble cave just outside the city. The night of Jesus's birth was marked by celestial ecstasy, as Mary remained in a state of divine rapture, her heart and soul united with the miracle of the Savior's birth. Jesus was miraculously delivered, preserving Mary's virginity in a sign of God's miraculous grace. According to Church tradition, Jesus was born at midnight on a Sunday, in the year 5199 Anno Mundi (the year of the world). After the birth of Jesus, the Holy Family fled to Egypt to escape King Herod's decree, seeking refuge until it was safe to return. They returned to Nazareth when Jesus was seven years old, where they lived quietly and humbly for the next twenty-three years, nurturing and protecting the Son of God, awaiting the time when His mission would be revealed to the world.

At thirty, Jesus sought Mary's permission to begin His public ministry. As His mother, she understood the gravity of His mission and gave her consent, fully supporting Him in His divine calling. Mary, along with many other devout women, accompanied Jesus throughout His ministry, providing support to Him and His Apostles. Her presence was a testament to her unwavering faith and her unique role in God's plan. During the Last Supper, a profound moment occurred when Mary received the Eucharist from the angel Gabriel.

This sacred event underscored her singular participation in the divine mysteries and her intimate connection to the work of salvation. Before Jesus's Passion, Mary made a heartfelt request to share in His sufferings. She longed to experience the depth of His physical and emotional anguish, so that she might fully unite with Him in His redemptive sacrifice. God granted this request, and Mary endured a level of suffering so intense that it could have been fatal had not divine intervention mitigated it. Despite her profound sorrow at witnessing her Son's suffering and death, Mary retained her awareness of the promise of His resurrection. She knew when and where the risen Christ would appear to her.

In 40 A.D., following the persecution of early Christians, Mary, along with Saint John, moved to Ephesus, where they continued to live in prayer and service. As Mary neared the end of her earthly life, she shared her wisdom, insights, and memories with the Gospel writers, providing them with invaluable perspectives on the life and teachings of Jesus. At the age of 67, the angel Gabriel came to Mary, informing her that her time on earth was ending. When the moment came, at the age of 70, Mary peacefully passed away at 3 p.m. on Friday, August 13. God offered her the choice of entering heaven immediately or passing through death as her Son had done. In perfect union with Jesus, Mary chose death, desiring to follow him and experience the fullness of her participation in the salvation story.

As Mary's earthly life concluded, a radiant light enveloped her body. A procession of angels carried her sacred body to her tomb, and the people of Jerusalem were divinely inspired to witness this miraculous event. Along the route, many miracles occurred, as the sick and afflicted were healed simply by being in the presence of Mary's body. The Apostle Saint Thomas, who seemed to have missed the funeral, requested to see Mary's body. When the tomb was opened, it was found empty—her body had been assumed into heaven by God, in a glorious moment that mirrored the resurrection of her Son. This miraculous assumption into heaven occurred precisely now Jesus had risen from the grave, completing the divine circle of life,

death, and resurrection that was fulfilled in both Mother and Son. This event, known as the Assumption, is a powerful reminder of the unique role Mary plays in salvation history—her complete cooperation with God's will, her total faith in His promises, and her share in the glory of eternal life. For me, this story affirms the beauty and truth of the Catholic faith, which celebrates the dignity of Mary as the Mother of God, and her continuing role in bringing us closer to her Son, Jesus Christ.

To all my Protestant friends, I understand that the Catholic veneration of Mary might confuse you a bit, but I want to clarify that Catholics do not worship Mary. Instead, we venerate her. Veneration is a profound expression of respect, admiration, and reverence for someone who holds a special place in God's plan. Worship, on the other hand, is reserved for God alone. When Jesus says in John 14:6, *"I am the way, and the truth, and the life. No one comes to the Father except through me,"* I agree wholeheartedly. Jesus is indeed the only mediator between God and man. Again, to my Protestant friends, it's never about Mary! It's through her intercession that many suffering souls are brought closer to God. Consider the story of the Wedding at Cana. Mary tells Jesus, *"They have no wine."* (John 2:3) Jesus responds, *"What is this to me? My hour has not come."* (John2:4) But Mary, with a sense of urgency, essentially says, "If not now, when?" She then instructs the servants, *"Do whatever He tells you."* (John2:5) Mary's role here shows how her intercession leads others to Jesus, guiding them toward God's grace. This passage shows that through Mary intercession one can find Jesus.

In the Catholic faith, we understand the communion of saints to mean that those who are united with God, both in heaven and on earth, can intercede on our behalf. The Bible itself supports the idea of intercessory prayer, and there are several passages that encourage us to pray for one another and seek the intercession of others:

- **Romans 15:30**: "Join me by your prayers to God on my behalf."

- **2 Thessalonians 3:1**: "Brothers, pray for us."

- **Ephesians 6:18-19**: "Pray for all the saints and for me."

- **Tobit 12:12**: The angel presents Tobit and Sarah's prayers to God.

- **Matthew 18:10**: "Angels in heaven always behold the face of God."

- **Revelation 5:8**: "The angels offer the prayers of the holy ones to God."

These verses indicate that prayer and intercession are central to the Christian life. Just as we ask our friends and family to pray for us, so too can we ask the saints in heaven—those closest to God—to intercede on our behalf. The veneration of Mary and the saints is not about placing them above God, but about recognizing their holiness and their unique role in leading us closer to Christ. For me, the practice of seeking the intercession of Mary and the saints enriches my faith. It does not take away from Christ's significant role in salvation but rather deepens my understanding of the Christian family—those on earth, in heaven, and in purgatory—united in prayer and love. Mary, as the Mother of Jesus, holds a special place as our spiritual mother, and her intercession is a powerful gift that brings us closer to her Son. I believe that asking for her prayers, and those of all the saints, strengthens my relationship with God and helps me grow in faith.

Mary and Jesus' hearts are deeply intertwined. Wherever Mary's heart goes, so does Jesus's, and vice versa. This profound unity is central to my understanding of the relationship between Mary and her Son, Jesus. When I pray to Mary for intercession, I am asking her to bring my petitions before Jesus, much like when my young

children would hesitate to ask their mother directly but would ask me to make the request for them. In the same way, seeking the intercession of Mary or the saints is not about bypassing Jesus or God but about recognizing the saints' intimate connection to the Divine. Their prayers, offered on our behalf, are a way of joining in the communion of saints, all of us united in Christ. In this sense, our prayers to Mary and the saints are fully aligned with the spirit of John 14:6, where Jesus tells us, *"I am the way, and the truth, and the life. No one comes to the Father except through me."* I believe that asking Mary to intercede on our behalf does not diminish Christ's vital role as the Mediator between God and man, but rather acknowledges the saints' special role in leading us closer to Jesus. Just as we ask our friends and family to pray for us, we ask the saints, who are already in the presence of God, to join in our petitions, trusting that they, too, will direct us to the heart of Christ. Mary is much more than just the Mother of God. In her, we see the fullness of grace, a woman completely open to God's will.

According to the mystic Mary of Agreda, Mary's conception and development in her mother's womb were marked by extraordinary gifts. God imparted to her profound insights into His creation, the angels, heaven, earth, and the divine plan for her to become the Mother of the Savior. From the very moment of her conception, Mary was granted a unique understanding of everything that would unfold in her life and in the life of Jesus. She was born without sin, free from original sin, and endowed with extraordinary gift; gifts that included the ability to read minds and even heal others. I believe that Mary's special role in salvation history is a testament to God's love and plan for humanity. Her free and total cooperation with God's will—her fiat, her "yes" to the angel's message—set in motion the course of salvation. Her sinlessness, her deep connection to Jesus, and her role as our spiritual mother make her the perfect intercessor for us. I believe that her intercession brings us closer to Jesus, who is the way, the truth, and the life. Through Mary, we find a pathway to deeper intimacy with Christ and a greater understanding of God's love for all of us.

As Mary and Joseph fled to Egypt to escape King Herod's decree, their presence brought about profound and dramatic disruptions in the local idolatry. According to various mystical accounts, the idols in the temples fell, altars were shattered, and false gods were overthrown as Mary, embodying the Wisdom of God, began to reveal the truth of the one true God. Her very presence caused a ripple effect, leading to conversions as people witnessed the power of God manifest through her. Miracles occurred, demons were cast out, and many were healed as Jesus, Mary, and Joseph moved through Egypt, bringing divine grace wherever they went.

Despite her extraordinary gifts—gifts that included her immaculate conception, profound wisdom, and special relationship with God—Mary remained humble and obedient throughout Jesus's ministry. She never sought to draw attention to herself but instead dedicated her life to supporting and nurturing Jesus, fully aware that her mission was to bring others closer to Him. Mary, the perfect model of humility, never used her supernatural gifts for personal gain or glory, but always in service to God's will. Before His ascension, Jesus entrusted Mary to the care of the Apostles and disciples, calling her to be their mother, Mediatrix, and Advocate. In this role, Mary continues to intercede for us, guiding us toward Christ with the same maternal love and care she showed to the early Church. I believe that Mary's role as Mediatrix and Advocate reflects her profound connection to Jesus, her Son, and her continued participation in God's plan of salvation. For me, this understanding of Mary's role deepens my belief in the beauty and truth of the Catholic faith. Mary is not merely a passive figure in the background of the Gospel story; she is an active participant in God's redemptive plan, and her intercession continues to draw us closer to Christ. Through her example of humility, obedience, and love, Mary teaches us how to live out our faith more fully, pointing always to her Son, the Savior of the world.

At the moment of Mary's creation, Lucifer recognized a threat he could not overcome: a woman who would become the Mistress and Queen of all creation, the one destined to bring forth the Savior of the

world. This knowledge filled him with intense fear and hatred, fueling his bitter opposition to both Christ and His Holy Mother. This ancient enmity is foretold in the vision of the Apocalypse, where a woman clothed with the sun stands poised to crush the serpent's head—a symbol of Mary's ultimate triumph over evil.

In the mystical writings of Mary of Agreda, we gain a deeper insight into Mary's role in Heaven. Upon her entrance into the celestial realm, Mary is immediately exalted to the right hand of her Son, sharing in the divine throne alongside the Holy Trinity. In this exalted position, she is crowned as the Empress of Heaven, granted authority over all creation, and given dominion over hell and its demons. The Lord decreed that Mary would be the Empress and Mistress of the Church, a Protectress, Advocate, Mother, and Teacher. In this role, she watches over all of humanity, especially those who call upon her with sincerity, offering her powerful intercession in their trials and struggles.

This vision of Mary as the Queen of Heaven and Earth empowers my belief in the beauty and truth of the Catholic faith. It highlights not only Mary's unique dignity as the Mother of God but also her active and ongoing participation in God's plan of salvation. I believe that Mary's role as the Protectress and Advocate of the Church is not just a symbolic title, but a very real and powerful presence in our lives. As Catholics, we recognize her as a mother who deeply cares for us, offering her guidance, protection, and intercession in a way that draws us closer to her Son. I understand that there are significant differences between how Protestants and Catholics view Mary, and these differences can be contentious at times. However, I believe that Mary's role as the Mother of the Church and her special relationship with God is a truth that resonates deeply within the Catholic faith. It is not about elevating Mary above Christ but recognizing the unique role she plays in pointing us to Him. Through Mary, we see an example of perfect obedience, humility, and love. Her life shows us how to say "yes" to God's will, and in doing so, she helps us draw nearer to Jesus, the way, the truth, and the life.

I've observed that some Protestant writers, like John MacArthur, offer strong critiques of Catholic veneration of Mary. In his book *Twelve Ordinary Men* and *Twelve Extraordinary Women*, MacArthur provides valuable insights into many biblical figures, including several women of the Bible. However, his treatment of Mary seems to carry a dismissive tone. MacArthur argues that various extrabiblical traditions have elevated Mary to an undue status, attributing to her titles and attributes that he believes should belong solely to God. He suggests that some Catholics view Mary as more approachable and sympathetic than Christ, which he finds problematic. In his view, Catholic dogma—such as the belief in Mary's perpetual virginity, her immaculate conception, and her bodily assumption into heaven—represents an exaggerated elevation of her role. He also critiques the devotion shown to Mary by some Catholics, including beliefs in her apparitions and prophecies. MacArthur goes further to criticize the emphasis placed on Marian devotion by figures like Pope John Paul II, claiming that it may distract from the centrality of Christ. He expresses concern that such reverence for Mary could overshadow the worship of Jesus and diminish His supremacy.

These criticisms reflect a broader divide between Protestant and Catholic perspectives on Mary. While Catholics view her as an essential figure in salvation history—honoring her with deep veneration and recognizing her unique role in God's plan of redemption—some Protestants see these practices as excessive or inconsistent with their interpretation of Scripture. This difference underscores a theological divergence about Mary's role in Christianity. It's disheartening to see the misunderstandings surrounding Marian devotion. Contrary to what critics like MacArthur suggest, Catholics do not idolize Mary or view her as a deity. Rather, we honor her as a beloved and significant figure in salvation history. Her role as a messenger of love, grace, and warning is firmly rooted in both Catholic tradition and Scripture.

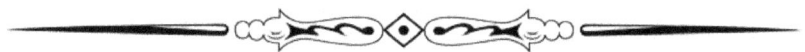

Mary's significance in Christianity is profoundly reflected in her role as the New Eve, whose obedience in accepting the mission to become the Mother of Christ counteracts the disobedience of Eve in the Garden of Eden. As the Mother of Christ, she becomes the Mother of the Church, symbolizing the reversal of Eve's fall through her faithful acceptance of God's plan. Her pivotal role was recognized early on in Christian history, with references to her found in texts like the *Protoevangelium of James* and in the writings of early Church Fathers such as Ignatius of Antioch, who lived around A.D. 110. By the fourth century, long before the Protestant Reformation, Mary was already venerated as *co-redemptrix* in Syrian Christian devotion.

Mary's humility and purity have stirred hatred in Satan, who cannot endure her goodness and compassion. Throughout history, she has come to us in times of societal turmoil, offering comfort and guidance in moments of crisis. Her apparitions are not just relics of the past but ongoing events, with the International Marian Research Institute at the University of Dayton noting thousands of significant Marian apparitions, many of which have gone unreported. Mary's presence has been felt during times of intense suffering, such as early Christian persecutions, the Council of Nicaea, and periods of plague and war.

In the Americas, Mary's influence has been equally profound. Christopher Columbus invoked her as he sailed the *Santa Maria*, and the first Christian prayer in the Western Hemisphere was the *Salve Regina*. The Mississippi River was originally named the "River of the Immaculate Conception," and Los Angeles was once known as "Saint Mary Queen of the Angels of the Portiuncola." From the very beginning of Christian history, Mary has been a beacon of hope and faith, helping to replace paganism with the worship of the one true God.

Mary's role in Christianity is not to draw attention to herself, but to point us toward her Son, Jesus, guiding us on the path to eternal life. Her veneration is widespread across the Christian world, with her

images and churches serving as a testament to her continued significance in the lives of countless believers, pointing to her leading role in God's redemptive plan for humanity.

In his book *The Last Secret*, Michael Brown recounts a fascinating account of a Marian apparition involving George Washington. During the harsh winter of 1777 at Valley Forge, Washington experienced a profound and unsettling encounter. As he prepared a dispatch, a remarkably beautiful woman unexpectedly visited him. Despite his strict orders to avoid disturbances, Washington found himself unable to speak or move, captivated by her gaze. The apparition, described as having a mysterious and irresistible presence, did not respond to his repeated questions. Washington then reportedly heard a voice instructing him, "Son of the Republic, look and learn," as the apparition extended an arm eastward. He then witnessed a vision of a white vapor that gradually revealed a panorama of the world, showing a cloud rising from Europe and America that moved westward.

Another compelling story of Marian intercession occurred close to home. On the frosty night of January 7, 1815, in New Orleans, the Ursuline Sisters and many local citizens gathered in the Ursuline Chapel of Our Lady of Consolation. They fervently prayed before a golden-painted statue of the Blessed Mother, known as "Our Lady of Prompt Succor." Their prayers were for the protection of New Orleans, as the city faced an imminent threat from a British force of over 7,500 soldiers preparing to attack a much smaller, poorly equipped American army of about 4,000 under General Andrew Jackson. Mother Superior Marie Francis Olivier de Vezin vowed to hold an annual Mass of thanksgiving for Our Lady of Prompt Succor if the American forces were spared significant losses. Despite being heavily outnumbered, the American troops experienced a miraculous turn of events. A dense fog rolled over the battlefield, obscuring the American positions from the advancing British troops. The ensuing battle was swift and decisive, with General Pakenham and 2,000 British soldiers killed, while the American casualties were minimal—

only eight killed and thirteen wounded. On January 23, 1815, a Mass of Thanksgiving was celebrated at Saint Louis Cathedral, attended by General Jackson and his staff. General Jackson also personally visited the Ursuline Sisters to thank them for their prayers. To this day, a Mass is held every January 8 at Saint Louis Cathedral, honoring the promise made by Mother Superior. Visitors can still see the golden statue of Our Lady of Prompt Succor, the "Patroness of Louisiana," at the National Shrine on State Street in uptown New Orleans. Remarkably, despite the extensive damage caused by Hurricane Katrina, the statue remained unharmed.

I want to share a very personal and remarkable experience involving a private Marian apparition. On April 27, 2013, I was part of a small group—ten of us in total—gathered at the home of a devout friend, Patty Ardoin, to attend a private Mass. Two priests celebrated the Mass: my godfather, retired Monsignor Charles Mallet, and Father Joseph Fazio. We had come together to meet an elderly woman named Claire Rose Champagne, who had been receiving private Marian apparitions since the age of twelve. Mrs. Claire, who was well-known to the Bishop of Houma, Louisiana, had received official approval from the Church for her revelations. Prior to that day, only Patty and her daughter Danielle were familiar with Mrs. Claire's experiences.

Before the Mass began, we were offered the opportunity to go to confession. I was quietly reciting the Rosary next to Mrs. Claire when something extraordinary happened—she suddenly went into a trance and began writing. It was clear that she was experiencing a vision of the Blessed Mother. After confession, Claire set down her pen, and the Mass continued as planned. But during the consecration of the Eucharist, she entered another trance. After the Mass, Mrs. Claire whispered something to Danielle, who then approached Father Fazio. After listening to Danielle, Father Fazio's eyes widened, and he responded, "Yes, by all means!" Danielle then informed us that Mrs. Claire had received a letter from the Blessed Mother, but before it could be read, Father Fazio's permission was needed. After

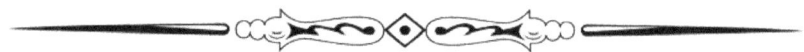

receiving his approval, Danielle read the astonishing letter aloud to us.

To fully appreciate this experience, I need to share an earlier event. About a year prior, I had attended a retreat at the Cajun Dome in Lafayette, Louisiana, led by Immaculée Ilibagiza, a survivor of the Rwandan genocide and a renowned author. During the retreat, I heard a quiet cry for help from a woman several rows behind me. Upon reaching her, I found an elderly woman collapsed on the floor, unresponsive, with her daughter in a panic. At first, I thought the woman had passed away, as I couldn't detect a pulse. But by the time EMS arrived, she had begun to revive. This event led to a deep friendship with the woman, Patty Ardoin, who later shared that she had, in fact, died during that moment and had found herself in the "Throne Room" of God, where He told her it wasn't her time yet.

In time, Patty introduced me to Mrs. Claire, which eventually led to our meeting and the remarkable letter from the Blessed Mother. After Patty passed away, Mrs. Claire said to me, "When Danielle called me that morning to inform me of Patty's death, I already knew. Patty came to me around 2 a.m. to tell me she was in Heaven. At Patty's funeral, Mrs. Claire described seeing her as "beautiful, luminous, and covered in gold." Mrs. Claire Rose Champagne passed away last year, and I believe she is now in Heaven, alongside the Blessed Mother and Patty.

As promised, here are the four pages of the letter dictated by the Blessed Mother to Claire Rose Champagne on April 27, 2013. Whether you believe it or not, I share this story as part of my journey of faith and devotion.

April 29, 2013   Last Saturday   Lafayette, La.

" My Beloved Children,

My Priest Sons and all of My children — I love you! I love you! I love you!

I have chosen and called each one of you to be here today.

This particular day was chosen from long ago as you each were chosen and called from long ago. Thank you My priest sons and My other children for your yes! — Thank you for all you do for My Son Jesus and for your Mother. All that you do for your Mother you do for My Son Jesus.

I love you — I offer to you My Immaculate Heart. I ask

gently - most tenderly for your
heart in return.
Come to your Mother My children.
give to Me all that worries you -
all that troubles you - all that
you are concerned about -
Place all your families and
your lives - all your concerns
into My Hands - Surrender
all My Beloved ones -
surrender all to your Mother.
Consider well My little ones
the greatest mystical gift that
will take place in your midst
in a little while - the transformation
of simple bread and simple
wine into the Body, Blood, Soul
and Divinity of My Beloved Son

Jesus - all for you My children and all through the sacred and holy hands of My priest son e. This is the greatest gift you are given My children -

Prepare your hearts and your souls

I ask you most gently and tenderly to remember My Words to you every time you attend Holy Mass - the Holy Sacrifice.

Keep in mind that where Jesus is Our Father is and The Holy Spirit is - They are One and cannot be separated -

I love you My priest sons and My children - I love you

I love you.

   I have many titles - I am
One Mother - your Mother -
   Mother of Divine Love,
      Patroness of Priests

I ask you to faithfully pray for
holy priests - Your prayer is heard
and will be answered -
I love you. "

"Thank you all for coming."

Blessed Mother appeared twice during the
   Gospel - 1 time during Father's Homily.

During the Chaplet I saw Jesus on the Cross.

3rd Mystery of the Rosary I saw
   Holy Father John Paul II - Padre Pio -
   Mother Theresa and my sister who died last

Purgatory · Hell · Heaven

Chapter Fourteen
Purgatory Is for Real

My eldest sister-in-law has lately been preoccupied with the concept of Purgatory, likely due to her diagnosis of pulmonary fibrosis and her advancing age. During a recent phone call, she joked about the suffering she might face in Purgatory and asked if there was any way to avoid it entirely. In response, I lightheartedly suggested she aim to live a saintly life. Still, I also shared with her what I've come to understand about Purgatory, drawn from the writings of saints and the visions of mystics like those from Medjugorje and Kibeho.

From what I've learned, very few souls are granted the grace of bypassing Purgatory and going straight to Heaven. These are extraordinary individuals, like Mother Teresa or Pope John Paul II, who led lives of exceptional holiness. For most of us, Purgatory is a necessary step—a process of purification before entering the fullness of God's presence. It's said that Purgatory has different stages, with the most intense involving fiery purification. Naturally, you would want to avoid reaching that final, most painful layer. In that context,

I mentioned the 12-Year Prayer of Saint Bridget, which, if prayed with sincere devotion for twelve consecutive years, is believed to spare souls from suffering in Purgatory. My sister-in-law, concerned about her health and the possibility of not completing the full twelve years, asked, "What if I don't make it?" I reassured her that, according to Saint Bridget's revelation, if someone praying this prayer dies before completing the full term, God would accept it as if the full twelve years had been prayed. She immediately requested the prayer, finding comfort in this beautiful grace. In addition, I shared a profound near-death experience involving a dear friend's husband, Bernie, which serves as a powerful testimony about Purgatory, Heaven, and Hell. One day, as I was entering the hospital, I noticed Bernie looking pale and unwell. I greeted him, but he didn't respond. Later, I learned he had just finished a stress test and then suffered a massive heart attack. His wife later shared Bernie's experience with me.

Bernie had been in a coma for about a month, and the doctors had little hope for his recovery due to the severity of the heart damage. But when he finally regained consciousness, he described his experience as either a vivid dream or a near-death encounter. Bernie explained that he was aware of his soul leaving his body and being drawn toward a heart. This heart was mostly purple, with a small section of gold. He was drawn toward the golden side and found himself standing at the gates of Heaven. What he experienced there was beyond description: the beauty, peace, and love were so overwhelming that it was more real than anything he had ever known. Then, Bernie encountered Jesus, who said, "Bernie, you don't belong here." In an instant, Bernie was transported to Hell, where he experienced incredible horrors, one might expect. In desperation, he cried out to Jesus for salvation, and immediately he found himself in Purgatory. There, Bernie was treated kindly, offered food and drink, and found peace and comfort in the loving environment. It wasn't the fiery torment he had feared, but rather a time of gentle purification. Jesus then told him, "It's not your time yet. You must return and make amends before you can return to Me." In the weeks following his experience, Bernie reached out to everyone he knew, sharing his profound revelation: simply being a good person was not enough to enter Heaven. Despite not regularly attending Mass, though he had never cheated in business, loved his family, and treated others with respect, Bernie realized that a deeper, more intimate relationship with God was essential. He made amends and sought reconciliation. On the day of his funeral, Bernie's wife, moved by her faith, prayed for a sign of his heavenly status. During the service, she described feeling, "golden glitter" falling upon her, completely covering her. She felt a deep sense of peace, knowing that Bernie had indeed reached Heaven.

This powerful testimony further affirms the beauty and truth of the Catholic faith. It underscores the importance of purification, not just through the sacraments, but also through the grace of intercessory prayers and penance. Purgatory is not a punishment but a loving, necessary preparation for the beatific vision of God in Heaven. It's a testament to the mercy of God, who offers us a way to become holy even after death, if we have not fully purified ourselves on earth. This story also highlights the profound reality that Heaven, Hell, and Purgatory are not abstract concepts, but real experiences that shape our eternal destinies. It reminds me that salvation isn't simply about avoiding Hell but striving for holiness and union with God— living a life of faith, love, and transformation in Christ. In a world where these truths can seem distant or unacknowledged, stories like Bernie's reaffirm my belief in the beauty of the Catholic faith, in the power of prayer, and in the promise of God's mercy and justice. And, as I share these reflections, I'm reminded of the importance of living each day with the awareness that we are, as the Catechism of the Catholic Church teaches, always on a journey toward God, preparing ourselves for the eternal life He offers.

Many of my Protestant and Catholic friends challenge the doctrine of Purgatory, often arguing that it is a later Catholic invention created to instill guilt and strengthen Catholic beliefs. They frequently point out that the word "Purgatory" is not explicitly found in the Bible, and, therefore, they conclude that the doctrine must be a human-

caused construct. Martin Luther, the key figure in the Protestant Reformation, is often cited in these discussions, as he initially believed in Purgatory but ultimately rejected it. In his "95 Theses" of 1517, Luther made several references to Purgatory, which suggest that, at that time, he still acknowledged its existence:

- "Hell, Purgatory, and Heaven seem to differ the same as despair, fear, and assurance of salvation."

- "Who knows whether all souls in Purgatory wish to be redeemed, since we have exceptions in St. Severinus and St. Paschal, as related in a legend."

- "As a matter of fact, the pope remits to souls in Purgatory no penalty which, according to canon law, they should have paid in this life."

However, by 1521, Luther began to shift his view, suggesting that Purgatory was a personal matter. He argued that praying for the dead could be beneficial but was not essential. He wrote: "Dear God, if this soul is in a condition possible for mercy, be thou gracious to it." By 1524, Luther removed a prayer for the dead from his prayer book, and by 1528, he explicitly rejected the concept of Purgatory altogether. He denounced it as "the greatest falsehood," claiming it was based on "ungodliness and unbelief," as it denied the sufficiency of Christ's sacrifice and instead suggested that satisfaction for sins was required for salvation. Luther's objections are clear: He saw Purgatory as a doctrine that diminished the centrality of faith in Christ for salvation. He also argued that it was a tool for the Church to profit from the faithful by selling indulgences and prayers for the dead, a practice he strongly opposed. He famously declared, "One will search for the Scriptures in vain to find a doctrine of Purgatory," calling it a "lie of the devil" designed to entrap the faithful and enrich the papacy.

While I contemplate Luther's concerns, I find myself wondering: if he rejected Purgatory, where did he believe the souls of the righteous went after death before the resurrection of Christ? If Purgatory, as Luther contended, was a false doctrine, then how did he reconcile the fate of those who died before Christ's redemptive sacrifice on the cross? Consider the righteous figures of the Old Testament—Abel, Melchizedek, Abraham, Noah, Sarah, David, Solomon, and many others. All these people lived lives of faith and virtue, but the gates of Heaven were close to them following the original sin of Adam and Eve. If they were not in Heaven, and Purgatory was not a valid concept, where did their souls reside after death?

Catholic teaching on Purgatory offers a helpful answer, rooted in both Scripture and tradition. Purgatory is not a place of eternal damnation but a temporary state of purification for those who die in God's friendship but still need to be purified before entering Heaven. It is a mercy, not a punishment, allowing us to be fully sanctified before standing in the presence of God. Catholics believe that this doctrine, while not explicitly named in Scripture, is supported by biblical principles like the purification described in 1 Corinthians 3:15, where Paul speaks of a purifying fire that will test each person's works. The question of where the righteous went before Christ's resurrection is also addressed in Catholic theology. The Church teaches that the souls of the righteous—those who lived before Christ—were not damned but were held in a temporary state called the "Limbo of the Fathers" or "Abraham's Bosom." This state was not Heaven, but it was a place of rest and peace, where the righteous awaited Christ's sacrifice. When Jesus descended to the dead after His crucifixion, He opened the gates of Heaven, bringing these souls with Him into eternal glory.

Thus, Purgatory is not some late invention by the Church, but a doctrine deeply rooted in Scripture and the lived experience of the Church. It is a doctrine that acknowledges the holiness of God and the need for purification before entering His presence. It answers the questions about the fate of the righteous before Christ and emphasizes God's mercy and justice in dealing with the souls of the faithful.

Ultimately, I believe in the beauty and truth of the Catholic understanding of Purgatory. It is not a doctrine meant to cause fear, but one meant to encourage holiness and hope—assuring us that, through Christ's grace, we are all given the opportunity to be purified and made worthy to enter the fullness of God's love in Heaven. While the term "Purgatory" is not found in the Bible, it is worth noting that the terms "Incarnation" and "Trinity" are also not biblical in their specific nomenclature but represent doctrines that the Church teaches.

While Martin Luther ultimately rejected the doctrine of Purgatory, several prominent Protestant thinkers have expressed views that are more in line with the concept. For instance, C.S. Lewis once wrote in a letter, "Our souls demand purgatory, don't they?" and he also remarked, "Of course I pray for the dead." In a similar vein, Jerry Walls, a Protestant theologian, delves into the concept of Purgatory in his book *Purgatory: The Logic of Total Transformation*. Walls argues that Purgatory should not be understood as a form of divine retribution or punishment, but rather as a process of sanctification. He acknowledges that this process may be painful, as the experience of God's holy love often exposes the vast difference between divine purity and human imperfection. Karl August von Hase, a 19th-century German Protestant theologian, offered a more nuanced perspective, saying, "Most people when they die are probably too good for Hell, yet surely too bad for Heaven." He further admitted, "It must be frankly confessed that the Protestantism of the Reformers is unclear on this point, its justified denial not yet having advanced to the stage of affirmation."

The Bible contains several passages that many interpret as indirectly referencing Purgatory. For instance, Revelation 21:27 states, "*nothing unclean will enter heaven*," while 1 John 5:16-17 speaks of "*degrees of sins*." In 1 Corinthians 3:15, Saint Paul mentions suffering loss but being "*saved as through fire*," which some see as suggesting a purifying process. Additionally, 1 Peter 3:18-20 describes Jesus preaching to "*the spirits in prison*," and Matthew 5:26 says, "*you will not be released until you have paid the last penny.*"

The Old Testament also offers glimpses of this belief, as seen in 2 Maccabees 12:43-44, where Judas Maccabeus prays for the dead and offers a sin offering, implying a practice of posthumous purification. Saint Paul's words in 1 Corinthians 3:12-15 further hint at Purgatory: *"Now if anyone builds on that foundation with gold, silver, and precious stones, or with wood, hay, and straw, the work of each person will become known. For the day will disclose it, because it will be revealed with fire, and the fire itself will test the worth of each person's work. If what has been built survives, the builder will receive a reward. If it burns up, the builder will suffer loss, but will be saved, yet only as through fire."*

The concept of Purgatory often causes confusion among both Catholics and non-Catholics. Some view it as a temporary hell, while others argue that there is insufficient scriptural evidence for its existence. However, the Catechism of the Catholic Church clarifies the teaching: "All who die in God's grace and friendship, but are still imperfectly purified, are indeed assured of their eternal salvation; but after death, they undergo purification to achieve the holiness necessary to enter the joy of heaven. The Church calls this final purification Purgatory, which is entirely different from the punishment of the damned" (Catechism 1030-1031). Catholic doctrine distinguishes between two types of sin: mortal sin, which severs the soul from God's grace, and venial sin, which only weakens it. Those who die without any sin or need for reparation enter Heaven directly, while those with unrepentant mortal sin go to Hell. Purgatory exists for those who die in a state of grace but still require purification from venial sins or unfinished penance. It is not optional, but a necessary process for those not yet fully purified, as Hebrews 12:14 states: *"Strive for peace with everyone, and for the holiness without which no one will see the Lord."*

Blessed Anne Catherine Emmerich, in her book *The Life of Jesus*, describes a vision of a place of purification. She saw the soul of Jesus entering a realm where the righteous souls awaited their final entry into Heaven. Her vision included different spheres, each representing souls at varying stages of purification or awaiting redemption. While "Purgatory" may not be explicitly used in Scripture, the doctrine is supported by various biblical passages and theological reflections. The Church teaches that Purgatory is a final stage of purification for those who are assured of their ultimate salvation but still require cleansing before they can fully enter the presence of God in Heaven.

In the book "Get Us Out of Here," Nicky Eltz presents an intriguing account of Maria Simma, a mystic from Sonntag, Austria, whose experiences with the souls in Purgatory offer profound insights into this often-misunderstood doctrine. Since 1940, Maria Simma reported that souls in Purgatory visited her to request prayers and intercession. Her encounters were scrutinized by theologians, psychiatrists, her parish priest, and the local bishop, all of whom deemed her sane and credible. The Catholic Church confirmed that her revelations align with Church teachings. Maria passed away in 2004 at the age of eighty-nine. Here are some key excerpts from the book:

- **Who are the Poor Souls?**

  o *Maria's Answer:* The Poor Souls are all the deceased who have not yet entered Heaven. They are those still in Purgatory, awaiting final purification.

- **What exactly is Purgatory?**

  o *Maria's Answer:* Purgatory is both a place and a condition experienced by souls who need to make atonement and reparation for their earthly sins before they can join Jesus in Heaven. It represents a time of waiting and yearning for God, which is their greatest suffering. Purgatory is divided into three main levels, each with further subdivisions. In the lowest level, souls are subject to attacks from Satan, which is not the case in the higher levels. The deepest level involves intense suffering and purification, whereas the higher levels are less severe. This suffering is compared to different kinds of earthly illnesses, where the lowest levels resemble a consuming fire.

- **Do the Poor Souls experience joy and hope?**

- *Maria's Answer:* Yes, the souls do experience joy and hope. Despite their suffering, no soul wishes to return to earth, as their understanding of God is much clearer than ours. The souls long for God and are content in their yearning, which is a sign of their profound realization of divine truth.

- **Does God put the Poor Souls in Purgatory to cleanse them of their sins?***Maria's Answer:* No, this is a misunderstanding. God does not place souls in Purgatory. Instead, the souls choose their Purgatory level based on their desire to be purified. They willingly undertake this purification process to prepare themselves to join God

- **.How long do souls spend in Purgatory before they can enter Heaven?**

- *Maria's Answer:* The duration varies widely. Some souls may spend only a short time, such as half an hour, while others may remain there for centuries. On average, souls report spending about forty years in Purgatory. Maria recounted assisting a soul from 1660 and another from 555.

- **Isn't it said that time no longer exists after death? How does this fit with Purgatory being described as a time of yearning?**

- *Maria's Answer:* This is a complex issue. While time as we understand it may not exist after death, the experience of Purgatory is described in terms of time to convey the process

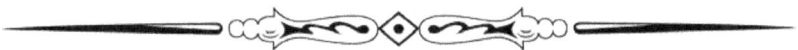

of purification and the depth of the souls' yearning. In their state, the souls experience a form of time as part of their purification journey, even if this concept differs from our earthly understanding of time.

- **Does time exist in Purgatory?**

  o *Maria's Answer:* After death, time as we know it no longer exists. However, when souls refer to needing to suffer for a certain period, this is translated into terms we can understand. These references to time symbolize the intensity and duration of their suffering. The idea of suffering for a certain amount of time or requiring a specific number of Masses is a way to express the level and type of purification they are undergoing.

- **Do the souls in Purgatory have bodies?**

  o *Maria's Answer:* Souls in Purgatory possess transfigured bodies, which can appear similar to healed and dressed human bodies.

- **Do the Poor Souls experience regret?**

  o *Maria's Answer:* Yes, the souls in Purgatory have deep regrets. They lament missed opportunities to do good and help others. Once deceased, they can no longer perform good deeds or earn merits, leading to a profound sense of loss.

- **How much do the souls know about their families?**

  o *Maria's Answer:* The souls in Purgatory are aware of everything concerning their families. They see and hear all that happens, including our words and actions towards them. They even observe their own funerals

and know who is praying for them versus those who are merely present for appearances. However, they do not have access to our inner thoughts.

- **Do the souls appear to their families?**

    o *Maria's Answer:* Yes, but such appearances are rare. Souls typically manifest to those who were particularly caring, sensitive, loving, or prayerful during their lifetime.

- **What about those who knowingly sin, believing they can rely on Purgatory for purification?**

    o *Maria's Answer:* Such individuals will deeply regret their actions. The regret will be more intense for those who knew about Purgatory and chose to sin anyway, compared to those who were unaware of its existence.

- **Are there specific times when more souls are released from Purgatory?**

    o *Maria's Answer:* Yes, certain days see more souls delivered to Heaven. The most significant is Christmas, followed by Good Friday, Ascension Day, and All Saints' Day.

As understood in Catholic teaching, Purgatory is not a belief confined solely to the Catholic tradition. Across various religious and cultural contexts, there are remarkably similar ideas of temporary suffering and purification in the afterlife, even though these concepts may take different forms and names. This shared understanding underscores a universal longing for purification and redemption after death, which aligns beautifully with the Catholic view of Purgatory.

In Karlo Broussard's book, *Purgatory Is for Real*, he explores how the idea of purgation after death appears in several major world religions. This broader perspective deepens my belief in the truth and beauty of Catholic teaching, as it suggests that the Catholic understanding of Purgatory may reflect a deeper, divinely inspired truth about the afterlife.

Hinduism: In Hinduism, the Vedas, which are the ancient sacred texts, refer to *Naraka*, a realm of temporary suffering after death where souls undergo purification for their past misdeeds. Souls in Naraka are not condemned forever but are eventually reborn, depending on the consequences of their actions. This cycle of purification, followed by rebirth, resonates with the Catholic view that souls may undergo purification before they can enter the fullness of Heaven. The use of fire as an agent of purification in both Hinduism and Catholicism, particularly in the imagery of Purgatory, highlights a common theme of refining the soul through trial.

Buddhism: In Buddhism, the concept of *Naraka* is similarly a temporary state, where beings are punished for their negative actions. The duration and nature of their suffering depend on the karmic consequences of their actions. Once their karma is exhausted, they are released to continue their spiritual journey. This aligns with the Catholic understanding of Purgatory, where souls who are not yet pure are temporarily cleansed before being fully united with God. The idea that purification is a necessary step before entering a higher state of being resonates with the Catholic view that we must be purified before entering Heaven.

Zoroastrianism: In Zoroastrianism, at the final judgment, all souls must pass through a river of molten metal. The righteous will find it harmless, while those needing purification will experience it as a test of their soul's worthiness. This process transforms them into pure beings. The imagery of fire as a means of purification here echoes the Catholic teaching of Purgatory, where fire is often used symbolically to represent the refining process through which souls are made pure before entering the presence of God.

Tengrism: In Tengrism, an ancient Central Asian belief system, wicked souls undergo punishment in a realm called *Tamag*. This fire-filled realm serves as a place of purification. After their punishment, the souls are believed to ascend to the third level of the sky. The fire as a means of purification is consistent with the Catholic understanding of how suffering and purification prepare the soul for its final union with God.

Judaism: In Jewish tradition, particularly during the Second Temple and Talmudic periods, there is a belief in a postmortem purification process. The Tosefta, an early Jewish text, describes how some souls undergo purification in *Gehenna* before eventually entering *Gan Eden* (the Garden of Eden). This echoes the Catholic teaching of Purgatory, where souls who have died in God's grace but still need purification undergo a process of cleansing before being allowed into Heaven. Jewish thought on Gehenna suggests a similar belief in a temporary state for souls that are ultimately destined for eternal peace, which aligns with the Catholic vision of Purgatory as a final purification before eternal union with God.

Eastern Orthodox Church: The Eastern Orthodox Church also acknowledges a process of purification for souls after death. The Synod of Jerusalem teaches that souls undergo temporary punishment for their sins, a purification process that prepares them to enter Heaven. This understanding further reinforces the universality of the idea that purification, in some form, is necessary for spiritual perfection and readiness to behold God.

Islam: In Islam, the term *Barzakh* refers to the intermediate state between death and resurrection. In this state, souls who have committed bad deeds endure spiritual suffering in a fire, which purifies them before the final judgment. This intermediate stage serves a similar function to Purgatory in Catholicism, where purification prepares the soul for eternal life in Paradise. The use of fire in both traditions underscore the theme of suffering as a means of purification.

When I contemplate the concept of Purgatory in the broader context of world religions and cultures, I am struck by how universally the idea of purification after death seems to resonate. From Hinduism to Islam, there is a common thread that emphasizes the need for purification, whether through fire, suffering, or a temporary state, before the soul can reach its destination in the presence of God. This universal theme reinforces the beauty and truth of the Catholic understanding of Purgatory, which teaches that God, in His mercy, offers souls a chance to be purified and made holy before entering Heaven. In the Catholic faith, Purgatory is not a punishment but a merciful means of purification for those who have died in God's grace but are not yet perfectly purified. It is an expression of God's love, offering souls the opportunity to be refined and sanctified before they enter eternal joy in Heaven. This understanding brings depth to my belief that God's justice and mercy are perfectly balanced, and that Purgatory is not only a possibility but a necessity for souls who are destined for Heaven. When I see how this concept is reflected across different religions and cultures, it becomes clear to me that the Catholic doctrine of Purgatory aligns with a deeper, shared understanding of the afterlife that transcends individual traditions. This gives me confidence in the beauty and truth of the Catholic faith, knowing that it reflects a universal longing for purification, redemption, and eternal union with God. As part of this grand narrative, Purgatory is a testament to the depth of God's mercy and His desire to see all souls healed and made perfect in His love.

The concept of final purification, akin to Purgatory, has deep historical roots, predating Christianity. Philosophers such as Plato and Heraclides Ponticus wrote about a similar notion known as "Celestial Hades." This intermediary realm was envisioned as a temporary state where souls resided after death before either ascending to a higher existence or being reincarnated. The exact location of Celestial Hades varied among thinkers. Heraclides of Pontus located it in the Milky Way, while the Academicians, Stoics, Cicero, Virgil, Plutarch, and Hermetical writings placed it between the Moon and the Earth, or around the Moon. In contrast, Numenius and the Latin Neoplatonists positioned it between the sphere of the fixed stars and the Earth.

In Jewish tradition, the belief in purification after death is evident in texts such as 2 Maccabees 12:43-44. This tradition persists in modern Orthodox Judaism, where the Mourner's Kaddish is recited for eleven months following a loved one's death to aid in the purification of the deceased's soul.

According to Catholic legend, in the fifth century, Saint Patrick sought to convert the Irish from paganism. The Irish challenged him to prove his divine authority by crossing into the unseen world and returning. One night, Saint Patrick was transported by God to a desolate place and was told that anyone who spent one day and night there would receive absolution. Upon awakening, Saint Patrick found a staff and a book left by God, symbolizing the authenticity of the divine promise. This event is said to have given rise to the legend of Saint Patrick's Purgatory. Regardless of the veracity of this legend, many saints have had visions or experiences related to Purgatory. Here are some accounts from such saints:

St. Maria Faustina Kowalska

St. Faustina, also known as St. Maria Faustina Kowalska, described a vision where she was guided by her guardian angel to a misty, fiery place filled with suffering souls. These souls were fervently praying

but could not aid themselves; only the living could help them. She observed that their greatest torment was the profound longing for God. St. Faustina saw the Virgin Mary visiting these souls, bringing them comfort, and she was deeply moved by this encounter. Afterward, she heard an interior voice indicating that while God's mercy desires their relief, justice demands their purification. This experience led her to a deeper communion with the suffering souls in Purgatory.

St. Catherine of Genoa

St. Catherine of Genoa spoke about the indescribable suffering of Purgatory, noting that the pain there was as intense as in Hell. However, she observed that souls with even the slightest imperfection considered this suffering as a form of mercy compared to the anguish of remaining distant from God. She believed that the pain in Purgatory came from the souls' awareness of their imperfections and their longing to be united with God.

St. Lidwina of Schiedam

St. Lidwina of Schiedam was shown a terrifying part of Purgatory by her angel, which bordered on Hell. She saw a dreadful prison surrounded by high, dark walls, filled with lamenting souls and chaotic sounds of suffering. Lidwina witnessed a soul in a fiery pit, whose intense suffering deeply shocked her. This experience made her realize the gravity of Purgatory and she continued to pray and offer her sufferings to help that soul move to a less severe state of Purgatory. Her prayers eventually helped the soul transition to a more peaceful condition.

Saint Padre Pio

Saint Padre Pio had a notable encounter when Pietro di Mauro, a man who had died in a friary fire. He appeared to him, asking for prayers to free his soul from Purgatory. Padre Pio promised to celebrate a

Mass for him, which he believed successfully released the man from Purgatory. The next day, a priest confirmed the man's death under the described circumstances. Padre Pio often spoke of his interactions with souls from Purgatory, noting that more souls came to his Masses than living people. He advised that accepting everything from God with love and gratitude would help avoid Purgatory and move directly to Paradise.

Saint Catherine of Siena

Saint Catherine of Siena revealed to Blessed Raymond Capua that she had witnessed the immense sufferings of Hell and Purgatory, describing them as so severe that human language could not fully convey their intensity. She contrasted this with the profound joy and glory of Heaven and her Divine Spouse, which made her view earthly things with utter disdain.

St. Gertrude of Helfta

St. Gertrude of Helfta had a vision during the elevation of the Host, where she saw Christ descending into Purgatory with a golden rod. The rod had many hooks representing the prayers offered for the souls in Purgatory. By these hooks, Jesus appeared to draw souls into a place of rest. St. Gertrude understood that prayers made from charity for these souls, especially those who lived lives of charity, significantly helped in their release. Her prayer, known as the Prayer of Saint Gertrude the Great, is believed to free 1,000 souls from Purgatory each time it is said: "Eternal Father, I offer You the most Precious Blood of Your Divine Son, Jesus, in union with the Masses said throughout the world today, for all the Holy Souls in Purgatory, for sinners everywhere, for sinners in the universal Church, those in my own home and within my family. Amen."

Our Lady of Fatima

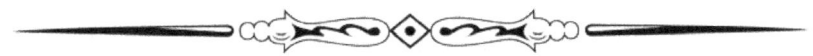

During her first apparition at Fatima on May 13, 1917, Lucia inquired of the Blessed Virgin about her friend Amelia, who had recently passed away. Our Lady responded that Amelia would remain in Purgatory until the end of the world. This response highlighted that entering Heaven is not an easy feat; it requires immense effort and heroic generosity. Our Lady's message underscores that while God's ultimate purpose is the salvation of souls and their union with Him, most souls are not entirely pure at the moment of death. Therefore, Purgatory exists as a means of purification through intense spiritual suffering. Our Lady's mention of Amelia's prolonged suffering "until the end of the world"—illustrates the severity of Purgatory. It emphasizes that even a moment in Purgatory can equate to centuries of suffering on earth, reminding us of the profound importance of striving for purity and understanding the gravity of our earthly lives. Life on earth can be likened to a small hill overlooking a vast valley engulfed in a raging fire where countless souls suffer. Among these souls are our ancestors, relatives, and friends, all gazing towards Heaven and Earth with a hope that their suffering might be alleviated. If only people were more concerned with aiding these souls rather than focusing solely on their own lives, immense relief could be granted. Our Lady, from the onset of her apparitions, draws our attention to this immense realm of Purgatory, filled with billions of souls. She does this to inspire us to assist them, as they are dearly beloved children of hers. Additionally, she reminds us that, without paying attention to our own spiritual state, we too might find ourselves in Purgatory after our earthly lives. Contemplating Purgatory helps us detach from our worldly distractions and gain a perspective on the "other world"—the essential and true reality.

Sister Lucia of Fatima

Lucia de Jesus Rosa dos Santos, known as Sister Lucia of Fatima, who became a Carmelite nun on June 13, 1929, reflected deeply on the visions she received from the Holy Mother. She grappled with understanding Purgatory and shared her insights: "I have pondered what Purgatory truly means. The term 'Purgatory' signifies 'purification,' and since we are all imperfect and sinful to varying degrees, we all need purification before entering the eternal glory of God's Kingdom. This purification can occur during our earthly lives if God grants us the opportunity.

Through sincere repentance, confession, and penance, we can begin this process here and now. Purgatory is a place where the souls are purified of sins, faults, and imperfections for which they have not made complete reparation. The duration of this purification depends on the gravity of these imperfections and the extent to which reparation has been made. Traditionally, it was believed that souls were purified by being subjected to a fiery ordeal akin to Hell. However, contemporary interpretations suggest that it is the fire of divine love that purifies the soul. If a soul dies with a perfect act of love, it is said to be entirely purified and admitted directly into Heaven. This suggests that love and contrition for sin are what purify the soul, allowing it to enter the presence of God. Though I am not certain of all the details, I believe that our purification is linked to our love and sorrow for having offended God and our neighbors. As we strive to love God with our whole being, even the smallest spark of love can grow, leading to complete purification and admission into the divine presence of God."

Visionaries of Medjugorje

In Medjugorje, visionaries have also shared insights into Purgatory. They describe it as having various levels: the lowest being closer to Hell, and the highest nearing Heaven. Most souls undergo a period in Purgatory before reaching Heaven, with only a few ascending directly to Heaven and many others descending to Hell. Marija Pavlovic-Lunetti, a visionary from Medjugorje, conveyed a message from the Blessed Mother on November 6, 1986: "Dear Children, I urge you to pray daily for the souls in Purgatory. Every prayer and grace are essential for these souls to reach God and experience His love. Through your prayers, you will also gain new intercessors who will support you in your life, helping you recognize that earthly matters are insignificant compared to the pursuit of Heaven. Pray unceasingly to help yourselves and others, as your prayers bring joy and grace."

For me, it is a deep source of comfort to know that my loved ones, if they are not yet fully purified, can be made ready before entering Heaven. The mystery of Purgatory and Heaven, while beyond our full understanding, fills me with hope because I trust in Jesus' promise: *"In my Father's house, there are many dwelling places. I go to prepare a place for you."* (john14:2) This assurance of a place prepared for us in the presence of God, despite the imperfections we may carry, is a beautiful expression of God's mercy and love. I also find great solace in the words of my favorite Saint, Padre Pio, who reminds us: "Death is not always a free pass to Heaven. Many souls need our prayers to receive the gift of entering there." These words resonate deeply with me, affirming that our prayers and sacrifices can help our loved ones on their journey to eternal happiness. This truth underscores the power of intercession and the communion of saints, which I find the most beautiful aspects of the Catholic faith. It is through the prayers of others, especially those of the saints and of the Church, that souls can be helped along the path to Heaven, reminding me of the profound interconnectedness of the Body of Christ.

The Catholic teaching on Purgatory offers not only a profound understanding of God's mercy but also a call to action: to pray for the departed, to offer sacrifices for them, and to recognize that God's love extends beyond death, allowing us to continue helping those we love. It is this belief in the beauty of God's justice and mercy that strengthens my faith and my trust in the profound truth of the Catholic faith.

Chapter Fifteen
Satan

In a chilling exchange from the 1997 film, *The Devil's Advocate*, Kevin Lomax asks, "What are you?" to which John Milton replies, "Oh, I have so many names..." When Lomax exclaims, "Satan!" Milton coolly responds, "Call me Dad." This unsettling dialogue serves as a stark reminder of the spiritual battle that exists beyond the superficial world—a battle between good and evil, between God and Satan.

I remember in 1973, at the age of fourteen, the release of *The Exorcist* had a profound impact on both viewers and the culture at large. The film, based on William Peter Blatty's novel, brought to life the terrifying story of a young girl possessed by a demon named Pazuzu, and the priests who risked everything to save her. The fear it evoked was so intense that audiences were physically and emotionally shaken, with reports of people fainting, vomiting, and even being hospitalized after seeing it. I recall hearing about the strange and unsettling reactions to the film, which some claimed left behind a dark, lingering presence, as though the movie carried a malevolent

force. There is something deeply revealing about how *The Exorcist* affected so many people. It brought to the surface an undeniable truth—that evil exists, and it can manifest in ways we cannot easily explain. Despite the modern skepticism that pervades much of our culture, especially in a society that prides itself on scientific explanations and self-reliance, the reality of spiritual warfare cannot be dismissed. While Hollywood has often softened and popularized images of the supernatural, making demons and evil forces seem less threatening, the message of *The Exorcist* and related stories serves as a sobering reminder: evil is real and seeks to destroy.

The novel *The Exorcist* was so disturbing to some readers that they reportedly stored it in isolated spots like garages or linen closets to keep its influence at bay. Footage from the film's release on YouTube captures the eerie atmosphere, showing long lines of eager moviegoers. However, the initial excitement quickly turned to palpable fear as audiences exited the theater visibly shaken, with some even fainting. A local newspaper even reported that some moviegoers were so overwhelmed by the experience that they collapsed upon leaving the theater. This reaction mirrored the infamous joke in *Friends*, where Joey Tribbiani hides *The Shining* in a freezer for fear of its content. When the film adaptation hit theaters, it amplified these fears to an entirely different level. Some viewers were so disturbed by the film that they believed it contained a real, malevolent force within its film stock. Although it's not uncommon for certain films to push the boundaries of viewers' comfort, *The Exorcist* remains a particularly intense example. The impact of the movie's release was marked by widespread reports of its terrifying effect on audiences, with news footage showing theatergoers struggling to regain their composure after the film. This wasn't just part of the marketing hype—*The Exorcist* genuinely caused many viewers to become physically ill. In his book *Laughing, Screaming*, William Paul recalls that the bathrooms at his theater were so overwhelmed with vomit that the sinks were completely blocked. The sheer volume of such incidents became as notorious as the film itself, even inspiring a parody cover in *MAD* magazine featuring an "Exorcist" vomit bag.

In a culture where many profess belief in God yet often live as if they are untouched by the reality of spiritual forces, there is a pervasive tendency to underestimate the power of the unseen world. We may acknowledge the concept of Satan, but how often do we recognize his influence in our daily lives? The idea that we must choose between God and Satan, without any middle ground, is a stark, yet essential, truth of the Christian faith. It's easy to be lulled into complacency in a world that emphasizes self-sufficiency, material success, and comfort. Yet, as *The Exorcist* so chillingly demonstrates, evil can break through even the most carefully constructed facades, revealing that we are not as in control of our lives as we may think. I believe in the truth and beauty of the Catholic faith precisely because it recognizes this cosmic battle between light and darkness, between God and Satan. It teaches that the choice to follow Christ is not just an abstract idea or moral guideline—it is a life-altering decision that shapes our eternity. The Catholic Church reminds us that spiritual vigilance is necessary. We are called to prayer, to sacrament, and to remain grounded in the truth of Christ, not just for our own sake, but for the sake of others, and the sake of the world. While many might dismiss the reality of evil or the possibility of demonic influence, I find in the Catholic faith a powerful antidote to this skepticism. The Church does not shy away from the truth of spiritual warfare but faces it with the full power of prayer, the sacraments, and the authority of Christ. This is why I believe in the beauty and truth of the Catholic faith—it doesn't just acknowledge the existence of evil; it offers the grace, the means, and the hope to overcome it, in this life and the next.

In Scripture, Satan is referenced more frequently than all but Jesus Christ, appearing across both the Old and New Testaments under various names, each shedding light on several aspects of his nature and role. From Genesis to Revelation, these names serve to highlight his function as the ultimate adversary to God's plan for humanity. The Greek word *diabolos* and the Latin *diabolus* are often

translated as "devil" and describe the accuser or slanderer. These terms are intricately linked to Satan's role in opposing God and leading others astray, as we see in Matthew 25:41, where Jesus speaks of "the devil and his angels." In Hebrew, *Satan* itself means "adversary" or "accuser," further emphasizing his role as the one who challenges, accuses, and attempts to deceive God's people. Understanding these various names and titles for Satan strengthens my belief in the reality of spiritual warfare and the need for God's grace and protection. From *Lucifer* (meaning "light-bearer") in Isaiah 14:12, referencing his fall from grace to *Beelzebul* (lord of the flies) in the Gospels, and *the tempter* in Matthew 4:3, Satan's titles all remind us that his influence is both deceptive and pervasive. These names deepen my understanding of the battle between good and evil and affirm the importance of turning to God for strength and guidance in our journey toward holiness.

These biblical descriptions reveal that Satan is not merely a mythical figure or a symbolic force of evil, but a real and active presence whose purpose is to undermine our relationship with God. Yet, in knowing the power of his name and how it is used in Scripture, I find comfort in knowing that Jesus Christ has already conquered him. His victory over sin and death, through His life, death, and Resurrection, assures me that while Satan may seek to destroy, Christ has already triumphed over all the forces of darkness. Satan, known by various names throughout the Bible, is depicted in numerous passages under different titles, each reflecting a different aspect of his malevolent nature:

- **The Serpent**: In Genesis 3:1, Satan is described as "the serpent, more cunning than any of the wild animals the Lord God had made." This title reflects his role in tempting Eve and introducing sin into the world.

- **King of Babylon**: Isaiah 14:4 refers to a taunt-song against the "king of Babylon," often interpreted as a symbolic reference to Satan's pride and downfall.

- **Lucifer**: Isaiah 14:12 speaks of "Lucifer, son of the morning," who has "fallen from heaven." The term "Lucifer" means "light-bringer" or "morning star," symbolizing Satan's initial grandeur and subsequent fall.

- **Leviathan**: In Isaiah 27:1, Satan is likened to "Leviathan, the fleeing serpent," and "Leviathan, the coiled serpent," depicting him as a powerful and chaotic force.

- **King of Tyre**: Ezekiel 28:12 includes a lament for the "king of Tyre," which many interpret as an allegory for Satan, emphasizing his pride and subsequent fall.

- **Little Horn**: Daniel 8:9 mentions "a little horn" that emerges, often seen as a symbol of a powerful and corrupting force, representing Satan's influence.

- **Beelzebub**: In Matthew 12:24, Satan is referred to as "Beelzebub," which means "lord of the flies" or "lord of dung," signifying his role as the prince of demons.

- **Satan**: Mark 1:13 states that Jesus was "tempted by Satan in the wilderness," directly naming him as the adversary.

- **Prince of Demons**: Luke 11:15 refers to Satan as "Beelzebub, the prince of demons," highlighting his leadership role among the fallen angels.

- **Thief**: John 10:10 describes Satan as "a thief who comes only to steal, kill, and destroy," emphasizing his destructive intentions.

- **Evil One**: In Ephesians 6:16, believers are advised to use faith as a shield to "extinguish all the flaming arrows of the evil one," referring to Satan's malicious attacks.

- **Antichrist**: 1 John 4:3 mentions "the spirit of the antichrist," indicating a force opposed to Christ, often associated with Satan's influence in the world.

- **Beast**: Revelation 14:9 warns against "worshipping the beast," a symbol of evil power and opposition to God, often linked with Satan's schemes.

These various names and titles reflect the multifaceted nature of Satan's role as depicted in the Bible, illustrating his influence and opposition throughout Scripture. The concept of the Devil and fallen angels is dispersed throughout the Old and New Testaments, but a comprehensive account is not provided in any single passage. Instead, understanding these entities is pieced together from various scriptural references, from Genesis to Revelation, and further illuminated by patristic writings and theological traditions. Private revelations from saints also offer additional insights. The Bible does not give a detailed narrative of the fallen angels in the Old Testament; this story is more fully developed in the Book of Revelation.

According to Christian tradition, God created angels as pure and good beings, each with free will. Lucifer, the most brilliant and radiant among them, was endowed with immense beauty and intelligence. However, Lucifer's pride and desire for autonomy led him to rebel against God's divine plan. Along with one-third of the heavenly host, he sought to overthrow God's authority, believing that he should reign supreme rather than submit to God's will. This act of defiance resulted in their fall from grace, and Lucifer, now known as Satan, and his followers were cast out of Heaven into Hell, a place of eternal torment and separation from God. The traditional account holds that Lucifer's pride was not merely a rejection of God's authority but also a refusal to accept God's plan for creation, particularly humanity's role in Heaven. Lucifer, created as a being of fire, could not bear the idea of a lesser creature—humanity—being destined for Heaven alongside the angels. In his arrogance, he rejected the idea that God's love and redemption could extend to fallen humans in a way that would not be extended to him or the other angles. His rebellion wasn't simply against God, but also against the idea of grace and redemption that would ultimately come through Jesus Christ, who, as a descendant of Adam, would save humanity. The rebellion of Lucifer and his followers is not just an ancient story, but a reality that affects us today. The fallen angels now exist with a single purpose: to lead humanity away from salvation. Their mission is to tempt, confuse, and deceive, aiming to thwart our relationship with God and to prevent us from attaining the eternal joy of Heaven. Their constant warfare against our souls is a stark reminder of the need for vigilance, prayer, and the strength of God's grace in the daily spiritual battle.

This account boosts my belief in the beauty and truth of the Catholic faith. It reminds me that the struggle between good and evil is real and that my choices have eternal consequences. Yet, it is also a source of hope because the ultimate victory belongs to Christ, who has already triumphed over Satan and death. Through His passion, death, and resurrection, Jesus has opened the gates of Heaven and offers each of us the possibility of redemption. Knowing this, I am reassured that despite the presence of evil in the world, God's love, mercy, and the promise of eternal life with Him are far greater. This truth fuels my faith and trust in God's ultimate plan for good.

Blessed Maria of Agreda provides a profound glimpse into Satan's animosity towards God and humanity through her private revelations from the Blessed Mother, as detailed in her work *City of God*. According to her account, in the beginning, God created Heaven for the angels and humanity, with Earth serving as a temporary pilgrimage for mortal beings. The angels were fashioned in the empyrean heavens, blessed with grace, and designed to merit the glory of God. They were created in three distinct phases:

1. **First Instant:** The angels were created as the most beautiful and perfect beings, endowed with divine gifts and graces.

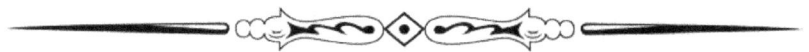

They were introduced to God's will, which included acknowledging Him as their Creator and Supreme Lord.

2. **Second Instant:** The angels were informed that God would create human beings who were lower but were to love, fear, and reverence Him as their Creator. Furthermore, the second Person of the Holy Trinity would incarnate as a human, and the angels were instructed to honor Him as both God and man, acknowledging His authority as their Head. However, they would remain His inferiors in dignity and grace. They were to serve Him and recognize that all creations, including themselves, existed for His glory.

The obedient and holy angels accepted this divine plan with humility and love. However, Lucifer, consumed by envy and pride, resisted. He incited other angels to join him in rebellion, promising them leadership and a separate dominion from Christ. This pride and envy blinded Lucifer and spread sin among many angels, leading them to follow him in defiance of God's command.

3. **Third Instant:** The angels were then informed that a woman would be exalted as Queen and Mistress of all creation, and that the Only Begotten of the Father would assume flesh in her womb. This woman would be instrumental in the redemption of humanity. The good angels accepted this revelation, but Lucifer and his followers grew increasingly proud and rebellious. They demanded that if a divine union were to occur, it should be with him, not with this woman. This arrogance provoked God's wrath, who declared to Lucifer, "This woman whom you refuse to honor shall crush your head, and through her humility, life and salvation for humanity shall be secured."

Infuriated, Lucifer vowed to destroy humanity and harbored relentless hatred against Christ and His most holy Mother. The fallen angels, spurred by their leader's fury, became implacable enemies of

God and humanity, seeking to thwart the divine plan and perpetuate their rebellion through eternal malice. When Jesus uttered the words, "Father, into Your hands I commend My spirit," Lucifer and the evil spirits were thrown into the deepest depths of Hell with a violence and swiftness surpassing their initial expulsion from Heaven. This route was more catastrophic than their first banishment. From the creation of the first man, I have ceaselessly sought to find and destroy them. Although I could not annihilate them, I aimed to bring ruin upon all of God's creatures and persuade them not to acknowledge Him as their God, ensuring that none would benefit from His works. This was my sole intent, primary concern, and the focus of all my efforts. I have always viewed humanity as my greatest adversary, a source of intolerable loathing. Men, who are so favored and cherished by God, whom I detest and whose love I cannot endure—how will I thwart your blessed destiny? How can I inflict misery upon you, knowing that I cannot erase your existence? In response to this grim objective, several principal demons devised plans to obstruct the fruits of the Redemption among humanity. They conceded that while it was impossible to harm Christ Himself, they could shift their focus to harming men. Content with these diabolical strategies, Lucifer saw fit to assign tasks to his minions. Some demons were tasked with thwarting the inclinations of children from the moment of their conception and birth. Others aimed to induce parents to neglect their children's proper education and guidance, whether through excessive indulgence or aversion, and to foster discord between parents and their offspring. Some were assigned to sow discord between spouses, to tempt them into adultery, or to diminish their commitment to marital fidelity. All agreed to cultivate seeds of strife, hatred, and revenge, and to inspire pride, sensuality, and greed by misleading reasoning against the virtues Christ taught. Above all, they sought to weaken the memory of Christ's Passion and death, diminish the awareness of salvation's means, and obscure the eternal suffering of Hell. By these tactics, the demons hoped to distract humanity with earthly concerns and

In a world increasingly dominated by transient pleasures and distractions, it's evident that the more profound truths of our faith are often overlooked. Many have turned away from the path of spiritual reflection and personal salvation, preferring the fleeting satisfactions of the flesh. Yet, in the heart of the Catholic faith, we find the eternal beauty and truth that can lead us to true fulfillment, not through indulgence in worldly desires, but through the embrace of the Cross and the transformative power of Redemption.

The Blessed Mother, in her maternal wisdom, reminds us of the profound significance of the Cross, a symbol of both suffering and salvation. While the forces of darkness—embodied by Lucifer and his legions—fear the power of the Cross, many of the faithful have forgotten its blessings. In their pursuit of vanity and carnal inclinations, they have become deceived by falsehoods, clouding their vision of the Savior's glory. In doing so, they risk falling into the traps set by the enemies of our soul, who seek to lead us astray. Yet, this moment of spiritual crisis also calls us to awaken. The Church, in its purity, is the body through which Christ's love and sacrifice continue to reach us. Through the Church, we can receive the fruits of the Cross—grace, redemption, and the power to overcome sin. This is the beauty and truth of the Catholic faith: that we are offered a new life through the blood and death of our Redeemer. Even when the world around us may seem consumed by pride and confusion, the Church stands as a beacon of hope, inviting us to return to the truth of our salvation. Through its sacraments, its teachings, and the wisdom of the saints, the Catholic faith offers a path to true peace and joy—one that transcends the empty promises of a world that is passing away. This is why I believe in the beauty and truth of the Catholic faith: it is a light that shines in darkness, a source of eternal hope, and a call to live with purpose, guided by the love of God.

In a time when the spiritual landscape seems increasingly chaotic and distorted, the truth of the Catholic faith shines ever more brightly as a beacon of clarity and hope. The reality of Satan and his work in the world is not a mere relic of ancient myth or the exaggerations of popular culture. He is a real and active force, actively seeking to deceive and lead souls away from the truth of God's love, distorting the divine and the sacred with lies and empty promises. As Catholics, we are called to stand vigilant, recognizing how Satan seeks to infiltrate every corner of society, whether through media, politics, or even in the hearts of those who should be guardians of spiritual truth. One only needs to look at the events unfolding today to see the evidence of this ongoing spiritual battle. For instance, the disturbing spectacle of the 2023 Grammy Awards, where Sam Smith's performance was drenched in overt satanic symbolism, offers a stark illustration of how cultural institutions are embracing darkness. Smith's portrayal of the devil, surrounded by figures dressed in demonic garb, received praise from the secular media, more interested in entertainment than the moral implications of what was being celebrated. In its endorsement of the performance, CBS crossed a line that, for many, can only be seen as a blatant compromise with evil. This is not just a matter of sensationalism or passing trends. It is part of a larger movement where the forces of darkness, disguised as art, politics, or personal expression, are becoming normalized in society. Events like SatanCon in Boston and the "After School Satan Club" in Virginia reveal the growing public embrace of satanic ideology. These are not just fringe activities; they reflect a broader cultural trend that seeks to undermine traditional values and spiritual truths. In this context, it becomes clearer than ever that the Catholic faith, rooted in the love and truth of Christ, offers a refuge from the confusion and darkness surrounding us.

We also see this distortion in the twisting of religious symbols and concepts, such as when a Lutheran pastor reimagines God as "nonbinary" and Jesus as having "two dads" during a Pride Month service. While this may be intended as a form of inclusivity, it ultimately misrepresents the divine reality of who God is—Father, Son, and Holy Spirit—by politicizing and secularizing the core tenets of the Christian faith. It is precisely in moments like these that we are reminded of the beauty and truth of the Catholic faith, which preserves the fullness of God's revelation through Sacred Scripture,

Sacred Tradition, and the Magisterium of the Church. Finally, the response of two pro-life students during Vice President Kamala Harris' rally is a powerful testament to the courage of those who stand for truth in a world that often mocks or dismisses it. Their shout of "Jesus is Lord!" and "Christ is King!" in the face of a political narrative that seeks to erase the sanctity of life is a clear reminder of the authority of Christ in all things. In moments like these, we see the clash of two vastly different worldviews—the secular and the sacred—and the Catholic faith is a firm witness to the eternal truth of Christ's kingship and the dignity of every human life.

In a world where Satan is actively at work, trying to lead souls astray, the Church offers us the light of Christ, which is never dimmed by the darkness of evil. The Catholic faith preserves the fullness of God's truth, which is unchanging and unshakeable, even during a culture that increasingly seeks to redefine and distort the sacred. It calls us to stand firm in our faith, to resist the temptations and lies of the world, and to proclaim boldly the truth of the Gospel—now, more than ever, we are called to be the light in the darkness.   To combat the influence of Satan, the Blessed Mother has been appearing to visionaries in Medjugorje, Bosnia, since 1981, offering messages of hope and warnings to the world. In her June 25, 2021, message to Marija, one of the Medjugorje visionaries, she issued a stern warning: "Pray with me for peace and freedom, because Satan is strong and, through his deceptions, aims to lead more souls away from my motherly heart. Our religious freedoms are under threat from what is now called atheistic ideology, often referred to as 'Wokeism.' For many years, Our Lady has alerted us to this scourge, which she also identifies as 'Modernism.' She warns that these influences are driven by Satan, who is more active now than ever before." Echoing the Blessed Mother's concerns, author A.J. Rice argues that "Woke faith" (Modernism) is fundamentally incompatible with Christian faith. He explains, "It is atheistic and denies both God and Christ. It replaces the path of sin and salvation with its own, which leads only to ongoing conflict. He references 1 Peter 5:8: "Be sober and vigilant. Your

opponent, the devil, prowls around like a roaring lion, looking for someone to devour."

Why I believe in the beauty and truth of the Catholic faith is rooted in the unwavering clarity of Christ's revelation, especially regarding the reality of Satan and the deception he seeks to spread. Jesus Himself calls Satan "the father of lies" (John 8:44), revealing the essence of evil as a distortion of truth. Satan's primary and most insidious lie is that there is something better than developing an intimate, life-giving relationship with God through His Son, Jesus Christ, and the grace of the Holy Spirit. This lie seeks to pull us away from the source of all truth, beauty, and love.

The tactics Satan uses to seduce souls away from God are as varied as they are effective. They often begin subtly, working within the human heart to plant seeds of doubt, discouragement, and division. First, Satan fosters **doubt**—the question that undermines trust in God's goodness: "Is God good? Does He absolutely love you?" This is the first crack in the foundation of faith, and once doubt takes root, it can grow into a deep sense of distance from God. It is a lie that suggests that we cannot fully trust in God's providence and mercy, and that we are alone in our struggles. If doubt doesn't succeed, Satan often moves to **discouragement**—shifting the focus away from God's power and grace to our own weaknesses, failures, and trials. He tempts us to fixate on our problems, our imperfections, and the seeming impossibility of overcoming our struggles. This leads to feelings of despair, as if God is absent or uninterested in our lives, when in truth, He is always present, patiently waiting to lift us up. The lie of discouragement seeks to make us believe that our spiritual journey is futile or beyond our reach.

Next, there is the tactic of **diversion**—the seductive lure of sin disguised as something desirable or fulfilling. Satan makes immoral or wrong things seem more attractive, as if they offer a quick fix to our deepest desires for love, acceptance, or purpose. In this deception, we are drawn away from God's truth, lured into temporary pleasures

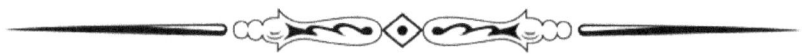

312

that ultimately leave us empty. This is the great illusion: that earthly satisfaction can provide what only God can fulfill. Finally, Satan uses **defeat**—the lie that we are beyond redemption, that we have failed so many times that it's not worth trying anymore. This lie paralyzes the soul, convincing us that we are unworthy of God's grace and that we are irredeemable. It whispers that we should give up, that our efforts to grow in faith are futile. Yet this is the greatest lie of all, for in Christ, there is always hope, always forgiveness, and always the opportunity for renewal. These are the lies that Satan promotes, designed to slowly erode the foundation of our faith and our relationship with God. They are subtle, but they are deadly, because they lead us away from the truth of God's love and mercy, and from the transformative grace that He offers us in the sacraments, in prayer, and through the Church.

But, this is precisely why I believe in the beauty and truth of the Catholic faith. In the face of these lies, the Church holds fast to the truth of Christ, the eternal Word, and the living reality of His grace. Through the Church, we are constantly reminded of the truth: that God is good, that He loves us beyond measure, and that no matter how many times we fall, He is always ready to forgive and restore us. The sacraments, especially the Eucharist and Reconciliation, are powerful means through which God offers His grace, helping us to overcome doubt, discouragement, diversion, and defeat. The Catholic faith does not shy away from the reality of evil, but rather, it equips us to stand firm in the truth. It teaches us to recognize the lies and reject them, and to embrace the freedom that comes from knowing and loving the one true God. In a world full of deception, I find strength and peace in the truth of the Catholic faith—where Christ is the way, the truth, and the life. This is why I believe, now more than ever, in the beauty and truth of the Catholic faith.

In Matthew 7:13-14, Jesus warns that many will fall victim to Satan's lies, leading to suffering and punishment: *"Enter through the narrow gate; for wide is the gate and broad is the road that leads to destruction, and many enter through it. But small is the gate and*

narrow the road that leads to life, and only a few find it. " However, it's crucial to remember that Satan is neither omniscient nor omnipresent. With God, all things are possible, including Satan's defeat. While Satan was defeated by Jesus' crucifixion, his ultimate defeat came with the resurrection at the empty tomb. Just as Daniel had faith and trust in God and survived the lions' den, and David overcame Goliath with his faith, so too can we find strength and protection in God. David proclaimed, "You *come against me with sword, spear, and javelin, but I come against you in the name of the Lord Almighty, the God of the armies of Israel, whom you have defied. This day the Lord will deliver you into my hands, and I will strike you down and cut off your head"* (1 Samuel 17:45-46). If God protected Daniel and David, He would protect us as well. Without fear, we are encouraged to face challenges and adversaries, including demonic forces. Strengthen your faith, trust in God, and equip yourself with the armor of God. When feeling overwhelmed by spiritual attacks, I turn to Ephesians 6:10-16 for guidance and protection in spiritual warfare:

Be strong in the Lord and His mighty power, believe that no power can harm you as long as God protects you. Put on the full armor of God so that you can stand firm against the devil's schemes. Our battle is not against flesh and blood, but against the rulers, authorities, and powers of this shadowy world, and against the spiritual forces of evil in the heavenly realms. So, take up the full armor of God, so that when the day of evil comes, you can stand your ground. And after you have done all you can, you will still be standing. Stand firm, then, with the belt of truth fastened around your waist, the breastplate of righteousness in place, and your feet ready with the gospel of peace. Above all, take up the shield of faith to extinguish all the fiery darts of the enemy. Put on the helmet of salvation and take the sword of the Spirit, which is the word of God. For additional support in combating the forces of evil, invoke the protection of Michael the Archangel and the Heavenly Choir of Angels. Embrace the light of freedom, forgiveness, and humility, rather than the darkness of resentment, bitterness, oppression, hatred, and malice. A powerful prayer for

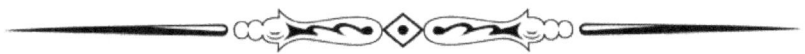

protection is the one composed by Pope Leo XIII: "Saint *Michael the Archangel, defend us in battle. Be our safeguard against the wickedness and snares of the devil. May God rebuke him, we humbly pray, and do thou, O Prince of the heavenly host, by the power of God, cast into hell Satan and all the other evil spirits who prowl through the world seeking the ruin of souls.*"

Pope Leo XIII wrote this prayer after a disturbing vision he experienced in 1884 while attending Mass. In his vision, Pope Leo overheard a conversation between God and Satan. Satan requested a period of 75 to 100 years to wreak havoc on the Catholic Church. God granted this period, and Satan chose the twentieth century for his work. The vision so shocked Pope Leo that he reportedly turned pale and collapsed, causing alarm among the Cardinals who feared he had died. Upon regaining consciousness, Pope Leo described the vision and instructed that the Saint Michael Prayer be recited at the end of every Mass.

Reflecting on the twentieth century, it becomes clear why Pope Leo XIII's vision was so unsettling. This period witnessed catastrophic events: World War I and World War II, which caused immense loss of life and destruction. The century also saw other significant conflicts such as the Korean War, Vietnam War, Arab-Israeli War, Gulf War, Balkan War, Iran-Iraq War, Falklands War, and the Rwandan Civil War, among others. These wars led to unprecedented atrocities, including the Holocaust, genocides, and atomic bombings. The development of atomic weapons resulted in the immediate vaporization of approximately 214,000 people in Japan, with many more suffering from radiation sickness. The Cold War followed, characterized by an arms race between the United States and the USSR, amassing thousands of nuclear weapons. By 1990, the U.S. possessed 10,904 nuclear weapons, while Russia had 37,000. By the early 21st century, these numbers were reduced but remained significant, with the U.S. having 5,800 and Russia 6,375 nuclear warheads. Communism spread rapidly, overthrowing governments and suppressing religious practices. In communist countries, anti-

Catholic policies led to the closure of churches and schools and the persecution of the faithful. Meanwhile, in non-communist nations, secularism gained momentum, leading to the banning of prayer in schools and the removal of religious symbols from public spaces. This secularism gradually eroded the influence of religion, causing a decline in church attendance and a decrease in religious vocations. The Catholic Church faced scandals, including a worldwide pedophile crisis that persisted into the 21st century.

Pope John XXIII convened the Second Vatican Council (1962-1965), which, according to some, led to significant changes and controversies within the Church. Pope Paul VI later discontinued the recitation of the Saint Michael Prayer in 1968. The sexual revolution of the 1960s introduced birth control and legalized abortion, further challenging traditional moral values. Additionally, in 1981, Pope John Paul II survived an assassination attempt by a lone shooter linked to the Soviet Union. These events illustrate the profound and unsettling impact of the twentieth century, affirming, perhaps, the accuracy of Pope Leo XIII's vision. The turbulence of the century and the ensuing challenges of the 21st century underscore the continued relevance of seeking divine protection and remaining vigilant in the face of evil. The devil remains as active in the 21st century as in previous eras. Today's conflicts, often termed "armed conflicts," continue the legacy of violence. The Global Slavery Index reveals that approximately 27.5 million people are trapped in modern slavery, including forced labor and sex trafficking. Of these, 17.3 million are subjected to forced labor, while 6.3 million face sexual exploitation. Additionally, about 22 million people are in forced marriages, with women, migrants, and refugee children disproportionately affected. Violent crime rates are at historic highs, and homelessness is at a critical level. Pornography is rampant, with millions of websites dedicated to it, offering every conceivable depraved, immoral, and perverted content. Accessibility is unprecedented, with explicit material readily downloadable to personal devices. Drug overdose deaths now surpass fatalities from violent crime, with seven out of ten

overdose deaths occurring daily, according to the National Center for Drug Abuse Statistics.

Moral and societal norms are also rapidly shifting. For instance, the definition of marriage has evolved significantly since the Netherlands became the first country to legalize same-sex marriage in 2000. This change spread quickly, with countries like the United States, France, and Germany following suit. Terminology itself has become fluid, with debates over gender identity leading to new definitions. Transgender men claim the ability to give birth, while transgender women argue for the right to use women's facilities and compete in female sports. This shift in understanding has led to questions about fundamental definitions; for example, during her Supreme Court confirmation hearing, Senator Marsha Blackburn asked Justice Ketanji Brown Jackson to define "woman." Jackson's response, "I am not a biologist," was widely supported by some as reflecting the complexity of gender identity.

The COVID-19 pandemic, which claimed approximately 6,951,664 lives globally, profoundly impacted people's attitudes toward God. As the world grappled with the pandemic, a German survey revealed a troubling trend: faith in a higher power declined significantly. According to research published in the *Journal of Religion and Health*, the longer the pandemic persisted, the more individuals lost faith in God. Nearly 5,000 people in Germany were surveyed over 18 months, and findings indicated that with the second wave of infections and lockdowns, trust in a higher power and practices such as praying and meditation diminished. The study noted that increasing stress related to the pandemic was linked to a decline in well-being and faith, affecting both Catholics and Protestants across various age groups. In the post-pandemic era, a poll of 1,871 individuals identifying as Christians revealed that only 78% believed in God as depicted in the Bible. The remaining 22% described God in ways inconsistent with traditional biblical teachings. Additionally, 40% of those surveyed rejected the existence of Satan, viewing him merely as a symbol of evil.

317

Pope Francis has been outspoken in reminding us that the presence of the devil is not a relic of the past, but a real and present threat to our spiritual lives, even in the 21st century. In his teachings, he has rejected the idea that speaking of Satan is outdated, and instead, he calls us to be ever vigilant in the face of temptation and evil. Pope Francis has made it clear that we, as Christians, constantly struggle against the forces of darkness. During a Mass at the Vatican, he urged believers to turn to the Gospel for guidance in combating the devil's temptations. "The devil is present... even in the 21st century," he said, warning us not to underestimate the enemy. This message resonates deeply with me because it reminds us that we cannot afford to be naïve about the spiritual battle we face. The devil's temptations are subtle and often come gradually, leading us to justify them little by little, until we find ourselves far from the path of holiness. Reflecting on the Gospel, Pope Francis highlighted how temptation often begins with small compromises that grow over time. He recalled the biblical account of Jesus' temptations in the desert, particularly when Satan tried to convince Him to throw Himself from the Temple to prove His divinity. In this, we see how the devil works to twist God's truth, using subtle lies to create doubt and to lead us away from God's plan for our lives. This reminds us that we must resist allowing small temptations to take root, for they can quickly escalate, drawing us further away from Christ.

It is the Church that teaches us to be vigilant, to recognize the subtle ways in which evil can infiltrate our lives, and to turn to the Gospel for strength and guidance. The spiritual life is a struggle, as Pope Francis has said, and our fight is not against flesh and blood, but against the spiritual forces that seek to separate us from Christ. The Church gives us the tools we need—the sacraments, prayer, and the wisdom of the saints—to resist temptation and to stand firm in our faith. The devil does not want our holiness, but the Catholic faith empowers us to draw closer to God and to remain steadfast in the battle for our souls.   Through the teachings of Pope Francis and the strength of the Church's tradition, I am reminded that the beauty and truth of the Catholic faith offer a powerful antidote to the lies of the

enemy. By staying close to Christ, living out the Gospel, and putting on the armor of God, we can stand firm against the devil's schemes and grow in holiness, knowing that we are never alone in this struggle. This is why I believe, with all my heart, in the transformative power of the Catholic faith.

Back in 1965, Paul Harvey, a famous radio commentator, gave us this warning that is still relevant today. It is title "If I was the Devil':

"If I were the devil ... If I were the Prince of Darkness, I'd want to engulf the whole world in darkness. And I'd have a third of its real estate, and four-fifths of its population, but I wouldn't be happy until I had seized the ripe apple on the tree. So, I'd set about, however necessary, to take over the United States. I'd subvert the churches first — I'd begin with a campaign of whispers. With the wisdom of a serpent, I would whisper to you as I whispered to Eve: 'Do as you please.'

"To the young, I would whisper, ' The Bible is a myth.' I would convince them that man created God instead of vice versa. I would confide that what's bad is good, and what's good is 'square.' And the old, I would teach to pray, after me, 'Our Father, which art in Washington...'

"And then I'd get organized. I'd educate authors in how to make lurid literature exciting, so that anything else would appear dull and uninteresting. I'd threaten TV with dirtier movies and vice versa. I'd pedal narcotics to whom I could. I'd sell alcohol to ladies and gentlemen of distinction. I'd tranquilize the rest with pills.

"If I were the devil, I'd soon have families that war with themselves, churches at war with themselves, and nations at war with themselves; until each in its turn was consumed. And with promises of higher ratings, I'd have mesmerizing media fanning the flames. If I were the devil, I would encourage schools to refine young intellect, but neglect

to discipline emotions — just let those run wild, until before you knew it, you'd have to have drug sniffing dogs and metal detectors at every schoolhouse door.

"Within a decade, I'd have prisons overflowing, I'd have judges promoting pornography — soon I could evict God from the courthouse, then from the schoolhouse, and then from the houses of Congress. And in His own churches, I would substitute psychology for religion and deify science. I would lure priests and pastors into misusing boys and girls, and church money. If I were the devil, I'd make the symbols of Easter an egg and the symbol of Christmas a bottle.

"If I were the devil, I'd take from those who have, and give to those who wanted until I had killed the incentive of the ambitious. And what do you bet? I couldn't get whole states to promote gambling as the way to get rich? I would caution against extremes and arduous work, in patriotism, and in moral conduct. I would convince the young that marriage is old-fashioned, that swinging is more fun, that what you see on TV is the way to be. And thus, I could undress you in public, and I could lure you into bed with diseases for which there is no cure. In other words, if I were the devil, I'd just keep right on doing on what he's doing.

Saint Padre Pio was intimately familiar with the presence of the devil throughout his life. Numerous accounts reveal that Satan visited him repeatedly over six decades, manifesting in various forms: as a devil, a beast, a man, a woman, a friar, a Crucifix, Our Lady, an angel, Saint Francis, and many others. These visits were often accompanied by temptations and physical assaults aimed at undermining Padre Pio's faith, hope, and trust in God, thereby hindering his mission to lead countless souls to salvation. Padre Pio could immediately discern the demonic nature of these manifestations because they always instilled a profound sense of disgust in his soul. The temptations he faced were diverse and insidious. They included assaults on his purity, such as visions of a seductive woman intended

to provoke impure thoughts. They challenged his faith, with the devil suggesting he deny Catholic truths, planting blasphemous thoughts, or urging him to conceal his spiritual struggles from his spiritual director. The devil even attempted to disrupt his sacramental duties by appearing as a penitent during confession, trying to convince Padre Pio that sin did not exist and that the Church's teachings on morality were merely "natural" and "normal" human behaviors.

How to Defeat Satan and His Temptations, according to St. Padre Pio

"The devil is like a rabid dog tied to a chain; beyond the length of the chain, he cannot seize anyone. And you: keep a distance. If you approach too near, you let yourself be caught. Remember that the devil has only one door by which he enters the soul: the will. There are no secret or hidden doors."

To overcome Satan and his temptations, St. Padre Pio offers these insights:

- **Avoid Dwelling on Satan's Insinuations:** Focus on fleeing from temptation rather than dwelling on what the devil suggests. Victory comes from avoiding engagement with these thoughts.

- **Don't Fixate on Weakness and Sinfulness:** Satan uses our awareness of our own weaknesses to undermine our courage and perseverance in pursuing holiness. Resist these discouraging thoughts.

- **Be Ever Vigilant:** Satan is constantly active, waiting for the opportune moment to strike. Stay alert to his tactics at all times.

- **Pray Continuously:** Despite being a fallen angel, Satan's intelligence surpasses that of humans. To combat him, divine

assistance is essential. Maintain a close relationship with God through continuous prayer.

- **Cultivate Humility and Trust in God:** St. Padre Pio emphasized that "Satan fears and trembles before humble souls." Arrogance and self-reliance make one vulnerable, but humility and trust in God provide protection. Satan avoids humble souls because they rely on God's strength rather than their own.

- **Lean on the Cross of Jesus:** "The best way to avoid falling is to lean on the cross of Jesus," St. Padre Pio advised. Even the fiercest temptations cannot shake a soul firmly attached to the Cross. Embrace Jesus crucified as your source of hope and safety.

- **Seek Help from Saint Michael the Archangel and Your Guardian Angel:** Guardian Angels are assigned to protect us from dangers, including the temptations of Satan. Invoke their protection at the first sign of temptation, or even before it begins. Archangel Michael, who led the faithful angels in battle against Satan, can also assist in driving the devil away from your soul.

- **Deepen Your Devotion to Our Lady:** According to St. Padre Pio, Our Lady provides strength and courage in the fight against Satan. He often referred to the Rosary of Mary as a powerful weapon against evil. St. Padre Pio recounted a vision in which he was given the Rosary as a weapon by the Madonna, which immediately vanquished a multitude of devils. He urged his spiritual children to love and recite the Rosary frequently, as it is a formidable defense against demonic forces.

In the Book of Revelation, God ultimately triumphs over all evil. When the weight of spiritual warfare feels overwhelming or

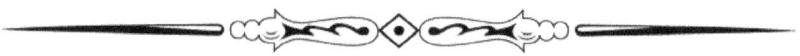

anxiety-inducing, I find solace in the words of the Apostle John. His vision reminds us that God's victory is certain, offering hope and peace in the face of struggle. There, he reveals the ultimate victory of God over Satan and all the forces of darkness. God's power and sovereignty are not just present now—they are eternal, and His triumph is assured. The Catholic faith teaches us that while we are called to engage in the spiritual battle, we do not fight alone. God has already secured the victory through Jesus Christ, who conquered sin, death, and the devil. The cross, though it was a moment of apparent defeat, was in fact the decisive victory over Satan's power. Through Christ's resurrection, the gates of hell have been defeated, and the promise of eternal life has been made secure for all who follow Him. This assurance of God's final victory gives me great peace, knowing that no matter how intense the battle against evil may seem in our lives, we are part of a larger story—one in which God's light will ultimately overcome the darkness. The Catholic Church continually reminds us of this promise through its sacraments, its teachings, and the witness of the saints. We are not alone in our struggles, and we can stand firm in the hope that, in the end, God will make all things right. This is why I believe in the beauty and truth of the Catholic faith. It is a faith that gives us the strength to endure in the face of temptation, doubt, and suffering, while also offering us the hope of final victory in Christ. It assures us that, no matter how difficult the spiritual battle may be, the outcome is certain: God will triumph, and we, through His grace, will share in that victory. This is the hope and beauty that the Catholic faith offers, and it is why I believe in it with all my heart.

The Role of Satan and Demons:

One of the more difficult yet necessary truths of the Catholic faith is the reality of spiritual warfare—our ongoing battle against forces of evil, led by Satan, the prince of hell. In the beauty of the Catholic tradition, we are taught not only of God's infinite love and mercy but also of the dangers that arise when we stray from His

protection and guidance. The existence of Satan and his demonic followers is an integral part of this spiritual reality, and understanding their influence is key to appreciating both the depth of our human freedom and the power of God's grace to protect and save us. Satan, also known as Lucifer, was once a beautiful angel, but through his pride and rebellion, he fell from grace and became the prince of hell. He commands a vast army of demons, each falling from grace and bound in their malevolence. As the mystic St. Padre Pio explained, the number of demons is so great that if each one were reduced to the size of a grain of sand, they would blot out the sun. Their power, their malice, and their cunning are real, and they constantly seek to exploit human weaknesses, feeding off sin and turning human hearts away from God.

I recognize that these demonic forces are not some abstract concepts but real threats that seek to destroy souls. Satan and his legions are adept at finding openings in our lives—whether through direct invitation via occult practices or through the vulnerabilities created by grave sin. Practices such as witchcraft, astrology, fortune-telling, or engaging with the occult can serve as gateways for demonic influence. The Catholic Church warns us to avoid these practices, not out of superstition but because they open the door to forces far greater than we can comprehend. Even areas of addiction, sexual immorality, and unrepentant sin provide demons with opportunities to bind us in spiritual darkness. Perhaps the most tragic invitation to demonic influence is abortion. The Church has long taught that abortion is not only a grave moral sin but also an act that profoundly offends the sanctity of life and opens the door to spiritual harm. Those involved in the abortion industry or who support abortion are urged to seek repentance, for this sin carries an immense weight, both in the spiritual and natural order. Satan delights in destruction, and the taking of innocent life is one of the ways he furthers his diabolical designs.

Pope Francis has consistently warned against engaging with Satan, cautioning that even the smallest conversation with him is a

grave error. Satan is far more intelligent and manipulative than any human being can imagine. As the father of lies and an expert in deception, his influence is insidious. He doesn't present himself as the overt monster we might expect, but instead as a whisper, a temptation that seems reasonable, appealing, and right. His goal is always to lead us away from the truth and God's love. This is why I believe in the beauty of the Catholic faith, for it gives us the armor of truth to recognize and resist these deceptions. Even more compelling is the power of God's grace and the strength of the Church in combating these forces of evil. One of the most striking aspects of the relationship between demons and hell is their fear of it. In exorcisms, demons often resist being cast out, begging to remain in their human victims rather than face the abyss of hell. This is reminiscent of the biblical account of the demons in the Gerasene man, known as Legion, who, when confronted by Jesus, begged not to be cast into hell but instead to be allowed to enter a herd of swine (Mark 5:1-20). The demons' fear of hell reveals just how horrific and agonizing their eternal fate truly is. It is a place of total separation from God, a prison of torment from which there is no escape.

This fear of hell reinforces why I believe in the power of God's mercy and the importance of spiritual vigilance. The demons themselves know the horror of hell intimately, and their goal is to bring as many souls with them as possible. This is why the Church, through the power of the sacraments, especially the Eucharist, Confession, and the Rite of Exorcism, provides us the means of grace to resist these spiritual attacks. Through prayer, especially the Rosary, and a life lived in union with Christ, we are protected from the enemy's influence. These tools of grace are not just symbolic; they are powerful means by which we can participate in the victory of Christ over sin, death, and the devil. In recognizing the reality of spiritual warfare, I also come to a deeper appreciation of the profound beauty of our faith. It is a faith that does not shy.

Finally, to end this chapter is a fascinating and disturbing true story from Germany in 1975 that revolves around Anneliese Michel,

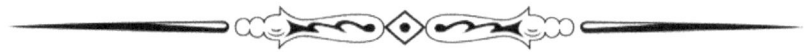

a 23-year-old woman raised in a deeply devout Catholic family. At a time when the Church was undergoing significant changes, both legitimate and controversial, Anneliese had a profound experience. The Blessed Mother appeared to her and asked if she would be willing to suffer for the youth of Germany and its clergy. After some contemplation, Anneliese agreed, and she was aware that this suffering would manifest in the form of demonic possession. The Blessed Mother revealed that Anneliese would become a victim soul, enduring possession to show the world that demons are real. As the possession unfolded, it is believed Anneliese was tormented by up to ten demons, some of whom identified themselves, including Lucifer, Cain, Nero, Judas, Hitler, and a demonic priest named Father Fleischmann. The story of Anneliese Michel serves as a chilling reminder of the existence of evil forces, according to those who witnessed her ordeal. The following quotes are taken from an interview with Father Joseph Fortea in his book *Anneliese Michel: A true story of a case of demonic possession* by Fr. Jose Antonio Fortea and Lawrence E.U. LeBlanc

Lucifer:

> "I want to conquer the earth for myself. In the meantime, I make a rich booty. I am filling up my kingdom. I take whatever I can take; I must convince you of this."

> "The majority have abandoned the Nazarene. How foolish! Those still faithful are a small flock."

> I took Judas with me! He is always at my service. He is damned. He could have saved himself, but he did not follow the Nazarene."

> The enemies of the Church belong to us."

> "O, if you had an idea of how things stand below! The visionary children of Fatima have seen it. If you had an idea...

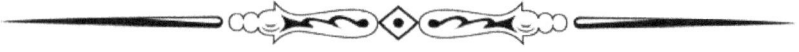

you would be on your knee's day and night at the tabernacle. I had to say it because the High Lady compels me to."

➤ "I am responsible for heresies."

➤ The Priests should say that I exist or else they will go down."

➤ "The apparitions of San Damiano and Montechiari are true. The Church did not approve them, but this is the fruit of our work."

Judas:

➤ "I am damned for all eternity! You careless people, if you could just imagine what it is to be damned for eternity, I am damned!"

➤ "I will not come out of this girl. Down there it is too tormenting."

➤ If people knew what was in store for them by not going to church it will fair then extremely bad."

➤ "These modernists are the result of my work and they all belong to me."

➤ "They no longer obey the Pope in Rome. It is the one in Rome who still keeps the Church going."

➤ "The religious in monasteries watch tv and don't pray enough, do not kneel down and they extend their paws, receiving Holy Communion in the hand."

➤ "The giving of Communion in the hand was my work."

➤ "Holy water should come back to houses. Also, the crucifix should return to its place in the home."

- ➢ "The Holy Face should be venerated."

- ➢ "The Divine Mercy image should be propagated."

- ➢ "It is very important to pray to Saint Joseph. Rather, it is most important."

- ➢ "If the message of Fatima is not given due importance and Humanae Vitae, a new punishment will come."

- ➢ "It won't last much longer. The chastisement is coming.

- ➢ "Everyone has a Guardian Angel. Guardian Angels are my enemies. I hate them."

- ➢ "People standing during Holy Communion pleases me more than kneeling. I do everything possible so that no one is on his knees."

- ➢ "We are very happy with the new reform of the Church. We are most happy with these changes."

- ➢ "Many do not go to church any longer. No one kneels down to the Blessed Sacrament. And the Church is not doing well since the time it was founded. The churches are so modern! The Nazarene and His Mother are now attacking"

Cain:

- ➢ "I have killed my brother; I am burning."

Father Fleischmann:

- ➢ "I was a priest at Ettleben. I am damned. It is horrible down there. Judas pulled me down there."

- ➢ "I am damned because I fulfilled my duties very badly."

- ➤ "I have killed one person and I have had women."

- ➤ "I prayed too little. I was always in a hurry to finish my sacred duties. Now I am down there languishing for eternity."

- ➤ "No priest should marry."

- ➤ "If the bishops did not permit communion in the hand, this would not have happened."

Nero:

- ➤ "You should follow the message of Fatima."

- ➤ "Humanae Vitae is decisive, the whole Humanae Vitae!"

- ➤ "The Rosary should be recited or else it is the end."

- ➤ "The Dutch bishops are heretics. They have become unfaithful to the Pope."

- ➤ "Catholics have the true doctrine, and they run after the Protestants like prostitutes."

- ➤ "People should go to confession."

- ➤ "Abortion is homicide."

Miscellaneous things demons said:

- ➤ "The modernists are killing the Church. We are hard at work at this."

- ➤ "No one speaks any longer of us, especially the parish priests."

- ➤ "The bishops are so foolish as to believe the theologians like Kung rather than the Pope."

> This is the month of the rosary but very few recite it because the parish priests think it's not modern. They are so foolish! IF they knew its importance! It is a strong weapon against Satan and against us."

After enduring 67 exorcism sessions, Anneliese Michel passed away on July 1st, 1976. Since her death, her grave has become a place of pilgrimage, with people visiting it regularly, drawn by the significance of her story. The site has gained a reputation as a spiritual destination for many. More information about this story can be found on the internet. Her mother stated that her daughter received the Stigmata during the procession. The cause of death was dehydration and malnutrition secondary to Anneliese's stopping eating during this time. Her parents and the two priests were charged with her death. The charges were later dropped. I assure you, there is more information one can read regarding this story.

"Red Forman: "Eric what did I tell you about calling your sister the Devil"?

Eric Forman: "It's offensive to the Devil"? [15]

---

[15] www.TV fanatic.com/70 show quotes.

Chapter Sixteen
Hell

The Catholic faith, in its fullness, holds together both the astonishing beauty of God's mercy and the sobering reality of His justice. While the concept of hell is difficult and sobering, it is through these warnings that Jesus, in His infinite mercy, calls us to choose life and to live in right relationship with God. His teachings on hell are not meant to instill fear but to encourage us to avoid the eternal separation from God that comes from rejecting His love.

Jesus speaks about hell multiple times in the Gospels—23 times, to be precise—highlighting its gravity and urging us to take our spiritual lives seriously. He does not shy away from describing hell as a place of eternal suffering and separation from God, where *"the worm does not die, and the fire is not quenched"* (Mark 9:48). Yet, in these warnings, we also see the mercy of Christ, who desires that no one should perish but that all should come to repentance (2 Peter 3:9). His warnings about hell are an invitation to conversion, a call to turn away from sin, and to live in accordance with God's will. In the Gospel of Matthew, Jesus speaks of hell in the context of judgment,

where those who have rejected God's commandments and lived in unrepentant sin will be cast into "the outer darkness," a place *"where there will be weeping and gnashing of teeth"* (Matthew 25:30). These stark words remind us of the consequences of turning away from God. Still, they also remind us of the beauty of God's justice and His invitation to choose righteousness. Jesus' teachings on hell, while sobering, are always framed within the context of God's loving desire for our salvation. Hell exists, not as something God wants for us, but as the tragic consequence of freely choosing to reject His love and grace. Yet, in the Catholic faith, we are constantly reminded that God, in His mercy, provides us with all the means to avoid hell—the sacraments, prayer, the grace of the Holy Spirit, and the constant invitation to conversion. It presents the fullness of truth, including the reality of hell, but it does so with the loving invitation to come back to God, to seek forgiveness, and to embrace the grace that leads to eternal life with Him. The Catholic faith does not shy away from brutal truths, but rather, it offers them in the context of God's abundant mercy. And it is in this mercy that I find the true beauty of our faith: a faith that calls us to holiness and eternal happiness, while offering us the strength and grace to avoid the darkness and despair of hell.

Similarly, the Blessed Mother, in her appearances throughout history, has echoed Jesus' warnings about hell, particularly in her messages at Fatima and Medjugorje. She spoke of the reality of hell as a place where souls suffer, and she urged us to pray for the conversion of sinners and to embrace penance. Through her maternal love, the Blessed Mother doesn't seek to frighten us, but to guide us toward holiness, offering us a path of hope, repentance, and salvation.

Blessed Bishop Fulton Sheen once shared a story about a man who visited hell. He asked Saint Peter for permission to see hell, and Saint Peter granted his request. Upon his return to heaven, the man described his visit with enthusiasm, saying it was a fantastic party. A few weeks later, he requested another visit to hell, and again, Saint

Peter allowed it. Once more, the man reported an amazing time, enjoying the revelry. When he asked for a third visit, Saint Peter agreed, but this time, the experience was drastically different. The man found himself in a fiery cell with a terrible stench, tormented by demons. In agony, he asked the devil why he was being treated so harshly. The devil replied, "The first two times you were here, you were just a tourist. Now, you are a resident!"

One of the greatest aspects of the Catholic faith is its ability to speak truthfully about the beauty of God's love and the sobering reality of His justice. Central to Catholic teaching is the understanding of hell, a reality that has been revealed in Scripture and illuminated by the Church's Tradition. While the concept of hell may seem unsettling or even foreign to some, it is, in fact, an essential part of understanding the fullness of God's plan for humanity—a plan rooted in both His infinite love and His unyielding justice.

The term "hell" appears in various forms throughout sacred Scripture. In the Latin Vulgate, it is referred to as *infernos*, while in the Greek texts of the New Testament, the word *Hades* is used, and in the Hebrew Scriptures, *Sheol* often appears. Each of these terms conveys a depth of meaning that reflects distinct aspects of the human condition—both the consequences of sin and the potential for eternal separation from God.

Jesus, in His compassion, speaks of hell to warn us of its reality. According to the different translations of the Bible, the word "hell" appears numerous times. In the King James Version (KJV), it is mentioned 54 times, emphasizing the gravity with which the concept is treated. The New International Version (NIV) mentions it 13 times, and the English Standard Version (ESV) mentions it 14 times. Still, the message remains consistent: hell is a real and terrifying possibility for those who choose to live in defiance of God's will. Jesus' teachings on hell—particularly in the New Testament—

are sobering and direct. In fact, in my catholic bible, He speaks about it 22 times, emphasizing its reality and the need for vigilance in our faith.

But, it is not only the warnings that speak to me; it is the broader context of Jesus' message—the Good News—that makes the truth of hell so powerful. Hell exists not because God wants to condemn, but because God respects human freedom. He desires that all should be saved and come to the knowledge of the truth, and it is this very freedom that allows us to choose Him or reject Him.

The beauty of the Catholic faith lies in its offering of redemption: a way to avoid hell, not by mere avoidance of sin but through the transformative power of God's grace and mercy. The Catholic Church teaches that through the sacraments, prayer, and acts of charity, we are continually invited to turn towards God, to repent and believe in His love. The Eucharist, the source and summit of the Christian life, is a testament to God's immense desire for communion with His people. When we receive the Body and Blood of Christ, we are reminded that He has conquered sin and death, offering us a path to eternal life. It is this offer of grace, this constant invitation to return to Him, that underscores the beauty of the Catholic faith. The reality of hell does not negate the goodness of God—it highlights the depth of His love and the seriousness of our spiritual journey. Hell is not the ultimate desire of God; rather, it is a consequence of rejecting His mercy, a mercy that is boundless and ever available to those who repent and seek His forgiveness. In embracing the beauty and truth of the Catholic faith, I come to understand that hell is not a threat to keep us in line, but a stark reminder that our choices matter. It is a call to seek the fullness of life in Christ, to live in the light of His truth, and to participate in the eternal joy He desires for us. The Church's teachings on hell are not a denial of God's love, but a reaffirmation of the reality of His justice and the unrelenting beauty of His mercy.

Jesus emphasized the reality of hell, offering multiple warnings throughout His teachings. Here are a few notable references:

- **Matthew 5:21-22:** "*You have heard that it was said to the people long ago, 'You shall not murder, and anyone who murders will be subject to judgment.' But I tell you that anyone who is angry with a brother or sister will be subject to judgment. Again, anyone who says to a brother or sister, Raca, is answerable to the court. And anyone who says, 'You fool!' will be in danger of the fire of hell.*"

- **Matthew 23:15,33:** "*Woe to you, teachers of the law and Pharisees, you hypocrites! You travel over land and sea to win a single convert, and when you have succeeded, you make them twice as much a child of hell as you are. You snakes! You brood of vipers! How will you escape being condemned to hell?*"

- **Matthew 5:29:** "*If your right eye causes you to stumble, gouge it out and throw it away. It is better for you to lose one part of your body than for your whole body to be thrown into hell.*"

- **Matthew 25:41:** "*Then he will say to those on his left, 'Depart from me, you who are cursed, into the eternal fire prepared for the devil and his angels.'*"

- **Luke 12:5:** "*But I will show you whom you should fear: Fear him who, after your body has been killed, has authority to throw you into hell. Yes, I tell you, fear him.*"

- **Luke 16:28:** In the parable of the rich man and Lazarus, Jesus refers to "*this place of torment.*"

- **Luke 3:16-17:** "*John answered them all, 'I baptize you with water. But one who is more powerful than I will come, the straps of whose sandals I am not worthy to untie. He will baptize you with the Holy Spirit and fire. His winnowing fork is in his hand to clear his threshing floor and to gather the* *wheat into his barn, but he will burn up the chaff with unquenchable fire.'"*

- **Mark 9:43-48:** *"If your hand causes you to stumble, cut it off. It is better for you to enter life maimed than with two hands to go into hell, where the fire never goes out. And if your foot causes you to stumble, cut it off. It is better for you to enter life crippled than to have two feet and be thrown into hell. And if your eye causes you to stumble, pluck it out. It is better for you to enter the kingdom of God with one eye than to have two eyes and be thrown into hell, where 'the worms that eat them do not die, and the fire is not quenched.'"*

Saint John Chrysostom is reputed to have said, "We must not ask where hell is, but how we are to escape it." In 1916, near Fátima, Portugal, the Blessed Mother appeared to three shepherd children: Lucia (age 9), Francisco (age 8), and his sister Jacinta (age 6). She entrusted them with three secrets, the first of which was a horrifying vision of hell. Sister Lucy (Lucy Dos Santos) later described this vision in her memoirs: "Mary opened her hands once more, as she had done in the previous months. Rays of light seemed to penetrate the earth, revealing souls in torment. These souls appeared as transparent burning embers, blackened or burnished bronze, with human forms. They were floating in a fiery conflagration, sometimes lifted by the flames, then falling back amid shrieks and groans of pain and despair. This sight was so terrifying that it made us tremble with fear. The demons were distinguished by their dreadful resemblance to terrifying and unknown animals, black and transparent like burning coals. The vision lasted only a moment, thanks to Our Lady's promise to take us to Heaven, or I believe we would have died from fear and horror." The vivid descriptions and teachings about hell.

On June 24, 1981, the Blessed Mother appeared to six children in Medjugorje, Bosnia and Herzegovina. The visionaries were Ivanka Ivankovic-Elez, Mirjana Dragicevic-Soldo, Vicka Ivankovic-Mijatovic, Marija Pavlovic-Lunetti, Ivan Dragicevic, and Jakov Colo.

During these apparitions, only four of the six were permitted to witness hell. According to James Mulligan's book, *Medjugorje: What's Happening*, the Blessed Mother offered Mirjana and Ivanka the choice to see hell, which they declined. Ivan and Marija chose to view it, while Vicka and Jakov were physically taken to hell by the Blessed Mother. Below is a detailed description of what Vicka and Jakov experienced:

Vicka's Account:

- **On the Reality of Hell:** Vicka reported seeing many souls in hell, stating that some are already there, while others will join them after death. The Blessed Mother revealed that the souls in hell are there because they chose to be, rejecting God even in the face of His continual efforts to guide them toward holiness.

- **Description of Hell:** Vicka described hell as a place with a central, immense fire resembling an ocean of raging flames. The souls before entering the fire appeared human, but as they became more resistant to God's will, they descended deeper into the fire. The deeper they went, the more grotesque and inhuman they became. Upon emerging from the fire, they lost their human shape and appeared as grotesque, monstrous beings, each unique and horrifying. They were depicted as enraged and destructive, filled with fury, and making dreadful sounds.

- **Impact on Prayer:** Witnessing hell profoundly affected Vicka's prayer life. She now fervently prays for the conversion of sinners, understanding the dire consequences of rejecting God. She noted that individuals who turn away from God through their choices end up in hell, where they lose all connection to Him. Hell becomes their eternal state of separation from God's mercy, and they carry the consequences of their choices into eternity.

Marija's Account: Marija also shared her experiences of hell, further illuminating the horrors witnessed and the implications for the souls who find themselves there.

These accounts from Medjugorje emphasize the severity of hell and the importance of choosing a path aligned with God's will to avoid eternal separation from Him.

Marija Pavlovic-Lunetti's Vision:

Question: "Marija, have you ever seen hell?"

Marija: "Yes, I have. Hell is a vast expanse with a great sea of fire at its center, teeming with many souls. I distinctly remember seeing a beautiful young girl who, upon approaching the fire, lost her beauty and emerged as a monstrous, inhuman creature. The Blessed Mother explained that God grants everyone the freedom to choose their path. Those who end up in hell do so because they have chosen it. Hell is the result of their own choices."

Question: "Marija, how does a soul choose hell for eternity?"

Marija: "At the moment of death, God provides us with the light to see ourselves as we truly are. Throughout life, we have the freedom to make choices, and those who live in sin can recognize their true selves when faced with this divine illumination. Seeing themselves as they are, such souls find that hell is the only fitting place for them. It is not God who condemns them; rather, they condemn themselves. Our freedom of choice determines our eternal destination."

Vision from Kibeho, Rwanda: Beginning on November 28, 1981, the Blessed Mother appeared to eight children in Kibeho, Rwanda. One of the visionaries described her vision of hell as follows: "The last place we visited was a land of twilight, with only an unpleasant shade of red illuminating the scene, reminiscent of congealed blood. The heat was stifling and dry, brushing against my face like a flame,

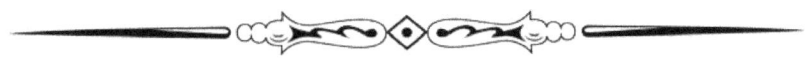

causing me to fear that my skin might blister. The suffering of the countless souls there was so intense that I could not bear to look at them. Mary did not need to name this place; I instantly knew it was hell."

Throughout history, many saints, such as St. John Bosco, St. Teresa of Avila, St. Hildegard of Bingen, and St. Catherine of Siena, have received visions of hell. These experiences were not meant to frighten, but to enlighten us on the gravity of sin and the importance of living a life of holiness. These saints, in their deep love for God, were granted extraordinary insights into the consequences of turning away from His love. One of the most poignant and vivid descriptions comes from St. Faustina Kowalska, whose visions of hell are recorded in her diary, *Divine Mercy in My Soul*. In these writings, St. Faustina describes an angel leading her to the "chasms of hell," a place of unspeakable torment. She recounts her experience of this horrifying vision, where the sufferings of the damned are almost too terrible to comprehend: "Today, an angel led me to the chasms of hell. It is a vast and horrifying place of great torment. The sufferings I witnessed include:

1. The loss of God, which is the most significant pain of all.

2. Perpetual remorse of conscience.

3. The unchanging nature of one's condition.

4. Spiritual fire that torments the soul without consuming it.

5. Continuous darkness, a suffocating stench, and the sight of both the devils and the damned, who see each other's and their evil.

6. The constant presence of Satan.

7. Horrible despair, hatred of God, vile words, curses, and blasphemies.

These are common tortures, but each soul experiences additional, specific sufferings based on their sins. There are various caverns and pits where each form of agony differs. I would have perished from these tortures if not for the omnipotence of God supporting me." In her vision, St. Faustina is struck by the profound loss of God, which she describes as the greatest pain of all. It is a loss that no other suffering could compare to, and it underscores the central teaching of Catholicism: the eternal happiness of the soul is found only in communion with God. The soul's separation from God, she reveals, is the ultimate torment of hell. This vision speaks to the great truth of the Catholic faith: that we were created for God and that the true fulfillment comes only through Him. What St. Faustina also highlights is the *unchanging* nature of one's condition in hell. There is no hope, no relief, no chance of escape.

The despair of the damned is unending. This perpetual state of suffering is aggravated by the continual presence of Satan, the father of lies, who is the cause of all evil and hatred towards God. The damned, in their final rejection of God's love, are bound by their own hatred, remorse, and blasphemies, each soul experiencing torments according to their sins. But while these accounts are undeniably sobering, they do not define the whole of our faith. The reality of hell is not a lesson in despair but a call to action—a call to live in the light of God's truth, to turn away from sin, and to embrace the grace He offers through the sacraments, prayer, and the works of mercy. Hell, in the vision of saints like St. Faustina, serves as a reminder of the stakes of the spiritual battle in which we are all engaged. The Church does not present hell to frighten us, but to warn us of the consequences of a life lived in separation from God. It is a call to conversion and repentance, an invitation to experience the infinite mercy of God before it is too late.

Jesus Christ, through His life, death, and resurrection, has opened the gates of Heaven to all who will accept His invitation to love and follow Him. The Sacrament of Confession is a gift of mercy, offering us a way to reconcile with God and avoid the eternal suffering that results from rejecting His grace. The Eucharist, the source and summit of Christian life, is the ultimate sign of God's desire for communion with His people. By partaking in the Body and Blood of Christ, we are drawn into union with Him, nourishing our souls and strengthening us for the journey ahead.

A German Augustinian nun, Blessed Anne Catherine Emmerich, offers a harrowing depiction of hell in her mystical experiences, detailed in *The Dolorous Passion of Our Lord Jesus Christ*: "My soul descended with Jesus to the very depths of the great abyss—hell itself. The exterior of hell was appalling and fearsome: an immense, heavy structure made of black granite with a metallic sheen. The doors of this grim edifice were secured with formidable bolts, their mere sight inducing trembling. Even through the tightly shut doors, the deep groans and cries of despair were audible. Yet, when the bolts were removed and the doors flung open, the horrendous cacophony of shouts and shrieks was unbearable. Hell presented itself like a city, but one filled with intense misery and confusion. Every corner of this dreadful place was designed to evoke pain and grief. The marks of divine wrath and vengeance were evident everywhere, with despair spreading to every heart. The city was a chaotic expanse of dismal dungeons, dark caverns, frightful wastelands, and fetid swamps teeming with revolting reptiles and poisonous creatures. Hell is a realm of eternal anguish and discord, where every form of sin and corruption is represented by ghastly torments. Comfort or consolation finds no place in this temple of despair."

Hell is real, but so is the mercy of God, which is greater than everything, all the powers of darkness. The teachings of the saints and the visions they received help us to understand the stakes of our spiritual lives—not to instill fear, but to encourage us to turn to God in faith and trust. When we align our lives with God's will, seeking His grace through prayer, penance, and the sacraments, we are assured that no torment, darkness, or evil can separate us from His love. As I reflect on these powerful testimonies of the saints, I am reminded that the Catholic faith is not merely a set of rules, but a profound invitation to experience the fullness of life in God, now and for all eternity. The truth of hell, while sobering, is balanced by the eternal beauty of God's mercy, which is always available to us, calling us back into His loving embrace. And this, above all, is the foremost reason why I believe in the beauty and truth of the Catholic faith.

Chapter Seventeen
Heaven

John Kinsella: "Is this heaven?

Ray Kinsella: "It's Iowa

John Kinsella: "Iowa? I could have sworn this was heaven."

Ray Kinsella: 'Is there a heaven?

John Kinsella: "Oh yeah. It's the place where dreams come true.

(Ray looks around......... seeing his wife playing with their daughter on the porch)

Ray Kinsella: "Maybe this is heaven."[16]

---

[16] Phil Alden Robinson, <u>Fields of Dream</u>, movie quote. 1989

As Catholics, we believe in the promise of eternal life with God, a promise that is rooted in the death and resurrection of Jesus Christ. Heaven, the ultimate goal of our existence, is a place of perfect peace, joy, and communion with the Divine. We know, through faith, that when our time on earth is over, we will be called into the presence of God, where *"Eye has not seen, nor ear heard, nor the human heart conceived what God has prepared for those who love Him"* (1 Corinthians 2:9). Yet, despite this certainty, many of us still find ourselves holding back from a wholehearted desire to go there—at least, not today.

Why is that? Why, when we profess faith in Jesus and His promises, do we hesitate at the thought of death? After all, Jesus Himself reassured us: *"Do not let your hearts be troubled. You believe in God; believe also in Me. My Father's house has many rooms... I am going there to prepare a place for you"* (John 14:1-2). If we genuinely believe in these words, if we hold firm to the hope that heaven is our destination, then why is there still a lingering fear of death in our hearts? As I reflect on this, I come to appreciate that the Catholic faith offers a profound understanding of the complexities of human nature—our bodies, our minds, and our souls. Yes, our ultimate destiny is with God in heaven, but we are also deeply connected to our earthly lives, the people we love, and the experiences that shape us. It is not simply fear of the unknown that keeps us from eagerly welcoming death; rather, it is our attachment to this world, our love for life, and our deep desire to fulfill God's will for us here, now.

In the beauty of the Catholic faith, we are reminded that life is a gift. The very fact that we are alive today, with all its joys and challenges, is a grace from God. The love we experience with family and friends, the work we do, the beauty of creation—all of these are glimpses of the goodness of God's plan for us. While we know that heaven is our true home, it is natural to feel a sense of reluctance to

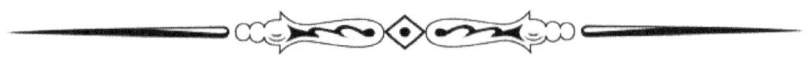

leave behind the things that we hold dear. We are called to love life in its fullness, to cherish the time we have, and to live with purpose. The fear of death is not always a lack of faith, but a natural human response to the reality of separation from the life we know and love. Yet, the beauty of the Catholic faith lies precisely in its ability to help us navigate this tension. We do not deny the reality of death, nor do we try to avoid it. But we also know that death is not the end. Jesus has conquered death, and through Him, we have the promise of eternal life. The resurrection of Jesus is the cornerstone of our faith—through His victory over sin and death, He has opened the gates of heaven for us. We are assured that death is not a tragedy, but a passage into something greater. At the same time, the Church teaches us that our journey towards heaven is not a passive waiting for the end, but an active participation in God's grace. We are called to live each day in faith, hope, and love, knowing that every moment is an opportunity to grow closer to God. The sacraments, prayers, and the works of mercy help us to remain focused on the eternal while still fully engaged in the present. As St. Paul writes, *"For to me, to live is Christ and to die is gain"* (Philippians 1:21). In the Catholic faith, we learn to live with the tension of being in the world but not of it, of living fully and joyfully while also longing for the life to come.

The fear of death, I believe, is also rooted in the uncertainty that surrounds the moment of our passing. Though we believe in God's mercy, we still face the mystery of our own personal judgment. We trust that God is loving and merciful, but the process of leaving behind our earthly attachments, confronting our imperfections, and facing our final judgment can stir anxiety. The beauty of the Catholic faith is that it gives us the tools to prepare for this moment: regular confession, the anointing of the sick, and the constant invitation to draw near to God. These sacraments help us to be ready, to die well, and to face death with peace, knowing that we are held in the arms of our loving Father. Furthermore, the Church's teachings on purgatory offer a beautiful perspective on the afterlife. While heaven is the goal, purgatory is not a place of punishment but purification. It is God's loving mercy at work, helping us to become fully cleansed and ready to enter His presence. This teaching reminds me that even though I may not feel ideally be ready to enter heaven, God is always at work in my soul, shaping me into the person He wants me to be.

In the end, I believe that the fear of death is not a sign of a lack of faith, but a reflection of our human nature—a nature that longs for both the beauty of this world and the promise of the next. The beauty of the Catholic faith is that it holds both these truths together: we are called to live fully, to love deeply, and to experience God's grace in the here and now, while also keeping our eyes fixed on the eternal life that awaits us. The Catholic faith teaches me that death is not to be feared, but embraced, not as an end but as a transition into the fullness of life with God.   I trust in the beauty of God's plan for me, knowing that He walks with me through every fear, every joy, and every moment. The promise of heaven, which Jesus Himself has made, is a reality I look toward with hope, not dread. And while I may not desire to leave this world today, I find peace in the truth that, when the time comes, I will be ready, held in the grace and mercy of a God who loves me beyond measure.

As Catholics, we believe in the promise of eternal life with God, a promise that is rooted in the death and resurrection of Jesus Christ. Heaven, the goal of our existence, is a place of perfect peace, joy, and communion with the Divine. We know, through faith, that when our time on earth is over, we will be called into the presence of God, where *"eye has not seen, nor ear heard, nor the human heart conceived what God has prepared for those who love Him"* (1 Corinthians 2:9). Yet, despite this certainty, many of us still find ourselves holding back from a wholehearted desire to go there—at least, not today. Why is that? Why, when we profess faith in Jesus and His promises, do we hesitate at the thought of death? After all, Jesus Himself reassured us: *"Do not let your hearts be troubled. You believe in God; believe also in Me. My Father's house has many rooms... I am going there to prepare a place for you"* (John 14:1-2). If we honestly believe in these words, if we hold firm to the hope that

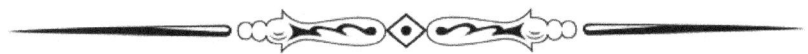

heaven is our destination, then why is there still a lingering fear of death in our hearts?

I come to appreciate that the Catholic faith offers a profound understanding of the complexities of human nature—our bodies, our minds, and our souls. Yes, our ultimate destiny is with God in heaven, but we are also deeply connected to our earthly lives, to the people we love, and the experiences that shape us. It is not simply fear of the unknown that keeps us from eagerly welcoming death; rather, it is our attachment to this world, our love for life, and our deep desire to fulfill God's will for us here, now. The love we experience with family and friends, the work we do, the beauty of creation—all of these are glimpses of the goodness of God's plan for us. While we know heaven is our true home, it is natural to feel reluctant to leave behind the things we hold dear. We are called to love life in its fullness, cherish our time, and live with purpose. The fear of death is not always a lack of faith, but a natural human response to the reality of separation from the life we know and love. Yet, the beauty of the Catholic faith is precisely in its ability to help us navigate this tension. We do not deny the reality of death, nor do we try to avoid it. But we also know that death is not the end. Jesus has conquered death, and through Him, we have the promise of eternal life. The resurrection of Jesus is the cornerstone of our faith—through His victory over sin and death, He has opened the gates of heaven for us. We are assured that death is not a tragedy, but a passage into something greater. At the same time, the Church teaches us that our journey towards heaven is not a passive waiting for the end, but an active participation in God's grace. We are called to live each day in faith, hope, and love, knowing that every moment is an opportunity to grow closer to God. The sacraments, prayers, and the works of mercy help us to remain focused on the eternal while still fully engaged in the present. As St. Paul writes, "For to me, to live is Christ and to die is gain" (Philippians 1:21). In the Catholic faith, we learn to live with the tension of being in the world but not of it, of living fully and joyfully while also longing for the life to come.

The fear of death is rooted in the uncertainty that surrounds the moment of our passing. Though we believe in God's mercy, we still face the mystery of our own personal judgment. We trust that God is loving and merciful, but the process of leaving behind our earthly attachments, confronting our imperfections, and facing our final judgment can stir anxiety. The beauty of the Catholic faith is that it gives us the tools to prepare for this moment: regular confession, the anointing of the sick, and the constant invitation to draw near to God. These sacraments help us to be ready, to die well, and to face death with peace, knowing that we are held in the arms of our loving Father. Furthermore, the Church's teachings on purgatory offer a beautiful perspective on the afterlife. While heaven is the goal, purgatory is not a place of punishment but a place of purification. It is God's loving mercy at work, helping us to become fully cleansed and ready to enter His presence. This teaching reminds me that even though I may not feel perfectly ready to enter heaven, God is always at work in my soul, shaping me into the person He created me to be. In the end, the fear of death is not a sign of a lack of faith, but a reflection of our human nature—a nature that longs for both the beauty of this world and the promise of the next. The beauty of the Catholic faith is that it holds both these truths together: we are called to live fully, to love deeply, and to experience God's grace in the here and now, while also keeping our eyes fixed on the eternal life that awaits us. The Catholic faith teaches me that death is not to be feared, but embraced, not as an end but as a transition into the fullness of life with God.

I trust in the beauty of God's plan for me, knowing that He walks with me through every fear, every joy, and every moment. The promise of heaven, which Jesus Himself has made, is a reality I look toward with hope, not dread. And while I may not desire to leave this world today, I find peace in the truth that, when the time comes, I will be ready held in the grace and mercy of a God who loves me beyond measure.

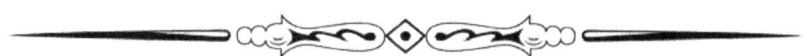

One of the most enduring and meaningful lessons I ever received came from my ninth-grade religion class, taught by Sister Christian Maria. It's been over fifty years, yet I can still recall her words clearly. She told us to pray for a "happy and holy death." I didn't fully grasp the weight of those words, but over the years, I have realized how profound and transformative that simple prayer would become in my life. I can say, without a doubt, that I have prayed for a happy and holy death every night since that lesson, and in doing so, I have come to understand more deeply the beauty and truth of the Catholic faith. In the beauty of the Catholic tradition, we are taught that death is not something to be feared, but rather a passage—a transition from this earthly life to the fullness of life with God. The prayer for a "happy and holy death" is a way of entrusting our lives to God, of acknowledging that every day, every breath is a gift from Him, and that when our time on earth comes to an end, we are ready to return home to Him, prepared in holiness and peace.

Why, you might ask, would I pray such a prayer every night? It's not because I'm morbid or focused on death itself, but because it reflects a deep trust in God's plan. We don't know when our time will come. We don't know what circumstances will surround our final moments, but what we do know that God desires us to live in harmony with His will—to love, to forgive, to serve, and to grow in faith. When I pray for a "happy and holy death," I am asking God to help me live each day with that same peace and trust in His plan. I am asking Him to guide me toward holiness, to make me ready to meet Him when the time comes. This prayer, as simple as it is, has also helped me to confront the fear that so many people have about death. In the world, there is often anxiety and uncertainty about what lies beyond this life. People worry about the unknown, the possible suffering, and the separation from loved ones. But as a Catholic, I believe that death is not an end, but a transformation—a return to the fullness of life in God. When I ask for a "happy and holy death," I am also asking for the grace to face death with the peace and assurance that come from trusting in Christ's promise of eternal life.

The beauty of the Catholic faith lies in its ability to comfort us, not just in life, but in death as well. We know that Jesus has conquered death. Through His Passion, death, and Resurrection, He has opened the gates of heaven for all who believe in Him. I believe that, because of Jesus' victory, death is no longer something to be feared. It is a gateway to eternal life, a reunion with God, and fulfillingour deepest hopes. And while we cannot know the exact moment of our passing, we can live each day in such a way that we are prepared to meet Him when He calls us home. The prayer for a happy and holy death also reminds me of the importance of living with intention, of keeping my heart and mind focused on the things that matter most: faith, love, mercy, and service. It is not just about the end, but about how I live each day, considering that end. As St. Paul wrote, *"For me, to live is Christ, and to die is gain"* (Philippians 1:21). I believe that this prayer, which Sister Christian Maria taught me so many years ago, is a way to continually align my life with Christ, to seek His grace daily, and to trust that when my time comes, I will be ready to embrace the eternal life He has prepared for me.

Over the years, I have come to realize that the prayer for a happy and holy death is not just about asking God to grant me peace at the end of my life. It is a prayer that shapes the way I live now. It reminds me that my life is not my own, but a gift given to me by God, and that each day is an opportunity to live in a way that prepares me for that final moment. It has taught me to be more present to those around me, to cherish each moment, to forgive quickly, to love deeply, and to surrender my life to God's will. As I reflect on this, I am filled with gratitude for the wisdom and guidance I received from Sister Christian Maria all those years ago. Her words, simple yet profound, have shaped my spiritual life in ways I never expected. And now, I can see that the prayer for a happy and holy death is not just a way to face the end with peace, but a reminder to live each day with purpose, with faith, and with the confidence that we are always in God's loving hands. In the beauty and truth of the Catholic faith, we are not alone in the face of death. The grace of God, the prayers of the saints, and the promise of eternal life accompanies us. And for all

these reasons, I believe with all my heart that the Catholic faith offers us not just a way to die well, but a way to live well—with faith, hope, and trust in the love and mercy of our Savior. I've wondered about what heaven is really like and what we'll do there. I've read accounts from saints and visionaries who describe heaven as a place of eternal singing and praising God. Revelation 7:9-10 depicts a scene of a vast multitude from every nation, standing before the throne and the Lamb, dressed in white robes, and holding palm branches, crying out in praise: "Salvation belongs to our God who sits on the throne and to the Lamb."

We all dream about heaven. I know I do. The idea of being in the presence of God, seeing Jesus' face to face, and experiencing the fullness of joy and peace is a hope that every Christian holds close. But, if I'm being honest, sometimes I wonder what heaven will be like. Is it just standing around in robes, singing praise songs forever? While I enjoy singing and praising God, the thought of doing so for eternity in a celestial choir doesn't quite capture the full scope of what my heart longs for. The good news is that the Catholic faith offers us a beautiful understanding of heaven, one that is far beyond anything we can fully grasp but still gives us glimpses of its truth. Here on earth, I take extraordinary joy in activities that nourish my body, mind, and soul. I love the simple pleasures of watching college football, biking through nature, hiking in the mountains, and spending time in quiet reflection at the beach. I savor tasty food—gumbo, pasta, pizza, Oreos, and ice cream—and appreciate the simple joys of being with family and friends. From reading to traveling, fishing, playing with my grandson, walking my dogs, and spending time with my wife and children during Christmas. Life on earth is filled with these small yet significant moments. And, of course, there's the deeper joy I find in my faith—praying, going to the adoration chapel, and attending Mass. These activities, these connections, are what make life rich and meaningful.

But, what about heaven? Will it be a place where these joys are amplified and transformed? Will we still enjoy the things we love,

only in a deeper and more perfect way? And will we really recognize our loved ones? Will we get wings and halos, like in the pictures, or become like angels? Will there be Monday Night Football? I once had a conversation about heaven with my godfather, Monsignor Charles Mallet, who is now ninety-three years old. He's a man of deep wisdom, and our conversation turned to the nature of heaven—what it will be like, and what we will do there. After listening to my many questions and musings, he said something that took me by surprise: "Let me put it another way that you might understand. Do you enjoy making love with your wife?" Caught off guard, I responded affirmatively, as you might imagine. Ugh! Can you say something else? With a laughing smile, he continued, "Well, then heaven will be like an eternity of endless bliss." While his analogy was unexpected—and, if I'm honest, a bit overwhelming—it made me pause and think deeply about heaven. Perhaps heaven is not something we can fully understand with our human minds, but it's a reality that surpasses everything we know, a place of joy and fulfillment beyond our current comprehension. Heaven, I now realize, is not just an endless church service, but an eternal experience of God's love, peace, and beauty—unimaginably rich and satisfying, like an endless feast of the soul.

So, what is heaven like? In truth, it's beyond anything we can fully comprehend, no matter how vivid our imagination or advanced our technology. Even the best special effects or the most vivid descriptions fall short of the reality of heaven. St. Paul writes in Romans 8:18, *"I consider that the sufferings we presently endure are not worth comparing with the glory to be revealed to us."* What we experience in this life, even in our most joyful moments, will seem trivial compared to the glory that awaits us in heaven. Heaven is not a static place, a simple "reward" for living a good life. It is a dynamic, living reality where we will be in perfect communion with God and with all the saints and angels. We will recognize our loved ones, not as they were on earth, but as they were always meant to be—fully healed, fully alive, and fully who God created them to be. It's not about wearing robes or becoming angels; rather, we will be fully

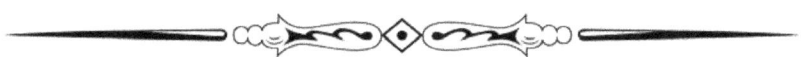

ourselves, but in the fullest, most perfected sense. We will be in bodies that are transformed, glorified, and imperishable. The love we experience on earth—through family, friendship, and even in the beauty of creation—will be magnified in heaven, beyond what we can even imagine. In heaven, I believe we will be completely free to enjoy God's presence in a way we never could here on earth. While I may not fully understand how, I trust that the joys I experience now—whether in nature, in family, or in simple pleasures—are mere glimpses of the much greater joys to come. Heaven is not a place of drudgery or endless work, but an eternal rest in the presence of God, where every desire of the heart is fulfilled, and all things are made new. But what about activities like eating, sleeping, or sports? I don't have all the answers, but I trust that heaven will not be boring or monotonous. We will be in the presence of the Creator, who made us to be creatures of joy, creativity, and love. Whether it's enjoying the beauty of a celestial landscape, engaging in some form of eternal work, or celebrating with friends, I believe that heaven will be full of the kind of fulfillment that we only taste on earth in fleeting moments. Will there be a perfect game of football? Maybe not as we know it, but there may be a perfect way to enjoy everything that brings us joy now, without the limitations of time, fatigue, or sin.

The real beauty of heaven lies in its eternal relationship with God. In heaven, we will experience perfect union with the Creator, a communion so deep and satisfying that no earthly joy will ever be equal to that. We won't need to worry about the ordinary things—food, sleep, or time—because we will be in God's presence, and He will be our everything. Our hearts will be full, our desires delighted, and our capacity for love and joy will be endless. There will be no more tears, no more suffering, and no more separation—only the purest, most complete communion with God and with those we love. In the end, what I believe about heaven is this: it is a place that surpasses our ability to understand or imagine. It will be an eternal experience of love, joy, and fulfillment beyond anything we have known on earth. While I don't know all the details, I trust that it will be perfect designed by God to fulfill us in ways we cannot yet comprehend. And so, while I may wonder about things like Monday Night Football, I know that heaven will be filled with something far better: an eternal union with the God who created me, who loves me, and who promises that the joy of heaven will never end.

What excites me most about heaven can be summed up in Jim Hill's poem, "What a Day That Will Be": "What a day that will be When my Jesus I shall see. When I look upon His face, The one who saved me by His grace. When He takes me by the hand and leads me to the promised land. What a day, glorious day that will be." Yes, it's the idea of spending eternity with Jesus that fills me with hope. Revelation 22:4 assures us: *"They will see His face, and His name will be on their foreheads."*

The late Reverend Billy Graham once described heaven as a place where all the fears and insecurities that trouble us in this life are wiped away. There will be no more energy crises, no economic worries, no fear of personal or physical harm, and no fear of failure. Our relationship with God will be direct and intimate, and heaven will be everything we've ever longed for—a perfect order of peace and justice, free from the pain, loss, and suffering that we endure here on earth. As Revelation 21:4 promises, *"God shall wipe away all tears from their eyes; and there shall be no more death, neither sorrow, nor crying, neither shall there be any more pain: for the former things are passed away."* This vision of heaven offers us comfort, hope, and peace. But while we may have a clear understanding of hell, heaven remains somewhat elusive. Jesus often described the Kingdom of Heaven through parables rather than giving us a literal, physical picture. Through these vivid and powerful stories, He invited us to imagine the beauty, the mystery, and the joy of this eternal reality.

In the Gospel of Matthew, Jesus uses these images to describe the Kingdom of Heaven:

- A man who sowed good seed in his field

- A mustard seed that grows into a large tree

- Yeast that leavens a batch of dough

- A treasure hidden in a field, purchased out of joy

- A merchant searching for fine pearls

- A net cast into the sea, gathering all kinds of fish

- A landowner hiring laborers for his vineyard

- A king hosting a wedding feast for his son

- Ten virgins waiting for the bridegroom, with only five prepared

These parables paint a picture of heaven through images of growth, value, preparation, and inclusion. They speak of treasure, of joy, of the fulfillment of purpose, and of the invitation to share in God's eternal feast. But none of these parables give us a straightforward, physical description of what heaven will look like. Instead, they point us toward the deeper truths of the Kingdom—what it means to belong, to be ready, to be filled with God's grace, and to experience the fullness of His love.

What I find so beautiful about these parables is that they reveal the nature of heaven as something that is not just a place we go, but a reality we enter. It's not simply about the end of our journey but about a transformation that happens within us. Heaven is not merely a destination; it is a state of being, a state of communion with God. It's about being part of a greater whole, where every person, every soul, is united in perfect harmony with God and one another. It's about the fulfillment of all our deepest longings—peace, joy, purpose, and love. The mystery of heaven is that it is more than we can grasp with our limited human understanding. The Bible invites us to imagine heaven, to long for it, but not to be able to fully comprehend it. It's a place of *"unspeakable joy,"* as St. Peter writes (1 Peter 1:8), where every tear will be wiped away and every sorrow will be healed. It's a reality so glorious that we cannot even begin to describe it in human terms. We are told that *"eye has not seen, nor ear heard, nor the heart of man imagined, what God has prepared for those who love Him"* (1 Corinthians 2:9). In this way, heaven calls us to a deeper kind of faith. The parables Jesus shared encourage us to be active participants in the Kingdom here and now. They invite us to seek the treasure of the Kingdom with joy, to grow in our relationship with God, to prepare ourselves for the wedding feast of the Lamb, and to be ready for the day when the Kingdom of Heaven is fully revealed to us.

What heaven will be like, in its fullness, is still a mystery—but it's a mystery filled with hope. We know it will be a place of perfect peace and joy, where every mistake is made right, every sorrow healed, and every longing fulfilled. Heaven will be everything we've hoped for and so much more. We will be in the presence of the One who made us, who loves us, and who promises us eternal life in His glory. And though we may not fully understand what that will look like, we can trust that it will be beyond anything we can imagine—a place where all our fears, insecurities, and struggles will be transformed into perfect peace and joy. In this sense, heaven is not just a future promise; it is something that is already taking root within us. The Kingdom of Heaven is at hand, and as we live out our faith, love, and service to others, we experience glimpses of that eternal reality. Through prayer, through the sacraments, through acts of charity and kindness, we begin to enter the joy of heaven here on earth, preparing ourselves for the fullness of that joy in the life to come.

I believe that while the details of heaven remain a mystery, the hope it offers is clear. Heaven is where we are free from every burden, our hearts are united with God in perfect love, and we experience eternal joy and peace. And though the journey of life on earth is often filled with challenges, we hold on to the promise that heaven is a place where all the former things—our pain, our struggles, our fears—will

pass away, and we will be with God forever in a glory that surpasses all understanding. In the end, the beauty of heaven is not in the details we can picture, but in the certainty that it is a place where we will finally be home—united with our Creator, our loved ones, and the whole communion of saints. Heaven is the fulfillment of every desire, the realization of every hope, and the eternal joy of being with God forever.

Ultimately, heaven is a realm of unimaginable joy and fulfillment, a place where our deepest desires, hopes, and longings will be fully realized. It's a perfect communion with God and with one another, where love and peace abound, far beyond the limits of our understanding. But let's be honest: talk of heaven can sometimes feel abstract, even confusing. We're told it's beautiful and glorious, but what does that mean? What does heaven *look* like? What will we do there? How can we even comprehend something so far beyond our earthly experience? Interestingly, when Jesus spoke about hell, His descriptions were vivid and explicit. He used stark, graphic imagery to warn of its consequences. Hell was real, and He wanted us to understand the grave reality of its horrors. However, His descriptions are much more enigmatic when it comes to heaven. Instead of concrete details, He often communicates the nature of the Kingdom of Heaven through parables—stories that invite us to ponder and imagine but don't offer a direct blueprint for heaven. For example, in the Gospel of Matthew, Jesus describes heaven as a mustard seed, yeast, a hidden treasure, or a wedding feast. These parables are rich with meaning, yet they are also mysterious. The mustard seed grows into something large, the yeast transforms the dough, the treasure is worth everything, and the wedding feast is the ultimate celebration. But none of these descriptions gives us a clear picture of heaven. Instead, they describe the process of growth, transformation, and the value of the Kingdom, which are all deeply spiritual truths. But they leave us wondering: If Jesus came to open the gates of heaven, why doesn't He provide a clearer, more straightforward description?

It does seem curious, doesn't it? Heaven is the place He opened for us through His suffering, death, and resurrection. You would think He'd want to give us a full and detailed explanation of what we're hoping for. Why not lay it out for us, especially after all He did to make it possible? But instead, we get these symbolic and abstract comparisons. Imagine if I tried to describe the Superdome in New Orleans using parables instead of facts. Instead of telling you it's a massive steel structure, covering thirteen acres with seating for over seventy thousand people, I described it as a buried treasure or rising yeast. How would that help you understand what the Superdome truly looks like?

The difference between the clarity of hell and the mystery of heaven can make us uncomfortable. We long for certainty, and Jesus' parables don't provide that. Yet perhaps that's the point. Heaven is beyond our full comprehension. No matter how many details we might wish for, words, even Jesus' words, can only hint at what heaven really is. Its beauty, joy, and fulfillment cannot be captured fully in human language, no matter how much we try. Heaven is not something we can measure or quantify with our senses; it is something we must embrace with our hearts, our imaginations, and our faith. In fact, I found it interesting when I searched online for, "What does heaven look like?"—there were over 687 million results! Many of these sites offer subjective opinions, theories, and interpretations, while others focus on "Near Death Experiences" (NDEs), where people claim to have glimpsed heaven in moments of crisis or clinical death. One such account comes from the book *Heaven is for Real*, in which Colton Burpo, a three-year-old boy who had a near-death experience, describes meeting deceased relatives and even an unborn sibling he had never known about. His descriptions of heaven included details that he couldn't have known, leaving his family and many others questioning whether his experience was a true glimpse of the afterlife.

Such stories are powerful and moving, and they do make us wonder about the nature of heaven. But they don't provide the

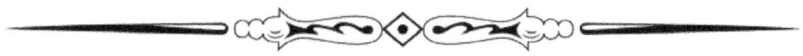

definitive answers we seek. We cannot base our faith on NDEs or personal revelations; they are only partial glimpses of a reality that is still shrouded in mystery. Yet they do give us a sense of the profound longing we all have for heaven, a place where love, peace, and joy are unbroken, and where the brokenness of this world is made whole. Ultimately, I believe that the mystery of heaven is part of its beauty. Heaven cannot be contained in a simple description, nor is it a destination that can be fully captured in human terms. It is a reality that invites us to hope, too long, and to trust. Jesus may not have given us a clear map of what heaven looks like, but He has shown us the way through His life, death, and resurrection. The parables of heaven speak to us of a Kingdom where growth, value, and transformation abound—where every soul is invited to find its deepest fulfillment in the presence of God.

As a Catholic, I trust that heaven will be more wonderful than anything I can fully imagine. It will be a perfect union with God, where all pain and suffering are washed away, and where our hearts are fulfilled in a way that nothing on earth can replicate. The mystery of heaven draws me closer to God because it is a reminder that His ways are far beyond my own. Heaven is not something I can control, but it is a promise—a promise that, in the fullness of time, I will experience the eternal joy and peace that God has prepared for those who love Him. Though heaven remains a mystery, it is a mystery that I trust with all my heart. And while I may not fully understand what it will be like, I know it will be everything I've ever hoped for—and so much more. That hope gives me peace in this life, even as I continue to seek God's presence and grow in my relationship with Him. Heaven may be mysterious, but it is also real, and it is the fulfillment of all that we desire and dream of in our hearts.

Numerous modern near-death experiences share strikingly similar elements: entering a tunnel, approaching a bright light, reviewing one's life, reconnecting with loved ones who have passed away, and experiencing a profound sense of love and peace. Dr. Jeffrey Long, who has documented thousands of these experiences,

observes that individuals from various religious backgrounds consistently describe these phenomena similarly. This suggests that what they encounter might be a transcendent experience that is way beyond traditional spiritual teachings. Common themes include reunions with loved ones, heightened senses, and an overwhelming feeling of unconditional love. Many people find it challenging to articulate the depth of these emotions and sensations, as they transcend the limits of earthly language. In many of these accounts, individuals report encounters with angels or even with Jesus Himself, offering them brief but powerful glimpses into heaven. These glimpses are awe-inspiring but often beyond full comprehension. While the imagery and descriptions of heaven may remain mysterious and elusive, these near-death experiences and Jesus' parables point to a far greater reality than we can grasp in this life. It is a reality filled with unimaginable joy, love, and peace—an existence that we can only begin to understand as we look toward eternity.

In 1990, while serving as the nurse manager of a hyperbaric-wound clinic in New Orleans, Louisiana, I had a profound encounter with a man whose story would leave an impression on my faith. Our clinic, located near the Gulf of Mexico, treated commercial and sport divers who suffered from injuries, many of which were life-threatening. One case stands out—an experience that marked the first time I encountered the mysterious and transformative power of near-death experiences. A fifty-year-old French diver, whom I'll refer to as F.C., came to our clinic after a harrowing incident. Commercial diving is a grueling and dangerous profession, and divers like F.C. spend extended periods offshore, enduring the physical toll it takes on their bodies. By their forties, most divers transition to less physically demanding roles. But F.C. had been engaged in a deep-sea saturation dive at 300 feet when an explosion occurred nearby. He was pulled from the water, clinically dead—no pulse, no respiration. Emergency efforts included CPR, recompression to 165 feet in a diving chamber, and, against all odds, F.C. was revived. He was later transferred to our hospital, where my team treated him for decompression injuries. As he recovered, I noticed a profound shift in F.C.'s demeanor. The once

boisterous, hard-living man who had been defined by heavy drinking, drug use, and womanizing was now withdrawn and profoundly depressed. His personality had changed so dramatically that he was eventually admitted to the psychiatric unit. Concerned, I visited him to see if he was willing to open up about what had happened during his near-death experience. At first, he claimed he didn't recall anything unusual. But a week later, he shared a story with me that I will never forget.

F.C. explained that, before the accident, he was not a religious man. His life had been one of excess and recklessness, and faith had never been a part of it. But what he experienced during his near-death encounter changed him in ways he could scarcely explain. He recounted the moment when he left his body and observed the entire rescue process from above, detached and calm. He was able to identify each rescuer and describe their actions in detail, even though he was technically dead at the time. He spoke of being drawn toward a brilliant, warm light that seemed to envelop him, a light that he believed led him directly to heaven. In heaven, he felt an overwhelming sense of love—an intense, pure love that transcended anything he had ever known on Earth. He encountered relatives who had passed away, but they appeared to him to be youthful and vibrant, radiating peace. He struggled to describe the beauty of the place—the colors, the sounds, and the appearance of Jesus—but what he did convey was clear: the love he experienced there was unlike anything he could put into words. It was a profound love that left him longing to stay. But F.C. also understood something deeper: his time in heaven was not meant to be. And with that realization, he found himself back in his body, returned to the world of the living.

After sharing his experience with me, F.C. looked at me earnestly and said, "Of course, I want to die. I don't want to be here on earth after seeing what heaven is like." He spoke with a depth of emotion that I had never witnessed in him before. His whole perspective on life had shifted. Heaven, for him, was no longer just an abstract idea; it was a real place of unimaginable beauty and love.

And he knew, without a doubt, that he had glimpsed something that far surpassed anything this world could offer. After our conversation, F.C. was discharged and returned to France. I often wonder what happened to him after that. How did his experience continue to shape his life? Did it deepen his faith? Did it help him find a new purpose, or did he struggle to reconcile his newfound understanding with the life he had lived? I'll never know. But what I do know is that his experience left me with an undeniable sense of the reality of heaven— a reality far greater than I had imagined, and one that I now believe in with all my heart. That moment with F.C. reaffirmed for me the truth of our faith. Heaven is not some distant, abstract hope, nor is it a place we can fully describe with our earthly words. It is real, and it is filled with love and peace beyond our comprehension. When I reflect on F.C.'s story, I am reminded that Jesus opened the way for us to experience this reality. His sacrifice on the cross made it possible for us to know that heaven is a place of true fulfillment, where we will be embraced by God's love in a way that transcends everything we've known on earth.

I firmly believe that, one day, we too will experience this joy, just as F.C. did, when our time comes to be with Him. In the end, what F.C. shared with me was not just a glimpse of heaven; it was a witness to the power of God's love and the profound truth that the life to come is more beautiful, more real, and more fulfilling than we can ever fully understand on this side of eternity. And that is why I believe— because I know, deep in my heart, that heaven is real, and it is waiting for us.

Over the years, many of the visionaries from Medjugorje have shared extraordinary testimonies of their encounters with heaven. These testimonies offer profound glimpses into the reality of the afterlife, and they deepen my faith in the existence of heaven as a place of unimaginable beauty and peace. The visionaries—who began receiving apparitions of the Blessed Virgin Mary in 1981—have not only spoken about their experiences of seeing Our Lady, but also about their glimpses into heaven. Their testimonies often recount

profound moments when they felt a deep sense of God's love, encountered heavenly beings, or were shown the eternal life awaiting those who follow Christ. These experiences reveal a heaven far beyond our earthly comprehension—a place where joy, love, and peace abound. They describe a realm where suffering and pain are no more, and where the beauty of God's presence fills every part of existence. Some of the visionaries have spoken about their visits to heaven, where they have witnessed the incredible joy and harmony of those who are with God. They speak of the peace that surpasses understanding and love so pure that it's impossible to fully explain in human terms.

Vicka's Description:

In an interview with Fr. Livio for Radio Maria, Vicka described her vision of heaven. She recalled arriving at a large wooden door, which was closed until Our Lady opened it, allowing them to enter. St. Peter stood by the door, and Vicka immediately recognized him: "He had a small key, a beard, was a bit sturdy, and had hair." When asked by Fr. Bubalo to describe heaven, Vicka said: "…it is beyond description. It is filled with indescribable light, people, flowers, and angels. Everything is imbued with joy that cannot be put into words. Your heart feels still when you behold it."

Question: "Vicka, tell us more about heaven."

Vicka: "Heaven is a vast space with a brilliant light that never fades. It represents a life completely different from what we know on Earth. We saw people in gray, pink, and yellow robes, walking, praying, and singing. Small angels flew above them. The Blessed Mother showed us how profoundly happy these people are."

Question: "How could you tell they were happy?"

Vicka: "It was evident from their faces. Although it's impossible to describe in words, the happiness in heaven is overwhelming. When

the Blessed Mother passed by, everyone responded to her, and she responded to them. There was a sense of recognition among them. They communicated in a way that resembled a tunnel, though it wasn't exactly like a tunnel. People were praying, singing, and engaging with one another. In heaven, beings experience the absolute fullness of existence."

Question: "How long were you there?"

Vicka: "Maybe twenty minutes."

Question: "Did the people talk to you?"

Vicka: "It was unusual. They spoke, but I couldn't understand them. People were in small groups. I was with Jakov and the Blessed Mother, and we communicated, but there was no interaction with others. The Blessed Mother pointed out how happy the people in heaven are."

Mirjana's Description:

Mirjana did not physically visit heaven but saw it during an apparition. Here is her account:

Mirjana: "I saw heaven as if it were a movie. The first thing I noticed was the faces of the people there; they radiated an inner light that conveyed immense happiness."

Question: "Is heaven an actual place?"

Mirjana: "Yes. The trees, meadows, and sky are entirely different from anything on Earth. The light is much more brilliant. Heaven's beauty surpasses anything I've seen on Earth."

Question: "Did the people you saw have bodies?"

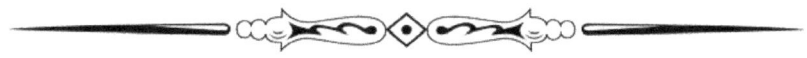

Mirjana: "Yes."

Question: "What ages were they?"

Mirjana: "They appeared to be around thirty years old, different from how we are now. They were walking in a beautiful park, fully content and needing nothing. They wore clothing similar to what Jesus wore."

Mirjana's Insight:

When asked why Our Lady showed her Heaven, Mirjana explained:

"She told me that many people today do not believe Heaven exists. Our Lady said God has chosen us six visionaries to be instruments of His love and mercy. I have personally seen Heaven—it is real! Those who remain faithful to God until the end will be rewarded with the vision of Heaven."

Ivanka's Experience:

Question: "Did you see Heaven, hell, and Purgatory, Ivanka?"

Ivanka: "I saw Purgatory and Heaven in a vision. I told the Blessed Mother I did not wish to see hell."

Question: "What did Heaven look like?"

Ivanka: "Heaven is an incredibly beautiful place, more beautiful than anything I can describe. Everyone I saw there was filled with a profound happiness that I can't put into words—and it's something I can't forget."

Question: "Do you long for that happiness yourself?"

Ivanka: "I experience some of that happiness when I am with the Blessed Mother and when I pray."

Question: "Can you tell us more about Heaven?"

Ivanka: "God created us for Heaven. If you pray, you will come to understand that."

Marija's Vision:

Question: "Were you taken to Heaven, or did you have a vision of Heaven?"

Marija: "I had a vision of Heaven, while Jakov and Vicka were physically taken there."

Question: "When you saw the vision, were you in the rectory room or somewhere else?"

Marija: "It was at Jakov's house. It was like watching a movie on a screen or looking out a window. I saw a vision; I wasn't there like the other visionaries. The vision was unlike anything I had ever seen; it's beyond what anyone can imagine. Flowers surrounded the people, and all appeared to be the same age—no one was older than the age of Christ. They were filled with joy, constantly thanking God for His gifts. Every day, they experience the depth of God's love. There was a multitude of people."

Ivan's Perspective:

Question: "What can you tell us about Heaven?"

Ivan: "Heaven is worth any sacrifice! Jesus demonstrated this with His death on the Cross. His death was not the end but a gateway to eternal life. He rose from the dead, glorified, to end death forever for God's children. The people in Heaven are profoundly happy, living in the fullness of God."

Jakov's Reflections:

Jakov, who, along with Vicka, was physically taken to Heaven at the age of eleven, shared his thoughts in a series of interviews:

Question: "Will you describe Heaven to us?"

Jakov: "When you get there, you will see for yourself."

Question: "You mentioned that the Blessed Mother took you there to show you what it will be like for those who remain faithful to God. Can you elaborate?"

Jakov: "If I dwelled on it too much, I would be overwhelmed by loneliness."

Question: "What is your understanding of Heaven?"

Jakov: "Having been there, it's hard for me to express it in words."

Question: "Is it challenging to live on Earth after having been to Heaven?"

Jakov: "That's an understatement."

Question: "Jakov, you mentioned that thinking too much about Heaven makes you feel lonely. How do you cope with the memories of Heaven, hell, and Purgatory?"

Jakov: "The Blessed Mother advises us to guard against the burden of memories. She encourages us to trust in God's love to make everything right and entrust the past to her maternal care, remembering only through God's love."

The testimonies of the visionaries from Kibeho, Rwanda, who began experiencing apparitions of the Blessed Virgin Mary in 1981,

have left a lasting imprint on my belief in the reality of heaven. These visionaries, like those from Medjugorje, were blessed with extraordinary encounters that revealed not only the presence of the Virgin Mary but also glimpses into the beauty of the afterlife. Their descriptions of heaven resonate deeply with my faith, bringing me closer to the profound truth that heaven is not merely a hopeful dream but a real, tangible reality that awaits us. The Kibeho visionaries were given vivid visions of both heaven and hell, showing them the contrasts between the eternal joys of heaven and the unthinkable suffering of hell. These experiences were meant to call us to repentance and inspire us with the beauty and hope of life to come. The visionaries describe heaven as a place of peace, light, and profound beauty, where the souls of the righteous are in perfect communion with God. They have spoken of a peace so deep and joyful that it is beyond earthly comprehension, that fills every part of the soul, leaving no room for anxiety, sadness, or fear.

Alphonsine Mumureke's Vision

Alphonsine Mumureke described her experience as follows:

"Our travels were numerous, moving across the stars until we reached a place of golden light, brimming with happiness. The air was filled with laughter and songs sung by countless joyous voices. It felt as though the souls of everyone who had ever lived were floating around, singing praises to God."

Anathalie Mukamazimpaka's Encounter:

Anathalie Mukamazimpaka shared her vision of Heaven:

"The Holy Mother took me to extraordinary places. The first was a realm where shifting shades of vivid color and light replaced mountains and valleys. People traveled by gliding through the light. Mary then led me to a realm illuminated solely by white light. There, I saw seven majestic figures in white cloaks, standing in a circle,

creating beautiful music without instruments. Each note brought a unique sensation of contentment and joy. When I asked, 'Where are we, Mother?' she replied, 'This is Isangano, the focal point; the place of communion.' I inquired about the seven figures, and she told me they were angels who praised God, watched over Earth, and assisted humanity when needed. Next, we visited three distinct worlds, each bathed in its own color and light. As we moved farther from the angels, the colors and light became dimmer. In one realm, I saw millions of people in white garments. They appeared overwhelmingly happy, though not as blissful as the angels. This was Isenderezwa z'ibyishimo, the place of the cherished of God. Finally, we reached a realm with light as dim as twilight, where people wore dull, dreary clothes. Some seemed content, but many were sad and suffering. Mary told me this was Isesengurwa, a place of purification; the people here are Intrambira, those who persevere."

Vestine Salina's Experience:

Vestine Salina recounted her experience after being resurrected: "Jesus took me to Heaven, but I struggle to describe it. There were colors I had never seen, which sounded like music, and those that felt like color. It was beyond any earthly comparison. Describing the feeling of being there is as impossible as explaining how breathing water or drinking air feels. I begged Jesus to let me stay, but He said it was not my time. Leaving Heaven was the saddest moment of my life."

Ruminating on the Kibeho visionaries' testimonies and the rich imagery in Revelation, I am filled with awe and longing. Heaven is a reality far beyond our earthly understanding—an existence filled with peace, love, and eternal joy, where we are in perfect union with God. I believe that these visions, both the ones from Kibeho and the biblical account from Revelation, are not simply symbolic representations but glimpses into the truth of what awaits us. Heaven is real, and it is promised to us by God as our eternal home. These descriptions remind me of why I believe in the beauty and truth of the

Catholic faith. It is a faith that reveals the profound love of God, who desires us to be with Him forever in heaven. Heaven is not an abstract concept or a distant dream; it is a real, eternal destination for those who remain faithful to God's call. Through the Virgin Mary's intercession and God's grace, we are invited to prepare for this ultimate joy, to live in a way that makes us worthy of that eternal home. And I trust, with all my heart, that heaven is waiting for us—a place of unimaginable beauty, peace, and love, where we will experience the fullness of God's presence forever.

When I reflect on the beauty and truth of heaven, I am drawn to the powerful descriptions in Scripture, particularly in the Book of Revelation. In Revelation 21:11-27, the Apostle John provides a vivid and awe-inspiring picture of heaven that affirms my faith and deepens my understanding of the eternal home that awaits us. John's vision of heaven in these verses is physical and spiritual, giving us a glimpse of the splendor, purity, and divine glory that will fill the New Jerusalem, the eternal dwelling place of the righteous. This heavenly city is described as having "the glory of God" shining so brightly that it radiates like the most precious jewels (Rev. 21:11). It is a city of unimaginable beauty and radiance, where the light of God's presence illuminates everything, making the sun and the moon unnecessary. The physical world we know is marked by darkness, decay, and limitation, but heaven is where God's glory fills every corner, and there is no need for darkness. The city itself is described with such vivid and captivating imagery. It is built with pure gold, clear as glass (Rev. 21:18), and its streets are paved with gold. This golden city is not just an idea or metaphor but an actual place, a physical manifestation of divine perfection. The city's foundations are adorned with every kind of precious stone—jasper, sapphire, emerald, and amethyst—each symbolizing the fullness and richness of God's creation, and the glory that will be fully revealed in heaven. It is a place of unparalleled beauty and majesty; beyond anything we can experience here on earth.

The city's gates are made of a single pearl (Rev. 21:21), symbolizing the preciousness of our access to God's presence and the unity and wholeness of all who dwell there. There are twelve gates, each guarded by an angel, emphasizing the holiness and divine protection surrounding heaven. The number twelve in Scripture often symbolizes perfection and completeness, reminding us that heaven is the fulfillment of all God's promises. Furthermore, the city does not need a temple because God Himself is its temple (Rev. 21:22). God's immediate presence will be so encompassing that there will be no separation between His divine nature and the people who dwell there. The glory of God will be ever-present, and all who inhabit the city will worship Him continually. This speaks to the deepest longing of the human soul—to be in complete union with God, to experience His love and presence without any hindrance or separation. Perhaps one of the most profound details in this passage is the assurance that there will be no more suffering, death, or pain. Revelation 21:4 promises, "He will wipe every tear from their eyes. There will be no more death or mourning or crying or pain, for the old order of things has passed away." This is a promise that heaven will be a place of complete peace and joy, where the burdens of this world are no more. All that is broken, and imperfect will be healed, and the former struggles of this life will be forgotten in the face of God's eternal love.

As I concentrate on these words from Revelation, I am filled with a deep sense of hope and anticipation. Heaven, as described in the Bible, is not a distant, abstract concept, but a real place where we will experience the fullness of God's glory, peace, and love. It is a place where the limitations of this world no longer bind us, and we are free to live in perfect communion with God and with one another. The physical beauty and divine perfection described in Revelation only enhance the spiritual reality of heaven. I believe, with all my heart, that this vision is not just symbolic but a true representation of the eternal home that awaits us. As Christians, we are called to keep our eyes fixed on this eternal reality, knowing that, through Jesus Christ, we have been promised a place in this glorious city. This vision of heaven inspires me to live in a way that aligns with God's

will, knowing that my goal is not the fleeting pleasures of this world but the eternal joy of being with Him forever. Heaven is real, and it is waiting for us—a place of beauty, peace, and eternal life, where we will dwell in the presence of God for all eternity. And that, to me, is why I believe in the beauty and truth of the Catholic faith, with all my heart.

In John 14:2-3, Jesus speaks to His disciples with profound comfort and promise: *"In my Father's house there are many dwelling places. If there were not, would I have told you that I am going to prepare a place for you? And if I go and prepare a place for you, I will come again and will take you to myself, so that where I am, you may also be."* This passage is deeply personal and filled with hope. Jesus tells us that the House of God—Heaven—is vast, and within it, there are many dwelling places, each prepared for those who love Him. It is a comforting reminder that heaven is not a one-size-fits-all place but a realm where God, in His infinite love, has crafted a unique and specific space for each believer. This assures me that heaven is not just a distant idea but a tangible, personal reality—a place where I, and everyone who follows Christ, will find a home, perfectly suited to us, in the presence of God.

What's even more reassuring is Jesus' promise that He is preparing this place for us is even more reassuring. The thought that He is actively preparing a home for me and for all believers fills me with awe and peace. The fact that Jesus Himself will come back to take us to this eternal home shows the intimate nature of this promise—it's not just about reaching heaven; it's about being in His presence, united with Him forever. In this passage, I see the promise of eternal communion with God— *"so that where I am, you may also be."* This is the essence of heaven: to be with Christ, in His glory, for all eternity. Similarly, in Luke 23:43, we hear Jesus' comforting words to the good thief on the cross: *"Amen, I say to you, today you will be with me in Paradise."*

This powerful promise is made in the decisive moments of Jesus' earthly life, offering hope even during suffering and death. Despite the thief's past sins, Jesus assures him of a place in Paradise, emphasizing that redemption and eternal life are available to all who repent and trust in Him, no matter their past. For me, this passage is deeply moving because it shows the boundless mercy and love of Jesus. It is a reminder that heaven is not reserved for the perfect but for those who, in their hearts, turn to God in faith and repentance. Jesus' promise of Paradise reveals the essence of heaven: it is a place of complete peace and fulfillment, where we will be with Him forever. It is not just a vague spiritual state; it is a real, personal experience of God's love and presence. These passages give me confidence and peace in the certainty of heaven. Heaven is not a distant, unclear dream but a place prepared by Christ Himself, where we will experience His love, joy, and presence. And just like Jesus promised to the good thief, He promises us that those who trust in Him will be welcomed into the eternal joy of Paradise—to be with Him, in the Father's house, forever. I believe in the beauty and truth of the Catholic faith: it offers the hope of eternal life with God, a life beyond what we can fully comprehend, where we will dwell in the peace and glory of the Father's house. It's a hope that shapes how I live today and fuels my longing to draw closer to Christ each day, knowing that He has prepared a place for me and for all who trust in His promises.

Quotes from Saints Who Had Visions of Heaven:

- **Saint John of the Cross**: "The soul that is in love with God knows that the beatific vision will be its ultimate end, the supreme fulfillment, and the eternal union with the Divine."

- **Saint Teresa of Ávila**: "I saw the soul in its glory and splendor, as in Heaven, the divine light and the divine love embrace all the souls who have reached their ultimate destiny."

- **Saint Augustine of Hippo**: "The vision of God will be the beatific sight, where the soul will find the rest, it has longed for, in perfect and eternal bliss."

- **Saint Thomas Aquinas**: "In Heaven, the blessed will be in the full presence of God, experiencing infinite joy and peace, and sharing in the divine nature in a way beyond earthly comprehension."

- **Saint John Bosco**: "As I stood there, enveloped in the splendor of the celestial gardens, I was suddenly captivated by a melody so sweet and enchanting that it defies description. The music was beyond anything I could ever convey with words."

- **Saint Faustina Kowalska**: "Today, in a spiritual vision, I was granted a glimpse of Heaven's unimaginable beauty and the joy that awaits us after death. I saw how all creation perpetually praises and glorifies God. The happiness that comes from God permeates every creature, spreading divine joy that returns to God in a never-ending cycle of glory and praise. In Heaven, creatures gaze into the depths of the divine life of the Father, Son, and Holy Spirit, a mystery beyond human comprehension. This source of joy is eternal and continually renews itself, pouring out happiness for all. I now understand Saint Paul's words: 'Eye has not seen, nor ear heard, nor has it entered into the heart of man what God has prepared for those who love Him.' The greatest treasure in God's eyes is pure love, and nothing compares to a single act of sincere love for Him. The majesty of God, which I glimpsed more profoundly, was not terrifying but filled my soul with peace and joy. The more I comprehend His greatness, the more I rejoice in His nature and in the closeness He offers to those who are humble. I pray earnestly that those who do not believe in eternal life may also experience His mercy and be embraced by His love."

- **Saint Seraphim of Sarov**: "If you could know the sweetness awaiting the just in Heaven, you would willingly endure all the trials, sufferings, and insults of this earthly life with gratitude. Even if your cell were infested with worms and they tormented you continuously, you would accept it gladly rather than forfeit the heavenly joy prepared by God for those who love Him."

- **Saint Ann Schaffer**: "The heavens opened to reveal a marvelous garden of flowers, extending as far as the eye could see. I cannot fully describe God's wonders for those He loves. The landscape includes meadows, forests, rivers, and mountains, with homes and buildings that are transparent and imbued with a spiritual quality. Everything there is pure and vibrant, unlike earthly things' tainted and limited nature."

- **Saint Teresa of Ávila**: "During prayer, Jesus graciously revealed His hands to me. They were so beautiful that I find it impossible to describe them fully. A few days later, I saw His divine face, which left me utterly enraptured. Jesus unveiled Himself to me gradually, in a way that suited my natural weakness, so that I could endure His divine presence. How could a wretched and insignificant being like myself withstand such overwhelming glory without this divine preparation? Despite my yearning to behold His radiant hands and beautiful face, the exalted beauty of His glorified body is so profound that it surpasses all human understanding. On the Feast of Saint Paul, while attending Holy Mass, the complete and whole sacred Humanity of Jesus Christ appeared to me, more magnificent than any earthly depiction of the Resurrection. The beauty and majesty of His form were beyond any comparison. If His presence on Earth, adjusted to our frailty, is so awe-inspiring, imagine how much more splendid He must be in Heaven, where His glory is fully revealed. The light of Heaven is unlike any earthly light, surpassing even the brightness of the sun, to the point where the sun seems dim by comparison. It is a light so pure and intense that it blinds the eyes, an eternal radiance that no earthly light can resemble. This divine illumination is eternal and undisturbed, its brilliance beyond anything a human mind can conceive."

It becomes clear that no matter how much Scripture reveals to us, the full essence of heaven remains beyond our grasp. It's as though the human mind is too limited to fully comprehend the beauty and majesty that awaits those who love God. Yet, the Bible offers us glimpses, tantalizing us with images of heaven that speak to our deepest longings for peace, joy, and union with God. In 1 Corinthians 2:9, we are reminded that the splendor of heaven is beyond anything we can even imagine: *"What no eye has seen, what no ear has heard, and what no human mind has conceived—the things God has prepared for those who love him."*

This passage captures the truth that heaven, in all its glory, surpasses our current understanding. What God has prepared for us is so extraordinary that our earthly experiences—no matter how beautiful—are faint shadows of the reality awaiting us. Heaven is beyond comprehension, but it is promised to those who love God, and that promise fills me with hope and anticipation. In Isaiah 65:21, we get a glimpse of the peace and restoration that heaven brings: *"They will build houses and dwell in them; they will plant vineyards and eat their fruit."* This image speaks of a life of fulfillment, free from the struggles and heartaches we face on earth. Heaven will be a place of fruitful labor and rest, where we can enjoy the bounty of God's creation in perfect harmony. It will be a place where our desires and needs are fully satisfied, where the sweat and toil of this life are replaced with peace and joy in God's presence.

Revelation 21:4 offers another glimpse into heaven's nature, focusing on the relief from suffering:

"He will wipe away every tear from their eyes. There will be no more death or mourning, crying or pain, for the old order of things has passed away." Heaven is a place where suffering is no more. The burdens of this world—the grief, pain, and loss—will be wiped away, replaced by perfect peace. The brokenness that marks our earthly existence will be healed, and we will experience eternal joy in the presence of God. In Isaiah 65:25, we see the perfect harmony of God's kingdom: *"The wolf and the lamb will feed together, and the lion will eat straw like the ox, but dust will be the serpent's food. They will neither harm nor destroy on all my holy mountain,"* says the Lord.

Heaven will be a place of peace, where all creations live in harmony. There will be no more violence, no more strife between creatures, and no more destruction. This vision points to the ultimate reconciliation of all things in God, where harmony and peace reign forever. In Revelation 21:22, we are told that in heaven, *"I did not see a temple in the city, because the Lord God Almighty and the Lamb are its temple."*

This passage underscores the central truth of heaven: it is not about physical structures or rituals, but about the unbroken communion with God. He will be the focus of all worship and adoration, and we will live in His presence, with no barriers between us and Him. Heaven is where we are fully united with the source of all life and love. In Revelation 21:23, we learn that, *"The city does not need the sun or the moon to shine on it, for the glory of God gives it light, and the Lamb is its lamp."* This is a powerful reminder that God Himself is the source of all light, joy, and illumination in heaven. The darkness of sin, suffering, and confusion will be no more, and the radiant glory of God will be our eternal light. Throughout Scripture, we are also reminded that *heaven is the dwelling place of God* (Deuteronomy 26:15; Matthew 6:9). It is where the saints live in perfect communion with Him, free from the corruption of sin and death (Revelation 4-5; Hebrews 12:23). It is a place of great joy and pleasures for the redeemed (Psalm 16:11), and it holds the promise of unhindered life

and ultimate reunion with loved ones who have gone before us (1 Thessalonians 4:14-18).

I remember reading from one of the visionaries (though I can't recall exactly which one) that in heaven, everyone is restored to the age of thirty-three, the age at which Jesus died and was resurrected. This age, said to be the prime of life, full of strength and vitality, is an intriguing idea. I must admit, I certainly hope it's true! At thirty-three, I felt physically strong and vibrant, different from how I felt at sixty-four. But regardless of the details, what matters is that heaven will be a place of restoration. We will be made whole, free from the ravages of time, and united with God in perfect joy and peace. In the end, while we may not have a complete picture of heaven, these biblical glimpses fill me with wonder and awe. I believe that heaven is a real, tangible place where God's love and glory shine forth in ways we cannot fully grasp now but will one day experience in their fullness. Heaven is the fulfillment of every desire, the restoration of all things, and the place where we will be in eternal communion with God and those we love. And for all these reasons, I believe in the beauty and truth of the Catholic faith, and the hope of eternal life in the presence of our Creator.

Chapter Eighteen
Heaven on Earth

One of my favorite musicians, the late Dan Fogelberg, captures a sentiment that resonates deeply with me in his song *"The Wild Places"*: *"There's a heaven on earth that so few ever find, though the maps in your soul and the roads in your mind."*

I feel as though I have that map within me, the kind of road that leads to heaven on earth. And no GPS is necessary because I know where it leads. I've traveled this road many times, both physically and in the quiet moments of my heart. Whenever I leave my home in Covington, Louisiana, I take the familiar route eastbound on I-12, merging onto Interstate 10. I know that after a few hours of driving, I'll arrive at a slice of paradise: the beautiful beaches of Florida. In less than three hours, I can walk along the shores of Pensacola, Destin, or Perdido Key, and each time, I feel as though I've arrived at a personal heaven. There's something profound about the peace that floods over me as soon as my feet hit the soft, white sand and I gaze out at the clear, aquamarine waters. The troubles and worries of daily life melt away in an instant. It's in these moments of

stillness, watching the waves roll gently in, that I feel closest to heaven on earth. The people closest to me, my wife, my children, and my friends—know that I can lose track of time on the beach. Hours seem to vanish, especially in the evening when the crowds have thinned, and the beach becomes a quiet retreat. I savor those moments, usually around six p.m., when the sky is painted with brilliant reds and oranges as the sun sinks below the horizon. The cool breeze whispers through the air, and the peaceful rhythm of the waves is a balm for my soul. It's the kind of paradise that fills me with a deep sense of gratitude and wonder—true heaven on earth.

I am treated to something even more spectacular on rare occasions: a brilliant yellow moon rising just off the horizon as the fiery sunset takes its final bow. To witness such a sight, so beautiful and so fleeting, reminds me that heaven is all around us. It's a glimpse of the divine, a moment of grace in the midst of creation. It's in these moments that I experience the beauty and truth of the Catholic faith. For me, these fleeting instances of peace are reminders of the eternal joy that God has promised to those who seek Him. While heaven may be beyond our full comprehension, I believe that these moments of beauty on earth are like little windows into that ultimate paradise.

In the Catholic faith, we believe that heaven is not just some far-off place, but also something that we can experience here and now, through glimpses of God's presence in our lives. Whether it's in the beauty of nature, the love of family and friends, or the quiet moments of prayer, we are surrounded by the goodness of God. We are invited to find heaven on earth, even in the midst of life's challenges, because God is with us, revealing His love in the most ordinary and extraordinary ways. Just as I find peace on the beach, in the beauty of the sunset, and the sound of the waves, I believe that every moment of joy and peace is an invitation to draw closer to God. These moments remind me of the beauty of His creation, the goodness of His plan, and the promise of eternal life with Him. Heaven is a place of ultimate fulfillment, but we are given glimpses of that reality here on earth. These glimpses—whether in nature, relationships, or

moments of grace—inspire my faith and fill me with hope. So, in every peaceful sunset, every gentle breeze, and every beautiful moment, I am reminded of the beauty and truth of the Catholic faith. Heaven is real, and I believe that it is not only a future promise but a present reality that can be experienced in the here and now. These moments remind me that the road to heaven on earth is already open, and all we need to do is follow one step, one moment, one prayer at a time.

In truth, the most profound place where heaven and earth meet are in the Catholic Church, during the celebration of the Mass. As Pope John Paul II beautifully expressed, "The liturgy we celebrate on earth is a mysterious participation in the heavenly liturgy." These words carry a deep truth that resonates with me every time I step into the church and kneel before the altar, knowing that I am partaking in something far greater than myself, something that reaches across time and space and touches the divine. I believe in the beauty of the Mass because it is more than just a ritual or tradition. It is an encounter with God Himself, made possible by the incredible reality of the Eucharist—the Real Presence of Christ. Father John Hardon, in his *Pocket Catholic Dictionary*, explains that Christ is "really present in His humanity, in heaven, and on the altar," which is why He can offer Himself to the Father at every Mass as He did on Good Friday. This is not just a symbolic act; it is a true participation in the sacrifice of the Cross, made present for us now.

The Catholic doctrine of the Real Presence is the foundation of my belief. When the bread and wine are consecrated during the Mass, they become the true Body and Blood of Christ. This is not just a commemoration; it is a participation in the eternal act of Christ's sacrifice for the salvation of the world. If the Eucharist were merely a symbol, the Mass would be nothing more than a memorial of the Last Supper, but instead, it is a living reality, the source of grace, and a powerful means of encountering Christ. The Mass, as the Church teaches, is both a memorial and a sacrifice. As Christ instructed at the Last Supper, "Do this in remembrance of Me." It is a sacred banquet where we, as the faithful, participate not just in listening to the prayers but in receiving Holy Communion, the true Body and Blood of Christ. This participation in the Eucharist draws us closer to Christ, providing us with the grace He won for our salvation. Saint Paul's words in *1 Corinthians 5:7-8* help illuminate this further: "Throw out the old yeast so that you may become a fresh batch of unleavened dough. As you really are. For Christ, our Passover lamb, has been sacrificed. Therefore, let us celebrate the feast, not with the old yeast, the yeast of depravity and wickedness, but with the unleavened bread of sincerity and truth." The Mass is the new Passover feast, where Christ, our Passover Lamb, has given Himself for us, replacing the old system of sacrifice with a new and living sacrifice that unites us to God.

In the Mass, we are invited to participate in this new covenant, a covenant sealed by the Blood of Christ. We don't bring animal sacrifices as the Israelites did in the Old Testament; instead, we present simple gifts of bread and wine. But through the mystery of Transubstantiation, these offerings are transformed into the true Body and Blood of Christ. The priest, acting *in Persona Christi* (in the person of Christ), is the one who brings about this sacred transformation. Through this, we, the faithful, can partake in the same sacrifice that Christ made for us on the Cross. This connection between the Old Testament and the New is something that strengthens my belief. Just as the Israelites knew that God dwelled in the Holy of Holies, we Catholics believe that God now dwells in the Tabernacle, present in the consecrated Eucharist. The Holy of Holies, once separated by a veil, is now accessible to us every time we approach the altar. We are invited into that sacred space, not only to witness the offering of Christ but to partake in it ourselves, uniting our hearts and lives with Him.

Every time, I attend Mass, I am reminded of how this participation in the divine liturgy allows me to experience heaven on earth. It's not a place I will only experience in the afterlife; it is something I can touch and taste now, in the mystery of the Eucharist.

It is a gift given to us, here and now, to bring us closer to God and transform us from within. Through the Mass, I believe I am united with all of heaven. As the saints and angels praise God in the heavenly liturgy, we join them on earth, offering our prayers, praises, and lives to Him. In that moment, the veil between heaven and earth seems to disappear, and we, in our humble way, partake in the eternal praise of God. This is why I believe in the beauty and truth of the Catholic faith—because it brings heaven to earth in a way that touches my soul and transforms my life. Heaven is not a far-off, abstract place, but a reality that we can experience now, in the Mass. And for that, I am profoundly grateful.

If you've never experienced a Catholic Mass, let me share with you the beauty and depth of this sacred celebration. For me, attending Mass is an encounter with God, a moment where heaven touches earth, and where I am united with Christ and the Church in a way that transcends words. The Mass begins with the priest's entrance procession, where he walks to the altar and the Tabernacle, symbolizing Christ's triumphant entry into Jerusalem on Palm Sunday and His journey to the Cross. This initial moment is a reminder that our faith is rooted in the life, death, and resurrection of Jesus, and we are invited to walk with Him through this sacred ritual. Next, the priest leads the congregation in the Penitential Rite, a prayer of contrition where we ask for God's forgiveness for our sins. This humble act of repentance prepares our hearts to receive the grace of the Eucharist, as we acknowledge our need for God's mercy and love. The service continues with four Scripture readings. We begin with a reading from the Old Testament or the Acts of the Apostles, followed by a Psalm, a letter from Saint Paul, and finally, a Gospel reading. These readings are not just historical accounts but living words, speaking to us in the present moment. They are meant to guide, inspire, and draw us closer to God. After the readings, the priest or deacon delivers the homily—a reflection on the Gospel, helping us to understand how God's Word applies to our lives today.

Following the homily, the gifts of wine, unleavened bread, and financial offerings are brought forward to the altar. These gifts symbolize our lives, which we offer to God. The priest, acting *in Persona Christi* (in the person of Christ), then performs the sacred act of Transubstantiation, when the bread and wine are transformed into the true Body and Blood of Christ. This moment is central to the Mass—this is not a mere symbol, but a real, profound mystery, where Christ becomes present to us in the Eucharist. Before receiving Communion, the congregation joins in the Nicene Creed and the Our Father, reciting the core beliefs of the Catholic faith and praying the prayer that Jesus taught us. The priest then distributes the consecrated Eucharist, inviting us to receive Christ Himself in the Body and Blood. This moment is an intimate encounter with Jesus, a true communion with Him and the Church, the Body of Christ. The Mass concludes with a final blessing, sending the congregation out into the world to live the message of salvation. As we leave the Church, we are called to carry the love, peace, and grace we've received back into our daily lives to witness Christ's presence in the world. This brief overview captures the essence of the Mass, but even this cannot fully express the deep spiritual significance it holds for us as Catholics. The Mass is a living encounter with God—a place where we are nourished, healed, and empowered to live the Gospel. It is a foretaste of heaven, where we are invited to join in the eternal praise of God with all the saints and angels. Through the Mass, we come to understand more fully why I believe that the Catholic faith holds the truth and beauty of God's love for us.

I highly recommend watching the short film *The Veil Removed*, written by Branden J. Stanley, Chris Magruder, Julie Nelson, and Greg Krajewski. This film profoundly illustrates the intersection of Heaven and Earth during the celebration of the Mass, offering a powerful visual representation of the spiritual reality that unfolds each time we gather to worship. Drawing on insights from Scripture, the Catechism, and the wisdom of saints and mystics, it helps us glimpse the awe-inspiring truth of the Eucharist. Imagine for a moment being able to see what is truly happening during Mass—

the presence of Jesus Himself, the choirs of angels, and the saints joining with us in prayer and worship. This reality is not just a distant theological concept, but a powerful truth that occurs at every Mass, in every Catholic Church, and worldwide. *The Veil Removed* offers a visual expression of this mystery, helping us better understand the incredible, transformative event when the bread and wine become the true Body and Blood of Christ.

In the film, we begin with two individuals bringing gifts of wine and unleavened bread to the altar, surrounded by angels. As the priest begins the Eucharistic prayers, a miraculous transformation occurs: the priest himself is revealed as Christ, who performs the miracle of Transubstantiation. When Jesus raises the Chalice of wine, His crucified Body is shown above it, with His blood flowing into the Chalice, signifying the reality of His sacrifice. As this unfolds, the scene reveals the heavenly realm: choirs of angels, the saints, and God Himself all present, participating in this sacred moment alongside us on Earth. This is not simply a symbolic gesture or a metaphor—it's a profound reality. Heaven and Earth are united in the celebration of the Mass, where we, the faithful, are invited to enter the divine presence and join in the eternal worship of God. Watching *"The Veil Removed"* can be a transformative experience. It helps us see with new eyes the power of the Eucharist, reminding us that every Mass is a participation in the eternal worship that takes place in Heaven. Through this film, we are reminded of the depth and beauty of the Catholic faith and how every celebration of the Mass brings Heaven to Earth in a way that is beyond our full comprehension but entirely real.   The Mass is not just a human activity; it is where we encounter God, and *The Veil Removed* gives us a glimpse into that sacred mystery. Through this powerful depiction, we understand more fully why I believe the Catholic faith is the path that leads to true communion with God, where heaven and earth meet, where Christ offers Himself to us, and where we are invited to participate in the divine life.

In the end, the Mass is nothing less than Heaven on Earth. Saint Padre Pio, renowned for his deep mystical experiences, often found himself in ecstasy during the celebration of the Mass. On several occasions, he was even seen levitating, experiencing vivid visions of Heaven. Padre Pio once remarked, "If men only appreciated the value of a holy Mass, they would need traffic officers at church doors every day to keep the crowds in order." His words remind us that the Mass is far more than a ritual—it is a direct participation in the heavenly realities, a glimpse into the eternal worship of God. Yet, despite the profound beauty of the Mass, I must admit that I sometimes struggle to appreciate its power fully. Distractions often pull me away from the sacredness of the moment—whether it's the chatter of a woman and her daughter in front of me, or people around me checking their phones or scanning the room for familiar faces. These distractions, though human, can be a challenge to overcome. It's important to remember, however, that distractions during Mass are not a new phenomenon. They are, in fact, a deliberate tactic of the enemy, designed to keep us from fully engaging with the divine mystery unfolding before us. One mystic observed that the devil and his demons endure great suffering to enter a church and distract the faithful from focusing on God during the Mass. This insight highlights the spiritual battle in every church, urging us to remain vigilant and attentive as we participate in sacred liturgy.

Many Catholics, it seems, are content to attend Mass only on Christmas and Easter, but there is so much more to be gained from making Mass a regular part of our lives. Why is this so important? For starters, attending Mass is a direct commandment from God— "Remember to keep holy the Lord's Day" (Exodus 20:8). But, beyond that, the Mass is a Sacrament—one of the greatest gifts Jesus has given us. It is through the Mass that we, united with the priest acting "in Persona Christi," offer our praises, thanksgiving, and sorrows to the Father, in union with Christ's perfect offering of Himself on the Cross. As Jesus promised in Matthew 18:20, "Where two or three are gathered in my name, there am I with them." This is the great mystery of the Mass: Christ is truly present, not just in spirit, but in the fullness of His Body and Blood, and when we gather in His name, He is there, offering Himself to us, inviting us into eternal communion. The Mass is an act of heaven breaking into our lives, where we join the angels and saints in worship, participating in the divine liturgy of the Kingdom of God. Even when distractions arise, I know that the Mass is far more than the sum of its parts. Despite my struggles to remain fully attentive, I trust that by attending regularly, I will continue to be drawn closer to God. There, in the sacred space of the church, Heaven touches Earth, and we are allowed to be part of something far greater than ourselves. Through the Sacrament of the Eucharist, I believe we are not only spiritually nourished but are invited to enter the divine life of the Trinity itself—now and for all eternity.

According to the Pieta Prayer Book, Pope Paul IV noted that "The Mass is also the most perfect and powerful form of prayer." Here are some insights from saints and other figures regarding the significance of attending Mass:

Saint Gertrude the Great: "For each Mass we hear with devotion, Our Lord sends a saint to comfort us at death." "Each time we look at the Most Blessed Sacrament, our place in Heaven is raised forever."

Saint Padre Pio: "Every holy Mass, heard with devotion, produces in our souls' marvelous effects and abundant spiritual and material graces that we ourselves do not know. It is easier for the earth to exist without the sun than without the holy Sacrifice of the Mass."

Saint John Vianney: "If we knew the value of the Mass, we would die of joy."

"Your prayers are strongest at the Consecration in Holy Mass."

Saint Teresa of Avila: Overwhelmed by God's goodness, she asked, "How can I thank you?" The Lord replied, "Attend one Mass."

Blessed Alain: The Blessed Mother once told her, "My Son so loves those who assist at the Holy Sacrifice of the Mass that, if it were necessary, He would die for them as many times as they've heard the Masses."

Pope Benedict XV: "The Holy Mass would be of greater profit if people had it offered in their lifetime, rather than having it celebrated for the relief of their souls after death."

The Pieta Prayer Book also lists sixteen graces received from attending Mass:

1. The Mass is Calvary continued; each celebration represents Jesus' sacrifice for our salvation.

2. Every Mass is worth as much as the sacrifice of Jesus' life, suffering, and death.

3. Holy Mass is the most powerful atonement for our sins.

4. At the hour of death, the Masses you have attended will provide the greatest consolation.

5. Every Mass accompanies you to judgment and pleads for your pardon.

6. Attending Mass devoutly can reduce temporal punishment for your sins, based on your fervor.

7. Assisting at Holy Mass pays the greatest homage to the sacred humanity of our Lord.

8. Attending Mass compensates for many of your negligence and omissions.

9. Jesus will forgive venial sins that have not been confessed, and the power of Satan over you is diminished.

10. You provide great relief to the souls in purgatory.

11. A Mass heard during your lifetime is more beneficial than many celebrated for you after your death.

12. You are preserved from dangers and misfortunes and shorten your time in purgatory.

13. Each Mass earns you a higher degree of glory in heaven.

14. You receive the priest's blessing, which is ratified by our Lord in Heaven.

15. You kneel amid a multitude of holy angels present at the Sacrifice with reverential awe.

16. You are blessed in your temporal goods and affairs, and in eternity, you will realize the worth of attending Mass daily.

Attending Mass regularly is far more than a routine or a ritual—it is a profound means of deepening our faith, receiving abundant graces, and participating in the eternal sacrifice of Christ. Each time we gather at the altar, we are invited into a sacred encounter with God, where heaven touches earth in a transformative and life-giving way. Through the Mass, we enter the heart of God's plan of salvation, experiencing Christ's life, death, and resurrection in a tangible way. One of the greatest benefits of attending Mass regularly is that, over the span of three years, the faithful can hear the entire Bible proclaimed. The readings from the Old Testament, the Psalms, the Epistles, and the Gospel deepen our understanding of God's Word and His covenant with us. This practice emphasizes the truth that when we enter a church for Mass, we are stepping into something greater than ourselves, something that transcends time and space. As one reflection beautifully states, *"Heaven is where we place ourselves under judgment, where we see ourselves in the clear morning light of eternal day, and where the Just Judge reads our works from the book of life."*

The Mass, in its entirety, is a meeting place between the earthly and the divine, where we are invited to place our lives before God and hear His judgment, not with fear, but with hope, because we know He is merciful. Our deeds and our choices, both good and bad, are laid bare before God in the light of eternity, and in the Mass, we receive the fullness of grace that flows from God's very life. This is not a metaphor or a symbol; this is a real encounter with the living God. We are offered the life of the Trinity in every Mass, and no power in heaven or earth can bestow anything greater upon us than what we receive when we partake of the Eucharist. In this sacred act, we receive God Himself—His Body, His Blood, His Soul, and His Divinity—into our very being. To understand the depth of this encounter, we must come to Mass with open eyes, ears, mind, and heart. We must allow ourselves to be present to the mystery unfolding before us, to grasp the profound truth that, in every Mass, God renews His covenant with each one of us. The Catholic Mass is not only a place of spiritual nourishment; it is a moment of choice. We are presented with life or death, blessings, or curses. As the Lord says in Deuteronomy 30:19, "I have set before you life and death, blessings, and curses. Now choose life, so that you and your children may live." In the Mass, we are given the opportunity to choose life, to choose Christ, and to reject the curse of sin.

The Book of Revelation captures the awe-inspiring nature of the Mass, where the faithful, along with the choirs of angels, unite their voices in praise and worship of God. "And so, with all the choirs of angels, we sing..." (Revelation 5:11-12). When heaven touches earth in the liturgy, we are privileged to join in that eternal song, praying alongside the angels and saints. The Mass is a solemn oath, not only to God but before countless witnesses—angels, saints, and all those who have gone before us. Every Mass is a witness to the reality of God's kingdom, and through it, we are drawn deeper into that eternal communion. This is why I believe in the power of the Mass. It is a heavenly encounter—a moment when God enters our lives in the most intimate way. The Mass is not just a reflection of heaven but heaven on earth. It is a gift, a sacrament, and a call to live

out the blessings of God's covenant. When we attend Mass, we are not merely fulfilling an obligation but entering a divine reality that transforms our lives and our hearts. We are invited to be part of something far greater than ourselves, something eternal, and something constantly renewing us in God's grace and love.

In the early days of Christianity, believers often risked their lives to gather in secret, celebrating the Mass in hidden, underground spaces to avoid persecution. Many were martyred for their unwavering commitment to the Eucharist. Despite the passage of time, this persecution continues to this day. According to the 2022 World Watch List compiled by Open Doors International, Christian persecution is on the rise, especially in regions such as Africa and Asia. The report reveals:

- **5,898 Christians were killed** in the past year, marking an increase of 23.8% compared to the previous year.

- **5,110 churches were attacked or closed**, a rise of 13.8%.

- **6,175 Christians were arrested** without trial, a shocking increase of 44.3%.

- **3,829 Christians were kidnapped**, an increase of 123.9%.

Countries such as Afghanistan, North Korea, Somalia, Libya, and Yemen report the most severe levels of persecution. At the same time, other nations like Nigeria, Pakistan, Iran, India, Saudi Arabia, Myanmar, Sudan, Iraq, China, and Syria also see significant restrictions on religious freedom. One alarming story from May 28, 2023, illustrated the harsh realities of Christian persecution when a family in North Korea, including a two-year-old child, was sentenced to life imprisonment for simply possessing a Bible. This kind of brutality highlights the relentless crackdown on religious freedom in many parts of the world, as reported by the U.S. State Department's International Religious Freedom Report. The suffering endured by our siblings in faith should serve as a sobering reminder of the precious gift we have—the freedom to gather and worship without fear of persecution. It's easy to take the Mass for granted in places where religious freedom is protected, but when we hear these stories of persecution, it reminds us of the value of what we have. Every Sunday, when we walk into our church, we do not just perform a ritual; we participate in the eternal sacrifice of Christ. The Mass, in all its beauty and reverence, is a profound opportunity to receive God's grace, to encounter His real presence in the Eucharist, and to unite with the global Church in prayer and worship. In a world where so many are willing to risk everything to practice their faith, we must never lose sight of the extraordinary privilege of attending Mass freely. We are called to honor the Mass, to live out its transformative power, and to cherish the gift of the Eucharist, especially as we stand in solidarity with those around the world who are denied this sacred freedom.

As we reflect on the courage of those who face extreme persecution for their faith, let us be inspired to live with greater devotion, to participate more fully in the Mass, and to support our siblings in Christ through prayer and advocacy. The Mass is not just a personal encounter with Christ—it is a communal act of worship that connects us with the suffering Church worldwide, and with the angels and saints who join us in praising God. We are called to value this gift, to protect it, and to ensure that, no matter the circumstances, we continue to live the truth of the Eucharist with love, reverence, and gratitude.

For me, attending Mass is a simple and integral part of my life. My home in Covington, Louisiana, is just a short 10-minute drive from Holy Trinity Catholic Church. I am fortunate to live in a place where I have access to several beautiful churches within a fifteen-minute radius—Our Lady of the Lake, Mary Queen of Peace, Saint Anselm, and Saint Peter. Recently, Our Lady of Mount Carmel has also opened its doors, offering the Latin Mass. While I deeply respect the beauty and tradition of the Latin Rite, it is not where I feel the

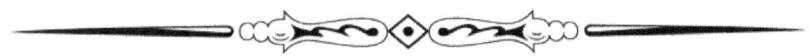

most personal connection to heaven on earth. But, wherever I choose to attend Mass, I am reminded of the incredible privilege we have as Catholics. The Mass is not merely a gathering; it is an invitation to join in the eternal worship of heaven itself. The sacred reality unfolding before us at every Mass is nothing short of a glimpse into the divine. We often take for granted the grace we are given to participate in this holy sacrifice, but a profound encounter with Christ connects us to the angels, the saints, and God Himself. The Mass is heaven on earth—every time we gather, we are given a glimpse of the eternal banquet, where we stand before the throne of God, united with the communion of saints. It's easy to forget that we are participating in such a profound mystery, but when we open our hearts and minds to the reality of what is happening, we find ourselves drawn into the divine presence. If we allow ourselves to experience this with reverence, we may even catch a fleeting glimpse of the divine kingdom, right here during our everyday lives. Ultimately, the Mass is not just a ritual or a weekly obligation. It is a sacred encounter where heaven and earth meet. And it is in these moments, as we receive the Body and Blood of Christ, that heaven genuinely touches us.

Next time you attend Mass, and if you find your mind wandering or your thoughts drifting, try to bring them back into focus. Look beyond the familiar surroundings of the church building. Imagine the many angels surrounding you, their voices joining in praise as the Eucharist is consecrated. Look above the Chalice, and imagine the Saints, both known and unknown, uniting in worship alongside the priest. And most importantly, imagine God, present among us in the Most Holy Eucharist. It is in that moment that heaven touches earth.

Chapter Nineteen
Powerful Weapons

The Brown Scapula of Mount Carmel

I still vividly remember the first time I learned about the brown scapular of the Blessed Mother. It was in first grade at Mount Carmel Elementary School, and Sister Fatima was teaching us about this special devotion. She showed us a short film that told the true story of a group of people aboard a ship caught in a violent storm at sea. The ship was sinking, and panic was spreading among the passengers. But one man, who was wearing a brown scapular, did something remarkable: he said a prayer to Mary and, in an act of faith, threw his scapular into the turbulent sea. Almost immediately, the storm began to calm, the waves settled, and the ship was saved. But then something extraordinary happened. A wave washed over the ship's railing and, to everyone's amazement, the very scapular the man had thrown into the water was returned to him, gently floating back to him on the calm sea. The film ended with the powerful message that, through the intercession of Mary, the man and the passengers were saved.

This story left an indelible impression on me, and from that day forward, I promised myself always to wear my brown scapular. I rarely take it off, as it has become more than just a piece of cloth—it is a tangible sign of my faith and trust in God's protection, as well as my devotion to the Blessed Mother. My wife continues to wear her scapula along with our daughter Alissa. Reflecting on this experience, I am struck by the deep beauty and truth that the Catholic faith offers. The story of the scapular reminds me that faith can move mountains—even still the stormy seas. It is a reminder that Mary, as our Mother, cares for us and intercedes for us in ways that often go beyond our understanding. This story, and the devotion it represents, embodies the core of Catholic belief: that God is with us in our trials, that Mary is always by our side, and that through small acts of faith, God can work great wonders. For me, the brown scapular is not merely a tradition or a symbol—it's a daily invitation to live my faith more fully. Wearing it is a reminder to turn to Mary in prayer, to trust in God's providence, and to be open to the ways God works in our lives, even in the most ordinary and simple things. It's a visible sign of my commitment to living a life of faith, rooted in prayer, humility, and devotion.

The brown scapular is a small but powerful symbol of that trust, a reminder that God works in our lives through grace and the intercession of His holy Mother. The story I heard as a child, and the devotion it inspired in me, continues to shape my faith to this day. Through this simple act of wearing the scapular, I am reminded that I am not alone on this journey—Mary's protection is with me, and God's love surrounds me, always. This is the beauty and truth of the Catholic faith: the loving presence of God, always with us, guiding us toward holiness and salvation. As a Catholic, I have often reflected on the beauty and depth of my faith, which is rooted in tradition, devotion, and the living presence of God. One of the most profound symbols of this faith is the brown scapular, a simple yet powerful sign of devotion to Mary, the Mother of God, and a commitment to living a life of holiness. The brown scapular, particularly in its association with the Carmelite Order, has always struck me as a remarkable

expression of the Catholic faith—its history, its symbolism, and the spiritual benefits it promises.

The brown scapular finds its origins in the 12th century, when the Carmelite Order was founded on Mount Carmel in the Holy Land. The early Carmelites wore a simple garment called a "scapular" as part of their religious habit. This piece of cloth, though modest, was a symbol of their total commitment to God, representing their life of prayer, penance, and contemplation. To me, this is a beautiful reminder that holiness is often found in the simplest of things. The scapular, a humble piece of clothing, became a profound sign of devotion—a way to dedicate oneself to God through the ordinary, day-to-day act of wearing it. The pivotal moment in the history of the brown scapular came in 1251, when St. Simon Stock, a Carmelite friar, is said to have received a vision of the Blessed Virgin Mary. In this vision, Mary presented St. Simon with the brown scapular, promising that those who wore it with devotion would enjoy her protection and be granted salvation. To me, this vision underscores the deep maternal love that Mary has for all of us and her desire to help guide us toward holiness. Through her intercession, we are invited to enter a closer relationship with God, relying on her maternal care and protection. The promise that Mary will be with us in life and especially at the hour of death brings a profound sense of peace and trust in God's grace. The brown scapular is much more than a physical object. It symbolizes a deeper spiritual commitment call to prayer, penance, and a life dedicated to holiness. For those of us who wear it, the scapular serves as a constant reminder of the need to seek God in everything we do. It calls us to a life of devotion, humility, and fidelity to God's will. In a world that often encourages distractions and superficiality, the scapular helps ground us in the reality of our faith, inviting us to focus on what truly matters: our relationship with God and our journey toward eternal life.

One of the most beautiful aspects of the brown scapular is the spiritual benefits and promises associated with it. Those who wear it faithfully are said to receive the protection of the Blessed Virgin

Mary, who intercedes on their behalf, especially at the moment of death. This promise, often referred to as the "scapular promise," offers profound comfort and assurance that, no matter what the trials or challenges we face in life, we are not alone. Mary, as our spiritual mother, walks with us every step of the way. This promise speaks to the Catholic belief in the importance of Marian intercession—how, through Mary's love and prayers, we can draw closer to Christ and experience His mercy. Even in today's world, the brown scapular continues to be a cherished symbol of Catholic devotion. Many Catholics still wear the scapular as a sign of their faith, a daily reminder of their commitment to God and trust in Mary's protection. The devotion to the brown scapular has also become a way for the faithful to renew their commitment to Carmelite spirituality, which emphasizes contemplation, prayer, and a deep sense of God's presence in our lives. For me, wearing the scapular is not just about adhering to a tradition, but embracing a lifestyle of prayer, humility, and true love for God.

The brown scapular is more than just an object, it is a pathway to holiness. It invites us into a deeper relationship with God and Mary, encouraging us to live lives of devotion, prayer, and fidelity. It reminds me that the Catholic faith is not simply a set of beliefs or rituals, but a living relationship with the Creator, sustained through grace, prayer, and the intercession of the saints. The brown scapular, with its rich history and spiritual promises, encapsulates the beauty and truth of the Catholic faith, offering us a tangible way to express our love for God and our trust in His mercy. In wearing the scapular, I am reminded that I am part of a long tradition of believers who have sought holiness through simple acts of devotion and trust in God's providence. And this, to me, is one of the most beautiful aspects of the Catholic faith: its ability to connect us to something much larger than ourselves—a communion of saints, a deep tradition of prayer, and the living presence of God in our lives.

On October 13, 1917, during the final apparition at Fatima, Our Blessed Mother appeared dressed as Our Lady of Mount Carmel,

holding out to the world the brown scapular as a sign of personal consecration and eternal salvation. This moment, when Mary entrusted this powerful symbol of devotion to the faithful, is a powerful reminder of the beauty of her love and the truth of her maternal care for us all. Mary's appearance at Fatima, where she presented the brown scapular, was not just a simple gesture. It was an invitation to all of us to draw closer to her, to be clothed in her grace, and to walk in the path of holiness. Saint Lucy of Fatima, one of the visionaries, later explained that the scapular and the rosary are inseparable—two powerful tools for our spiritual journey. The rosary is our prayer, a weapon of faith that connects us to God through Mary, and the scapular is a physical sign of our devotion, a spiritual garment that draws us into deeper union with her. The brown scapular carries with it a profound spiritual meaning. It is a sign of our consecration to Mary, a pledge of our commitment to live according to the teachings of Christ. When I wear my scapular, it reminds me daily that I am not alone on this faith journey. I am protected by the Blessed Mother, who lovingly guides me toward holiness and eternal life with God.

The significance of the brown scapular is even more clearly revealed when we look at the words of the devil, who revealed to Saint Francis of Yepes, the brother of Saint John of the Cross, that three things especially tormented him: the name of Jesus, the name of Mary, and the brown scapular. "Take off that habit," the devil cried, "which snatches so many souls from us. All those clothed in it die piously and escape us." To the devil, the scapular was a source of great torment because it represented the faithful's commitment to Mary and to living a life devoted to God. Souls who wear the scapular and live her message of holiness, prayer, and devotion are drawn closer to salvation and protected from the evil one's grasp. In these words, I hear a deep truth about the power of the scapular. It is not simply an ornament, but a spiritual shield, a reminder of our identity as children of Mary, and a sign of our commitment to live lives rooted in prayer, penance, and devotion to Christ. The devil fears the

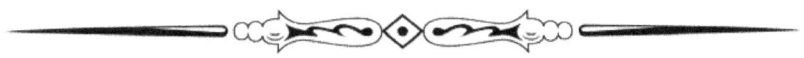

scapular because it symbolizes everything contrary to his influence—faith, hope, and love, lived through Mary, the mother of all grace.

Mary speaks to each of us through the brown scapular: "Wear it devoutly and perseveringly," she says, "It is my garment. To be clothed in it means you are continually thinking of me, and I, in turn, am always thinking of you and helping you to secure eternal life." These words are a call to all of us to wear the scapular with reverence, to allow it to deepen our relationship with Mary, and to live in constant awareness of her maternal love. Through the scapular, she invites us to think of her often and, in doing so, to be drawn closer to God and to His will for our lives. To wear the brown scapular, then, is to accept an invitation from Heaven itself—a call to live a life of holiness and devotion, to be continually mindful of Mary's presence in our lives, and to trust in her intercession as we journey toward eternal life. The scapular is a rich and powerful gift, brought down from Heaven by Our Lady herself, and it carries with it the promise of her protection, guidance, and the hope of salvation. The beauty of the Catholic faith is found in these simple yet profound truths. The brown scapular is a tangible reminder of Mary's love, symbolizing her call to holiness, and a tool for growing in grace. It invites us to deepen our relationship with God and to trust in His infinite mercy and love. Through the scapular, we are reminded of the truth that we are never alone—Mary is always with us, guiding us, praying for us, and helping us on our path to eternal life. This is the beauty and truth of the Catholic faith: the deep and abiding love of our Heavenly Mother, who leads us to her Son, and the promise of eternal salvation through faith and devotion.

Father Robert Levis, a Catholic exorcist, once described a powerful moment during an exorcism when the Brown Scapular was placed around the neck of a possessed person. The Devil, upon encountering the Scapular, could not contain its reaction. "It is fire! It is fire!" it screamed in agony. "Remove it, I beg of you! I cannot bear it! "In a similar experience, an anonymous exorcist priest recounted an instance when, during an exorcism, the demon spoke directly to him, saying, "Just take that Scapular off, and I will show you what I will do to you." The devil's hostility towards the Brown Scapular is consistent in such encounters. Exorcist Father Chad Ripperger has also spoken on the significance of the Brown Scapular. He explained that demons have a strong aversion to it, often attempting to dislodge it during expulsions. He emphasized that the Scapular provides a critical level of protection, noting a specific case where a demon of impurity would relentlessly attempt to remove the Scapular from the woman it was tormenting. In every manifestation, the demon first sought to take off the Scapular, recognizing its power to safeguard the wearer from its influence.

The Rosary

From an early age, I have been surrounded by the beauty and power of the Catholic faith, and one of the most profound sources of strength in my life has been the Rosary. While I was always aware of the brown scapular, I cannot pinpoint exactly when the Rosary became a central part of my spiritual life. I do, however, remember seeing it often, even as a child. I recall the Rosary on my parents' nightstand, a constant, quiet witness to their faith. Growing up in Mount Carmel Heights, a neighborhood filled with Catholic families, I was blessed to witness the way the Rosary brought people together in times of need. When a neighbor was struggling, the "Rosary warriors" were there—faithfully praying for and with them. In this environment, surrounded by a community of prayers, I came to understand the true power of the Rosary. My mother, a devoted woman of prayer, was part of a women's group that gathered regularly—either daily or weekly, I can't quite recall—to pray the Rosary together. I vividly remember these women, sitting under the carport at Mrs. Landy's house, united in prayer as they recited the decades of the Rosary. Their faith was palpable, and it was through them, along with my parents and the twelve years of Catholic education I received, that I grew to appreciate the profound depth of the Rosary. Over my sixty-five years, I've probably said the Rosary a billion times, and it has always been a source of comfort and solace.

The Rosary, with its rhythmic prayers and meditations, has been my constant companion through the highs and lows of life. Yet, it wasn't until I faced the deep pain of divorce that I truly began to experience Rosary's power on a deeper level. In the midst of my suffering, the Rosary became not just a prayer I said, but a prayer that told me. It offered me a refuge, a way to draw near to God and the Blessed Mother, who has always comforted those in pain. Each Hail Mary, each Our Father, each Mystery, became a lifeline, pulling me closer to the peace and healing I so desperately needed. The Rosary was no longer just a series of prayers—it became a conversation with God and Mary, a means of surrendering my suffering and trusting in divine providence.

However, the most profound experience I've had with the Rosary came when I met Immaculée Ilibagiza, the author of *Left to Tell*, *The Boy Who Met Jesus*, *The Rosary*, and several other inspiring books. Meeting Immaculée was, without a doubt, a God-given gift. Her story of surviving the Rwandan genocide and finding healing through faith, especially through the Rosary, is nothing short of miraculous. When I saw her pray the Rosary, I saw something extraordinary. It wasn't just words being recited—it was as though her entire being was immersed in the prayer. Her mind, body, and soul were completely united in the Rosary, as though she herself became one with prayer. It was a profound, living experience of prayer, a deep communion with God and the Blessed Mother. Immaculée's example taught me something essential: the Rosary is not simply a routine or a ritual, but a powerful means of connecting with God on a spiritual and emotional level. It's an opportunity to enter into the mysteries of Christ's life, death, and resurrection, to contemplate them with Mary, and to allow them to transform us. In seeing Immaculée pray the Rosary, I understood that it's not just about reciting prayers, it's about becoming one with the prayer itself. It's about opening our hearts to God and allowing Him to transform us through the power of the Holy Spirit, with Mary leading the way.

For me, the Rosary has become more than just a comfort prayer—it has become a tool of transformation. It's a prayer of healing, of surrender, of faith. When I hold the beads in my hands, I am reminded of the beauty and truth of the Catholic faith: that we are never alone, that Mary is always there to intercede for us, and that through prayer, we are drawn ever closer to Christ. The Rosary is a powerful reminder that God is with us in every moment of our lives, especially in times of pain and suffering. The beauty of the Catholic faith is revealed in the way the Rosary connects us to the mysteries of salvation and to the loving presence of Mary, our Mother. It's a prayer that invites us into deeper communion with God and offers us a path to healing and grace. Through the Rosary, I have experienced the transformative power of prayer, the kind of prayer that heals hearts, renews spirits, and draws us closer to God. And as I continue my journey of faith, the Rosary remains a constant source of strength and comfort, a reminder of the beauty and truth of God's love, which is always present, always sustaining, and always ready to lead us into the fullness of His peace.

I often feel a deep sense of compassion for my Protestant brothers and sisters who, out of a lack of understanding, miss the beauty and power of the Hail Mary. Over the years, many Catholics have been told by some Protestant friends that the Hail Mary is not found in the Bible, and this claim is, to me, incredulous. For those who hold the Bible as the sole authority in matters of faith, how can they overlook this beautiful prayer, which is so deeply rooted in Scripture? The Hail Mary is a powerful prayer, and it is both biblical and profoundly meaningful in the Catholic tradition. I believe it reveals the beauty and truth of the Catholic faith in a way that is sometimes misunderstood by those who do not know it.

The *Hail Mary* prayer is derived from several passages in Holy Scripture and can be divided into two parts:

Part One:

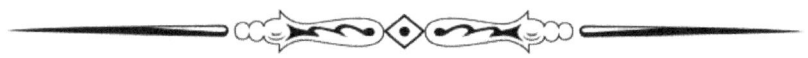

- **Luke 1:28**: *"Hail Mary, full of grace, the Lord is with thee."* – In this passage, the Angel Gabriel greets Mary, saying, *"Hail, favored one! The Lord is with you."*

- **Luke 1:42**: *"Blessed art thou among women."* – Elizabeth, filled with the Holy Spirit, cries out with a loud voice, *"Most blessed are you among women, and blessed is the fruit of your womb, Jesus."*

- **Luke 1:43**: *"Holy Mary, Mother of God."* – Elizabeth, amazed by Mary's presence, asks, *"And how does this happen to me, that the mother of my Lord should come to me?"*

Part Two:

- **James 5:16**: *"Pray for us sinners, now and at the hour of our death."* – In this scripture, James encourages believers to *"confess your sins to one another and pray for one another, that you may be healed. The fervent prayer of a righteous person is very powerful."* This echoes the final part of the *Hail Mary*, asking Mary to intercede on our behalf, especially in our time of need.

Together, these passages highlight Mary's honor, blessing, and intercessory power and the scriptural foundation of the prayer that has been cherished by Christians for centuries.

The first half of the Hail Mary is rooted in the Gospel of Luke, where the Angel Gabriel greets Mary with words and expresses who Mary is and honors her role in salvation history

"Hail, full of grace, the Lord is with you."

— Luke 1:28

This is the angelic greeting to Mary when the Archangel Gabriel appeared to her at the Annunciation. Gabriel calls Mary "full of grace," which emphasizes her unique role in God's plan of salvation. The phrase, "The Lord is with you," also speaks to Mary's divine favor and special relationship with God. For Protestants who take the Bible seriously, this verse is a direct scriptural foundation for the first part of the Hail Mary.

"Blessed are you among women, and blessed is the fruit of your womb."

— Luke 1:42

These words are spoken by Elizabeth, the mother of John the Baptist, as she greets Mary during her visitation. Elizabeth is filled with the Holy Spirit and recognizes the greatness of Mary's mission as the Mother of God. To say that Mary is "blessed among women" is not just an expression of respect but an acknowledgment of the extraordinary grace bestowed upon her to bear the Savior of the world.

"And how does this happen to me, that the mother of my Lord should come to me?"

— Luke 1:43

This is the continuation of Elizabeth's words, expressing awe that Mary, the Mother of the Lord, has come to visit her. Elizabeth's proclamation is powerful in affirming Mary's role as the mother of Jesus, the Lord and Savior.

The second half is our prayer to Mary, asking for her intercession. Both parts are firmly rooted in Scripture, with direct references to key moments in the Gospels and the New Testament.

"Holy Mary, Mother of God, pray for us sinners, now and at the hour of our death."

This part is rooted in both Scripture and Tradition. The phrase "Holy Mary, Mother of God" is a title that was formally recognized by the Church at the Council of Ephesus in 431 A.D. It is a declaration that Mary is truly the mother of Jesus, who is both fully God and fully man. The title "Mother of God" is not a claim about Mary's divinity, but rather an affirmation of her unique relationship with the divine Son, Jesus Christ.

James 5:16 prayer for Mary to *"pray for us sinners"* echoes the biblical call for the faithful to pray for one another. In, we read, "Confess your sins to one another, and pray for one another, so that you may be healed. The fervent prayer of a righteous person is immensely powerful." The prayer for Mary's intercession is consistent with the scriptural teaching that the prayers of the righteous, those united with God in grace, have great power. Catholics believe that Mary, as the Mother of Christ and one of the most righteous and holy of God's creatures, is uniquely positioned to intercede on our behalf, especially at the hour of our death.

The final petition— "now and at the hour of our death"—reminds us that we are always in need of God's mercy, and we ask Mary to pray for us at every moment of our lives, but especially at the end, when we need God's grace most profoundly. The beauty and truth of the Catholic faith are found in our deep reverence for Mary, who plays a vital role in God's plan of salvation. The Hail Mary is not just a prayer to a distant or passive figure; it is an invitation to draw close to the Blessed Mother, to entrust ourselves to her loving care, and to seek her intercession as we strive to live according to God's will.

For those who do not fully understand the role of Mary in the Catholic faith, it can be easy to misunderstand the Hail Mary as something that elevates her above Christ or diminishes the centrality of God in our faith. But in truth, the Hail Mary always points us to

Jesus. Mary is the perfect model of faith and obedience, and in honoring her, we are led to a deeper relationship with her Son. The Hail Mary is a prayer of humility, recognizing that Mary is "full of grace" because God chose her to be the mother of His Son, and we are called to imitate her trust in God's will. The beauty of this prayer, grounded in Scripture, is that it bridges the divine and the human. We pray with Mary, asking her to intercede for us, and in doing so, we become more deeply united to the great mysteries of our faith—the Incarnation, the life of Jesus, and the hope of eternal salvation.

The Hail Mary prayer draws us into the rich tapestry of God's love, showing us how His grace works through the lives of His faithful servants. By honoring Mary and seeking her intercession, we are not diverting our attention from God but rather growing in our devotion to Him, who has chosen to reveal His love through His Mother. The Hail Mary is a profound expression of our trust in God's plan and our belief in the power of prayer, both of which are essential to the Catholic faith. There's something profoundly beautiful about the Rosary that has drawn me in for as long as I can remember. For me, it's not just a string of beads or a set of prayers, it's a living tradition, rich with history, which reaches back over 800 years and connects us to the very heart of our faith. The Rosary is one of the most powerful prayers in the Catholic Church, and it speaks to me of the enduring beauty of our relationship with God, through the intercession of His Blessed Mother, Mary.

The story of the Rosary begins long before it became the prayer we know today. Early Christians, many of whom were poor and illiterate, had a deep desire to pray, but lacked the means to do so in the structured way we might think of today. In the absence of books or written prayers, they would use what was available to them—stones, beads, or simple knots—to count their prayers. They would often recite *the Our Father* or other prayers over and over, much as we still do today with the Rosary. These "prayer beads," as they were known, helped people keep track of their prayers, and this humble practice formed the foundation for what would become the Rosary.

This early form of prayer, though simple, was profound. The beads allowed the faithful to keep their focus on prayer and meditation, an act of devotion that, over time, would evolve into a powerful tool for reflection on the life of Christ and His Blessed Mother.

The next step in the Rosary's journey comes in the 12th century with St. Dominic, the founder of the Dominican Order. According to tradition, St. Dominic received a vision of the Blessed Virgin Mary in 1208. In that vision, Mary handed him a Rosary, telling him that it would be a powerful weapon to combat heresy and lead souls closer to God. In an age of spiritual unrest, when the Albigensian heresy threatened the faith in southern France, Mary instructed St. Dominic to use the Rosary to help people meditate on the life of Jesus and the mysteries of salvation. What strikes me most about this part of the Rosary's history is how it speaks to our need for prayer and protection in times of trial. Just as the early Christians used simple beads to keep count of their prayers, St. Dominic was given a prayer that would lead us deeper into the heart of God's plan for salvation. The Rosary, as it developed, would become much more than just a prayer; it would become a way to unite ourselves to the life of Christ and to the love of Mary, who is our mother.

As the centuries passed, the Rosary continued to evolve. By the 15th century, the Dominican Order formalized the structure of the Rosary, adding the concept of mysteries—specific events in the lives of Jesus and Mary—that would be meditated upon while praying the Rosary. These mysteries, grouped into three sets of five (the *Joyful*, *Sorrowful*, and the *Glorious* mysteries), allowed Catholics to contemplate the most important moments in the life of Christ. I find it incredibly powerful that the Rosary has always been more than just a prayer for personal devotion—it's a way to enter into the very story of our salvation, to walk alongside Jesus and Mary as we reflect on the central events of our faith: the Annunciation, the Crucifixion, the Resurrection. The idea of contemplating these mysteries—whether in joy, sorrow, or glory—reminds me that our faith is not just abstract; it's rooted in the lived experience of Christ and Mary. Through the

Rosary, we are invited to live that story again, to be part of the great drama of salvation. It's a constant invitation to draw closer to Christ.

The spread of the Rosary throughout the Catholic world was solidified in 1569, when Pope Pius V officially approved the Rosary as we know it today. His papal bull, *Consueverunt Romani*, not only declared the 15 mysteries, but it also affirmed the Rosary as a universal prayer for the entire Church. This papal approval marked a pivotal moment in the history of the Rosary, and it spread the prayer across the world. For me, this is significant. The Rosary was never meant to be a private or individualistic prayer. It's a prayer of the Church, a prayer meant to unite us all, from the most devout to the newest members of the faith. It speaks to the universality of our devotion to Mary and to Christ. Through the Rosary, we are part of a living tradition that stretches across centuries and continents. And in every bead, we are reminded that we are never alone—our prayers are joined with those of Catholics all over the world.

One of the most powerful moments in the history of the Rosary came in 1571, when Catholic forces, led by Pope Pius V, fought a crucial battle against the Ottoman Empire at Lepanto. The victory was attributed to the intercession of the Blessed Virgin Mary, and in gratitude, Pope Pius V established the feast of Our Lady of the Rosary. To this day, Catholics continue to celebrate this feast, remembering how the Rosary brought about not just personal peace, but a moment of global significance. To me, this story is not just about a historical event, it's about the Rosary's power to change hearts and circumstances. Whether it's a personal struggle, a family crisis, or a world-changing event, the Rosary is a tool of spiritual warfare. It's a way for us to call on Mary, our Mother, to intercede for us, just as she did for the soldiers at Lepanto. And when we pray for the Rosary, we are reminded that we, too, are part of the great spiritual battle for souls.

In 2002, Pope John Paul II introduced the *Luminous Mysteries*, adding five new mysteries that focus on the public ministry

of Jesus—from His Baptism in the Jordan to the institution of the Eucharist at the Last Supper. These mysteries, for me, help complete the picture of Jesus' life. The Rosary is no longer just a miracle, and the gift of His presence in the Eucharist. With the addition of these mysteries, the Rosary gives us a fuller, richer contemplation of the life of Christ—a life that is lived for us, in love, every day.

The Rosary is, without a doubt, one of the most cherished and powerful prayers in the Catholic Church. Today, it remains a source of comfort, strength, and peace, especially during times of difficulty and uncertainty. I can personally testify to the way the Rosary has brought me peace and clarity when life has felt overwhelming, or when I've been confronted with doubt, pain, or suffering. There is something deeply grounding about the repetition of its prayers. Each bead invites me to turn my focus back to the central mysteries of our faith—the life, death, and resurrection of Jesus—and in doing so, I rediscover a deep sense of calm and purpose.

The Rosary is not just a prayer; it is a powerful reflection of the beauty and truth of the Catholic faith. Its history, which stretches back over 800 years, reveals how God has used this prayer to draw us closer to His heart through the intercession of His Blessed Mother, Mary. The Rosary's roots in the early Church, its formalization by St. Dominic, and its eventual universal approval by the Church speak to a deep spiritual truth: that prayer, particularly through the Rosary, is a means of walking alongside Christ and His Mother as they invite us to contemplate the mysteries of salvation. The Rosary has evolved over the centuries into a beautiful structure—one that brings us into a deeper relationship with Christ. Each prayer, each bead, each mystery offers a new way to contemplate the great acts of love and redemption that define our faith. Whether reflecting on the joy of the Annunciation, the sorrow of the Passion, or the glory of the Resurrection, we are invited to meditate on the profound truths of our salvation. These mysteries are not just historical events; they are a call to join our hearts with the heart of Christ.

The power of the Rosary is also evident in how it has been used in times of trial and struggle. When Pope Pius V called for the faithful to pray the Rosary during the Battle of Lepanto, the victory of the Catholic forces was attributed to the intercession of the Blessed Virgin Mary. Throughout history, the Rosary has been seen as a spiritual weapon—one that unites us in prayer, helping us to overcome trials, to fight against evil, and to deepen our commitment to God.

One of the most striking aspects of the Rosary is the continued relevance it holds for Catholics today. In 1917, during the apparitions at Fatima, the Blessed Mother appeared to the children and identified herself as the "Lady of the Rosary." She urged the world to pray to the Rosary every day, to bring about peace for the world and to overcome the challenges facing humanity. This message was not only for the people of Fatima but for all of us. The Rosary is a prayer of peace, and through it, we unite ourselves with Mary's loving intercession to bring peace to our hearts, our families, and to the world. Similarly, the Medjugorje visionaries, who continue to receive messages from Our Lady, echo this same call: to pray the Rosary every day. These messages remind us that the Rosary is more than just a personal prayer, it is a communal prayer, a means of uniting the Church and the world in a shared mission of peace. Every time, I pray the Rosary, I feel connected not only to God and Mary, but also to the whole Church, the Body of Christ. It reminds me that prayer is never just about me; it's about us—about the whole world coming together in faith, hope, and love. I believe the Rosary is a spiritual journey—one that I am grateful to take every day. It's a journey that invites us to go deeper into the heart of God, to see the world through Mary's eyes, and to trust in the love and mercy of Christ. It's a prayer that doesn't just lead us to contemplation but transforms us. Each prayer of the Rosary is an opportunity to deepen our relationship with Christ and to invite Him more fully into our hearts.

The beauty and truth of the Catholic faith are deeply evident in the Rosary. It is a prayer that has been with the Church for

centuries, and it will continue to guide us toward the eternal love of God. Through the Rosary, we are invited to walk with Christ and His Mother on their journey of love, suffering, and glory, and in doing so, we come to know the profound peace that only God can give. In my life, I have experienced the truth of the Rosary's power and the beauty of its prayer. The words of Our Lady at Fatima, urging us to pray the Rosary for peace, and the continued call of the Medjugorje visionaries, remind me that this prayer is timeless. It is a prayer that continues to speak to our world today, calling us to peace, love, and unity with God. And it is a prayer that I will continue to turn to as a source of comfort, strength, and transformation in my own life. During an exorcism, Father Jose Syquia shared that the devil, in evident anguish, confessed that the Rosary is the most powerful of prayers, deeply feared in Hell. He also revealed that the Brown Scapular holds a similar power, dreaded by demonic forces.

The 15 Promises of the Rosary: A Path to Grace and Protection

The Rosary is more than just a prayer; it is a powerful means of grace, a source of spiritual strength, and a shield against the forces of evil. The 15 promises made by Our Blessed Mother to those who pray the Rosary devoutly highlight the profound beauty and truth of this devotion. These promises were first revealed to St. Dominic during the Albigensian heresy and later entrusted to Blessed Alan de la Roche, who helped renew devotion to the Rosary in the 15th century. These promises reveal not only the power of the Rosary but also the tender love that the Blessed Virgin has for those who entrust themselves to her through this prayer.

1. **Special Protection and Great Graces:**

   To all those who pray my Rosary devoutly, I promise my special protection and great graces. When we pray the Rosary, we invite Mary into our lives as a loving Mother who cares for us, intercedes for us, and shields us with her maternal protection.

2. **Special Grace for Perseverance:**

Those who persevere in the recitation of my Rosary will receive some special grace. The Rosary is a prayer that deepens with each repetition, and by persisting in this prayer, we are granted extraordinary graces to help us grow in holiness.

3. **Armor Against Hell:**

The Rosary will be a very powerful armor against hell; it will destroy vice, deliver from sin, and dispel heresy. The Rosary strengthens us spiritually, helping us resist temptation, overcome sin, and protect our hearts from worldly distractions.

4. **Flourishing of Virtue and Good Works:**

The Rosary will make virtue and good works flourish and will obtain for souls the most abundant divine mercies. As we meditate on the mysteries of Christ's life, we are transformed to live more like Him, performing acts of love, charity, and mercy.

5. **Elevation Toward Eternal Desires:**

It will draw the hearts of men from the love of the world and its vanities and will lift them to the desire of eternal things. In praying for the Rosary, we are reminded of the eternal life that awaits us in heaven, turning our hearts away from fleeting worldly pleasures to lasting spiritual joys.

6. **Assurance of Salvation:**

Those who trust themselves to me through the Rosary will not perish. When we place our trust in Mary and invoke her through the Rosary, we are assured of her intercession and protection, especially in moments of trial and danger.

7. Protection from Misfortune:

Whoever devoutly recites my Rosary, reflecting on the mysteries, shall never be overwhelmed by misfortune. They will not experience God's anger nor perish by an unprovided death. The Rosary offers peace and protection in the midst of life's challenges, giving us the strength to persevere with faith.

8. Conversion of Sinners and Perseverance in Grace:

The sinner will be converted; the just will persevere in grace and merit eternal life. Through the Rosary, many have experienced the grace of conversion, while the just are helped to stay strong in faith and grow in holiness.

9. Assurance of the Sacraments:

Those truly devoted to my Rosary shall not die without the sacraments of the Church. The Rosary is a powerful prayer, especially at the end of life, ensuring that we receive the grace of the sacraments when we most need them.

10. Light of God and Plenitude of Graces:

Those who are faithful to recite my Rosary shall have during their life and at their death the light of God and the plenitude of His graces and will share in the merits of the blessed. The Rosary brings light and grace into our lives, helping us remain focused on God's will and grow in holiness.

11. Deliverance from Purgatory:

I will deliver promptly from purgatory souls devoted to my Rosary. The Blessed Virgin promises to help release souls from purgatory, assisting them on their journey toward the fullness of heaven.

12. **Great Glory in Heaven:**

True children of my Rosary will enjoy great glory in heaven. Those who remain faithful to the Rosary will be rewarded with abundant glory in heaven, enjoying eternal communion with God and Mary.

13. **Your Requests Will Be Granted:**

What you shall ask through my Rosary you shall obtain. Mary assures us that when we pray the Rosary, with hearts truly devoted to God, our petitions will be heard and answered according to God's will.

14. **Aid for Those Who Spread the Rosary:**

To those who propagate my Rosary, I promise aid in all their necessities. Whether we share the Rosary with others, encourage others to pray for it, or support its spread, Mary promises to help us in all our needs.

15. **The Intercession of the Celestial Court:**

I have obtained from my Son that all the members of the Rosary Confraternity shall have as their intercessors, in life and in death, the entire celestial court. Those who devote themselves to the Rosary are promised the intercession of all the angels and saints, as well as Mary's constant help.

It is deemed that when we pray the Rosary, particularly the words, "Holy Mother of God, pray for us sinners now," the Blessed

Mother responds immediately, coming to our side to pray with us. And she does not come alone. As the Queen of Angels, she brings with her not just one or two, but choirs of angels—an awe-inspiring multitude of heavenly beings. But even more wondrous, she always brings Jesus with her. Since she and Jesus are forever united at the heart, they cannot be separated. And because Jesus is inseparable from the Holy Trinity, He brings with Him the Father and the Holy Spirit. Where the Holy Trinity is present, all of creation is made manifest, and in that sacred space, we are enveloped in a beauty and a light so pure and radiant that we cannot fully comprehend it in this life. This is a glimpse of the divine truth and beauty that the Catholic faith reveals—an encounter with the living God that transcends all earthly understanding. These are moments like these that strengthen my belief in the profound and unconditional love, grace, and mystery of our faith. It's amazing to reflect on how much grace and heavenly help we can receive from a practice as simple as praying the Rosary. It only takes about 15 minutes to pray, yet this prayer can transform lives, help us grow in holiness, and protect us from spiritual harm. If you feel that you don't have time for it, I encourage you to try praying the Rosary in the car on your way to work or set aside time alone or with your family to make it a daily habit. You will surely notice the grace it brings into your life, as promised by Our Lady. With each prayer, each mystery, each devotion, the Rosary becomes a source of peace and strength, drawing us ever closer to the heart of Christ and His Blessed Mother, and guiding us toward eternal life.

Seven Sorrows Rosary

The **Rosary of the Seven Sorrows** of the Blessed Mother dates back to the Middle Ages, though it was lost to history for a time. In recent years, however, this powerful devotion has been making a return among the faithful. Unlike the traditional Rosary, the Seven Sorrows Rosary focuses on seven key moments of suffering in the life of Mary, Mother of Jesus, drawing the faithful into meditation on her deep grief and her intimate participation in the Passion of Christ.

415

In the 1980s, during the Marian apparitions at **Kibeho**, Rwanda, the Blessed Mother appeared to a young visionary named **Marie Claire**. She entrusted Marie Claire with a mission to reintroduce the Seven Sorrows Rosary to the world. Marie Claire traveled widely, spreading the message and encouraging others to pray this special Rosary. Tragically, she lost her life during the Rwandan civil war. In 2001, the Catholic Church officially approved the Kibeho apparitions, affirming their authenticity. During these apparitions, the Blessed Mother revealed to Marie Claire that the Seven Sorrows Rosary holds great spiritual protection when prayed with an open and sincere heart. Mary also explained that this Rosary would help us understand more deeply why we sin, and that by meditating on these sorrows, we would gain the courage and wisdom to overcome our flaws and live more fully with God.

The Seven Sorrows of Mary:

1. **The Prophecy of Simeon** – (Luke 2:25-35)

   Simeon foretells that a sword will pierce Mary's soul, a prophecy that foreshadows her future sorrows.

2. **The Flight into Egypt** – (Matthew 2:13-15)

   Mary and Joseph flee to Egypt with the infant Jesus to escape King Herod's violent decree.

3. **The Loss of Jesus in the Temple** – (Luke 2:41-50)

4. Mary and Joseph search frantically for three days when they realize Jesus is missing, only to find Him in the temple teaching.

5. **Mary Meets Jesus on the Way to the Cross** – (Luke 23:27-31)

As Jesus carries His cross to Calvary, He meets Mary on the way, sharing in each other's sorrow.

6. **Mary Stands at the Foot of the Cross** – (John 19:25-30)

Mary watches helplessly as her Son is crucified, enduring the agony of witnessing His suffering and death.

7. **Mary Receives the Dead Body of Jesus** – (Luke 23:50-54; John 19:31-37)

After His death, Mary receives the lifeless body of Jesus into her arms, experiencing the depth of her grief.

8. **Jesus is Placed in the Tomb** – (Luke 23:50-56; Mark 15:40-47)

Mary witnesses the burial of her Son, a moment of intense sorrow as she faces the silence of His death.

The Promises Associated with the Seven Sorrows Rosary:

According to the Blessed Mother's message to Marie Claire, those who pray the Seven Sorrows Rosary will receive immense spiritual blessings, including the following promises:

1. **Conversion of Even the Hardest Hearts**

Whether prayed for yourself or for others, this Rosary has the power to soften even the hardest of hearts.

2. **Freedom from Addictions and Obsessions**

The Rosary helps to free individuals from spiritual and psychological bonds, including addictions and unhealthy attachments.

3. **True Repentance and Healing of Guilt**

Praying this Rosary leads to true repentance for sins, freeing the soul from guilt and remorse, and bringing inner peace.

4. **Understanding and Overcoming Weaknesses**

By praying this Rosary, especially on **Tuesdays and Fridays**, you will gain greater insight into your weaknesses and the flaws that lead to sin. Through Mary's intercession, those things about yourself that you once thought were unchangeable can begin to transform.

5. **Inner Transformation and Spiritual Healing**

The Seven Sorrows Rosary brings about real, lasting change in your character. What you once thought were unchangeable aspects of yourself can shift as you grow in virtue and holiness.

6. **Graces and Blessings Granted through Heartfelt Prayer**

When prayed sincerely and from the heart, this Rosary brings powerful graces and can obtain for you what you ask of God, according to His will.

The **Seven Sorrows Rosary** is a beautiful and transformative devotion that allows us to unite our suffering with Mary's and find healing, protection, and the grace to change. Through its prayers, we reflect on the Blessed Mother's sorrows and experience the wisdom and strength needed to grow in holiness and overcome the obstacles that keep us from God.

Chaplet of Divine Mercy

The **Chaplet of Divine Mercy** has a rich history rooted in **Catholic devotion** to God's mercy, and it was given to the world through **Saint Faustina Kowalska**, a Polish nun and mystic, in the early 20th century. Here's an overview of its origins and development:

1. The Apparitions of Jesus to Saint Faustina

In the 1930s, **Saint Faustina Kowalska** (1905–1938), a member of the Congregation of the Sisters of Our Lady of Mercy in Poland, began receiving mystical visions and revelations from Jesus Christ. These messages were recorded in her diary, *"Divine Mercy in My Soul."* Jesus instructed her to spread the message of Divine Mercy to the world, urging people to trust in God's infinite mercy, particularly in times of sin and despair.

One of the key elements of Jesus' message to Saint Faustina was the **Chaplet of Divine Mercy**. In one of her visions, on **September 13, 1935**, Jesus appeared and instructed her how to pray the Chaplet. He explained that the Chaplet was a powerful prayer that would bring great grace to those who prayed it, especially at the hour of their death. Jesus also promised that it would be a means of obtaining mercy for souls, and that it was an effective way of seeking divine assistance in times of need.

2. The Divine Mercy Message

The central message of the **Divine Mercy** devotion focuses on the boundless mercy of God, which is available to all who turn to Him with trust. This message is expressed in a series of **devotional prayers** (including the Chaplet) and in the **Divine Mercy Image**, which features Jesus with rays of light streaming from His Sacred Heart—one red, representing His Blood, and the other pale, representing His Water. The inscription beneath the image reads:

"Jesus, I trust in You", a reminder of the need for trust in God's mercy.

Jesus also gave Faustina a specific prayer, the **Jesus, I Trust in You** prayer, to be prayed regularly as a profession of trust in God's mercy.

3. The Prayer of the Chaplet

The Chaplet itself was revealed to **Saint Faustina** in a vision on **September 13, 1935**. She was told to use a set of **rosary beads** to pray it. The Chaplet consists of specific prayers to be said on the **five decades of beads**, which are structured in a way that reflects the **sacrifice of Christ**. It includes a key prayer offered to God the Father, acknowledging Christ's Body, Blood, Soul, and Divinity of Christ in atonement for the world's sins. The second prayer of the Chaplet, "For the sake of His sorrowful Passion, have mercy on us and the whole world," focuses on the suffering and death of Jesus and calls on God's mercy for all humanity.

Jesus explained to Faustina that the Chaplet would be especially powerful for interceding for others, particularly for the souls in purgatory and for those who would be dying. He promised that when the Chaplet is prayed in faith, it can save souls and obtain graces, even for those who seem most distant from God.

4. The Spread of the Chaplet

After Faustina's death in **1938**, her writings, including the **Divine Mercy Chaplet**, were published posthumously, and they soon began to inspire many people worldwide. **Father Michael Sopocko**, Faustina's spiritual director, played an instrumental role in the dissemination of her messages and in promoting the Chaplet. He was also central in the process of spreading devotion to **Divine Mercy** after her death and in having her writings approved by the Church.

The **Chaplet of Divine Mercy** became a central part of the broader **Divine Mercy devotion**, which includes the **Divine Mercy Sunday** (celebrated on the Sunday after Easter), the **Divine Mercy Image**, and the daily prayers of the Divine Mercy novena.

5. The Recognition by the Catholic Church

The message and devotion to Divine Mercy were initially met with some skepticism within the Church, as is often the case with private revelations. However, in the 1950s, the devotion began to gain recognition, thanks to the efforts of **Father Sopocko** and other supporters.

In 1978, the **Congregation for the Doctrine of the Faith** in Rome lifted the ban on the publication of **Saint Faustina's Diary**, and the **Divine Mercy devotion** was further promoted, particularly by **Pope John Paul II**, who had a strong personal devotion to the message of Divine Mercy. On **April 30, 2000**, during the canonization of **Saint Faustina Kowalska**, Pope John Paul II declared **Divine Mercy Sunday** to be a universal feast in the Catholic Church, to be celebrated on the Sunday after Easter. In his homily, he spoke of the Chaplet of Divine Mercy as a powerful prayer of intercession, offering the faithful the opportunity to encounter God's mercy in a special way.

6. Today's Popularity

Since its introduction, the Chaplet of Divine Mercy has become one of the most widely-prayed devotions in the Catholic Church. It is often prayed at 3:00 p.m. (the Hour of Mercy, when Jesus died on the cross) and frequently used for personal petitions and intercessions. Many people pray it daily, individually or in groups, and it is commonly prayed during the **Divine Mercy Novena** (a nine-day prayer period leading up to Divine Mercy Sunday).

The Chaplet of Divine Mercy has transcended national and linguistic boundaries, touching the hearts of millions around the world, and continues to inspire Christians to place their trust in God's infinite mercy.

Summary of Key Dates

- **1931**: Saint Faustina begins receiving revelations from Jesus.

- **1935**: Jesus reveals the Chaplet of Divine Mercy to Saint Faustina.

- **1938**: Saint Faustina dies; her Diary is published posthumously.

- **1978**: The Church lifts the ban on Faustina's Diary.

- **2000**: Saint Faustina is canonized by Pope John Paul II, and Divine Mercy Sunday is established.

The Chaplet continues to be a profound prayer of **trust** and **mercy**, offering solace and peace to all who pray it with a sincere heart.

To say the **Chaplet of Divine Mercy**, you'll need a set of **rosary beads** or a string of 59 beads (standard rosary beads with five decades). The Chaplet is made up of specific prayers that you say on the beads, and it can be prayed individually or as a group. Here's a step-by-step guide on how to pray it:

Prayers

1. **Begin with the Sign of the Cross:**

   In the name of the Father, and of the Son, and the Holy Spirit. Amen.

2. **Pray the Apostles' Creed**:

3. **Pray the Our Father**:

4. **Pray the Hail Mary**:

5. **Pray the Glory Be**:

The Chaplet Prayers (on the beads)

The Chaplet consists of **five decades** (each having one large bead and ten small beads), with specific prayers said on each.

1. On the large bead before each decade:

- **Say the following prayer:**

Eternal Father, I offer You the Body, Blood, Soul, and Divinity of Your dearly beloved Son, our Lord Jesus Christ, in atonement for our sins and those of the whole world.

2. On each of the ten small beads (within the decade):

- **Say the following prayer:**

For the sake of His sorrowful Passion, have mercy on us and on the whole world.

Repeat the second prayer on all ten small beads for each of the five decades.

Concluding Prayers

After completing the five decades, there are three final prayers:

1. **On the three beads (after the five decades):**

   o **Say the following prayer three times:**

      Holy God, Holy Mighty One, Holy Immortal One, have mercy on us and on the whole world.

2. **Conclude with the Sign of the Cross:**

      In the name of the Father, and of the Son, and of the Holy Spirit. Amen.

Optional Prayer (to end the Chaplet)

You may also say the following closing prayer, which is often added as an act of trust and dedication:

Eternal God, in whom mercy is endless and the treasury of compassion inexhaustible, look kindly upon us and increase Your mercy in us, that in difficult moments we might not despair nor become despondent, but with great confidence submit ourselves to Your holy will, which is Love and Mercy itself. Amen.

Time of Prayer

The **Chaplet of Divine Mercy** is traditionally prayed at **3:00 p.m.**, the **Hour of Mercy**, when Jesus died on the cross. However, you can pray at any time of day.

Promises of the **Chaplet of Divine Mercy**:

1. The Promise of Mercy for Sinners

"The soul that will say this Chaplet will be embraced by My mercy during their lifetime and especially at the hour of death."

- **Promise #1** assures that anyone who prays the Chaplet, particularly at the hour of their death, will be embraced by God's mercy. Jesus emphasizes trusting in His mercy at the end of life. This promise is a great comfort for those who are suffering or dying, as it offers hope for salvation.

2. A Great Promise for the Dying

"When this Chaplet is said by the bedside of a dying person, I will stand between My Father and the dying person, not looking at the poor soul, but at My own wounds. This is a powerful prayer for the dying, and I will grant the soul a great amount of mercy."

- **Promise #2** is particularly focused on those who are dying. The Chaplet of Divine Mercy is powerful for the souls at their hour of death. Jesus promises that He will intervene directly on their behalf, standing between the Father and the soul, showing His wounds as a plea for mercy.

3. The Promise of Peace

"I will grant peace to the whole world, and the entire world will know My mercy."

- **Promise #3** speaks of global peace and the spreading of God's mercy. Jesus promises that by praying the Chaplet, peace will be granted not only to individuals but also to the world, as His mercy flows out to all.

4. The Promise of Help in Time of Need

"Through the Chaplet, you will obtain everything if your request is compatible with My will."

- **Promise #4** assures that whatever we ask for will be granted as long as it aligns with God's will. This reinforces the idea that the Chaplet is a prayer of great intercession, and we can ask for help in all matters, whether spiritual, physical, or emotional.

5. A Promise of a Special Grace for Those Who Trust

"The prayer of the Chaplet will be especially powerful when said on behalf of the sick and dying, as it draws down mercy from heaven."

- **Promise #5** highlights the effectiveness of the Chaplet in bringing mercy, especially for the sick and dying. It's a prayer that brings God's grace and mercy into situations where help is most needed.

6. A Promise for the Faithful

"The soul that prays the Chaplet will be protected by the Divine Mercy in all moments of life."

- **Promise #6** speaks of God's protection over those who regularly pray the Chaplet. The soul is guarded from spiritual and physical harm by invoking Divine Mercy, ensuring God's watchful care.

7. The Promise of Salvation for Souls

"In a special way, I will protect the souls of the faithful who recite the Chaplet and will lead them to eternal life."

- **Promise #7** is a promise of eternal life. Jesus promises that those who pray the Chaplet with devotion will have their souls protected, and they will be led to eternal salvation.

8. The Promise of Special Protection at the Hour of Death

"The Chaplet will be a powerful weapon at the hour of death. Whoever will recite it will receive great mercy at the hour of death."

- **Promise #8** is a particularly comforting promise, emphasizing that the Chaplet is especially powerful at the hour of death. By praying it, one receives God's mercy at a crucial moment, helping ensure a peaceful passage into eternal life.

These promises are a beautiful invitation to experience God's infinite mercy and to rely on it in times of need, especially in the moments when we are most vulnerable—whether in life or at the hour of death.

SAINTS & APOSTLES

Chapter Twenty
Conclusion

The day before we celebrated Mass at my friend Patty Ardoin's home with the mystic Claire Rose Champagne, I had the privilege of sitting outside with Claire and my godfather, Father Charles Mallet. I felt a deep awe as I listened to Claire share captivating stories of her encounters with the Blessed Mother. For over an hour, Claire spoke of her profound experiences and how the Mother of Jesus had appeared to her. I found myself moved; struck by the grace she had been given. At one point, I said to Claire, "How blessed you must be to have been chosen to see the Blessed Mother in person." Claire responded unexpectedly: "You are more blessed than I am." Perplexed, I asked her to explain further, especially since she had the unique gift of seeing the Blessed Mother while I had not. With gentle wisdom, Claire quoted the Gospel of John: "Blessed are those who have not seen and yet have come to believe." She went on to say that while she had experienced a vision, the faith I carried without having seen was, in a sense, a greater blessing.

This moment of insight left me reflecting on my own journey of faith. As a child, my belief in God was largely shaped by my Catholic upbringing and my parents' example. I believed because they believed. But over time, as I faced the trials and tribulations of life, I began to realize that my faith was not merely inherited—it was forged in the fire of personal experience. There were times when life felt unbearable, when everything seemed to be falling apart, and I could have easily turned to destructive coping mechanisms like alcohol or drugs, as many do. Instead, I chose to turn to God. During those moments of darkness, when I felt most vulnerable and broken, my faith was truly tested and deepened. Through those trials, I understood the value of having a relationship with God—not one based on comfort or easy circumstances, but one that is strengthened in the storms of life.

Whenever my children or friends face difficulties, I often turn to a passage from Matthew 14:27-31. In this story, Peter steps out of the boat and begins walking toward Jesus on the water. But as soon as he takes his eyes off Jesus and notices the fierce storm around him, he begins to sink. Overcome with fear, Peter cries out, "Lord, save me!" And Jesus immediately reaches out and lifts him up. I remind my loved ones that life is much like that storm—filled with distractions, challenges, and temptations that pull us away from focusing on God. There are moments when it feels as though the waves are crashing over us and we're sinking. But the lesson here is clear: when we call out to Jesus, He is always there to lift us up. Our faith doesn't depend on how we feel in the moment, but on the assurance that Jesus is with us, even in the storm. This is why I believe. Faith isn't just a concept or something we inherit from living, breathing trust that grows through challenges. It's a recognition that even when we cannot see the way forward, we are not alone. Faith is a response to God's invitation to trust in His presence, in His love, and in His power to save us, especially when we feel as though we are sinking.

There's an old military adage that goes, "There are no atheists in a foxhole," and I've often thought of this phrase during my years working in trauma care. After over forty years in the field, I've witnessed countless moments of desperation in the emergency room, where life and death hang in the balance. In these intense moments, I've heard anguished cries for divine intervention, as we do everything we can to save lives. Sometimes, despite our best efforts, the damage is too great, and we must deliver the most painful news to families—that their loved one couldn't be saved. In those moments of heart-wrenching loss, I understand just how much faith is needed, not just for those facing the crisis, but for all of us. In trauma care and in life itself, faith becomes a lifeline. When we are drowning in despair or facing our deepest fears, it is our belief that we can serve as an anchor, like Peter's call for help when he was sinking in the storm. "Lord, save me!" he cried, and in that moment, Jesus reached out and pulled him from the waters. I think about the Apostles, and how much like them we are—human, frail, and often wavering in our faith. They had been in the very presence of Jesus for three years, witnessing His miracles firsthand—healings, exorcisms, and even raising the dead. But when their own storm hit—the arrest, crucifixion, and death of Jesus—they faltered in their faith. In the garden, they couldn't even stay awake to pray with Him, and when Jesus was arrested, they fled in fear, abandoning Him. They were left broken, scattered, and in despair. Despite all they had seen, their faith crumbled when the grief, doubt, and fear overwhelmed them. This reality forces us to ask: if the Apostles, who lived and walked with Jesus, who saw His divine power, could struggle with faith in the most trying moments, how can we, who do not have His physical presence, maintain our own? How can we hold onto our belief amid life's storms—personal, professional, or even spiritual?

It's both sobering and tragic to read the final words of those who spent their lives rejecting the reality of God and eternal life, only to realize too late that their understanding of the world was incomplete. The last words of figures like Caesar Borgia, Thomas Hobbes, Thomas Paine, and Voltaire—individuals who, during their lives, denied or dismissed God—serve as haunting reminders of the finality of death and the importance of faith in the face of eternity. Consider Thomas Paine, one of the most vocal atheists in early American history, who cried out for God's mercy in his final moments, expressing regret for having written *The Age of Reason*. Paine's anguished cries reflect a deep realization that no intellectual argument could save him from the terrifying reality of the afterlife. His words are a stark contrast to the confident atheism he championed during his life. Similarly, Voltaire, who spent much of his life mocking Christianity, found himself in desperation at the end, crying for forgiveness and lamenting the life he had lived. His final pleas reflect the tragic truth that all his earthly wisdom, wealth, and influence could not buy him the peace of mind he so desperately sought in his final hours. This pattern repeats across history. Sir Francis Newport, a prominent leader of the English Atheist club, found himself filled with dread and regret as he realized the truth of God's existence and the reality of hell in his last moments. David Hume, a philosopher known for his skepticism of religious belief, cried in agony that he was "in flames," a desperate image of a soul unprepared for the afterlife. Napoleon Bonaparte, whose life was marked by immense power and ambition, also faced his death with a stark awareness of the gulf between his worldly achievements and the eternal kingdom of Christ. These figures—each one a notable skeptic or enemy of Christianity—found themselves at the mercy of the very truths they had denied. Their final words serve as a cautionary tale about the importance of preparing for death with a living, enduring faith. The tragic irony is that, despite all their intellectual or political triumphs, they discovered too late that there are matters far greater than human power or reason.

In contrast to these men, my faith in God is not simply a theoretical belief or a set of intellectual arguments; it is a living relationship with the Creator, nurtured through prayer, the sacraments, and the Church. I believe in God not only because I see evidence of His presence in the world and in Scripture, but because of the peace that faith brings in the face of the uncertainties of life and death. When I reflect on these last moments of unbelief, I am reminded of how fragile life is and how critical it is to prepare for the inevitable reality of death with a heart open to God's mercy. Faith in God offers a refuge from the storms of life and the certainties of death. While the world offers many distractions and temptations to dismiss God, the final words of these men underscore the importance of being spiritually ready when our time comes. I believe that through Christ, we have been given the way, the truth, and the life—and that this is the most precious gift we can hold onto in life and in death. There is no greater peace than knowing that, regardless of what we face in this world, God loves us, and He has prepared a place for us in eternity. The contrast between their final regrets and my hope is profound. I believe in the salvation offered through Jesus Christ, and I am thankful that I can live with the confidence that death is not the end but

The answer to life's most profound questions, especially the questions of suffering, uncertainty, and death, lies in the promise Jesus made to His followers: He has gone to prepare a place for us. As He said to His disciples, "In my Father's house there are many dwelling places...I am going to prepare a place for you... so that where I am, you may also be." These words, spoken on the eve of His crucifixion, are a profound assurance that our faith may not be tested in vain. Jesus has not only prepared a place for us in eternity, but He also walks with us in this life, in every moment of joy and in every moment of suffering.

For me, the essence of faith is not about having all the answers or being certain at every moment. It is about trusting in His promises, even when the way forward is unclear or when we find ourselves in life's storms. Just as the Apostles, who had witnessed the miracles and resurrection of Jesus, struggled to hold onto their faith in the days after His crucifixion, we too can find our faith restored through the knowledge of His resurrection and the ongoing presence of Christ in our lives. In those moments of doubt, when we feel lost or alone, the truth of His promise shines the brightest: He is preparing a place for us, both here and in the world, to come. I have seen that in life's darkest moments, when I felt overwhelmed by grief or uncertainty, it is not the absence of trials that tests my faith, but my trust in Jesus' unwavering promise. I believe that even when my faith falters—when I feel weak or unsure—Jesus is there, reaching out to me, pulling me through, and leading me closer to that place He has prepared. Faith is not about never wavering or always feeling strong. It's about trust. Trust that even when we cannot see the path, He is with us, guiding us through the darkness. I believe not because I have all the answers, but because I trust in the One who holds the answers—and I trust in His promise that He will never leave me, even when I feel most alone. This is why I believe. Because in every storm, in every trial, I know that He is preparing a place for me, and He will carry me through to the end.

You may wonder, if even those who walked with Jesus in person struggled to maintain their faith, how can we, who have never seen Him, hold on to ours? The reality is that faith can be incredibly difficult—yet it is in those struggles that faith often grows deeper. Candy Arrington, in her insightful blog, *candyarrington.com*, highlights several reasons why faith is such a challenge, and why, despite these difficulties,

1. **Faith Requires Letting Go of Control**: We often try to organize and control every aspect of our lives—anticipating challenges and planning for every possibility. But life can suddenly shift, throwing us into situations beyond our control. Whether it's a health crisis, a financial hardship, or a personal loss, those moments when we realize we are powerless can either break us or draw us closer to God. When my grip on control slips, I have to lean into my faith, trusting that God is in control and that He holds my life in His hands. As Job 12:10 reminds us, "In His hand is the life of every creature and the breath of all

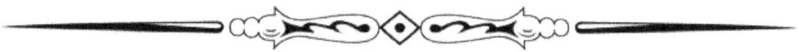

mankind." Trusting in God's sovereignty, even when I cannot see the outcome, is crucial to my belief.

2. **Faith Requires Trusting the Invisible**: When crises come, it's tempting to take action to solve the problem, but more often than not, that leads only to exhaustion and frustration. In those moments, doubt and fear try to convince me that there's no hope, no solution. But faith calls me to believe in what is unseen, to trust that God is working even when I cannot perceive it. Hebrews 11:1 says, "Faith is the confidence in what we hope for and assurance about what we do not see." It is this kind of trust that, over time, strengthens my belief. Faith is not about having all the answers; it's about trusting in God's promise that He is present, even in the unseen.

3. **Faith Requires Seeing with Spiritual Eyes**: Vision is something we often take for granted, until it's compromised. Similarly, spiritual blindness is something many of us struggle with. When we can't see God's hand in our lives, it becomes easy to rely on our own efforts or to focus only on the tangible. The healing of the blind man in Mark 8:22-25 is a powerful reminder that sometimes, we need a "second touch" from Jesus. Just like the blind man's sight was restored in stages, my own faith sometimes needs a second touch—more time, more prayer, more trust in God's process. This is why I believe: not because I can always see the way forward, but because I trust that God's vision for me is clearer than mine.

4. **Faith Requires Living in Uncertainty**: Life is filled with uncertainties, and often, we find ourselves in situations where we have no control, no answers. It's hard when the prayers we pray for seem unanswered,

our expectations aren't met, or things don't turn out as we hoped. But it's precisely in these moments that my faith is refined. I believe because I have learned to trust God, even when answers are unclear. As James 1:3 teaches, "The testing of your faith produces endurance." Through the trials, I find strength that grows my faith and peace that surpasses understanding.

5. **Faith Requires Patience and Perseverance**: Faith isn't about instant answers; it's about trusting in God through every waiting period. Patience is hard, especially when I want results now. Perseverance is even harder when doubts start to creep in and discourage me. Yet, through these struggles, I learn that patience and perseverance are not only essential for surviving the storms of life, but they are also what allow faith to deepen and mature. As James 1:3 says, "For when the way is rough, your patience has a chance to grow." I believe not because I have immediate answers, but because I trust that God's timing is perfect, and that He is working in the waiting.

Faith isn't about certainty; it's about trust. It's about believing in what we cannot always see or control, about choosing to walk in the dark, knowing that God's light is there to guide us. I believe, not because I have all the answers, but because I trust in the One who holds the answers and in His promises to be with me through every trial. Even when the path ahead is uncertain, I know He is preparing a place for me, and He is with me every step of the way. This is why I believe. Reflecting on my own journey, I recall a lesson from high school football practice that resonates with me. During one pivotal session, my coach noticed I kept lining up offside. He stopped the drill and scolded me, saying, "What you do in practice, you will do in the game." That Friday night, sure enough, I was flagged multiple times for being offside. This memory carries a powerful lesson: just as in sports, faith requires effort, discipline, and consistency.

Jesus taught that faith is like a mustard seed—small at first, but potentially growing into something great. "It is the smallest of all seeds, but when it has grown, it is the greatest of plants and becomes a tree large enough for the birds to make nests in its branches." (Matthew 13:31-32) In the same way, our faith may start small, like a tiny seed, but with time, dedication, and care, it can grow into something that can move mountains. If you feel like your faith is weak or nonexistent, don't be discouraged. Just as learning to swim or ride a bike takes practice, so does growing in faith. Start where you are. Read the Bible, pray, talk to a friend, attend church, or seek guidance from a spiritual leader. Every step, no matter how small, is part of the process of strengthening your faith.

The Saints, for example, didn't become Saints because their lives were free from struggles or doubts. Quite the opposite. They were human, just like us, and faced challenges, fears, and temptations. They became Saints not because they were perfect, but because they persevered in faith despite their difficulties. They trusted in God's grace and kept moving forward, step by step, just like practicing for a game. So, when my faith feels small or when I face doubts, I remember that faith isn't about being perfect from the start; it's about persistence. It's about continuing to show up, to practice, and to trust that, over time, God will grow that mustard seed of faith into something much greater. And that's why I believe—not because I have it all figured out, but because I trust in the power of persistence and the faithfulness of God to guide me through every season. Reflect on these saints and how their faith guided them through storm seas.

Saint Paul of the Cross: Saint Paul of the Cross offers a profound example of perseverance through spiritual darkness. An Italian saint from the 18th century, he founded the Passionists, a religious order dedicated to the Passion of Christ. His experience of spiritual darkness was extraordinary, lasting forty-five grueling years,

following twelve years of intense spiritual joy and five years of consolation. Paul viewed his suffering as a sharing in Christ's Passion, particularly the sense of divine abandonment. He recognized that his trials were a means of obtaining grace for others in need of spiritual assistance. Despite the darkness, he maintained his faith and avoided despair, confident that his trials would eventually lead to a realm of divine joy. Ultimately, his perseverance was rewarded with a five-year period of profound spiritual ecstasy, during which he received visions of the Virgin Mary, St. Michael, and the Christ Child. His life exemplifies the value of patient endurance and the joy that follows steadfast trust in God through periods of darkness.

Saint Thérèse of Lisieux: Saint Thérèse, a beloved French saint, was declared by Pope Pius X as the "greatest saint of modern times." This title was earned not only through her charm but through her virtuous life and deep wisdom. Her autobiography, *The Story of a Soul*, details her spiritual doctrine known as the Little Way, which emphasizes the trust and abandonment of a child who knows his Father loves him. However, this childlike faith was tested during the last eighteen months of her life as she battled tuberculosis. She experienced what she called a "trial of faith," describing how she felt engulfed in darkness and struggled with doubts about Heaven, which had once been a source of comfort. Despite her suffering, Thérèse remained steadfast. She devoted herself to practicing her faith even when it brought her no joy, making more acts of faith in her final year than ever before. She wrote out the Creed with her own blood as a testament to her enduring belief. Thérèse's approach to her torment was to avoid debating her doubts, instead turning to Jesus with courage. She believed her suffering was a form of atonement for those who had lost faith, likening her experience to sitting at a table with atheists and their bitter fare while clinging to God. Her struggles with doubt ultimately enabled her to support and intercede for those who continue to struggle. She expressed that the blessed in Heaven have deep compassion for our human struggles, remembering their own frailty and offering greater love and protection from their heavenly state.

Saint Teresa of Calcutta (1910-1997): When Sister Agnes Gonxha was preparing to make her religious vows as a Loreto Sister, she desired to take the name Thérèse, feeling a deep connection with the French saint of the same name. However, since another sister had already chosen that name, she opted for the Spanish equivalent, Teresa. Like her patron, Saint Thérèse of Lisieux, Mother Teresa faced significant challenges with doubt. On September 10, 1946, while traveling from Calcutta to Darjeeling for a retreat, she experienced a profound mystical encounter with Jesus, who called her to serve the poorest of the poor. Although she was content teaching as a Loreto Sister, she embraced this new "call within a call." Her spiritual life was filled with consolation for several months following this call. However, darkness soon fell upon her. Initially, she wondered if this darkness was her fault, but over time, she understood it as a way of sharing in Jesus' thirst on the cross. In her letters to spiritual directors, she described an aching thirst for God that mirrored Jesus' own thirst for souls. Despite the pain, she accepted her trial to imitate Christ's suffering on the cross and contribute to the salvation of souls. This concept, known in Catholic theology as "co-redeeming," recognizes that while Jesus is the sole Redeemer, His followers can participate in His redemptive work. Saint Teresa's experience demonstrates that suffering caused by doubt, when offered with love, holds value in God's eyes. Her story highlights that faith is not about feelings but about a conscious decision of will. If you find yourself walking a dark path, remember that those who have navigated similar trials can offer guidance.

Lessons from the Saints:

- **Saint Jane**: Emphasizes the importance of a spiritual guide and the virtue of trust.

- **Saint Paul**: Teaches patience, hope, and the rewards that follow periods of darkness.

- **Saint Thérèse**: Demonstrates the necessity of exercising faith and ignoring doubts.

- **Saint Teresa of Calcutta**: Shows that suffering caused by doubt has value when offered to God with love.

Inspirational Quotes from Saints:

- **Saint Augustine**: "There is no Saint without a past, no sinner without a future."

- **Saint Thomas Aquinas**: "Faith concerns things that are not seen, and hope relates to things that are not at hand."

- **Saint Bernard**: "I believe, though I do not comprehend, and I hold by faith what I cannot grasp with the mind."

- **Saint Elizabeth Ann Seton**: "I will go peaceably and firmly to the Catholic Church; for if Faith is so important to our salvation, I will seek it where true Faith first began, among those who received it from God Himself."

- **Saint Francis of Assisi**: "Where there is hatred, let me sow love. Where there is injury, pardon. Where there is doubt, faith."

- **Saint Faustina**: "When I immersed myself in prayer, I was spiritually transported to the Chapel, where I saw the Lord Jesus. He said to me, 'What you see in reality, these souls see through faith." How pleasing to Me is their great faith!' Although there seems to be no trace of life in the Host, it is present in its fullness. For Me to act upon the soul, the soul must have faith. Oh, how pleasing to Me is living faith!"

By reflecting on these examples and teachings, we find strength and inspiration for our own faith journeys. As I reflect on the depths of the Catholic faith, I find that all my reasons for belief can

440

be summed up in one powerful prayer—the **Nicene Creed**. This prayer encapsulates the heart of what the Catholic Church believes: it is the truth that has guided Christians for centuries, a beautiful expression of faith that unites us across time and space. The Nicene Creed is not merely an ancient declaration; it is the living foundation of my faith, and it expresses everything I believe about God, Jesus Christ, the Holy Spirit, and the Church.

The *Nicene Creed* begins with a profound affirmation: *"I believe in one God, the Father almighty, maker of heaven and earth, of all things visible and invisible."* These words resonate deeply with me because they remind me that God is both personal and powerful—Father Almighty. He is the Creator, the One who spoke the universe into being. His power is unmatched, but He is not distant or remote. As Father, He is close, nurturing, and sustaining all life. This vision of God as both transcendent and intimate is a truth that brings beauty and meaning to everything I see and experience in the world.

The Creed continues with the declaration that *"I believe in one Lord Jesus Christ, the Only Begotten Son of God, born of the Father before all ages."* This part of the Creed speaks to the uniqueness of Jesus Christ, God's Son, eternal and divine. It is through Him that the world was created, as the Creed affirms: *"Through him all things were made."* For me, this is a reminder that Jesus is not just a teacher or a prophet, but the very Word of God made flesh, the one who holds all creation together. The truth that Jesus is God from God, Light from Light, true God from true God strikes me with awe, for it reveals the depth of God's love and His desire to enter our human experience fully, while never ceasing to be divine. The heart of the Catholic faith lies in the Incarnation—the belief that God became man in Jesus Christ, *for our sake, for our salvation.*

When I pray for the Creed, I am reminded of the immense mystery and beauty of this truth. Jesus, the eternal Son of God, took on human flesh, lived among us, suffered for us, and died for our sins. The suffering of Jesus on the cross was not just a tragic event; it was

the perfect sacrifice that restored humanity to communion with God. *"For us men and for our salvation, he came down from heaven"*— these words speak to me of God's ultimate love for humanity. Jesus' death and resurrection are not abstract doctrines; they are personal, life-changing truths that make salvation possible. Because of His sacrifice, I hope for eternal life and the promise that death has been conquered.

'*The Ascension of Jesus into heaven, where He sits at the right hand of the Father",* reminds me that Jesus' work on earth did not end with His resurrection. He is now reigning as Lord and King, and one day He will return in glory to *"judge the living and the dead."* This promise of His Second Coming gives me hope, knowing that God's plan for the world is not finished. Christ will return to establish His Kingdom in its fullness, a Kingdom that will have no end. It's a future to look forward to, and a present reality that shapes my life now.

The *Holy Spirit*, as the Creed proclaims, is the *"Lord and Giver of Life."* This is where the beauty of the Catholic faith touches me personally. The Holy Spirit is not a distant force but the very presence of God at work in the world today. The Spirit empowers us, guiding us into all truth and leading us into a deeper relationship with God. The *Holy Spirit has spoken through the prophets* and continues to speak to us through Scripture, the Church, and our hearts. In times of uncertainty, the Holy Spirit is my Comforter, reminding me of God's love and truth.

The Creed also affirms the *"Church as one, holy, catholic, and apostoli.* I am deeply moved by the reality that the Church is more than a human institution—it is the living Body of Christ, a family that stretches across the globe and throughout history. The Church's unity in faith, its call to holiness, its universal mission, and its rootedness in the apostles make it a place where I can find connection with God and with Christians from all times and places. The Catholic Church is holy not because of the perfection of its members, but because it is set

442

apart for God's purposes. It is catholic in that it is open to all people, always, and in all places. It is apostolic because it carries forward the teachings and mission of the apostles, passed down through the centuries.

Through the *sacrament of baptism*, the Creed tells us, we are incorporated into this Church and receive the forgiveness of sins. This sacrament is not just a rite of passage; it is a deep, life-changing encounter with the grace of God. It marks the beginning of a new life in Christ, one that is continually nourished through the life of the Church, the Word of God, and the Eucharist. Baptism is a beautiful symbol of our *union with Christ in His death and resurrection,* and it is through the Church that I am continually reminded of this reality.

Finally, the Creed speaks of the *resurrection of the dead and the life of the world to come.* This promise of eternal life is the ultimate hope of the Catholic faith. It affirms that death is not the end, but the beginning of a new and glorious existence with God. The resurrection of the body is a reminder that the material world, our very bodies, have intrinsic value. The renewal of all things is spiritual and physical, affirming that God's plan for salvation involves the redemption of the entire created order.

For me, the Nicene Creed is a summary of everything I believe. It is a declaration of the beauty and truth of the Catholic faith, which speaks to the deepest longings of the human heart. It answers the fundamental questions about who God is, who we are, and our destiny. It speaks to the reality of God's love for us in Christ, and to the hope of eternal life that comes through Him. The Creed is not just something I recite. It is something I live. It is the framework through which I understand my place in the world, and the lens through which I see the truth and beauty of God's work in creation, in the Church, and in my own life. In this simple prayer, I find the fullness of the Catholic faith—the beauty and truth that has captivated my heart and shaped my life. The Nicene Creed is everything I believe, and through it, I am reminded that I am part of a story much larger than myself, a

story of God's love, redemption, and eternal glory. So, there it is for all to read my many reasons I believe in the beauty and truth of the Catholic faith. This faith offers not only a deep spiritual connection but also a way of life that aligns with the true meaning of love, compassion, and justice. At the heart of Catholicism is the life and teachings of Jesus Christ, whose message transcends time and place, offering hope and healing to all people. The Catholic faith invites each of us to live out the virtues of love, humility, forgiveness, and self-sacrifice—virtues that have the power to transform lives and communities. These teachings are not just abstract ideals but practical calls to action that challenge me to live more fully and authentically.

The beauty of the Catholic faith is evident in its rich liturgical traditions and sacred rituals, which provide a framework for encountering the divine in a personal and communal way. With its reverence and solemnity, the Mass is a place where I feel connected to the broader Church—past, present, and future—uniting believers in worship and devotion. The sacraments, especially the Eucharist, offer a profound encounter with God's grace and presence, a gift that nourishes the soul and strengthens the spirit. Through these sacraments, I am reminded of God's endless love for me, and I am inspired to live out my faith more fully, both in moments of joy and times of struggle. The Catholic faith also draws me with its intellectual depth. The Church's teachings on morality, justice, and the human condition offer clear guidance for navigating a complex world. Catholic social teaching challenges me to look beyond my comfort and work toward the common good, advocating for the marginalized and promoting peace.

The Church calls us to be a light in the darkness of suffering, injustice, and confusion, offering not just a moral compass and a vision for a more just and compassionate world. Above all, I believe in the truth of the Catholic faith because it answers life's most profound questions. What is the purpose of life? What is the meaning of suffering? How can we attain true peace and happiness? The Catholic Church provides a comprehensive and loving response to

these inquiries, rooted in the belief that God is with us in every moment, offering guidance, strength, and comfort. The truth of the faith is not merely a set of doctrines or rules to follow; it is a living relationship with God, made possible through Christ and the Church, which continues to be a source of hope, peace, and transformation in my life. In a world often filled with uncertainty, division, and fear, the Catholic faith remains a beacon of light, calling us to live lives of love, service, and truth. It offers a timeless and enduring path to understanding the deepest mysteries of human existence, providing a solid foundation of faith, hope, and charity.

The absolute beauty of the Catholic Church lies in its ability to unite people, heal brokenness, and reveal a deeper truth that transcends the limits of this world. I believe in this beauty and truth, and it continues to guide me toward a life of greater meaning and purpose. Ultimately, the main reason I believe in the beauty and truth of the Catholic Church is this: it is the one true religion that Jesus entrusted to humanity. Jesus said it, and I believe!

Footnotes

[1] Karen Danao. 25 Moonstruck Quotes.quoteambition.com2023

[2] John: 13 New American Bible. Catholic Translation. Catholic Bible Press. Nashville, Tn. 1987. Pp 1210

[3] Pieta Prayer Book. Hickory Corners, Mi. 2006. Pp 26

[4] Ibid.

[5] Joan Carrol Cruz. Eucharistic Miracles. Tan Books. Charlotte, Nc. 2010 pp 222

[6] Ibid. pp 223

[7] Ibid pp 223

[8] Ibid pp222

[9] Ibid. Pp222

[10] Saints' Quotes on the Eucharist. Wikipedia 2021

446

[11]Ibid

[12]Joan Carrol Cruz. Eucharistic Miracles. Tan Books. Charlotte, Nc. 2010 pp xiv

[13]Ibid. Pp XV

14. Rev. George J. Blatter. The Mystical City of God by Venerable Mary of Agreda. Tan Books. Charlotte, North Carolina. 1978. Pp367-373

15 www.TV fanatic.com/70 show quotes.

[16.]Phil Alden Robinson, <u>Fields of Dream</u>, movie quote. 1989

Book Back Cover

With over 43,000 Christian denominations, have you ever wondered which one truly represents the Church established by Jesus? *Why I Believe in the Beauty and Truth of the Catholic Faith* takes you on a journey through the core doctrines of Catholicism—faithfully handed down from the Apostles to the 1.2 billion Catholics worldwide today. In this book, the Catholic Church is contrasted with other man-made churches such as Lutheranism, Anglicanism, Presbyterianism, Quakerism, Methodism, Unitarianism, Jehovah's Witnesses, Mormonism, and many more.

Explore the origins of these denominations, uncovering the stories behind their founders, including one who was antisemitic, another who couldn't obtain an annulment, and the first to teach that the Last Supper was only a symbolic remembrance, rather than the real presence of Jesus' body and blood. Learn why Catholic Bibles differ from Protestant Bibles and dive into the history of the Bible's creation, including the roles various religions played in shaping the biblical canon and the reasons behind the different versions of the Bible.

Delve into profound truths about Jesus' family, including why He did not have siblings, the actual number of wounds He sustained, and the true meaning behind the Eucharist as the body and blood of Christ. Discover why priests have the authority to hear confessions and absolve sins, and understand the significance of the term "in Persona Christi."

This book also invites you to experience firsthand accounts from visionaries and mystics who have encountered Purgatory, Hell, Heaven, and Satan. You'll also learn about the fates of key biblical figures after Jesus' Resurrection—such as the Apostles, the Blessed Mother, Pilate, Claudia Procula (Pilate's wife), Caiaphas, Annas, Lazarus, Martha and Mary, Veronica, Mary Magdalene, Dismas (the good thief), Simon of Cyrene, Nicodemus, and Joseph of Arimathea.

Offering compelling answers to these questions and more, *Why I Believe in the Beauty and Truth of the Catholic Faith* reveals the depth and beauty of the Catholic Church. It's a must-read for anyone seeking to understand and confidently respond to anti-Catholic arguments with clarity and insight.

John Lawrence Fontana lives in Covington, Louisiana, with his wife, Joni, and their four dogs—a Poodle and three Pomskies. He is the father of five adult children and a proud grandfather. With over 40 years of experience as a Registered Nurse, John has specialized in trauma care, diving medicine, wound care, and medical sales. He served as a First Lieutenant in the U.S. Army Reserve and National Guard and currently works part-time as a clinical instructor for an LPN program. Beyond his medical career, John spent over ten years teaching CCD (Confraternity of Christian Doctrine) to tenth graders in local public schools and has participated in several medical mission trips to Guatemala and Mexico, providing care to underserved communities. He is also a volunteer for Sky High, a nonprofit organization dedicated to raising funds for St. Jude Children's Research Hospital in Memphis, Tennessee. John self-published his first book, "God & Free Will: True Stories of Sins, Faith and Redemptions," in 2024